Graphic Guide to
Interior Details

MW01043155

Graphic Guide to Interior Details

for builders and designers

Rob Thallon

*Drawings by Rob Thallon
and Jeff Stern*

The Taunton Press

Taunton
BOOKS & VIDEOS
for fellow enthusiasts

Printed in the United States of America

First printing: February 1996
Second printing: November 1996
Third printing: December 1997

A FINE HOMEBUILDING Book

FINE HOMEBUILDING® is a trademark of The Taunton Press, Inc., registered in the U.S.
Patent and Trademark Office.

The Taunton Press, 63 South Main Street, Box 5506, Newtown, CT 06470-5506

Library of Congress Cataloging-in-Publication Data
Thallon, Rob.
        Graphic guide to interior details : for builders and
designers / Rob Thallon ; author's drawings rendered by
Jeff Stern.
            p.   cm.
        "A fine homebuilding book"—T.p. verso.
        Includes index.
        ISBN 1-56158-143-7. — ISBN 1-56158-098-8 (pbk.)
        1. Building—Details. 2. Interior decoration. I. Title.
TH2025.T43 1995
729—dc20   95-25665
                                        CIP

FOR CARTER AND CLAIRE

ACKNOWLEDGMENTS

I am deeply grateful to Jeff Stern, my research assistant, who was devoted to the quality of this project far beyond the call of duty. In addition to researching many of the materials included in the book, Jeff graciously consented to write first drafts of several sections (plaster, tile, carpet and countertops) when deadlines interrupted our otherwise smooth process. Jeff has also lent a most valuable editing eye to both text and drawings.

This book has also been enriched by the invaluable comments of consultants from throughout the country. Drafts of the entire book were reviewed by:

Ed Allen
South Natick, Massachusetts

Dan Rockhill
LeCompton, Kansas

In addition, individual chapters or sections of chapters were reviewed by:

Don Bollinger (wood floors)
Seattle, Washington

Rick Gregory (GWB)
San Diego, California

Jeffrey Johnston (GWB & plaster)
Arlington Heights, Illinois

Herrick Kimball (trim)
Moravia, New York

Michael Luttrell (radiant floors)
Napa, California

Tom Meehan (tile floors)
Harwich, Massachusetts

Pat Morgan (cabinets)
Eugene, Oregon

Scott Schuttner (stairs)
Fairbanks, Alaska

Jim Tolpin (cabinets)
Port Townsend, Washington

I also gratefully acknowledge the contributions of the following individuals:

Dee Etzwiler, my wife, for her loving support;

Joanne Kellar Bouknight, my editor, for her patient and skillful editing;

Sarah Bernhard, graduate student, for drafting the appendices on paints and coatings and on sound reduction;

Peter Grimm, graduate student, for drafting the appendix on building codes.

I also express my appreciation to the University of Oregon for a New Faculty Research Grant, which provided funding to research the needs for this book and to do preliminary work on its organization.

I would also like to offer thanks to the many people in the Department of Architecture at the University of Oregon who contributed helpful suggestions and who otherwise supported this project in numerous small but important ways.

CONTENTS

Introduction   xi

1   WALLS & CEILINGS   1
Gypsum Wallboard Systems   3
Lath & Plaster   11
Masonry   15
Tile   25
Sheet Paneling   31
Board Paneling   36
Frame & Panel Systems   40
Suspended Ceiling Systems   42
Interior Doors   44

2   FLOORS   55
Carpet   60
Resilient Flooring   68
Wood Flooring   78
Tile & Masonry   92
Concrete   100
Terrazzo   103

3   CABINETS & COUNTERTOPS   107
Cabinets   109
Cabinet Cases   112
Cabinet Doors   114
Cabinet Drawers   116
Cabinet Shelves   118
Cabinet Hardware   120
Cabinet Installation   126
Countertops   128
Sinks & Countertops   131
Plastic Laminate Countertops   132
Tile Countertops   136
Stone Slab Countertops   140
Solid-Surface Countertops   142
Concrete Countertops   144
Metal Countertops   146
Wood Countertops   147

4   TRIM   149
Solid Wood Trim   150
Alternatives to Wood   152
Finishes   153
Trim Application   154
Fasteners   158
Door & Window Trim   159
Base Trim   162
Specialized Moldings   164

5   STAIRS   167
Safety   168
Structure   169
Spiral Stairs   173
Finish Materials   174
Banisters & Handrails   181
Handrails   186

Appendix A—Paints & Coatings   189
Appendix B—Composite Panels   191
Appendix C—Fire & Safety Codes   193
Appendix D—Sound Reduction   194
List of Abbreviations   197
Resources   199
Readings & Product Information   201
Index   203

INTRODUCTION

The best buildings, whether affordable or expensive, are made by people with a profound understanding of the materials used to make them. In the past, this understanding was common because the people who designed buildings were also intimately involved in constructing them. Today, the process of making buildings has been fragmented by specialization that separates material producers, designers and builders from one another. As a result, most buildings are constructed without an understanding of the materials or details that are used to make them. Even in this specialized industrial society, however, it is possible to make beautiful high-quality buildings if design and construction are integrated so that they reinforce each other.

Building materials are the common language that ties together the disciplines of design and construction. These materials, which ultimately form the substance of a building, must be thoughtfully selected and composed (detailed) if the building is to have authentic quality and character.

When designing the interior of a building, it is important to consider a variety of materials for the floors, walls, ceilings, cabinets, stairways and trim. Materials must be judged by how they are connected to the structure of the building, how they meet one another and how they may be finished. In addition, the comparative cost, durability, ease of maintenance and many other factors may need to be considered. Whether the primary goal is efficiency or elegance, detailing the interior of a building requires a multitude of complex, interdependent decisions about materials.

Graphic Guide to Interior Details compares the spectrum of available materials sufficiently to allow intelligent preliminary choices based on an understanding of the nature of the materials and the various ways of assembling them. Details showing connection to the structure and meeting of other materials are portrayed graphically. Whether the primary concern is durability, affordability or aesthetics, this book leads the reader to the most *appropriate* materials and details, narrowing the field so that further in-depth inquiry will be informed and meaningful.

The book is written from a designer's point of view in that it does not describe the construction process so much as the characteristics of the materials and their relationship to the structure and to each other. The term "designer" is used in its broadest sense to include everyone who selects materials and has a say in how they fit together. This book is intended, therefore, to be a reference and a resource for professional designers, builders, building owners and students.

The Scope of the Book

The materials and details discussed here are limited to those applied to the structural shell of a building in order to finish the interior spaces. Wall and ceiling paneling, finish flooring, cabinets, trim and stairways are the primary topics covered. Both residential and commercial construction are included because most interior finish materials are common to both types of construction, and many materials that have been traditionally used for one type may be appropriately used for the other.

The book's scope has been limited to new construction since the idiosyncrasies of remodeling tend to complicate detailing, and because it is a goal in most remodeling work to achieve conditions similar to new construction. Plumbing fittings, electrical fixtures and specialty hardware are not discussed since there is a wide variety of available choices, and the descriptions of these products are so technical that they cannot be fairly covered in a book of this length. A comprehensive discussion of paints and coatings has been excluded for similar reasons, but a brief overview is presented in Appendix A.

A sincere attempt has been made to describe all common materials from affordable to expensive. The more common materials such as drywall and carpet are discussed in more detail than seldom-used materials such as raised paneling or colored concrete flooring. Each material is described sufficiently to allow a thoughtful comparison with other materials.

A Note About Structure

The materials discussed in this book may be applied to buildings made using any standard structural system, including masonry, concrete, steel or wood frame. The structure of the walls, ceilings and floors of these various systems can be quite different, but the most common situation is for walls to be framed in wood or steel and for ceilings and floors to be either a concrete slab or wood framed.

Wall and ceiling materials are therefore discussed with the assumption that they will be attached to some kind of framing. For a wall that is not framed, such as a masonry bearing wall, furring at typical framing intervals is usually added to simulate the framing of interior partition walls. If framing is not required for the attachment of materials, such as for plaster or tile, this will be noted in the discussion of the material and shown in the details. Floors are assumed to be either wood framed or concrete, and each flooring material is discussed in relation to these two options.

Environmental Responsibility

Growing numbers of designers are becoming aware of the impact of their material choices on the environment at large. All building materials have some degree of environmental impact associated with their extraction from the earth, their manufacture, their transport to the building site and the disposal of their waste after installation. There is not space in this book to allow a detailed discussion of these issues, but materials that are cause for special concern are pointed out. There are many excellent publications about environmental concerns (see References), and new information is constantly being made available.

Toxicity

In addition to presenting global environmental threats, some materials pose health risks to people who handle them and/or to building occupants. Solvents, adhesives and several materials such as particleboard and carpet usually contain high levels of volatile organic compounds (VOCs), which when released into the air inside a building can become respiratory irritants and are suspected of playing a role in other physiological problems. Toxic compounds are at their highest concentration when a material is installed, but some compounds can be released at lower concentrations for months or even years.

Material choices can be made that will minimize the exposure of workers or occupants to high levels of toxicity. For example, carpet, tile and other materials can be installed with new adhesives that have very low VOC content. Fiberboard that is free of the most harmful chemical components of typical binders is now also available.

Building Codes

Every effort has been made to ensure that the details in this book are permitted by most building codes. Codes vary, however, so designers and builders must consult local codes and building departments to verify compliance with specific regulations. The materials used on walls, ceilings and floors are most likely to be affected by codes that govern their acceptability with respect to the spread of fire (see Appendix C). Cabinets may be subject to codes regulating dimensions, such as the ANSI standards for disabled persons. The dimensions of stairways are always regulated for the safety of the users, and there may also be special regulations that apply to the use of stairs by disabled persons.

How to Use the Book

The book is organized into five chapters that roughly follow the sequence of construction so that materials are described in the order that they would most likely be applied. The design process is not as linear as the construction process, however, so the book should not be read from cover to cover. Each drawing shows a particular detail of the material described but also shows generic interpretations of adjacent materials that are described in other chapters. By combining the details from various chapters, it is possible to integrate details and draw all the parts of an interior space.

Within each chapter, there is first a discussion of general principles followed by sections that describe specific materials or methods of application that affect finish details. A reference drawing at the beginning of most sections refers to the detailed discussions.

Chapter titles and subsections are called out at the top of each page for easy reference. All drawings and discussions are cross-referenced where appropriate. The pages are numbered and the drawings lettered so that a reference to "56A," for example, refers to drawing A on page 56.

Generally, the more common materials and details are located nearest to the beginning of each chapter or section with the more obscure or esoteric items at the end.

When possible, the details are drawn in the simple section format found in architectural working drawings. When a simple section drawing does not suffice, isometric drawings are used in order to convey the third dimension. Because of the range in size of the materials depicted, the details are not drawn to any particular scale although they are proportionally correct. Notes are used to describe the most important features of a detail. Abbreviations used in the notes are spelled out on page 197.

A Final Note

It has been my intention in writing this book to assist designers and builders who are trying to make the most appropriate choices for the details of interior spaces. It is my hope that the choices that are made will lead to beautiful, economical and durable buildings. With the discussion and drawings I have tried to describe the essence of each common material and the relationship between the parts of each common detail. I have included many alternative approaches as well, both from my own experience and from the expertise of others. To build on this endeavor, I would appreciate seeing your own details and critical comments. Please send them to: *Graphic Guide to Interior Details*, The Taunton Press, PO Box 5506, Newtown, CT 06470-5506.

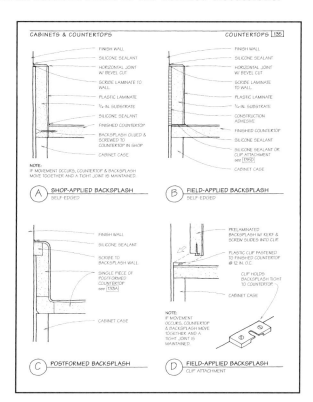

Walls & Ceilings

W alls and ceilings have many similarities. Their framing systems are often virtually identical, with stud spacing equal to that of joists or rafters. This wall and ceiling framing is frequently covered with the same finish material, which is directly applied to it. Unlike floors, both walls and ceilings are usually independent of the live load requirements imposed by people and furniture and do not require much abrasion resistance.

Yet walls and ceilings are quite different from each other in some respects. A wall, being a vertical plane, is appropriate for the application of heavy masonry veneer, while ceilings are more subject to the forces of gravity and are not usually made of masonry. Gravity also dictates that ceilings may need to accommodate deflection caused by floor loads above or by live roof loads, while walls do not receive such loads. People and furniture also occasionally bump into walls, while this is rarely the case with ceilings. The implications of such impacts and abrasion over the long term must therefore be considered when designing walls, but not when designing ceilings.

Coordinating with Framing

Most finish materials will attach directly to either wood or steel framing. Some materials (e.g., tongue-and-groove boards), however, are more compatible with wood framing than with steel framing, so coordination with framing should be considered when selecting finish materials.

Stud and rafter spacing can influence wall and ceiling finishes, too. For example, ⅜-in. gypsum wallboard is not recommended for application on studs spaced 24 in. o.c., while ½-in. and ⅝-in. wallboard can be used under most conditions. Consult product manufacturers for their recommendations regarding wall and ceiling finishes and framing.

Looking Forward to Trim

The materials used to make the surfaces of walls and ceilings are usually covered at the edges with trim, which spans any gaps between the wall surface and adjacent elements such as doors, windows and floors (chapter 4).

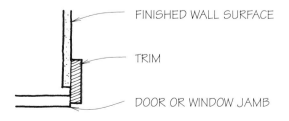

FINISHED WALL SURFACE

TRIM

DOOR OR WINDOW JAMB

The relationship of finish wall surface materials to trim should be considered when selecting these materials. This is especially important when using more than one surface material for the same wall or ceiling. As a rule, it is most expedient to maintain a continuous plane between two adjacent surfaces, since this will allow simple trim to be continuous across the two surfaces.

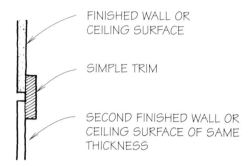

FINISHED WALL OR CEILING SURFACE

SIMPLE TRIM

SECOND FINISHED WALL OR CEILING SURFACE OF SAME THICKNESS

Alternatively, the extra thickness of built-up veneer may abut the trim or be lapped by rabbeted trim.

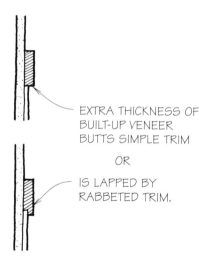

EXTRA THICKNESS OF BUILT-UP VENEER BUTTS SIMPLE TRIM

OR

IS LAPPED BY RABBETED TRIM.

In each case, the thickness of the wall or ceiling surface material must be coordinated with the trim that will ultimately finish its edges.

Designing the Ceiling

The ceiling, because it is often a simple plane contained within the boundaries of walls and uncomplicated by openings, can offer an opportunity for architectural expression. Since the ceiling is usually bounded by walls at its edges and generally has few interruptions, changing its thickness does not entail the same problems associated with the existence of doors and windows. Therefore, articulating the ceiling is a cost-effective way to add spatial drama to a room. Coffered and soffited ceilings are fairly easily achieved by following the building's primary structure or by adding simple framing to it.

For sound reduction in walls and ceilings see Appendix D.

For flame-spread ratings of wall and ceiling finishes see Appendix C.

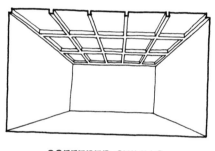

COFFERED CEILING

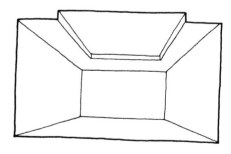

SOFFITED CEILING

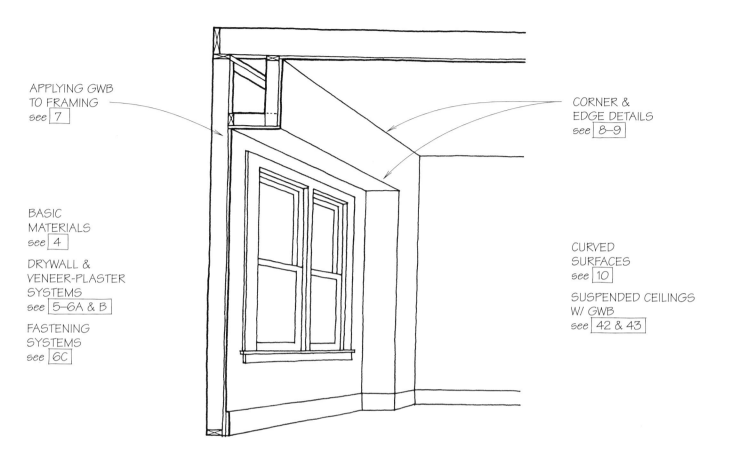

APPLYING GWB
TO FRAMING
see 7

BASIC
MATERIALS
see 4

DRYWALL &
VENEER-PLASTER
SYSTEMS
see 5-6A & B

FASTENING
SYSTEMS
see 6C

CORNER &
EDGE DETAILS
see 8-9

CURVED
SURFACES
see 10

SUSPENDED CEILINGS
W/ GWB
see 42 & 43

Developed originally as a cheaper alternative to the once ubiquitous lath and plaster, gypsum wallboard is now the most common finish material for walls and ceilings. Gypsum wallboard has replaced traditional lath and plaster because it takes less labor and time to install, requires less time to cure and generates less moisture during construction. Gypsum wallboard also provides excellent fire protection of the wall and ceiling structural systems (see Appendix C), and is an important component in most sound-control systems (see Appendix D).

Aside from traditional lath and plaster (see 11A), gypsum wallboard is the only interior finish system that provides a continuous surface without joints. The finished surface is usually planar (flat) but can also be curved within limits. Gypsum wallboard can be finished with a variety of textures, accepts paint readily, and is easily remodeled or repaired.

Drywall vs. Veneer Plaster

The two basic wall and ceiling systems that employ gypsum wallboard as a base are the drywall system (see 5A) and the veneer-plaster system (see 5B).

When choosing between drywall and veneer-plaster systems, consider relative costs, installation times, durability and appearance. For example, the higher cost of veneer plaster may be offset by its shorter construction schedule. Also consider the hardness of a wall or ceiling's finish surface in relation to the use of the space. Compared with drywall finish, a veneer-plaster finish on gypsum wallboard provides a harder surface more resistant to cracking and impact, but accepts tacks and pins less readily. Veneer plaster requires somewhat more skilled labor to finish than drywall. If a truly smooth surface is desired, it is more easily achieved with a veneer-plaster system, assuming that skilled craftspersons execute the work.

 GYPSUM WALLBOARD SYSTEMS

Gypsum Wallboard

Gypsum wallboard (GWB) comes with the edges of the long sides tapered and the short sides squared, and is available in the sizes shown below. It is manufactured in several grades for specific applications:

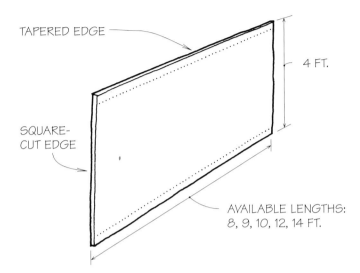

TAPERED EDGE

SQUARE-CUT EDGE

4 FT.

AVAILABLE LENGTHS: 8, 9, 10, 12, 14 FT.

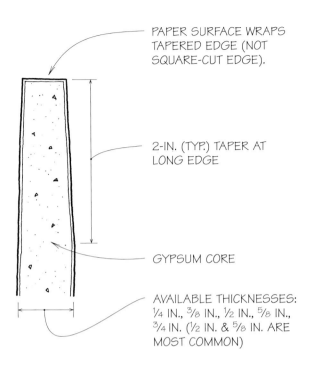

PAPER SURFACE WRAPS TAPERED EDGE (NOT SQUARE-CUT EDGE).

2-IN. (TYP.) TAPER AT LONG EDGE

GYPSUM CORE

AVAILABLE THICKNESSES: 1/4 IN., 3/8 IN., 1/2 IN., 5/8 IN., 3/4 IN. (1/2 IN. & 5/8 IN. ARE MOST COMMON)

Regular—for most work.

Type X—for locations where fire-resistant wallboard is required by code.

Water-resistant—often called "greenboard," for use in a moist location such as a bathroom, laundry room or kitchen. Not to be used in locations receiving constant moisture, such as spas or swimming pools.

Ceiling board—a high-strength, sag-resistant board for use where wide joist or rafter spacing (24 in. o.c.) is required or where high levels of moisture during construction might cause sagging (1/2-in. ceiling board has span capacity equal to 5/8-in. regular gypsum wallboard).

Veneer-plaster base—often called "blueboard," this board has a high-density gypsum core and an absorbent, textured paper surface that provides a good bond for veneer plaster and is treated with a chemical catalyst.

Combination types—most of the above types are available in combination, e.g., Type-X water-resistant or Type-X veneer-plaster base.

Foil-backed—for use as a vapor retarder in certain locations and regions.

Vinyl-faced—a prefinished board usually used only for commercial work (see 31A).

Joint Reinforcing

Reinforcing tape or mesh is located at the joints where gypsum wallboard panels meet to prevent cracking of the finished surface caused by any slight movement of the panels. Paper tape is embedded in taping compound with the drywall system while fiber-mesh tape is embedded in veneer plaster. The fiber-mesh tape is available with a self-adhering sticky backing or a plain backing, which requires the tape to be stapled in place.

Drywall Compound

Drywall compound, also called joint compound, is available premixed or as a powder to be mixed on site. The types of products are named according to function. Taping compound is designed specifically for embedding the reinforcing tape. Topping compound is designed specifically for the second and third coats. An all-purpose compound is manufactured for both taping and topping, but it does not perform as well as separate taping and topping compounds.

Veneer Plaster

Veneer plaster is generally available in powder form to be mixed on site. Silica sand or other textures can be added during mixing.

(A) GYPSUM WALLBOARD
BASIC MATERIALS

Gypsum wallboard finished with drywall compound is used in more than 90% of residential projects and in much commercial work. A drywall system, as it is commonly called, is a three-coat process, with texture applied as an optional fourth coat. Since each coat usually requires sanding to achieve a smooth surface and must dry by evaporation before sanding, the overall process consumes a significant amount of construction time (about a day for each coat).

With its hardness and finish texture that are the direct result of a hand-applied system, veneer plaster has both the quality and the appearance of traditional lath and plaster but is much less expensive to apply. The veneer-plaster system costs more than the drywall system (about 10% to 25%), but the additional cost can sometimes be justified by the quality of the finished surface and/or shorter construction schedule (one day as opposed to four).

PAPER TAPE IS EMBEDDED IN FIRST COAT OF DRYWALL COMPOUND APPLIED OVER JOINTS BETWEEN SHEETS.

SECOND COAT OF DRYWALL COMPOUND FILLS LOW SPOTS.

THIRD COAT OF DRYWALL COMPOUND SMOOTHS SURFACE AND IS SANDED TO A FEATHERED EDGE.

NOTE:
EACH COAT OF DRYWALL COMPOUND HARDENS BY EVAPORATION.

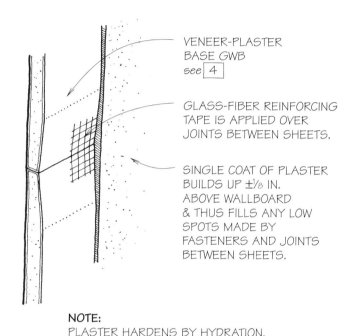

VENEER-PLASTER BASE GWB see │4│

GLASS-FIBER REINFORCING TAPE IS APPLIED OVER JOINTS BETWEEN SHEETS.

SINGLE COAT OF PLASTER BUILDS UP ±⅛ IN. ABOVE WALLBOARD & THUS FILLS ANY LOW SPOTS MADE BY FASTENERS AND JOINTS BETWEEN SHEETS.

NOTE:
PLASTER HARDENS BY HYDRATION.

Smooth, sanded drywall compound on gypsum wallboard makes an acceptable surface for paint, but the slightly different texture between the sanded compound and the exposed paper surface of the wallboard makes it difficult for paint alone to hide the distinction between these two surfaces. It is general practice, therefore, to hide the difference in the two surfaces by applying a special texture compound similar to but thinner than joint compound. Texture compound is commonly sprayed on, applied by hand with a trowel, roller or brush, or by a combination of techniques. More creative textures can be achieved with such applicators as a whisk broom, a sponge or crumpled paper. Sprayed-on acoustical textures are also available for ceilings or other locations where abrasion is unlikely to occur (see Appendix D for sound-attenuation details). Some textures, such as sand, may be incorporated into the paint (see Appendix A for paints).

The veneer-plaster system is a one-coat process with an optional texture coat applied over the first coat after it has set but not cured. The applied veneer plaster cures by hydration (chemical action) rather than evaporation, so the hardening process is much faster than for a drywall system. This rapid curing of the plaster is what allows the work to be completed in one day (and also what requires the craftsperson to be skilled). The actual sequence of application usually involves first filling out low spots at tapered wallboard joints, then floating the entire surface with a ⅛-in. thick plaster coat, then an optional texture coat. This covering of the entire surface with plaster is an important distinction between veneer plaster and the drywall system, which only covers joints and fasteners with drywall compound. The finish surface of veneer plaster may be smooth, have an integral sand finish, or have other textures intentionally created by the motion of the trowel.

 Ⓐ DRYWALL SYSTEM

Ⓑ VENEER-PLASTER SYSTEM

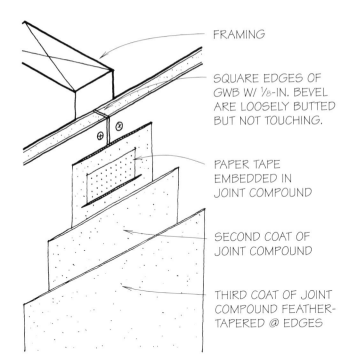

- FRAMING
- SQUARE EDGES OF GWB W/ 1/8-IN. BEVEL ARE LOOSELY BUTTED BUT NOT TOUCHING.
- PAPER TAPE EMBEDDED IN JOINT COMPOUND
- SECOND COAT OF JOINT COMPOUND
- THIRD COAT OF JOINT COMPOUND FEATHER-TAPERED @ EDGES

(A) DRYWALL
SEAM @ SQUARE-CUT EDGE

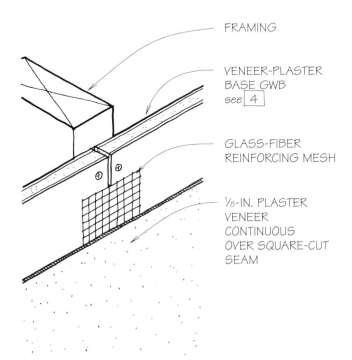

- FRAMING
- VENEER-PLASTER BASE GWB see [4]
- GLASS-FIBER REINFORCING MESH
- 1/8-IN. PLASTER VENEER CONTINUOUS OVER SQUARE-CUT SEAM

(B) VENEER PLASTER
SEAM @ SQUARE-CUT EDGE

Gypsum wallboard is fastened to the framing with nails or screws designed specifically for such a use. Nails, formerly the most common means of attachment, are losing favor to screws, which are stronger and more universally applicable (see chart below for fastener requirements). No matter which fastener is used, when a wooden building goes through a heating season, nail or screw pops may occur as framing shrinks, requiring spot repair.

Nails

A proper drywall nail has a concave- or dish-shaped head with a thin rim and annular rings on a short shank that is sized to penetrate only about ¾ in. into the wood. The annular rings and the short shank are designed to minimize popping caused by shrinking and swelling of wood framing. The head of the nail is sized and shaped to provide maximum contact area while lying flat against the surface of the gypsum wallboard. Nails can be used only for wood framing.

Screws

Screws can be used to attach GWB panels to virtually any surface, including wood or steel framing, metal-resilient channels or metal suspended ceiling. A drywall screw has a bugle-shaped head that depresses the paper surface of a GWB panel without tearing it. Screws have a greater withdrawal resistance than nails and therefore fewer fasteners are required per panel.

Adhesives

Adhesives can be used between panels in multilayered assemblies, and between panels and framing to reduce the number of fasteners required, as shown in the chart below.

FRAMING	Fastener type	Location	Max. spacing (in.)
Wood	Nails	Ceiling	7
		Walls	8
	Screws	Ceiling	12
		Walls	16
	Nails/screws with adhesive	Ceiling	16
		Walls	16
Steel	Screws	Ceiling	12
		Walls	16

(C) FASTENING SYSTEMS

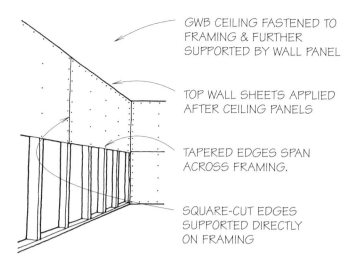

GWB CEILING FASTENED TO FRAMING & FURTHER SUPPORTED BY WALL PANEL

TOP WALL SHEETS APPLIED AFTER CEILING PANELS

TAPERED EDGES SPAN ACROSS FRAMING.

SQUARE-CUT EDGES SUPPORTED DIRECTLY ON FRAMING

GWB HORIZONTAL ON WALLS

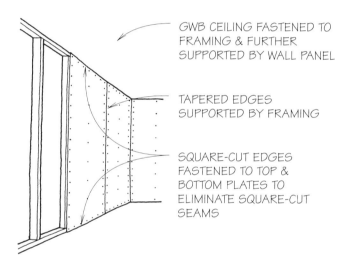

GWB CEILING FASTENED TO FRAMING & FURTHER SUPPORTED BY WALL PANEL

TAPERED EDGES SUPPORTED BY FRAMING

SQUARE-CUT EDGES FASTENED TO TOP & BOTTOM PLATES TO ELIMINATE SQUARE-CUT SEAMS

GWB VERTICAL ON WALLS

Gypsum wallboard is usually applied directly to framing. For ceilings, the wallboard should be oriented perpendicular to the framing so that butt joints always occur at a framing member. Walls are applied after ceilings in order to provide additional support to the ceiling boards at the perimeter. For walls, the board may be attached either vertically or horizontally. Drywall contractors prefer a horizontal application since this allows most of the taping and finishing to occur at the convenient 4-ft. level. The advantage of a vertical wall application is that square-cut seams may be avoided altogether. Because gypsum wallboard is relatively flexible, the final surface can only be as true as the framing to which it is applied.

(A) APPLYING GWB TO FRAMING
STANDARD SYSTEMS

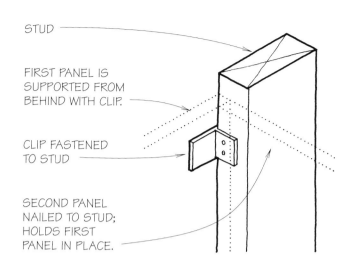

STUD

FIRST PANEL IS SUPPORTED FROM BEHIND WITH CLIP.

CLIP FASTENED TO STUD

SECOND PANEL NAILED TO STUD; HOLDS FIRST PANEL IN PLACE.

Corner Clips

Corner clips may be used to join GWB panels at inside corners in situations where it is desirable to minimize framing members (for economy or for increased insulation). These clips act as a substitute for a stud by supporting the edge of one inside corner panel (see above).

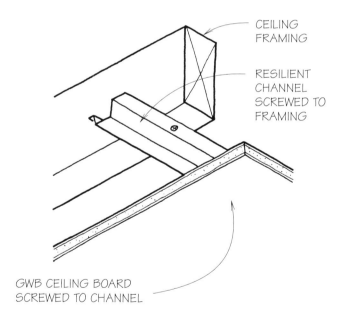

CEILING FRAMING

RESILIENT CHANNEL SCREWED TO FRAMING

GWB CEILING BOARD SCREWED TO CHANNEL

Resilient Channel

Metal sound-reducing resilient channels applied perpendicular to the framing of either walls or ceilings provide a framework to which wallboard may be attached if sound reduction is a goal (see Appendix D).

(B) APPLYING GWB TO FRAMING
ALTERNATIVE SYSTEMS

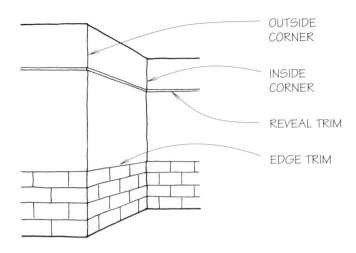

OUTSIDE CORNER

INSIDE CORNER

REVEAL TRIM

EDGE TRIM

Outside corners—A bead stapled or nailed to the GWB provides a straight edge and protects the corner (see 8B).

Inside corners—Reinforcing tape is applied to inside corners and finished similarly to seams (see 8C).

Reveal trim—This trim is fastened to parallel edges of GWB that have been spaced apart to allow for the trim (see 9A).

Edge trim—Where the edge of a GWB panel is exposed, edge trim, commonly referred to as "J-mold" (it can also be L-shaped), finishes and protects the fragile wallboard edge (see 9B).

Control joint—Usually occurring only in commercial work, a V-shaped flexible trim piece allows movement between two large areas of GWB (see 9C).

Radius trim—Available for inside corners, outside corners and edges, radius (also called bullnose) trim forms a soft, curved edge (see 10A).

Before the application of drywall compound or veneer plaster, metal or plastic trim is applied to the exposed outside corners and edges of wallboard. Such trim provides both a straight edge to which drywall compound or veneer plaster is finished and resistance to impact at particularly vulnerable locations.

 FINISHING CORNERS AND EDGES
TYPES OF TRIM

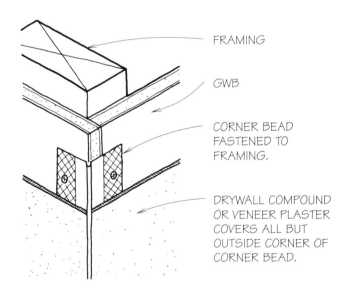

FRAMING

GWB

CORNER BEAD FASTENED TO FRAMING.

DRYWALL COMPOUND OR VENEER PLASTER COVERS ALL BUT OUTSIDE CORNER OF CORNER BEAD.

NOTE:
FOR ARCHED OPENINGS, AN ARCH CORNER BEAD IS AVAILABLE. THIS PERFORATED CORNER BEAD CAN BE SNIPPED AND CURVED.

 OUTSIDE CORNERS

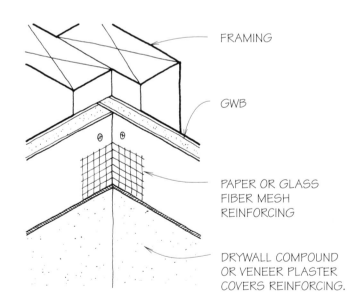

FRAMING

GWB

PAPER OR GLASS FIBER MESH REINFORCING

DRYWALL COMPOUND OR VENEER PLASTER COVERS REINFORCING.

NOTE:
FOR CORNERS LESS OR GREATER THAN 90° (SUCH AS A DORMER WALL), A FLEXIBLE JOINT TAPE WITH INTEGRAL METAL BANDS IS AVAILABLE.

 INSIDE CORNERS

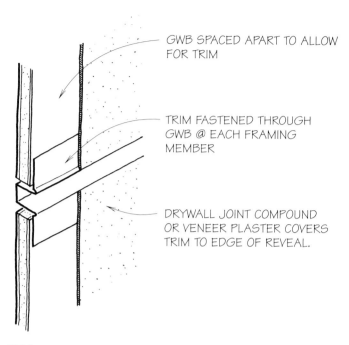

GWB SPACED APART TO ALLOW FOR TRIM

TRIM FASTENED THROUGH GWB @ EACH FRAMING MEMBER

DRYWALL JOINT COMPOUND OR VENEER PLASTER COVERS TRIM TO EDGE OF REVEAL.

NOTE:
SOME REVEAL TRIMS HAVE SNAP-IN FINISH TRIM.

 REVEAL TRIM

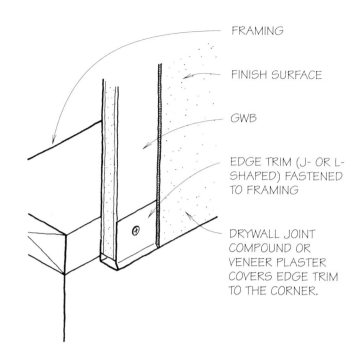

FRAMING

FINISH SURFACE

GWB

EDGE TRIM (J- OR L-SHAPED) FASTENED TO FRAMING

DRYWALL JOINT COMPOUND OR VENEER PLASTER COVERS EDGE TRIM TO THE CORNER.

 EDGE TRIM

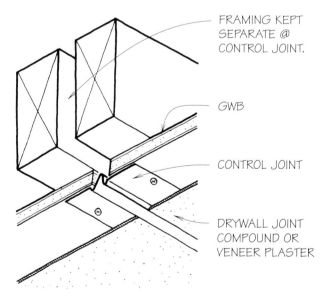

FRAMING KEPT SEPARATE @ CONTROL JOINT.

GWB

CONTROL JOINT

DRYWALL JOINT COMPOUND OR VENEER PLASTER

NOTE:
LOCATE GWB CONTROL JOINTS WHERE THERE IS LIKELY TO BE SIGNIFICANT MOVEMENT, WHERE EXPANSION OR CONTROL JOINTS EXIST IN BUILDING STRUCTURE, IN LARGE CEILINGS WITH T OR L SHAPES OR WITH EXPANSES GREATER THAN 30 FT.

 CONTROL JOINT

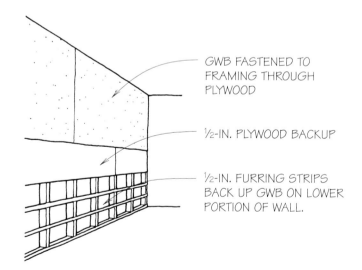

GWB FASTENED TO FRAMING THROUGH PLYWOOD

½-IN. PLYWOOD BACKUP

½-IN. FURRING STRIPS BACK UP GWB ON LOWER PORTION OF WALL.

NOTE:
IF EXTRA STRENGTH IS REQUIRED IN A WALL, SUCH AS FOR A GALLERY OR LIBRARY, GWB CAN BE BACKED UP BY PLYWOOD. FOR ECONOMY, FURRING STRIPS CAN BE ATTACHED TO THE STUDS, WHERE THE WALL IS LESS LIKELY TO NEED SUPPORT, AND FULL-SIZE PLYWOOD PANELS ADDED TO THE REMAINING PORTION.

 GWB W/ PLYWOOD BACKUP

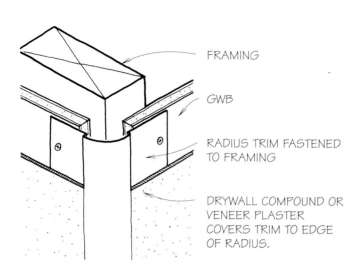

FRAMING

GWB

RADIUS TRIM FASTENED TO FRAMING

DRYWALL COMPOUND OR VENEER PLASTER COVERS TRIM TO EDGE OF RADIUS.

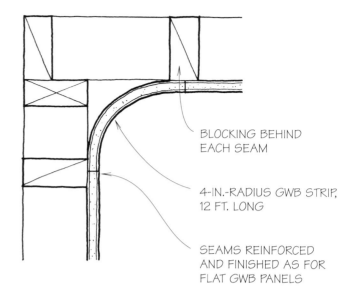

BLOCKING BEHIND EACH SEAM

4-IN.-RADIUS GWB STRIP, 12 FT. LONG

SEAMS REINFORCED AND FINISHED AS FOR FLAT GWB PANELS

Special fixed-radius strips are manufactured of gypsum wallboard to make coved ceilings. The strips may also be used for coved or radiused wall corners.

 A RADIUS TRIM

 B COVED GWB

Gypsum wallboard may be applied to curved surfaces by bending the panels into shallow curves, moistening panels to make a more pronounced curve, or building up with layers of very thin panels to make extreme curves. In most cases, the spacing between the framing members will need to be reduced to support curved panels.

Gypsum Wallboard thickness (in.)	Min. dry radius (ft.)	Min. wet radius (ft.)	Max. stud spacing for min. wet radius (in.)
½	20	4	12
⅜	7½	3	8
¼	5	2	6

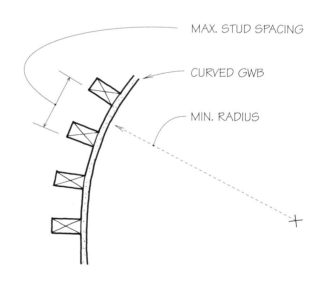

MAX. STUD SPACING

CURVED GWB

MIN. RADIUS

PLAN VIEW OF CURVED GWB WALL

C CURVED SURFACES

CURVED & COMPLEX SHAPES
see 14D

LATH
see 12

THREE-COAT PLASTER
see 13

EDGE DETAILS
see 14C

SQUARE CORNER
see 14A

RADIUS CORNER
see 14B

As recently as the early part of this century, virtually every interior wall and ceiling surface was made with wood lath and three coats of plaster. Wood lath has given way to metal lath, but even with this improvement, the lath and three-coat plaster system has largely been replaced with gypsum wallboard that is finished either with drywall compound (see 5A) or with veneer plaster (see 5B). Lath and plaster is rarely used because it is a more labor- and material-intensive process than a GWB system, and it costs up to several times more.

Lath and plaster is usually specified only where gypsum wallboard systems cannot perform. Tight curves required for intricate details such as a custom-coved ceiling or a fluted column can be formed with lath and plaster, whereas they cannot be made with GWB systems. In locations with high humidity such as a shower or steam room, portland cement/lime plaster on metal lath (see 13) is much more resistant to the effects of moisture and will perform much better than gypsum wallboard. Plaster may also be applied directly to the surface of a concrete-block wall without metal lath; the thickness of the three-coat plaster fills the mortar joints and creates a uniform surface.

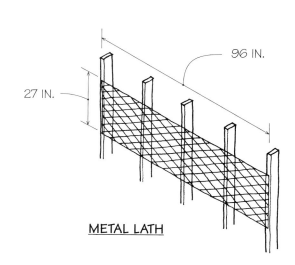

HISTORIC WOOD LATH

96 IN.

27 IN.

METAL LATH

A LATH AND PLASTER

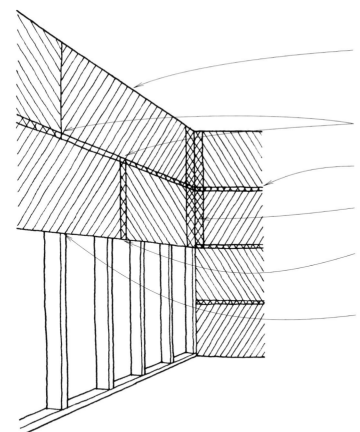

METAL LATH APPLIED WITH LONG DIMENSION ACROSS FRAMING. FASTEN TO WOOD FRAMING W/ NAILS OR STAPLES OR TO METAL FRAMING W/ 18-GA. WIRE.

STAGGER END JOINTS @ EACH COURSE.

LOWER COURSE LAPS OVER UPPER COURSE ½ IN.

LAP @ CORNERS 2 IN. MIN.

IF END JOINT OCCURS BETWEEN FRAMING MEMBERS, LAP 1 IN. MIN. AND LACE OR TIE W/ 18-GA. TIE WIRE.

TAR PAPER (NOT VISIBLE) PROTECTS FRAMING FROM MOISTURE (MAY BE BACKED W/ PLYWOOD OR WIRE).

Various types of lath can support plaster. The lath must be able to resist the application pressure of the first coat of plaster, support the wet plaster, and form an integral unit with the plaster when dry.

Wood and Gypsum-Board Lath

Wood lath is no longer used because of its limited strength, high labor cost and sensitivity to moisture. Metal and GWB lath replaced wood, but GWB lath has now virtually disappeared because it is not as durable as metal lath in moist conditions.

Metal Lath

Metal lath is made from cold-rolled, copper-bearing steel and is either galvanized or coated with rust-inhibitive paint. Metal lath is used almost exclusively because it has both the capacity to form tight curves and the ability to hold the portland cement/lime plaster required in moist locations.

Weight of metal lath (lb./yd.²)	Max. stud spacing (in. o.c.)
2.5	12
3.4	16

The lath is formed from sheet steel that is perforated with many small slits and then stretched to form a mesh with small diamond-shaped openings. This process produces a flat expanded lath commonly referred to as diamond mesh. It is also available in a self-furring type that has dimples that hold the lath ¼ in. away from the surface to which it is applied. Standard diamond mesh is used in new, planar construction, while self-furring diamond mesh is useful over existing or uneven surfaces, or over solid backing such as plywood. A separate tar paper moisture barrier is almost always used behind metal lath to protect the framing or backing from moisture. (The tar paper itself may be backed by plywood or wire.) Diamond mesh with an integral tar paper backing is available in regular and self-furring types.

FLAT EXPANDED LATH (DIAMOND MESH)

A plaster finish requires two general types of plaster in a three-coat application: two base coats (scratch coat and brown coat) and a finish coat (putty coat). The base coats are made of the same plaster but perform different functions. The scratch coat mechanically bonds with and stabilizes the lath and is scratched with a trowel to form a mechanical bond with the brown coat. The brown coat is a leveling coat and was originally brown because straw or horse hair was added to help it bond with the finish coat. The brown coat is floated to the desired thickness and left rough to receive the finish coat. The finish coat is similar to the thin coat of veneer plaster applied to gypsum wallboard (see 5B) and forms the final surface.

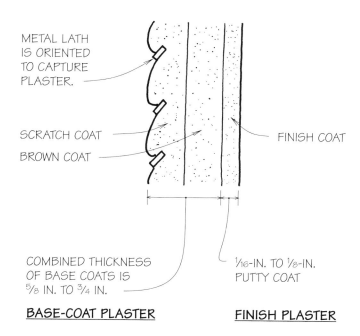

METAL LATH IS ORIENTED TO CAPTURE PLASTER.

SCRATCH COAT
BROWN COAT

FINISH COAT

COMBINED THICKNESS OF BASE COATS IS ⅝ IN. TO ¾ IN.

1/16-IN. TO 1/8-IN. PUTTY COAT

BASE-COAT PLASTER   **FINISH PLASTER**

Base-Coat Plaster

The two types of base-coat plaster are gypsum plaster and portland cement/lime plaster.

Gypsum plaster is most commonly used for base coats and is composed of gypsum, water and an aggregate (sand or perlite) to extend coverage, reduce shrinkage and lower cost. Plaster and aggregates can be mixed on site or are available premixed.

Portland cement/lime plaster is less commonly used and is composed of portland cement, lime, water and an aggregate, and is mixed on site. Suited for locations where moisture or humidity is high, such as showers, it is the same mix used outdoors as stucco.

Finish Plaster

Finish plaster is available as a prepared finish or as individual ingredients to be mixed on site. Prepared finishes are generally more economical and less time-consuming but lack the control of mixing on site. Finish plaster contains four primary ingredients: gauging plaster, finish lime, water and an aggregate (fine silica sand or perlite). Gauging plaster provides a controlled set, hardness and strength, and prevents shrinkage cracks; finish lime provides plasticity and workability; the aggregate adds texture.

Finish texture—Various materials and application techniques provide a range of textures and finishes. Straw, seeds and other materials have been used effectively, and sand gives a subtle texture that remains very popular. Troweled, floated or sprayed finish textures may range from smooth to coarse. Variety is limited only by the imagination of the designer or the ingenuity of the applier.

Trim—Because of its thickness and hardness, a lath-and-plaster wall or ceiling is very difficult to penetrate with a nail or screw without crumbling the plaster. Nailers must be provided for wood trim, or the trim must be eliminated. When using wood trim, wood grounds equal to the total thickness of the plaster and lath are secured to the framing, and then serve as nailers for the trim after plastering (see 14C).

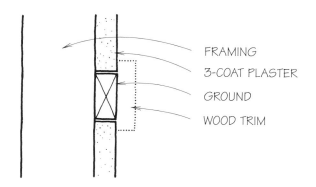

FRAMING
3-COAT PLASTER
GROUND
WOOD TRIM

Care must be taken in detailing how the plaster meets openings and other surfaces. If the plaster is run directly into wood jambs, slight cracking will occur at intersections of wood and plaster as the wood shrinks. Once all the materials become stable, the cracks can be filled with finish plaster to match. Whatever the finishing method, any wood that abuts plaster should be sealed completely before plastering begins.

(A) **THREE-COAT PLASTER**
MATERIALS & APPLICATION

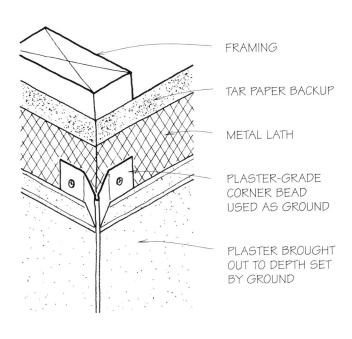

FRAMING

TAR PAPER BACKUP

METAL LATH

PLASTER-GRADE CORNER BEAD USED AS GROUND

PLASTER BROUGHT OUT TO DEPTH SET BY GROUND

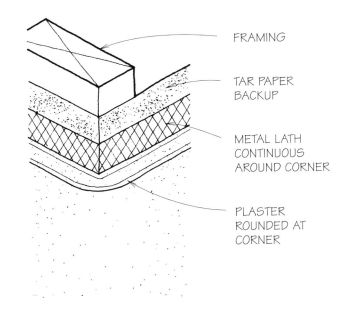

FRAMING

TAR PAPER BACKUP

METAL LATH CONTINUOUS AROUND CORNER

PLASTER ROUNDED AT CORNER

 A   SQUARE CORNER

 B   RADIUS CORNER

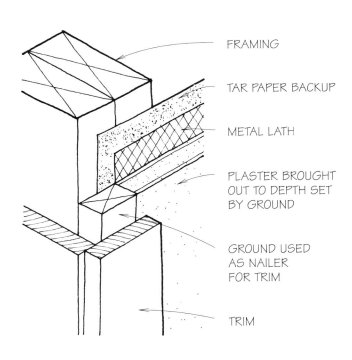

FRAMING

TAR PAPER BACKUP

METAL LATH

PLASTER BROUGHT OUT TO DEPTH SET BY GROUND

GROUND USED AS NAILER FOR TRIM

TRIM

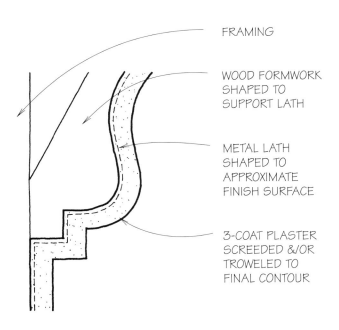

FRAMING

WOOD FORMWORK SHAPED TO SUPPORT LATH

METAL LATH SHAPED TO APPROXIMATE FINISH SURFACE

3-COAT PLASTER SCREEDED &/OR TROWELED TO FINAL CONTOUR

 C   EDGE DETAILS

 D   CURVED & COMPLEX SHAPES

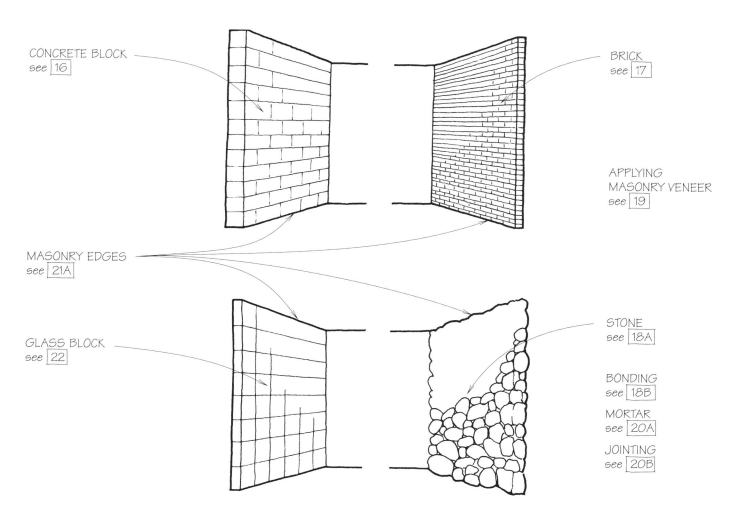

CONCRETE BLOCK
see | 16 |

BRICK
see | 17 |

APPLYING
MASONRY VENEER
see | 19 |

MASONRY EDGES
see | 21A |

STONE
see | 18A |

GLASS BLOCK
see | 22 |

BONDING
see | 18B |

MORTAR
see | 20A |

JOINTING
see | 20B |

Masonry materials are frequently used on the interiors of buildings. Masonry, which includes any durable unit material bound together with mortar, can make a beautiful finish surface and be reasonably priced. Masonry can also provide structural support, fire separation, thermal mass and very good sound reduction. The limitations of masonry include hardness, which makes attaching other materials to it difficult, and weight, which may require that its structural support be carefully considered.

The four types of masonry commonly employed as interior surfaces are concrete block, brick, stone and glass block. Concrete block is the only one of the group that is typically structural. For this reason, and because it is the least expensive, concrete block is the workhorse of the group. Brick and stone, although capable of being structural, are usually used as veneers in association with either concrete block or framed walls. Masonry veneer may require additional structural support, especially if used in conjunction with wood framing. Glass block is usually freestanding and will support its own weight.

In addition to its practical advantages, masonry is often chosen for aesthetic reasons. The color, texture and pattern of a masonry surface are extremely important to the overall aesthetic effect. While masonry patterns and textures can be reasonably simulated on paper, studying a sample of existing work is the best method for becoming acquainted with the features of various materials.

An important detailing consideration for any masonry surface is the condition at the edge where the masonry meets adjacent materials. The irregularity of the masonry surface usually makes a transition to other smoother surfaces a challenge (see 21A–D).

 MASONRY

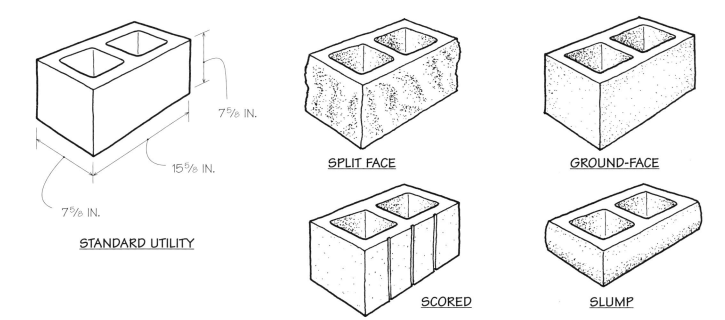

7⅝ IN.

15⅝ IN.

7⅝ IN.

STANDARD UTILITY

SPLIT FACE

GROUND-FACE

SCORED

SLUMP

Concrete block had its origin around the turn of the century when cast stone was developed as a less costly alternative to real stone for use in foundations and fireplaces. Today, an entire industry is based on the production of concrete blocks, which have come to be known as concrete masonry units (CMUs).

Concrete blocks are made of cement, sand, water and aggregate much like concrete. However, concrete blocks are made with a finer aggregate, formed under pressure and heat cured. The center of the block has large cavities to make it lighter and cure properly and for the placement of vertical steel reinforcement.

Surface Texture
The standard utility block has a relatively smooth surface, formed when the wet concrete mixture is forced into smooth-sided metal forms used in its manufacture. Many surface patterns are available:

Split-face—An irregular stonelike surface is achieved by manufacturing a double block and then cleaving it into two single split-face blocks.

Scored—Blocks are formed with vertical grooves. Grooves are available in various profiles and with spacing from 2 in. to 8 in. o.c.

Ground-face—The surface of the block is polished, removing the cement slurry and exposing the aggregate.

Slump—A half-high block that imitates adobe, made by removing forms before the block is cured. Only common in the Southwest.

The CMU surface is usually left exposed or painted but may also be plastered (see 11), furred for applying materials commonly applied to frame walls, or covered with a brick, stone or tile veneer (see 19).

Size
The most common block has an 8-in. by 16-in. face and is 8 in. deep. (The face is actually ⅜ in. undersized to allow for a mortar joint.) Half blocks with an 8-in. by 8-in. face are also common because they are almost

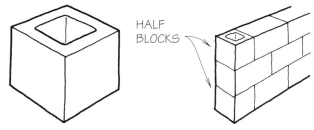

HALF BLOCKS

always required at openings and ends of walls. Deeper blocks (10 in. and 12 in.) are also available for structural purposes. Shallower depths (4 in. for veneer and 6 in. for partition walls) are also available. Half-height blocks are used for horizontal accents or to allow for module heights other than 8 in.

Color
Concrete block is naturally grey, the color of concrete. The color may be adjusted before the blocks are formed, however, by adding a coloring agent to the concrete mixture and/or by specifying a colored aggregate. The color of aggregate is especially important in ground-face block.

 CONCRETE BLOCK (CMU)

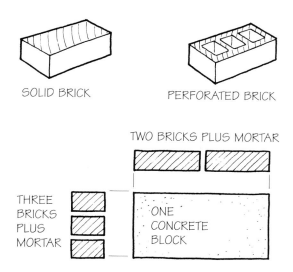

SOLID BRICK   PERFORATED BRICK

TWO BRICKS PLUS MORTAR

THREE BRICKS PLUS MORTAR

ONE CONCRETE BLOCK

MODULAR BRICK

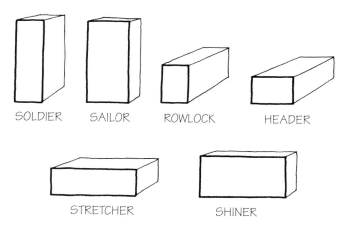

SOLDIER   SAILOR   ROWLOCK   HEADER

STRETCHER   SHINER

BRICK ORIENTATION

NOTE:

VIEWS REPRESENT SAME SIZE AND SHAPE BRICK SEEN FROM DIFFERENT ANGLES.

Bricks are usually made of clay mixed with sand and fired in a kiln. Originally, bricks were formed by hand and baked in the sun. Handmade bricks are the most expensive, but are still used occasionally because of their unmatched beauty. Clay is pressed by hand into a mold that has been wetted and sometimes dusted with sand. The bricks are then dried and fired. Bricks produced this way are called water-struck or sand-struck bricks. A smoother, more consistent machine-made version of this brick, called dry-pressed brick, is also available but not common.

The great majority of bricks made today are wire-cut bricks. These bricks are formed of clay that has been extruded through a rectangular die into long strips that are then cut into bricks by wires set at the desired spacing. The wire-cutting process produces drag marks along one face of the bricks. Bricks may be manufactured with or without perforations or cells, which reduce weight but minimize flexibility in choosing which surface of the brick to expose.

After bricks are formed, they are dried and then fired in a kiln for one to six days at temperatures greater than 2000°F. Generally, the higher the temperature and longer the firing, the harder and less porous the brick.

Size
The most common brick, a modular brick 2¼ in. by 3⅝ in. by 7⅝ in., is dimensioned so that it will lay up with concrete block, as shown above. The size of bricks, however, is determined by manufacturers more

than by logic, so bricks are made in a wide range of shapes and sizes. On the East Coast, for example, standard bricks tend to be longer than the standard modular size (8 in. or 8¼ in. long), while in the Northwest, bricks tend to be slightly shorter and taller (2½ in. by 3⅝ in. by 7½ in.)

Color
Color in clay bricks can be integral—the result of a reaction of the natural chemicals present in the clay to firing—or color may be applied by adding sand or oxide pigment to the bricks' surfaces before firing. Clay bricks often vary in color within one brick and from brick to brick, and are prized for this variation. There are five color designations for clay bricks: red, red multicolor, buff/yellow, grey/brown and blue. Bricks are also available glazed in an extremely wide range of colors for about ten times the cost of standard brick.

Alternatives to Clay Brick
Recently, concrete and calcium silicate have become less expensive alternatives to clay as the primary ingredient in bricks. Concrete bricks are machine pressed from a mixture of cement, sand, water and crushed stone. Calcium silicate bricks are machine pressed from a mixture of hydrated lime, water and either silica sand or crushed flint. Uniform color, although not necessarily desirable, can be better achieved with concrete or calcium silicate bricks than with clay bricks. Both alternative types have an inherent dull white color, but pigment can be added to simulate the color of clay bricks.

 BRICK

Stone, the oldest form of masonry, is available in a considerable range of materials and cuts. Sandstone, limestone, marble, slate and granite are widely available, with other types available regionally. Stone masonry is either laid up with unmachined, irregular pieces known as rubble masonry or with trimmed rectangular pieces known as ashlar masonry.

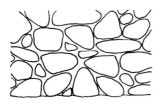

RUBBLE MASONRY

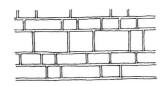

ASHLAR MASONRY

Rubble masonry can be made of rounded river rock, fractured igneous rock, slates, or other types of field-collected or unmachined stone. Ashlar masonry is made with any type of stone that has been cut to have parallel edges.

Like brick, stone is now employed primarily as a veneer. Consequently, there is a modern tendency toward smaller, thinner stone. Many stones, such as granite, marble and slate, are available as tile (see 25A). Stone veneers as thin as 1 in. have also been developed to simulate the appearance of full-thickness stone masonry at a fraction of the weight and cost. These materials are applied like tile.

Like any masonry, stone is difficult to detail at its edges as it makes a transition to another material. Natural stone, however, tends to be even more difficult than other masonry materials because the mortar joints are less uniform and the surface less smooth (see 21D).

 STONE

Bonding patterns were originally developed to tie two thin parallel brick walls (called wythes) into one structural unit.

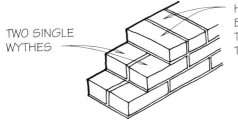

TWO SINGLE WYTHES

HEADER BRICKS TIE WYTHES TOGETHER.

Since bricks are now usually used as veneer, the formerly structural bonding patterns such as English bond and common bond are purely decorative. Running bond, which is a single wythe pattern, is now the most common brick bonding pattern.

Because of its practicality, running bond is also the most common bonding pattern for concrete block. Another bonding pattern is the stacked bond, which is inexpensive but relies on steel reinforcing for its integrity. The stacked bond is most common for glass block, but is also used for both concrete block and brick.

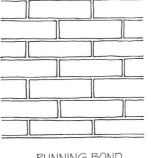
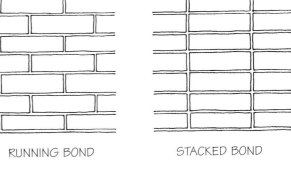

RUNNING BOND

STACKED BOND

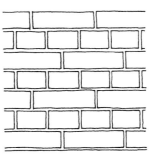
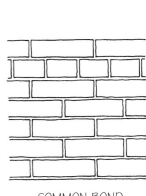

ENGLISH BOND

COMMON BOND

 BONDING PATTERNS

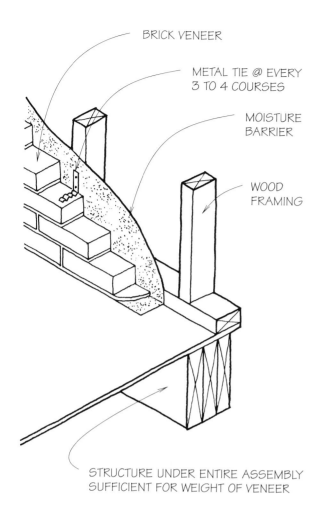

BRICK VENEER

METAL TIE @ EVERY
3 TO 4 COURSES

MOISTURE
BARRIER

WOOD
FRAMING

STRUCTURE UNDER ENTIRE ASSEMBLY
SUFFICIENT FOR WEIGHT OF VENEER

BRICK VENEER ON WOOD

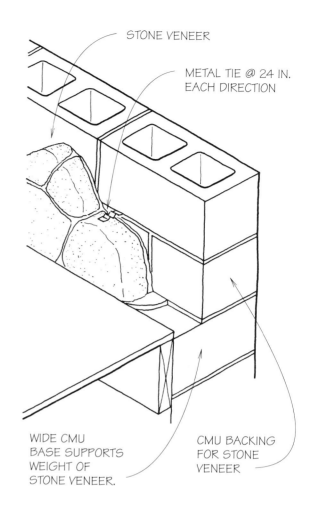

STONE VENEER

METAL TIE @ 24 IN.
EACH DIRECTION

WIDE CMU
BASE SUPPORTS
WEIGHT OF
STONE VENEER.

CMU BACKING
FOR STONE
VENEER

STONE VENEER ON CMU

Masonry veneers must be both supported from below and attached to the structure to keep from overturning. The support below the veneer assembly must be designed to hold its weight. Attachment of veneer to the walls of the structure is achieved with metal ties connected to the structure and embedded into the mortar joints of the veneer. For method used to span window and door openings in a brick-veneer wall, see drawing at right.

Since masonry is a material considerably thicker than most other finish materials and often uneven or irregular, it is imperative to consider carefully how the masonry meets other materials and how openings are made (see 21).

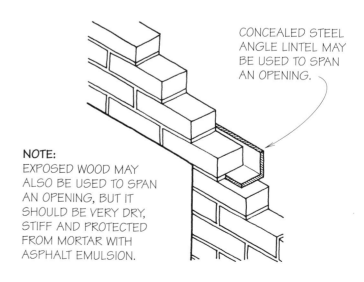

CONCEALED STEEL
ANGLE LINTEL MAY
BE USED TO SPAN
AN OPENING.

NOTE:
EXPOSED WOOD MAY
ALSO BE USED TO SPAN
AN OPENING, BUT IT
SHOULD BE VERY DRY,
STIFF AND PROTECTED
FROM MORTAR WITH
ASPHALT EMULSION.

SPANNING DOOR AND WINDOW OPENINGS

 MASONRY VENEER

Mortar fills the gaps between masonry units and serves to bind the units into a structural whole. Mortar must also support the weight of the masonry. Mortar strength is determined by the proportions of the mix.

The two common types of mortar are portland cement/lime mortar, which is a mixture of portland cement, hydrated lime, mason's sand and water, and is most common, and masonry cement mortar, a mixture of masonry cement, mason's sand and water. The addition of lime to the latter mixture is unnecessary because masonry cement is premixed with workability admixtures such as air entrainers.

Admixtures such as coloring pigments, agents to accelerate or retard curing, water repellents and fungicides to prevent mildew may be added to the mortar. A glass-block shower, for example, would likely have an accelerator, a water repellent and a fungicide added to the mortar.

The color of mortar is determined in part by all of its ingredients except water. Naturally pigmented mortar is grey and may be adjusted by the color of the sand used. Virtually any desired color may be achieved, however, by using white portland cement and adding pigment to the wet mixture. Premixed colored mortar is available in a number of colors and offers the best consistency from batch to batch.

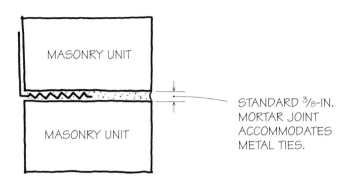

STANDARD ³/₈-IN. MORTAR JOINT ACCOMMODATES METAL TIES.

 MORTAR

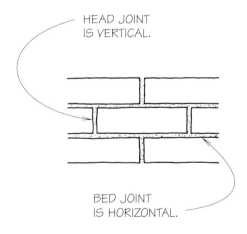

HEAD JOINT IS VERTICAL.

BED JOINT IS HORIZONTAL.

The exposed edge of the mortar joint can be finished with a variety of techniques, each producing a unique effect. The process of shaping the mortar edge when the mortar is fresh and wet is called jointing. Many of these methods were developed to minimize the effects of exposure to the weather, but this is not a factor in an interior veneer application, where appearance is the primary concern.

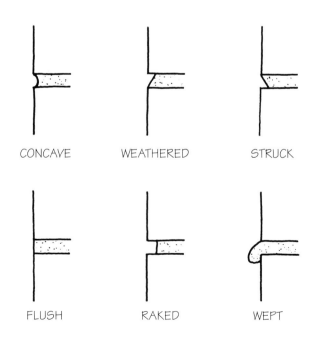

CONCAVE   WEATHERED   STRUCK

FLUSH   RAKED   WEPT

COMMON MORTAR JOINTS

 JOINTING

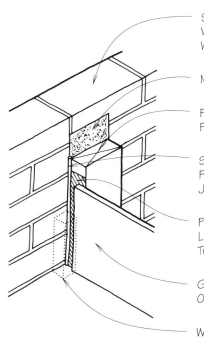

STRUCTURAL OR VENEER MASONRY WALL

MOISTURE BARRIER

FRAMING SPACED 1/8 IN. FROM MASONRY

SEALANT @ FRAMING/MASONRY JOINT

PLASTIC OR OTHER LAMINATE IS APPLIED TO FRAMING @ REVEAL.

GWB W/ EDGE TRIM OR OTHER FINISH WALL

WOOD TRIM MAY BUTT MASONRY IN PLACE OF REVEAL.

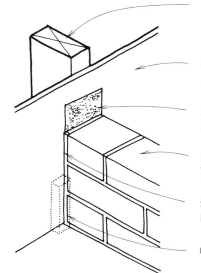

FRAMING KEEPS WALL STIFF ADJACENT TO MASONRY WALL.

GWB OR OTHER FINISH WALL

MOISTURE BARRIER

STRUCTURAL OR VENEER MASONRY

SEALANT REPLACES MORTAR @ END JOINT.

OPTIONAL WOOD TRIM

 FRAMING BUTTS MASONRY

 MASONRY BUTTS FRAMING

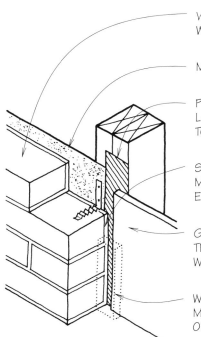

VENEER MASONRY WALL

MOISTURE BARRIER

PLASTIC OR OTHER LAMINATE IS APPLIED TO FRAMING @ REVEAL.

SEALANT REPLACES MORTAR @ EDGE JOINT.

GWB (W/ EDGE TRIM) OR OTHER WALL FINISH

WOOD TRIM MAY BUTT MASONRY IN PLACE OF REVEAL.

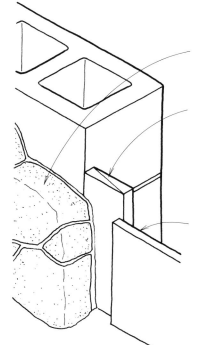

IRREGULAR STONE VENEER

TEMPORARY FORM SHAPES MORTAR INTO SMOOTH SURFACE TO WHICH FINISH PIECE MAY LATER BE APPLIED.

WALL (OR TRIM) LAPS FINISH PIECE TO CREATE REVEAL.

 EDGE OF MASONRY VENEER

 EDGE OF IRREGULAR STONE

Glass blocks are made from two halves of glass fused together to form a sealed hollow core with a partial vacuum inside. Geometric patterns and wavy surfaces can be pressed into the inside surface of the glass

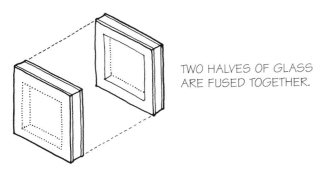

TWO HALVES OF GLASS ARE FUSED TOGETHER.

block prior to fusing to provide various levels of light transmission and distortion yet maintain an easily cleaned, smooth outer surface. Surface textures may also be achieved by etching or sandblasting the exterior faces.

The edges of the blocks are shaped to key the blocks into the mortar while providing space for reinforcing.

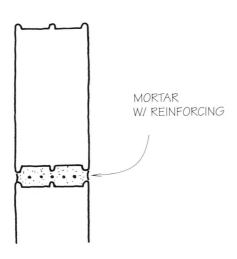

MORTAR W/ REINFORCING

CROSS SECTION OF GLASS-BLOCK JOINT

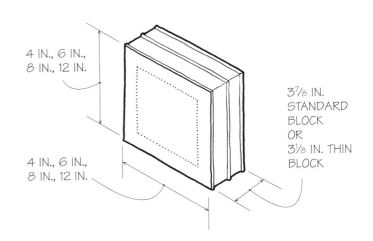

4 IN., 6 IN., 8 IN., 12 IN.

4 IN., 6 IN., 8 IN., 12 IN.

3⅞ IN. STANDARD BLOCK OR 3⅛ IN. THIN BLOCK

NOTE:
BLOCK THICKNESSES ARE ACTUAL DIMENSIONS. HEIGHT & WIDTH DIMENSIONS ARE NOMINAL. ACTUAL SIZES ARE ¼ IN. LESS TO ALLOW FOR MORTAR JOINT.

COMMON SIZES

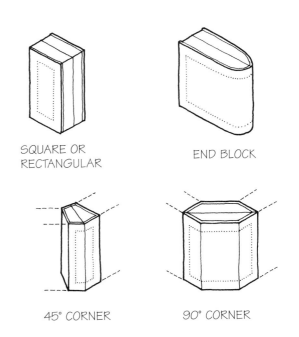

SQUARE OR RECTANGULAR

END BLOCK

45° CORNER

90° CORNER

COMMON SHAPES

Size
Glass blocks are available in two thicknesses: standard (3⅞ in.) and thin (3⅛ in.). Thin glass block is usually specified for interior applications. Most glass blocks are square (6 in., 8 in. or 12 in.), but rectangular shapes are also available (4 in. by 8 in. and 6 in. by 8 in.). Special shapes are available for making corners and ending panels. Not all sizes or shapes are available in either thin or standard thickness.

Special Blocks
When increased fire rating or sound reduction properties are desired, glass blocks with thicker faces may be used. These special blocks are heavier, making them more expensive to produce, transport and install. Solid glass blocks without cavities can provide more impact resistance for special situations but are much heavier than standard or special hollow blocks.

GLASS BLOCK

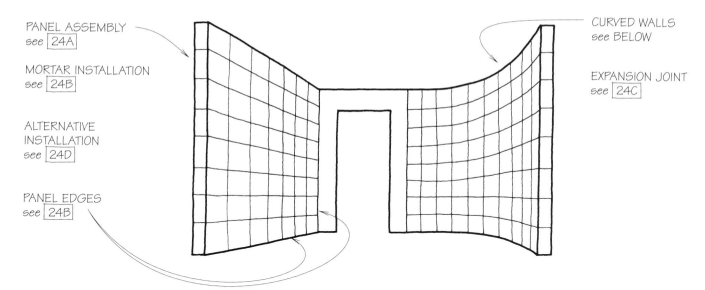

PANEL ASSEMBLY
see 24A

MORTAR INSTALLATION
see 24B

ALTERNATIVE
INSTALLATION
see 24D

PANEL EDGES
see 24B

CURVED WALLS
see BELOW

EXPANSION JOINT
see 24C

Typical glass-block walls are constructed like standard masonry walls, with blocks laid up in courses on beds of mortar. Glass-block walls are usually referred to as panels. Panel size must be coordinated with block thickness, anchoring and reinforcement (see chart below left). Joints are usually aligned both vertically and horizontally (stacked bond) for ease of installation, although other patterns are possible.

Mortar for Glass Block
Glass block doesn't wick away moisture so the mortar used must be drier than that for other masonry. Also, the mortar cures slowly, making it difficult to lay many courses simultaneously. Curing accelerators can counteract this phenomenon, and rigid joint spacers may be used for stability. White portland cement/lime mortar with silica sand makes a mortar color that best complements the color of glass block.

Reinforcement
Reinforcement of glass block panels is provided by galvanized steel reinforcing embedded into horizontal joints every other course (see 24A). Vertical

reinforcement is not necessary except for very large panels over 250 sq. ft. (see chart below).

Anchors
Panels are mortared solid at their bases but are anchored to the structure at their sides and tops with a flexible system of panel anchors, expansion strips and sealant (see 24A). This system allows for slight movement of the structure to occur without cracking the mortar joints. No more than one edge of glass-block panels may be free except for very small areas.

Curved Walls
Glass blocks are easily made into curved walls. The chart below shows the minimum inside radius for typical block widths. Expansion joints are usually required in conjunction with curved walls (see 24D).

Glass block width (in.)	Min. inside radius in inches (assumes ⅛-in. inside joint & ⅝-in. outside joint)
4	32
6	48
8	65
12	96

Alternative Systems
For panels of 85 sq. ft. or less, a mortarless system may be used. Metal channels are used in place of panel anchors to hold the panel edges. In place of mortar, clear plastic spacer strips combined with silicone sealant complete the system (see 24B).

Panel size (sq. ft.)	3⅞-in. block	3⅛-in. block	Flexible anchors	Vertical reinforcement
0–25	✔	✔		
25–150	✔	✔	✔	
150–250	✔		✔	
>250	✔		✔	✔

 INSTALLING GLASS BLOCK

³/₈-IN. FOAM EXPANSION STRIP REPLACES MORTAR @ JAMBS TO ALLOW EXPANSION AND CONTRACTION.

PANEL ANCHORS PLACED 16 IN. TO 18 IN. O.C. VERTICALLY. FASTEN TO FRAMING & SET IN MORTAR BETWEEN BLOCKS.

HORIZONTAL PANEL REINFORCING EVERY OTHER COURSE SET IN MORTAR BETWEEN BLOCKS.

MORTAR JOINT

CAULK COVERS EXPANSION STRIP.

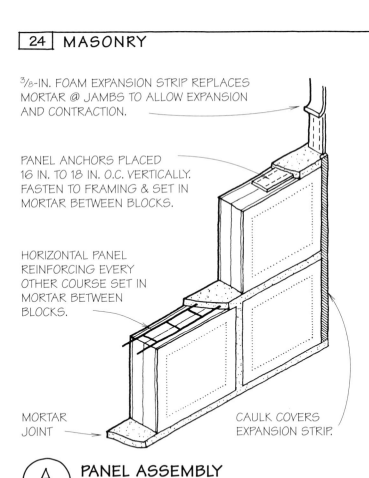

(A) **PANEL ASSEMBLY**
MORTAR INSTALLATION

FRAMING

PANEL ANCHOR @ JAMBS FASTENED TO FRAMING THROUGH SOLID BACKING.

FINISH WALL OR CEILING

EXPANSION STRIP @ JAMBS

CAULK OR TRIM COVERS EXPANSION STRIP.

GLASS BLOCK

MORTAR BED

SPACER OR STEM WALL

FINISH FLOOR

SUBFLOOR

STRUCTURE SUFFICIENT TO SUPPORT PANEL.

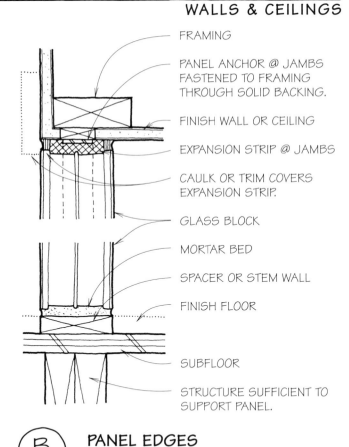

(B) **PANEL EDGES**
MORTAR INSTALLATION

DISCONTINUE HORIZONTAL REINFORCING.

ELASTIC CAULK

FOAM EXPANSION STRIP

GLASS BLOCKS

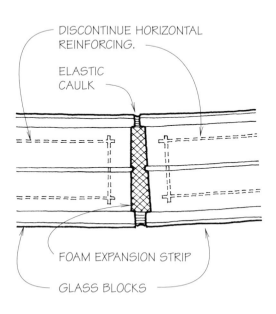

NOTE:
EXPANSION JOINTS REQUIRED @ INTERSECTION OF CURVED & STRAIGHT PANELS, @ EACH CHANGE OF DIRECTION IN MULTI-CURVED PANELS & @ CENTER OF CURVED PANELS GREATER THAN 90°.

(C) **EXPANSION JOINT**
MORTAR INSTALLATION

METAL CHANNEL PANEL RESTRAINT FASTENED TO FRAMING.

PLASTIC SPACER STRIPS

NOTE:
THIS SYSTEM IS SUITABLE ONLY FOR PANELS LESS THAN 85 SQ. FT.

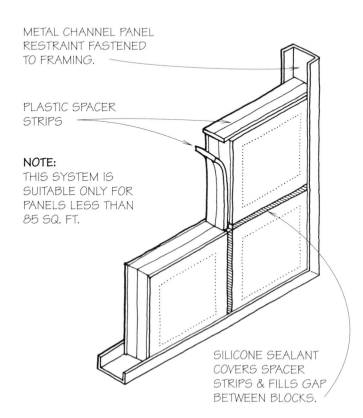

SILICONE SEALANT COVERS SPACER STRIPS & FILLS GAP BETWEEN BLOCKS.

(D) **PANEL ASSEMBLY**
ALTERNATIVE INSTALLATION

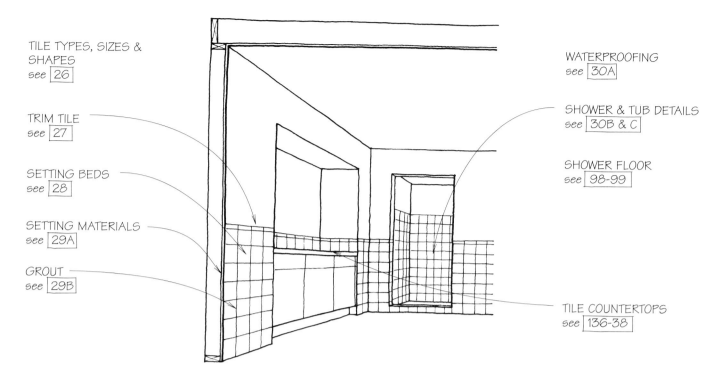

TILE TYPES, SIZES & SHAPES
see 26

TRIM TILE
see 27

SETTING BEDS
see 28

SETTING MATERIALS
see 29A

GROUT
see 29B

WATERPROOFING
see 30A

SHOWER & TUB DETAILS
see 30B & C

SHOWER FLOOR
see 98-99

TILE COUNTERTOPS
see 136-38

Although more labor-intensive to install than many other materials, tile has an enduring quality that is difficult to match. The aesthetic quality of a tile wall or ceiling is based on its surface alone, but it is the whole assembly that determines its performance. The basic components of a tile assembly are tile, setting bed (substrate), setting material, grout and waterproofing (if a wet application), as shown below.

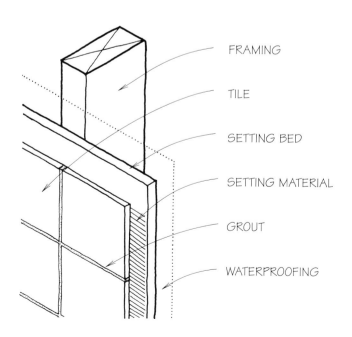

FRAMING

TILE

SETTING BED

SETTING MATERIAL

GROUT

WATERPROOFING

The most important factor related to a tile's performance is its degree of absorptivity. This is determined by the composition of the tile's ingredients, the temperature of firing in the kiln and the length of time it was fired. In general, the higher the temperature and longer the time in the kiln, the more dense, less porous and more costly the tile.

The following chart shows the four grades of tile recognized by the tile industry, with their respective absorptivity.

Grade	Absorptivity	Use
nonvitreous	7% or more	dry
semivitreous	3–7%	moist*
vitreous	.5–3%	wet
impervious	less than .5%	wet

*Up to 5% absorption OK for wet use.

It is important to match the grade of tile with its intended use. Dry installations are areas that rarely see moisture, such as fireplace surrounds, where any tile may be used. Semivitreous or better tile should be used in moist installations, such as showers, tub enclosures and steam rooms, which occasionally get wet. Vitreous and impervious tile are most suitable for wet installations, such as pools or spas, while semivitreous is acceptable for wet installations but not highly recommended, since it is more likely to harbor bacteria.

A TILE

Ceramic Tile

Originally made from pure clay, ceramic tile today is made from a composite of clay and shale or gypsum, plus other ingredients that control shrinking and provide body while reducing the amount of clay used. There are many types of ceramic tile, often categorized according to use or to principal ingredients. Paver tiles, for example, are categorized according to use, while porcelain tile is defined by its principal ingredient, china clay. There are many tiles, however, that do not fall into a specific category. Most tiles are graded by the American National Standards Institute (ANSI) for their water absorptivity. This absorption grading system should be the primary determinant when selecting tile for wet or damp locations.

The following types of tile are commonly accepted categories of ceramic tile. Remember that not all tile will necessarily fall into one of these categories.

Glazed wall tile—The major classification of ceramic tile is glazed wall tile. This nonvitreous tile is suitable for interior use on walls and ceilings. The glaze on the tile gives it color and surface texture and protects it. Glazed tile is made by brushing or spraying a coating of lead silicates and pigment on the tile and firing it in a kiln. Like the tile itself, however, the hardness and porosity of the glaze depend on its composition, the temperature of firing and the time in the kiln. The fact that a tile is glazed, therefore, does not necessarily make it suitable for wet locations. An enormous range of glaze colors is available commercially, and almost any color can be specially made.

Quarry tile—Originally quarried stone, quarry tile today is semivitreous or vitreous clay tile that is fired unglazed. Most commonly used for floors (see 92), quarry tile is also sometimes used for walls or ceilings.

Paver tile—These medium- to large-size ceramic tiles of varying hardness and absorptivity are usually used for floors (see 92).

Nonceramic Tile

A number of types of nonceramic tiles containing no clay can be used for walls and ceilings:

Stone—Flagstone, granite, marble, onyx and slate are the most common stones used as tiles. Stone tiles are either split from the stone (cleft), or cut to consistent dimensions (gauged). Since cleft stone is uneven and difficult to clean, it is not very practical for wet installations.

Cement-bodied tile—Cement-bodied tile is made of mortar that is extruded and cut into sheets. It is less expensive than ceramic tile, but is porous and should not be used for wet installations.

Glass tile—As its name suggests, glass tile is made primarily of glass, often recycled. It is available in many sizes and shapes, most commonly as a mosaic tile.

Solid-surface tile—A fairly new material made of mineral particles bound in plastic resin, solid-surface tile has gained tremendous popularity as a countertop material (see 128). The composition of this tile makes it very practical for wet installations.

Tile Size & Shape

Tile comes in a wide range of sizes (commonly up to 12 in.) and shapes (shown below), both as individual tiles and mounted on sheets. The larger the tile, the greater the chance of warping in production.

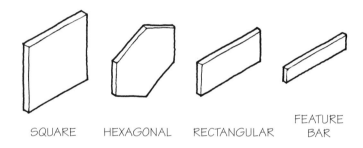

SQUARE   HEXAGONAL   RECTANGULAR   FEATURE BAR

TILE SHAPES

The smaller the tile, the greater the difficulty in handling. The smallest tiles are usually premounted on sheets (typically 12 in. square or larger) of paper, plastic or rubber backing, or with edge mounts as shown below. Tile less than 2 in. square is called mosaic tile.

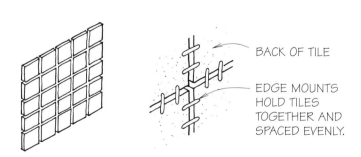

BACK OF TILE

EDGE MOUNTS HOLD TILES TOGETHER AND SPACED EVENLY.

PREMOUNTED SHEET   **BACK OF EDGE-MOUNTED SHEET**

 TILE TYPES, SIZES AND SHAPES

Corners and edges of tiled areas often require special trim tile. The availability of trim tile for these conditions often determines the selection of the field tile, which is most of the tile used in an installation. When stock trim tiles are unavailable, sometimes trim tiles can be made on site with simple tools. Some types of tile, such as stone, cannot be easily made in trim-tile configurations, so careful detailing is required to eliminate the need for trim tiles.

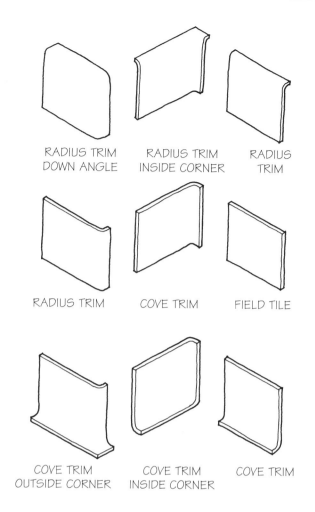

RADIUS TRIM DOWN ANGLE   RADIUS TRIM INSIDE CORNER   RADIUS TRIM

RADIUS TRIM   COVE TRIM   FIELD TILE

COVE TRIM OUTSIDE CORNER   COVE TRIM INSIDE CORNER   COVE TRIM

COMBINATION TRIMS

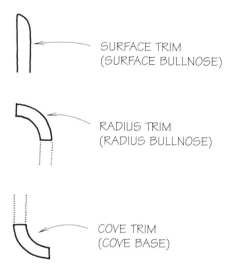

SURFACE TRIM (SURFACE BULLNOSE)

RADIUS TRIM (RADIUS BULLNOSE)

COVE TRIM (COVE BASE)

The major trim tile types are *surface trim* (also called surface bullnose), which is flat tile with one edge rounded over; *radius trim* (also called radius bullnose), which is curved trim tile with square edges for outside corners; *cove trim* (also called cove base), which is curved trim tile with square edges for inside corners.

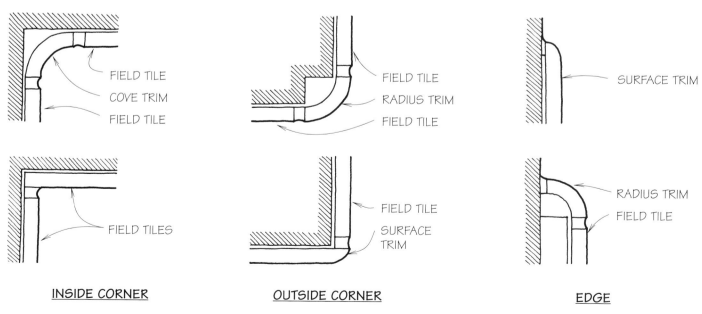

FIELD TILE
COVE TRIM
FIELD TILE

FIELD TILE
RADIUS TRIM
FIELD TILE

SURFACE TRIM

FIELD TILES

FIELD TILE
SURFACE TRIM

RADIUS TRIM
FIELD TILE

INSIDE CORNER   **OUTSIDE CORNER**   **EDGE**

A   **TRIM TILE**

The setting bed, commonly referred to as the substrate, is the rigid material to which the tile is bonded. The two general types of setting bed are thick-bed and thinbed.

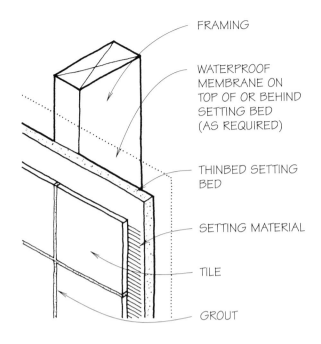

FRAMING

WATERPROOF MEMBRANE ON TOP OF OR BEHIND SETTING BED (AS REQUIRED)

THINBED SETTING BED

SETTING MATERIAL

TILE

GROUT

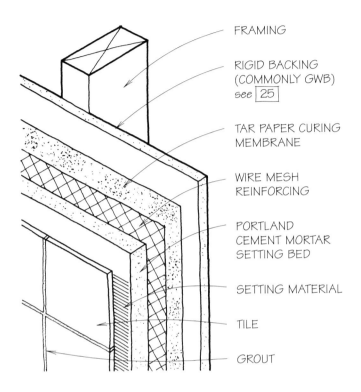

FRAMING

RIGID BACKING (COMMONLY GWB) see 25

TAR PAPER CURING MEMBRANE

WIRE MESH REINFORCING

PORTLAND CEMENT MORTAR SETTING BED

SETTING MATERIAL

TILE

GROUT

Thick-bed

Commonly referred to as "mudset," a thick-bed installation consists of a setting bed of reinforced portland cement mortar, typically ½ in. to 1½ in. thick. Although traditionally executed in two coats, it is typically floated in one coat over metal lath or wire mesh reinforcing fastened to a rigid backing, commonly gypsum wallboard or plywood. Tar paper or another suitable membrane is placed on top of the backing to protect it from the moisture in the mortar. Tile is bonded to the mortar setting bed with a setting material, either while the mortar is still workable or after the mortar has cured. A good-quality thick-bed installation is generally regarded as superior in performance to a thinbed installation. It is structurally strong, not affected by prolonged contact with water and can be used to provide a smooth, flat setting bed over an uneven surface, making it useful for renovation projects. It is, however, a more difficult and costly installation than thinbed.

Thinbed

A thinbed installation consists of a manufactured rigid backing attached either directly to the framing or to a rigid board attached to the framing. The tile is made to adhere to its surface with an appropriate setting material. The advantage of this system is its simplicity, but because it is thin in relation to a thick-bed, care must be taken to ensure its stiffness to avoid cracking the tiles or grout. The three most common thinbed backing materials are gypsum wallboard, plywood and cementitious backer board.

Gypsum wallboard is inexpensive but not moisture resistant. GWB is available with a variety of moisture-resistant coatings, but if any moisture should get past the coating, the gypsum core will disintegrate. It should therefore be avoided for moist installations.

Plywood is inexpensive but not very dimensionally stable, compared to cementitious backer board, and it doesn't bond well. It should be avoided for moist installations.

Cementitious backer board, a mortar core with glass mesh reinforcing on both faces, performs closest to a thick-bed installation. It is not affected by moisture, making it an ideal substrate for moist installations.

 SETTING BEDS

The setting material adheres the tile to the setting bed. Most installations are thinset, meaning the setting material is applied in one thin layer over a dry setting bed. The exception to the thinset installation is when tile is bonded to a still workable mortar bed, used traditionally but uncommon today. The two basic types of setting material are mortar and adhesive.

Mortar

A mixture of portland cement, sand and additives, mortar can be used for a variety of installations. A special latex is often added for increased flexibility. Mortar has a high bond and compressive strength and a quick setup time, and is more flexible than organic adhesive. It can be used for wet or hot installations and over almost any setting bed. Because it cures by hydration, thinset mortar is more forgiving of uneven setting beds than organic adhesive, but a relatively smooth setting bed is still required for a long-lasting installation. An epoxy mortar using epoxy resins and hardeners is available for increased bond strength.

Adhesive

The most common setting material is organic adhesive, also called organic mastic. It is a petroleum- or latex-based product with a bonding agent that holds the tile to the setting bed, and a liquid vehicle that provides the consistency necessary to spread the adhesive. Curing occurs when the liquid evaporates. Since it grips firmly before full curing, organic adhesive is ideal for wall and ceiling applications but doesn't have a bond strength as great as mortar. An epoxy organic adhesive is also available for installations requiring a high-bond strength.

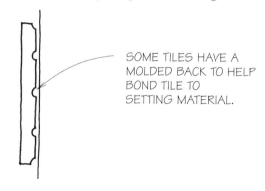

SOME TILES HAVE A MOLDED BACK TO HELP BOND TILE TO SETTING MATERIAL.

A   SETTING MATERIALS

A type of mortar, tile grout is portland cement mixed with water. It is used to fill the joints between tiles. Owing to its high density, grout aids in the prevention of water penetration, although it cannot be considered waterproof. Additives such as latex or epoxy may be included to increase flexibility, bond strength, water and stain resistance, mildew resistance and color retention. The two types of grout are plain grout, used for joints ¹⁄₁₆ in. or less, and sanded grout, which is simply plain grout with sand added for body and strength. Sanded grout is used for joints larger than ¹⁄₁₆ in. Grout is available in a number of premixed colors and can be custom mixed to make almost any color.

While grouting is generally the last step in a tile installation, mounted sheets of tile can be purchased pregrouted. These sheets are made using an elastomeric material such as silicone caulk rather than grout and are used in some commercial applications to save time, although the pregrouted sheets are more costly than standard tile sheets.

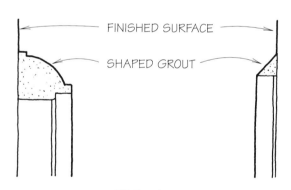

FINISHED SURFACE

SHAPED GROUT

EDGE TILES

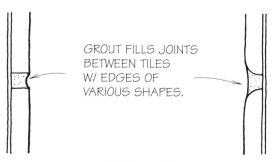

GROUT FILLS JOINTS BETWEEN TILES W/ EDGES OF VARIOUS SHAPES.

FIELD TILES

B   GROUT

When detailing a ceramic tile wall or ceiling for wet or damp locations (see 25), it is especially important to consider the performance of the entire assembly. Although ceramic tile, adhesives and grout aren't generally harmed by water, the setting bed and/or structure may be susceptible to moisture penetration. Keeping moisture out is usually achieved by the appropriate combination of setting bed and waterproofing membrane, which is generally either a flexible sheet or a trowel-applied system.

Flexible Sheets

The three common types of flexible sheet membranes are tar-saturated felt paper (also called tar paper), 4-mil polyethylene film and chlorinated polyethylene (CPE) waterproofing sheet. The tar paper and polyethylene are applied behind the setting bed, so the setting bed must be able to withstand exposure to moisture. They are attached with staples either directly to the framing or to a rigid backing. They are the least expensive, but also least reliable, waterproofing membranes.

CPE is laminated to the surface of the setting bed with an appropriate setting material. CPE sheets are the most expensive waterproofing membranes, but the most effective, and may allow the use of a less expensive setting bed.

Trowel-Applied Waterproofing

Single or multicomponent trowel-applied waterproofing membranes are available. The single-component system consists of a liquid or paste that cures into a continuous membrane. It is applied to the surface of the setting bed.

The multicomponent system is a combination of liquid latex and fabric applied to the surface of the setting bed. The liquid is first spread on the setting bed and the fabric is embedded in it. A second coat of liquid is then applied over the fabric.

Trowel-applied waterproofing typically costs about the same as the CPE membrane but is more versatile and effective in complicated installations.

(A) WATERPROOFING

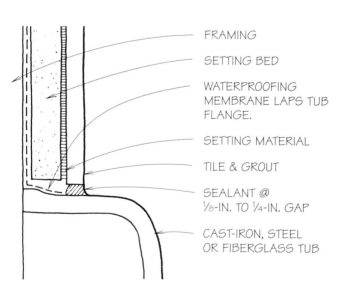

FRAMING

SETTING BED

WATERPROOFING MEMBRANE LAPS TUB FLANGE.

SETTING MATERIAL

TILE & GROUT

SEALANT @ ⅛-IN. TO ¼-IN. GAP

CAST-IRON, STEEL OR FIBERGLASS TUB

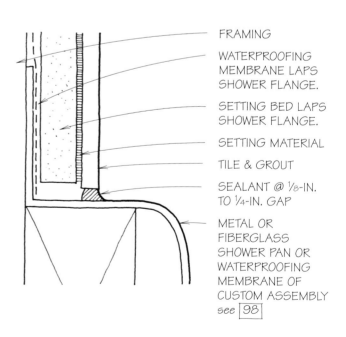

FRAMING

WATERPROOFING MEMBRANE LAPS SHOWER FLANGE.

SETTING BED LAPS SHOWER FLANGE.

SETTING MATERIAL

TILE & GROUT

SEALANT @ ⅛-IN. TO ¼-IN. GAP

METAL OR FIBERGLASS SHOWER PAN OR WATERPROOFING MEMBRANE OF CUSTOM ASSEMBLY see 98

(B) TUB DETAIL
TILE @ TUB EDGE

(C) SHOWER DETAIL
TILE @ SHOWER-PAN LIP

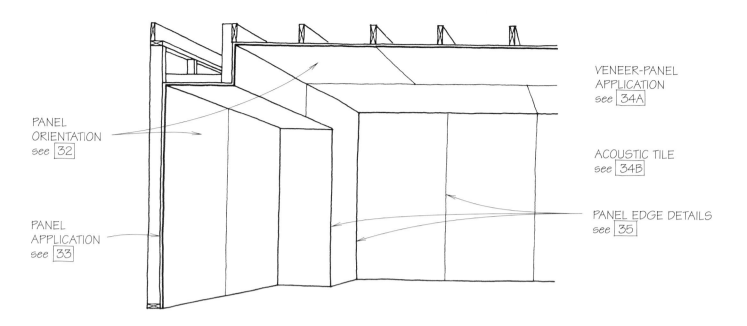

PANEL
ORIENTATION
see | 32 |

PANEL
APPLICATION
see | 33 |

VENEER-PANEL
APPLICATION
see | 34A |

ACOUSTIC TILE
see | 34B |

PANEL EDGE DETAILS
see | 35 |

There is a tremendous variety of manufactured sheet paneling designed to be used for interior finish surfaces. These products generally have a prefinished surface applied to a plywood, composition board or gypsum board core (see Appendix B for description of individual types of sheet paneling). Panels are usually 4 ft. by 8 ft. but may be found up to 5 ft. wide by 10 ft. long, and are available in a range of thicknesses from ⅛ in. to ¾ in. (as shown in the drawing at right). While most of the thicker panels may be fastened directly to the framing, a separate backing material is required for the thinnest panels (called veneer panels).

In addition to the products specifically manufactured for use as interior surfaces, several other panel products have been used creatively to make interesting and appropriate interior finishes. Some of these products include oriented-strand board (OSB), straw board, plastic board and unfinished hardboard (see Appendix B).

Finishes
Sheet panels most often have a visually desirable surface applied over the structural core. The applied surface may be a wood veneer, a paper overlay, a fabric overlay, a vinyl coating, a plastic coating or paint. Panels are frequently textured with shallow grooves cut into the surface to simulate individual boards or embossed to create other modular patterns. Some panels, such as oriented-strand board, have significant texture integral to the structural core.

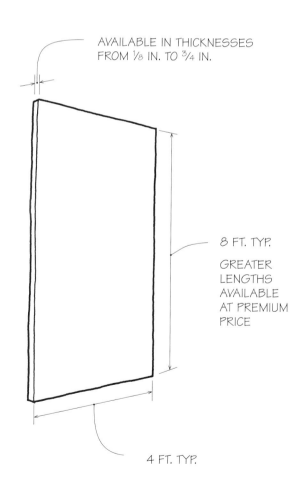

AVAILABLE IN THICKNESSES
FROM ⅛ IN. TO ¾ IN.

8 FT. TYP.

GREATER
LENGTHS
AVAILABLE
AT PREMIUM
PRICE

4 FT. TYP.

 SHEET PANELING

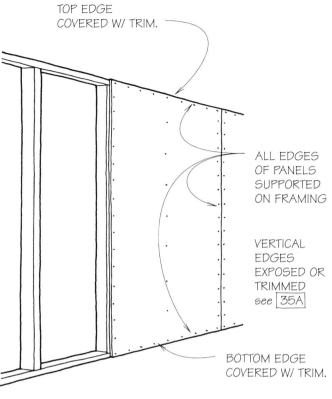

TOP EDGE COVERED W/ TRIM.

ALL EDGES OF PANELS SUPPORTED ON FRAMING

VERTICAL EDGES EXPOSED OR TRIMMED
see 35A

BOTTOM EDGE COVERED W/ TRIM.

TYPICAL VERTICAL ORIENTATION

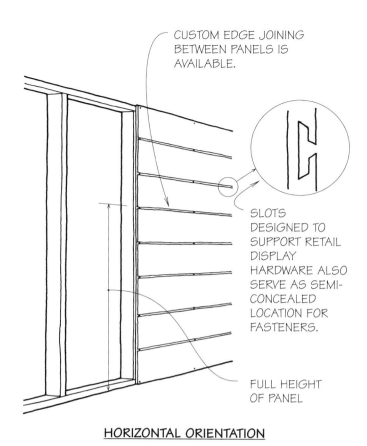

CUSTOM EDGE JOINING BETWEEN PANELS IS AVAILABLE.

SLOTS DESIGNED TO SUPPORT RETAIL DISPLAY HARDWARE ALSO SERVE AS SEMI-CONCEALED LOCATION FOR FASTENERS.

FULL HEIGHT OF PANEL

HORIZONTAL ORIENTATION

The fact that sheet paneling is usually prefinished has implications for its use. Since the edges of prefinished panels are always apparent after installation and it is generally desirable to minimize edge trim, the panels are most commonly found on walls in a vertical orientation. In this position, the panels touch each other only along their long edges (see drawing above left). Many manufacturers recognize this and detail the long edges of their panels with tongue-and-groove, or other profiles that interlock, or lap panels.

Another advantage of the vertical orientation of panels on walls is that all edges of the panel are supported by framing without the addition of blocking.

There are, of course, exceptions. Some specialized panels, such as the slot systems for retail display, are designed to be oriented horizontally on walls (see drawing above right). Panels may also be applied to the ceiling, but the perpendicular intersection of panel edges is inevitable so detailing is more difficult. Ceiling application also usually requires additional blocking located at panel edges.

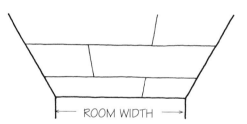

ROOM WIDTH

NOTE:
CEILING PANELS ARE USUALLY NARROWER THAN ROOM WIDTH SO PANEL EDGES WILL BE EXPOSED OR CAN BE TRIMMED IN BOTH DIRECTIONS.

ADDITION OF EXTRA TRIM CAN CREATE A REGULAR PATTERN.

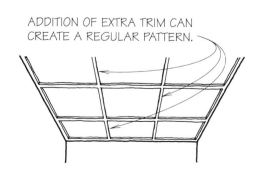

PANEL ORIENTATION

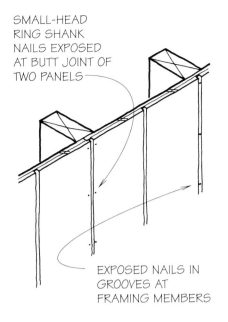

SMALL-HEAD RING SHANK NAILS EXPOSED AT BUTT JOINT OF TWO PANELS

EXPOSED NAILS IN GROOVES AT FRAMING MEMBERS

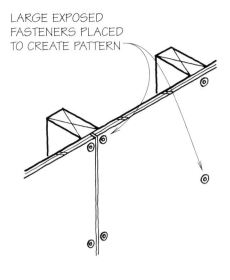

LARGE EXPOSED FASTENERS PLACED TO CREATE PATTERN

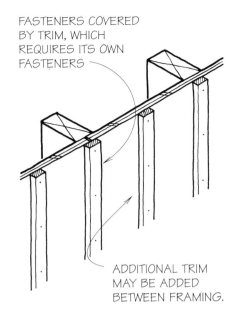

FASTENERS COVERED BY TRIM, WHICH REQUIRES ITS OWN FASTENERS

ADDITIONAL TRIM MAY BE ADDED BETWEEN FRAMING.

SMALL PAINTED NAILS

EXPOSED FASTENERS

FASTENERS COVERED BY TRIM

Since most panels are 4 ft. wide, they require fasteners both at the edges and in the field of the panel to connect them firmly to the frame of the building. There are two basic fasteners used to attach panel products: panel-penetrating fasteners and concealed fasteners.

Panel-Penetrating Fasteners
Panel-penetrating fasteners pass through the panel into the framing (drawings above). The standard approach is to leave these fasteners exposed but to make them small and unobtrusive. Alternatively, larger exposed fasteners may be applied carefully to make a pattern. The fasteners may also be covered with trim (which itself needs fasteners) to create a pattern reminiscent of board-and-batten siding.

Concealed Fasteners
Another method of connecting panels to the building frame is to employ a concealed fastener attached to the back of the panel. This fastener locks on to a complementary fastener attached to the wall framing (drawings at right). The entire system is held in place once the edges of the panel are fixed.

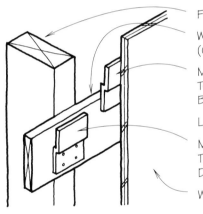

FRAMING

WOOD FURRING STRIPS (OPTIONAL)

METAL CLIP FASTENED TO PANEL FROM BEHIND

LOCKS ONTO

METAL CLIP FASTENED TO FURRING OR DIRECTLY TO FRAMING

WALL PANEL

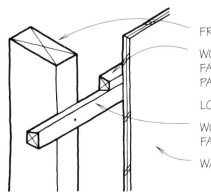

FRAMING

WOOD VEE HANGER FASTENED TO BACK OF PANEL

LOCKS ONTO

WOOD VEE HANGER FASTENED TO FRAMING

WALL PANEL

CONCEALED FASTENERS

(A) PANEL APPLICATION

Thin sheet panels (⅛ in. to 3/16 in.) are usually made of hardboard or three-ply plywood with an overlaid finish surface. Because buildup of materials is minimal, thin panels are generally designed for remodeling work but may also be used for new work. Panels are applied with adhesive to backing materials capable of spanning between framing members. The backing eliminates the need for panel edges to align with framing members, and the adhesive eliminates the need for exposed fasteners.

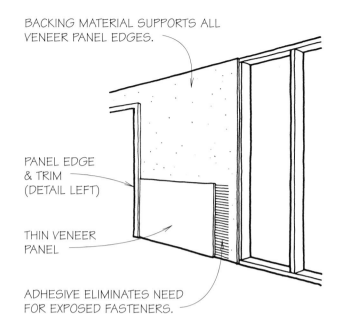

BACKING MATERIAL SUPPORTS ALL VENEER PANEL EDGES.

PANEL EDGE & TRIM (DETAIL LEFT)

THIN VENEER PANEL

ADHESIVE ELIMINATES NEED FOR EXPOSED FASTENERS.

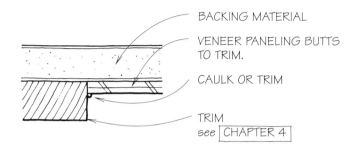

BACKING MATERIAL

VENEER PANELING BUTTS TO TRIM.

CAULK OR TRIM

TRIM
see CHAPTER 4

 VENEER SHEET PANELING

Acoustic tile, a common variety of sheet paneling, is . designed for use on ceilings. The tiles are typically 12 in. square and made of ½-in. to ¾-in. thick soundboard. Their prefinished white surface is either plain, perforated or embossed with a design for visual interest and to increase sound-absorption qualities.

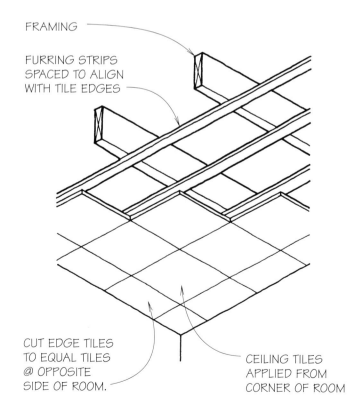

FRAMING

FURRING STRIPS SPACED TO ALIGN WITH TILE EDGES

CUT EDGE TILES TO EQUAL TILES @ OPPOSITE SIDE OF ROOM.

CEILING TILES APPLIED FROM CORNER OF ROOM

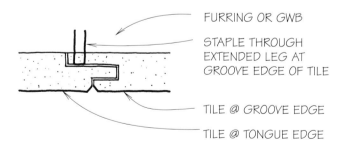

FURRING OR GWB

STAPLE THROUGH EXTENDED LEG AT GROOVE EDGE OF TILE

TILE @ GROOVE EDGE

TILE @ TONGUE EDGE

These tiles are furnished with tongue-and-groove edges so that they may be installed with concealed staples or nails. Tiles are commonly fastened to a furring strip system applied perpendicular to the framing. They may also be stapled or bonded with panel adhesive to a continuous surface such as GWB.

 ACOUSTIC TILE

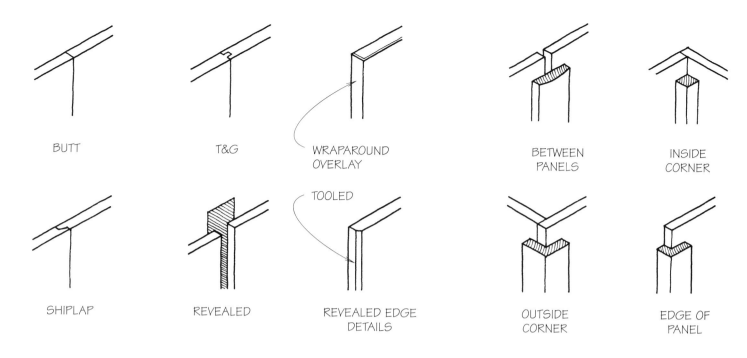

BUTT	T&G	WRAPAROUND OVERLAY	BETWEEN PANELS	INSIDE CORNER

TOOLED

SHIPLAP	REVEALED	REVEALED EDGE DETAILS	OUTSIDE CORNER	EDGE OF PANEL

EXPOSED EDGES

TRIMMED EDGES

The detailing of joints between panels and at the outer edges of panels is a significant factor in the overall appearance of a paneled surface. The joints may be either exposed or covered with trim.

Exposed Edges
Some panels are manufactured with a finished edge while others have a raw edge not designed for exposure. Unfinished edges may be detailed in a shop before installation to upgrade them to a visually desirable condition. The alignment of exposed edges of adjacent panels requires continuous framing and careful consideration of fastening systems.

Trimmed Edges
Custom-made or manufactured wood trim strips (drawing above right) are common for thick wood-product panels. These strips cover the edges of the panels and help hold them in line. Panel trim must be coordinated with other trim systems (see Chapter 4). There are also a number of manufactured edge trims designed specifically for veneer or gypsum panels (as shown at lower right).

BATTEN

INSIDE CORNER

OUTSIDE CORNER

PANEL EDGE

EXTRUDED PLASTIC TRIM FOR VENEER PANELS & GYPSUM PANELS

 PANEL EDGE DETAILS

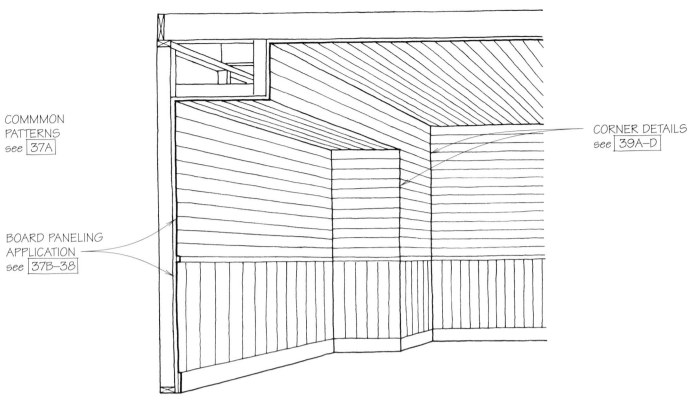

COMMMON
PATTERNS
see 37A

BOARD PANELING
APPLICATION
see 37B–38

CORNER DETAILS
see 39A–D

The development of tongue-and-groove (T&G) boards
before the beginning of the Industrial Age solved two
problems at once. First, the tongue-and-groove profile
locked adjacent boards together structurally so that
they could span greater distances with less deflection
than a single board. Second, the tongue provided a
location to nail the boards to the structure that is
covered by the next board, thereby eliminating
exposed fasteners.

The most common use of tongue-and-groove boards is
for flooring (see 90A), where it is important that the
boards fit snugly against one another to form a
continuous, smooth surface free of gaps. For walls and
ceilings, however, this continuous gap-free surface is
not as easily achieved, but fortunately it is not as
important. Gaps between boards on walls and ceilings
do not create maintenance problems and tend to go
unnoticed unless the boards are extremely light in
color. Tongue-and-groove or lapped profiles that create
a reveal between boards can eliminate concern about
gaps between boards by purposefully creating a wide
gap as a visual accent.

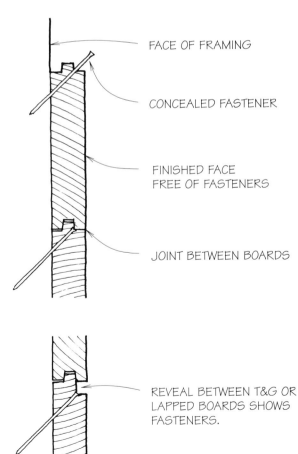

FACE OF FRAMING

CONCEALED FASTENER

FINISHED FACE
FREE OF FASTENERS

JOINT BETWEEN BOARDS

REVEAL BETWEEN T&G OR
LAPPED BOARDS SHOWS
FASTENERS.

 BOARD PANELING

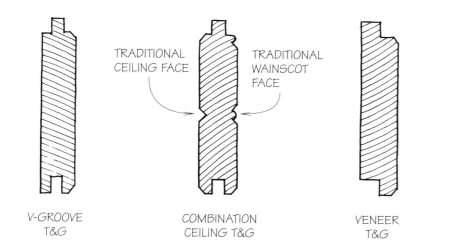

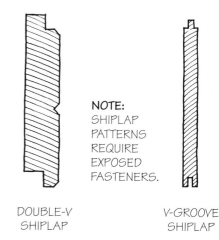

V-GROOVE
T&G

COMBINATION
CEILING T&G

VENEER
T&G

DOUBLE-V
SHIPLAP

V-GROOVE
SHIPLAP

TRADITIONAL
CEILING FACE

TRADITIONAL
WAINSCOT
FACE

NOTE:
SHIPLAP
PATTERNS
REQUIRE
EXPOSED
FASTENERS.

Both tongue-and-groove and lapped board paneling are available in the traditional (1-in. nominal) thickness capable of spanning between standard framing members (see 38A & B). Thin veneer boards (about ¼ in. thick) designed to be applied to a backing such as gypsum wallboard are also available in tongue-and-groove patterns (see 38C). Softwood—usually pine, cedar or fir—is used for all types. The most common board patterns used to panel entire walls and ceilings and as wainscoting are illustrated above.

 A COMMON BOARD PANELING PATTERNS

Because of the orientation of the grain and because the tongue-and-groove joints lock the boards together structurally, traditional tongue-and-groove boards can easily span across typically spaced framing members. Lapped patterns, although not as strong as T&G, can also generally span across framing. For these reasons, it is usually advantageous to orient board paneling perpendicular to framing (see 38B). When the boards are oriented parallel to the framing, blocking or strapping must be added for support (see 38A).

Spacing of blocking or strapping should either imitate framing spacing (24 in. max.) or be based on empirical deflection testing with the material to be used. No specific guidelines are available since boards used in this application are not structural.

Boards are normally attached to a wooden framing member (or furring, strapping or blocking) with a single fastener. Since a single pull of the trigger will now shoot a nail or staple diagonally into the proper position, pneumatically driven fasteners have almost totally replaced hand-driven nails for this formerly tedious task. One such fastener at each framing member will normally hold the board firmly to the structure and, in the case of T&G, will be concealed by the application of the next board.

Tongue-and-groove veneer (see 38C) may be applied to backing with adhesive, with pneumatically driven staples or with metal clips designed to fit into the groove of each board. The metal clips are designed for inexperienced homeowner/builders and allow the paneling to be removed for reuse.

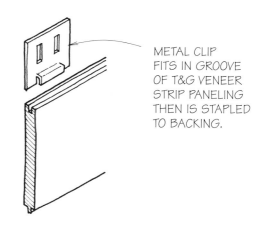

METAL CLIP
FITS IN GROOVE
OF T&G VENEER
STRIP PANELING
THEN IS STAPLED
TO BACKING.

B BOARD PANELING APPLICATION

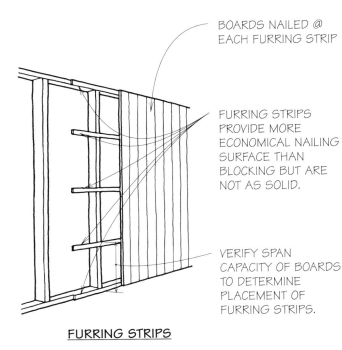

BOARDS NAILED @ EACH FURRING STRIP

FURRING STRIPS PROVIDE MORE ECONOMICAL NAILING SURFACE THAN BLOCKING BUT ARE NOT AS SOLID.

VERIFY SPAN CAPACITY OF BOARDS TO DETERMINE PLACEMENT OF FURRING STRIPS.

FURRING STRIPS

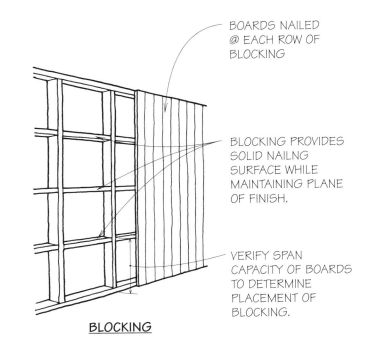

BOARDS NAILED @ EACH ROW OF BLOCKING

BLOCKING PROVIDES SOLID NAILNG SURFACE WHILE MAINTAINING PLANE OF FINISH.

VERIFY SPAN CAPACITY OF BOARDS TO DETERMINE PLACEMENT OF BLOCKING.

BLOCKING

 STANDARD BOARDS
BOARDS || TO FRAMING

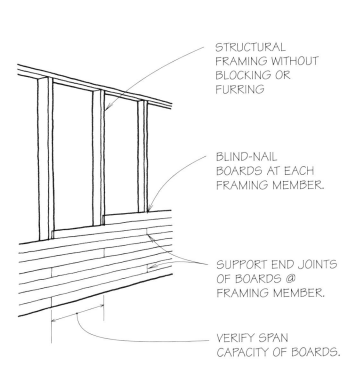

STRUCTURAL FRAMING WITHOUT BLOCKING OR FURRING

BLIND-NAIL BOARDS AT EACH FRAMING MEMBER.

SUPPORT END JOINTS OF BOARDS @ FRAMING MEMBER.

VERIFY SPAN CAPACITY OF BOARDS.

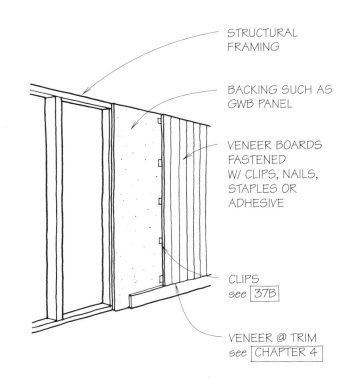

STRUCTURAL FRAMING

BACKING SUCH AS GWB PANEL

VENEER BOARDS FASTENED W/ CLIPS, NAILS, STAPLES OR ADHESIVE

CLIPS
see 37B

VENEER @ TRIM
see CHAPTER 4

 **STANDARD BOARDS**
BOARDS ⊥ TO FRAMING

 VENEER BOARDS

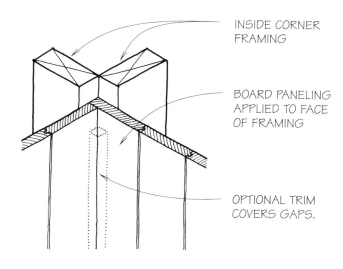

INSIDE CORNER
FRAMING

BOARD PANELING
APPLIED TO FACE
OF FRAMING

OPTIONAL TRIM
COVERS GAPS.

NOTE:
BOARDS ⊥ TO FRAMING MAY BE TRIMMED SIMILARLY.

A **INSIDE CORNER**
BOARDS ‖ TO FRAMING

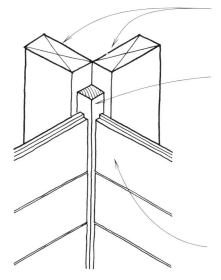

INSIDE CORNER
FRAMING

CORNER BOARD
TRIM INSTALLED
BEFORE PANELING
PROVIDES BUTT
SURFACE FOR
ENDS OF
PANEL BOARDS.

BOARD PANELING
APPLIED TO FACE
OF FRAMING

NOTE:
TRIM MAY BE ADDED TO CORNER.

B **INSIDE CORNER**
BOARDS ⊥ TO FRAMING

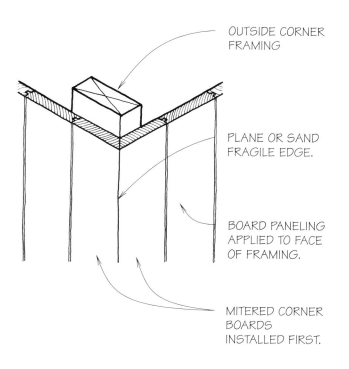

OUTSIDE CORNER
FRAMING

PLANE OR SAND
FRAGILE EDGE.

BOARD PANELING
APPLIED TO FACE
OF FRAMING.

MITERED CORNER
BOARDS
INSTALLED FIRST.

C **OUTSIDE CORNER**
BOARDS ‖ TO FRAMING

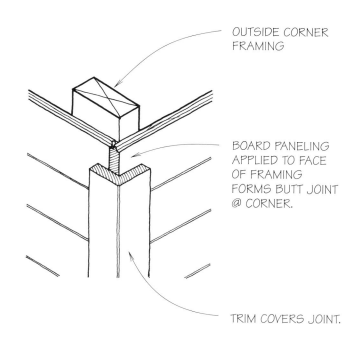

OUTSIDE CORNER
FRAMING

BOARD PANELING
APPLIED TO FACE
OF FRAMING
FORMS BUTT JOINT
@ CORNER.

TRIM COVERS JOINT.

D **OUTSIDE CORNER**
BOARDS ⊥ TO FRAMING

The frame-and-panel system is the oldest form of wall paneling, dating from the days before machinery was employed to manufacture building components. The system was developed to achieve a refined surface yet retain the warmth of wood. Examples of frame-and-panel systems can be found in the oldest buildings of many cultures.

Today, the frame-and-panel system is seldom used because it is so expensive. Occasionally, however, a designer may have the opportunity to express the rich pattern of naturally finished wood within the traditional frame-and-panel system. The most frequent use of the system today is for wainscoting or for repair or remodeling of existing work.

The Frame
The frame, made up of a top rail, bottom rail and stiles on the side, is traditionally a system of boards arranged to form rectangles. The boards are rigidly fixed at the joints (glued and/or pegged, doweled or biscuit joined). The horizontal frame members are usually continuous in order to support the panels when attached to the wall framing. The face of the frame is usually made with a simple profile so that joints between horizontal and vertical frame members can be easily made. The inside edges of the rectangular framed openings are grooved to accept the edges of the panels.

The Panel
The panel has traditionally been made of a single solid piece of wood profiled at the edge to fit into the grooves of the frame without glue. This arrangement allows the wood panel to float within the frame as it expands and contracts with changes in moisture content.

As alternatives to solid wood panels, plywood or a composite material with a veneered face may be used. Plywood and composite panels don't need to float because plywood and composite materials are dimensionally stable in both directions. As shown below right, a rabbet on the back of the frame can replace the traditional groove and the panel may be glued and/or nailed to the frame.

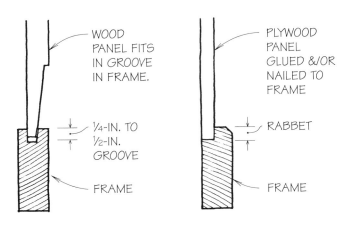

WOOD PANEL FITS IN GROOVE IN FRAME.

¼-IN. TO ½-IN. GROOVE

FRAME

PLYWOOD PANEL GLUED &/OR NAILED TO FRAME

RABBET

FRAME

FRAME W/ GROOVE   FRAME W/ RABBET

Panels may have any pattern carved into the surface as long as the edges are detailed to fit into the groove of the frame. Most common today are the raised panel and the flat panel, shown below. Composite panels may also be made of a number of small pieces.

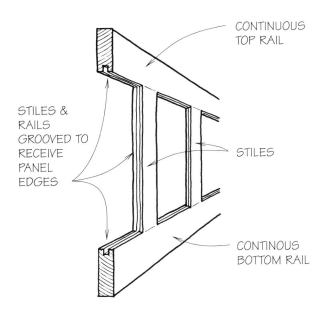

CONTINUOUS TOP RAIL

STILES & RAILS GROOVED TO RECEIVE PANEL EDGES

STILES

CONTINOUS BOTTOM RAIL

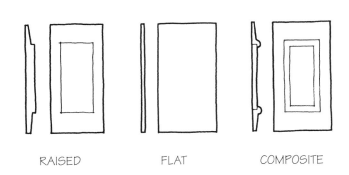

RAISED   FLAT   COMPOSITE

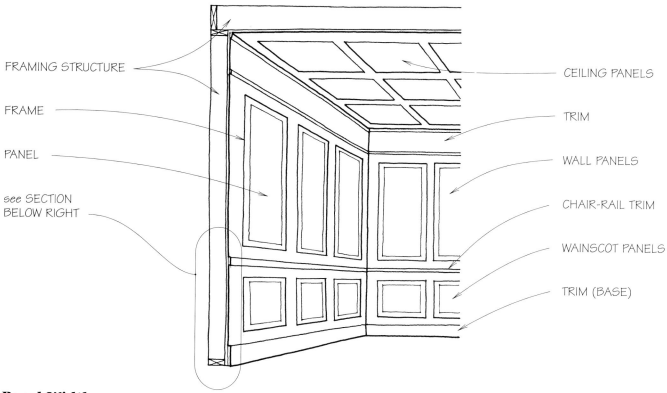

FRAMING STRUCTURE

FRAME

PANEL

see SECTION
BELOW RIGHT

CEILING PANELS

TRIM

WALL PANELS

CHAIR-RAIL TRIM

WAINSCOT PANELS

TRIM (BASE)

Panel Width

Determine panel width by the width of available
stock (if solid wood panels) and the overall width of
the space to which the paneling is to be applied.
Coordinating panel width on adjacent walls of
different dimensions is difficult, but it is not difficult
to achieve panels of similar (if not uniform) size if
relatively narrow panel widths are used throughout.

Integration with Trim

The integration of the frame with the finish system is
most easily accomplished if the face of the frame is in
the same plane as the other finish surfaces, as shown
at the top of the section at right.

Applying to Structure

A wainscot panel can usually be fastened directly
to the framing through the top and bottom rail. In
this case, the fasteners can be covered by base trim
at the bottom and a chair rail at the top. Alternatively,
very large panel systems may be attached to wall
framing through the back if the framing can be
left accessible.

When very large or long panels need to be joined
within the field of a wall or ceiling, tongue-and-
groove, spline or biscuit joinery at the edge between
frame and panel will allow large areas to be covered
without exposed fasteners.

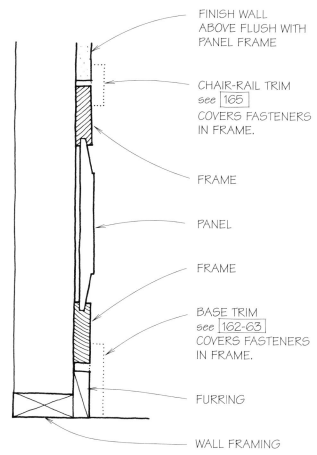

FINISH WALL
ABOVE FLUSH WITH
PANEL FRAME

CHAIR-RAIL TRIM
see 165
COVERS FASTENERS
IN FRAME.

FRAME

PANEL

FRAME

BASE TRIM
see 162-63
COVERS FASTENERS
IN FRAME.

FURRING

WALL FRAMING

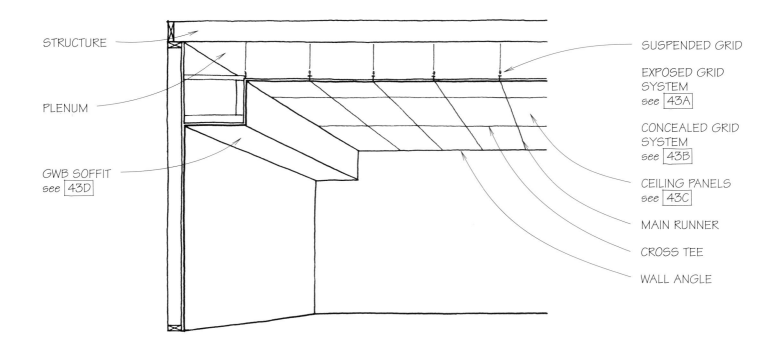

STRUCTURE

PLENUM

GWB SOFFIT
see 43D

SUSPENDED GRID

EXPOSED GRID
SYSTEM
see 43A

CONCEALED GRID
SYSTEM
see 43B

CEILING PANELS
see 43C

MAIN RUNNER

CROSS TEE

WALL ANGLE

Suspended ceiling grids with ceiling panels are used extensively in commercial building, and occasionally in residential construction, to create a finished ceiling while providing a plenum between the structure and the ceiling through which electrical, plumbing and mechanical services can pass.

Such a system has many advantages. A suspended ceiling system is relatively inexpensive, it can be hung at any height and the panels may be easily removed for plenum access. The system is modular and can be adapted to any size or shape room. Lights, air-duct grills, sprinkler heads and other systems can be directly integrated, and the ceiling panels generally provide good acoustical performance. Fire-rated suspended grid systems are also available.

Suspended Grid
The two widely used types of suspended grid systems are the exposed and the concealed. Exposed grid systems (see 43A) allow the ceiling panels to lie on top of the grid, leaving the grid visible from the room. Concealed grid systems (see 43B) fit into grooves at the edges of the panels, providing a continuous ceiling surface free of a visible grid. Semi-exposed systems exposing the grid in only one direction are also available. In all types of systems, the grid itself is typically made of steel, with exposed and semi-exposed grids available in an assortment of profiles and factory colors. Plastic grids are also available.

Ceiling Panels
Ceiling panels (see 43C) are typically made of mineral board or fiberglass and are available in a wide range of colors and surface patterns. Ceiling panels are also available in wood, metal or glass. Fluorescent light fixtures and air-duct grills the same size as panels are designed to integrate with the modular grid. Panels can easily be cut to accommodate the location of incandescent fixtures, sprinkler heads and other service elements, or to fit at the edge of a room.

GWB Grids
GWB suspended grid systems are often used in combination with suspended panel systems to create perimeter soffits (see 43D) that would be difficult to make with ceiling panels. GWB is applied directly to a special suspended grid, and edges and corners are finished like the standard GWB system (see 8A).

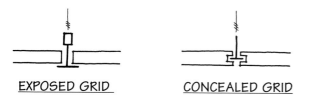

EXPOSED GRID   CONCEALED GRID

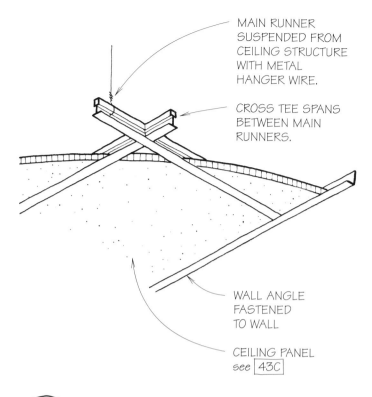

MAIN RUNNER
SUSPENDED FROM
CEILING STRUCTURE
WITH METAL
HANGER WIRE.

CROSS TEE SPANS
BETWEEN MAIN
RUNNERS.

WALL ANGLE
FASTENED
TO WALL

CEILING PANEL
see │ 43C │

 A **SUSPENDED GRID**
EXPOSED GRID SYSTEM

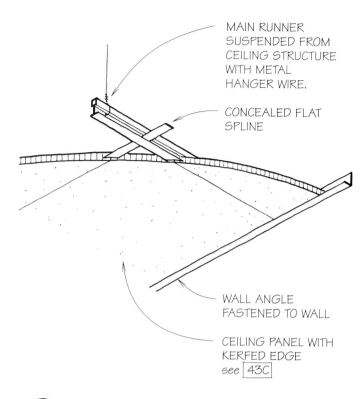

MAIN RUNNER
SUSPENDED FROM
CEILING STRUCTURE
WITH METAL
HANGER WIRE.

CONCEALED FLAT
SPLINE

WALL ANGLE
FASTENED TO WALL

CEILING PANEL WITH
KERFED EDGE
see │ 43C │

 **B** **SUSPENDED GRID**
CONCEALED GRID SYSTEM

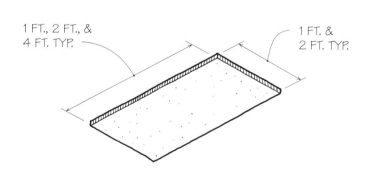

1 FT., 2 FT., &
4 FT. TYP.

1 FT. &
2 FT. TYP.

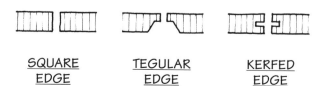

SQUARE
EDGE

TEGULAR
EDGE

KERFED
EDGE

 C **CEILING PANELS**

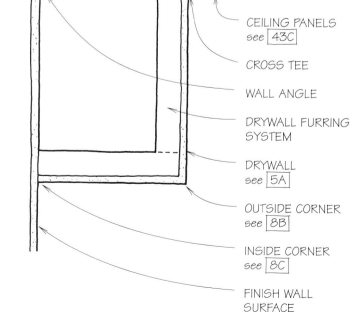

MAIN RUNNER

CEILING PANELS
see │ 43C │

CROSS TEE

WALL ANGLE

DRYWALL FURRING
SYSTEM

DRYWALL
see │ 5A │

OUTSIDE CORNER
see │ 8B │

INSIDE CORNER
see │ 8C │

FINISH WALL
SURFACE

 D **GWB SOFFIT**

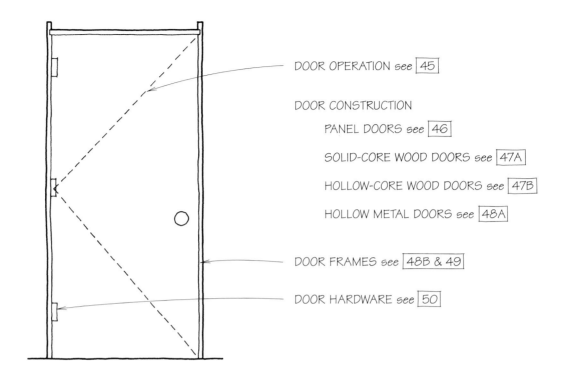

DOOR OPERATION *see* 45

DOOR CONSTRUCTION

    PANEL DOORS *see* 46

    SOLID-CORE WOOD DOORS *see* 47A

    HOLLOW-CORE WOOD DOORS *see* 47B

    HOLLOW METAL DOORS *see* 48A

DOOR FRAMES *see* 48B & 49

DOOR HARDWARE *see* 50

The earliest interior doors were plank doors hung with wooden or wrought-iron hinges and provided little else but visual privacy for the occupants of the space behind the door. Later, panel doors—made by hand until the mid-19th century and then with refined machinery—were fitted with improved hardware and added additional security and privacy. Now composite wood or steel doors combined with grouted metal frames, seals and sophisticated hardware provide high levels of security and fire protection.

Compared with exterior doors, interior doors are simple. Because they do not have to seal the building against the weather, all considerations of shedding water and sealing against air infiltration may be ignored. Interior doors are generally provided for privacy, security and/or acoustic separation. One exception is the fire door, which must be rated to withstand a fire on one side of the door for a specified time. All fire doors are self-closing. Some fire doors are self-closing only when coupled to an alarm system or a fused link (a heat-sensitive device that holds the door open under normal conditions).

Doors are manufactured in the stock sizes and widths shown at right.

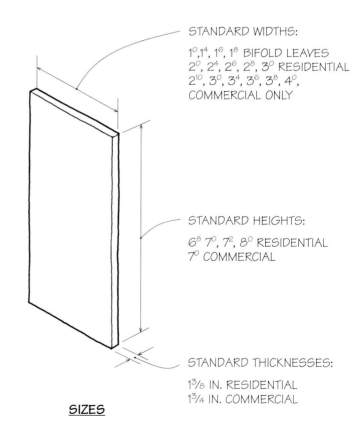

STANDARD WIDTHS:

$1^0, 1^4, 1^6, 1^8$ BIFOLD LEAVES
$2^0, 2^4, 2^6, 2^8, 3^0$ RESIDENTIAL
$2^{10}, 3^0, 3^4, 3^6, 3^8, 4^0$,
COMMERCIAL ONLY

STANDARD HEIGHTS:

6^8 7^0, 7^2, 8^0 RESIDENTIAL
7^0 COMMERCIAL

STANDARD THICKNESSES:

$1^3/_8$ IN. RESIDENTIAL
$1^3/_4$ IN. COMMERCIAL

<u>SIZES</u>

A INTERIOR DOORS

Doors may be classified by how they operate.

Hinged Doors
By far the most common of all doors is the hinged
door. Hinges located at one edge of the door allow it
to swing open 180° from its closed position in the
plane of the wall. A stop incorporated in or applied to
the door jamb prevents the door from swinging back
through the plane of the wall. In the case of the
double-acting door, the stop is eliminated so that the
door may swing through the plane of the wall in both
directions. The swing direction of hinged doors must
be specified.

Doors are classified as left-handed or right-handed so
that hinges may be located on the proper side of
prehung doors.

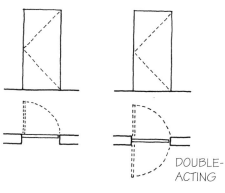

HINGED

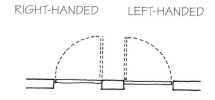

RIGHT-HANDED   LEFT-HANDED

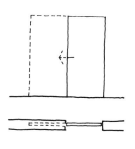

POCKET

Pocket Doors
Used when it is likely that a door will often remain
open and a hinged door left open would somehow be
in the way, pocket doors are hung on rollers from an
overhead track and roll into the thickness of the wall
to one side of the door opening. When planning for
pocket doors, it is essential to allow for a door-width
section of wall adjacent to the door opening that has
no wiring, plumbing or ductwork. This wall will house
the pocket frame into which the door rolls. The wider
and heavier a pocket door, the less likely it is to
malfunction because its rollers skip the track. For
pocket-door hardware, see 53A.

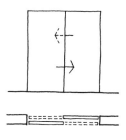

BYPASS

Bypass Doors
Typically used as residential closet doors, these doors
are always found in pairs and are hung on rollers from
overhead tracks that are offset to allow one door to
open over the other. Only one side of the double
opening may be opened fully at one time.

Bifold Doors
Consisting of two narrow doors hinged together,
bifold doors are often used to conceal storage areas.
They swing into the room, but project only half as far
as a simple hinged door of the same width. Bifold
doors are often used in pairs for residential closets,
and can reveal the entire double opening at one time.

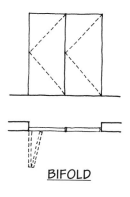

BIFOLD

 DOOR OPERATION

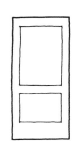
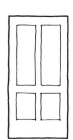
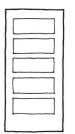
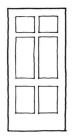
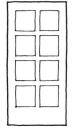
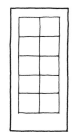
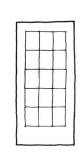

1-PANEL	2-PANEL	4-PANEL	5-PANEL	6-PANEL	8-PANEL	10-LITE	15-LITE
FLAT PANELS ONLY	FLAT PANELS ONLY	FLAT OR RAISED PANELS	FLAT OR RAISED PANELS	FLAT OR RAISED PANELS	FLAT OR RAISED PANELS	(8-LITE ALSO COMMON)	

COMMON DOOR PATTERNS

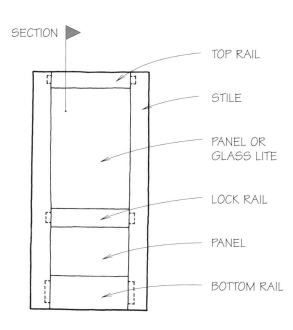

SECTION

- TOP RAIL
- STILE
- PANEL OR GLASS LITE
- LOCK RAIL
- PANEL
- BOTTOM RAIL

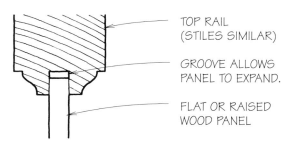

- TOP RAIL (STILES SIMILAR)
- GROOVE ALLOWS PANEL TO EXPAND.
- FLAT OR RAISED WOOD PANEL

SECTION @ WOOD PANEL

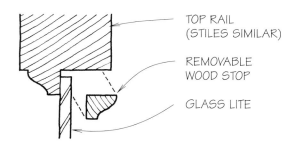

- TOP RAIL (STILES SIMILAR)
- REMOVABLE WOOD STOP
- GLASS LITE

SECTION @ GLASS LITE

The panel door is the traditional interior door. It has a framework made of 1⅜-in. or 1¾-in. thick stiles and rails and thinner panels filling the spaces. Stiles and rails in the highest quality panel doors are connected with glued mortise-and-tenon joints, but glued and doweled joints are also common. The panels, let into a groove at the edges of stiles and rails, are not glued so that they may expand and contract with changes in moisture content. Panels are either raised and made of solid wood or flat and made of plywood. The number of panels may vary. Most common are one-panel and two-panel doors with flat panels only, and four-, five-, six- and eight-panel doors with raised or flat panels.

Glass may be easily substituted for the panels in this door type, but glass is held in place with a stop rather than a groove so that broken glass may be replaced. Glass (called "lites") in standard interior doors is usually available in one-lite (storefront) or two-lite/two-panel, eight-lite, 10-lite or 15-lite configurations.

Louvers may also be inserted in place of a panel.

 PANEL DOORS

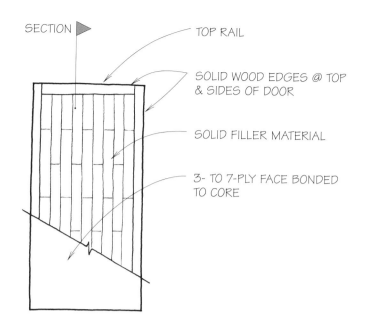

SECTION ▶

TOP RAIL

SOLID WOOD EDGES @ TOP & SIDES OF DOOR

SOLID FILLER MATERIAL

3- TO 7-PLY FACE BONDED TO CORE

ELEVATION

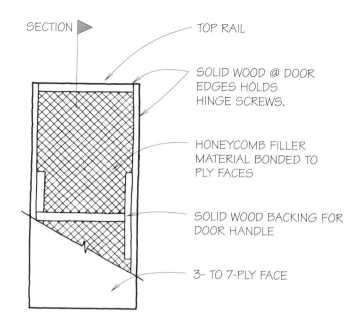

SECTION ▶

TOP RAIL

SOLID WOOD @ DOOR EDGES HOLDS HINGE SCREWS.

HONEYCOMB FILLER MATERIAL BONDED TO PLY FACES

SOLID WOOD BACKING FOR DOOR HANDLE

3- TO 7-PLY FACE

ELEVATION

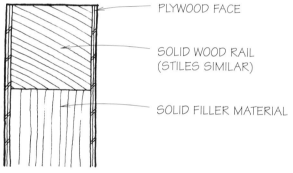

PLYWOOD FACE

SOLID WOOD RAIL (STILES SIMILAR)

SOLID FILLER MATERIAL

SECTION @ TOP RAIL

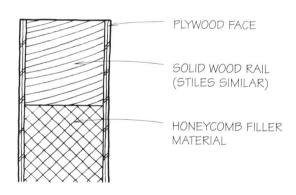

PLYWOOD FACE

SOLID WOOD RAIL (STILES SIMILAR)

HONEYCOMB FILLER MATERIAL

SECTION @ TOP RAIL

A solid-core wood door is a flush door entirely smooth on both faces. Most interior solid-core wood doors are made with a thin (1/16-in.) veneer of plywood on both faces glued to a solid interior core of wood products. The outer edge of the core (about 1½ in.) is made of continuous solid sawn lumber, while the remainder of the core may be made of various composite wood assemblies such as particleboard or bonded wood blocks. Solid-core wood doors may have glass panels, although there is usually only a single lite since multiple lites are more logically supported by the structure of a panel door. Solid-core wood doors may be fire-rated.

A hollow-core door can be identical in appearance to a solid-core door, but the core of the door is made of thin, lightweight spacers that hold the veneer plywood faces of the door parallel to one another. The doors are therefore much lighter and less of an acoustical barrier than solid-core doors. Hollow-core doors are the least expensive of the three wooden door construction types and are used extensively in residential construction.

 SOLID-CORE WOOD DOORS

 HOLLOW-CORE WOOD DOORS

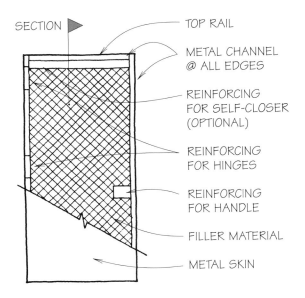

SECTION

TOP RAIL

METAL CHANNEL @ ALL EDGES

REINFORCING FOR SELF-CLOSER (OPTIONAL)

REINFORCING FOR HINGES

REINFORCING FOR HANDLE

FILLER MATERIAL

METAL SKIN

ELEVATION

SIDE JAMB PROJECTS ABOVE HEAD JAMB.

HEAD JAMB DADOED INTO SIDE JAMBS

SIDE JAMB

SECTION

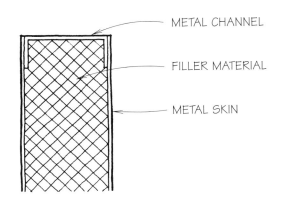

METAL CHANNEL

FILLER MATERIAL

METAL SKIN

TOP RAIL SECTION

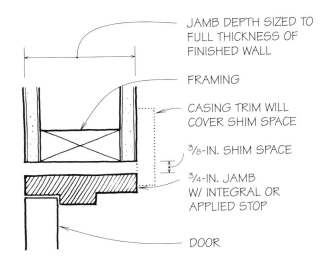

JAMB DEPTH SIZED TO FULL THICKNESS OF FINISHED WALL

FRAMING

CASING TRIM WILL COVER SHIM SPACE

3/8-IN. SHIM SPACE

3/4-IN. JAMB W/ INTEGRAL OR APPLIED STOP

DOOR

SIDE JAMB SECTION

Hollow metal doors are used almost exclusively for commercial work. They are made of 20- to 14-gauge steel or .025 to .060 in. thick aluminum and are filled with polystyrene, polyurethane, mineral board, fiberglass or the honeycomb material similar to hollow-core wood doors. Some metal doors are truly hollow and have only internal steel channel stiffeners to maintain the plane of the surface metal. Since metal doors cannot be altered at the site, coordination of metal doors with hardware is more critical than for wood doors. Except for aluminum doors, hollow metal doors are always painted and may be ordered primed or fully finished. Hollow metal doors may have glass panels or louvers and may be fire-rated.

Wood door frames are almost always used with wood doors (not metal doors). Door and frame usually arrive at the job site prehung, with the frames fully assembled and hinged to the door. The frame, which consists of head and side jambs, should be sized to be the full thickness of the wall from finish surface to finish surface. Split jambs that are adjustable to accommodate slight variations in wall thickness are available. After the walls are finished, the frame is shimmed to fit within the rough opening and nailed firmly to the structure with casing nails through the jamb. The shim space exposed on both sides of the wall will be covered later with casing trim (see 160-61).

 HOLLOW METAL DOORS

 WOOD FRAMES

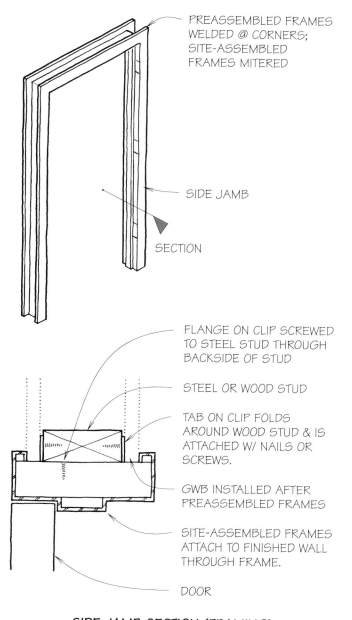

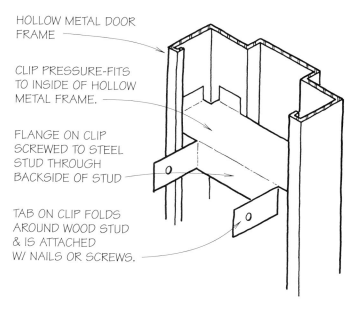

PREASSEMBLED FRAMES WELDED @ CORNERS; SITE-ASSEMBLED FRAMES MITERED

SIDE JAMB

SECTION

HOLLOW METAL DOOR FRAME

CLIP PRESSURE-FITS TO INSIDE OF HOLLOW METAL FRAME.

FLANGE ON CLIP SCREWED TO STEEL STUD THROUGH BACKSIDE OF STUD

TAB ON CLIP FOLDS AROUND WOOD STUD & IS ATTACHED W/ NAILS OR SCREWS.

FASTENING CLIP

FLANGE ON CLIP SCREWED TO STEEL STUD THROUGH BACKSIDE OF STUD

STEEL OR WOOD STUD

TAB ON CLIP FOLDS AROUND WOOD STUD & IS ATTACHED W/ NAILS OR SCREWS.

GWB INSTALLED AFTER PREASSEMBLED FRAMES

SITE-ASSEMBLED FRAMES ATTACH TO FINISHED WALL THROUGH FRAME.

DOOR

SIDE JAMB SECTION (FRAMING)

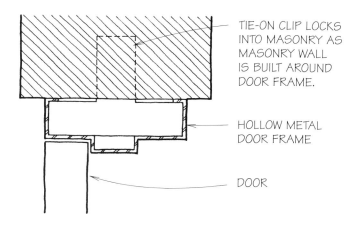

TIE-ON CLIP LOCKS INTO MASONRY AS MASONRY WALL IS BUILT AROUND DOOR FRAME.

HOLLOW METAL DOOR FRAME

DOOR

SIDE JAMB SECTION (MASONRY)

Hollow metal frames are used almost exclusively with solid-core wood doors or hollow metal doors. The frame is made of formed steel or extruded aluminum and can be either preassembled (welded) or assembled at the site.

Preassembled Frames
Often prehung, preassembled frames are installed simultaneously with the framing of the building. They are attached to either wood or steel framing with metal clips. Finish wall material (usually GWB) is then butted to or tucked behind the frame.

Site-Assembled Frames
Also called knock-down or K-D frames, site-assembled frames are installed after the walls are in place and finished. They are often used in remodeling work. Site-assembled frames may be fastened to the structure either through the sides of the frame or through the integral stop. Fasteners are then covered with snap-in trim.

 HOLLOW METAL FRAMES

Selecting the appropriate hardware for interior doors can be a complicated task. On a functional level, the hardware must be matched to the size, type, weight and frequency of use of the door. Aesthetically, there are many hardware styles and finishes from which to choose. For both commercial and custom residential work, numerous factors are involved in the selection of door hardware, and the designer would be well advised to work closely with an experienced wholesale hardware dealer.

Hardware choices are often quite limited at the lower end of the quality scale. Door manufacturers usually prehang their interior residential doors with hinges of the lowest quality, which are often quite adequate. A door handle, however, is the most complex part of a door assembly and is the only part consistently touched by the human hand, so the lowest quality will seldom endure as long as low-quality hinges. A higher-grade handle assembly should therefore be seriously considered.

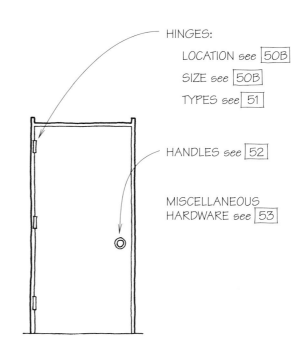

HINGES:
  LOCATION see | 50B |
  SIZE see | 50B |
  TYPES see | 51 |

HANDLES see | 52 |

MISCELLANEOUS
HARDWARE see | 53 |

 INTERIOR DOOR HARDWARE

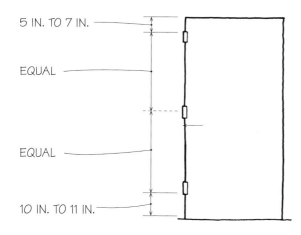

5 IN. TO 7 IN.
EQUAL
EQUAL
10 IN. TO 11 IN.

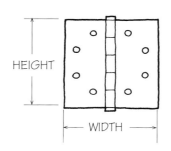

HEIGHT

WIDTH

STANDARD WIDTHS
3½ IN., 4 IN., 4½ IN.

STANDARD HEIGHTS
3½ IN., 4 IN., 4½ IN.,
5 IN., 6 IN., 8 IN.

The rule of thumb for specifying the number of door hinges is one hinge (called one-half pair) for every 30 in. of door height. This means that a standard 6 ft. 8 in. door would require three hinges (one and one-half pairs). Lightweight residential doors, however, often have only two hinges (one pair).

Hinge size is specified (in inches) as height followed by width. For example, a 4½ by 4 hinge is 4½ in. high and 4 in. wide. The height of a hinge is related to the

Hinge height (in.)	Door type
3½	Hollow-core or panel residential doors to 32 in. wide
4	Residential doors to 36 in. Light commercial doors
4½	Solid-core commercial doors to 36 in. wide
5+	Extra-heavy or wide doors

weight of the door (see chart above). The width of a hinge is related to the clearance required for door casings or other thick finish materials adjacent to the door (see 51).

 **HINGES**
LOCATION & SIZE

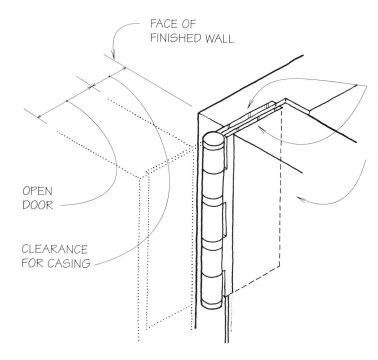

FACE OF
FINISHED WALL

OPEN
DOOR

CLEARANCE
FOR CASING

DOOR FRAME
see | 48B & 49 |

HINGE MORTISED
INTO BOTH FRAME
AND DOOR

DOOR

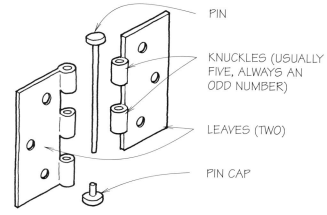

PIN

KNUCKLES (USUALLY
FIVE, ALWAYS AN
ODD NUMBER)

LEAVES (TWO)

PIN CAP

HINGE PARTS

Almost all door hinges are the full-mortise type. The hinge is designed to be set into a mortise in both the door and the jamb so that the exposed surface of the hinge is flush with the door edge and jamb surface. Following are three grades of hinges that can be specified, depending on the type of door and the frequency of its use.

Non–Bearing Hinge

The most economical choice is the non–bearing hinge used primarily for residential doors. The two halves (leaves) of the hinge rotate around the central pin, and friction between the two leaves is reduced only by the use of lubricant. There is a wide range of quality within this grade of hinge. The lowest-quality hinges have fast (nonremovable) pins, which make hanging and removing the door more difficult.

Standard-Weight Bearing Hinge

This hinge is used for commercial doors with an average frequency of use (up to 100 times per day) or for residential entry doors. Friction is reduced by the addition of either anti-friction self-lubricating bearings or ball bearings between the knuckles of the hinge.

Heavyweight Bearing Hinge

The heavyweight ball-bearing hinge is used for very heavy, oversized or frequently used doors. This grade of hinge is also usually used in conjunction with self-closers. The bearings are either anti-friction or ball bearings as for standard-weight bearing hinges.

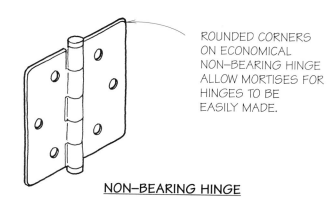

ROUNDED CORNERS
ON ECONOMICAL
NON–BEARING HINGE
ALLOW MORTISES FOR
HINGES TO BE
EASILY MADE.

NON–BEARING HINGE

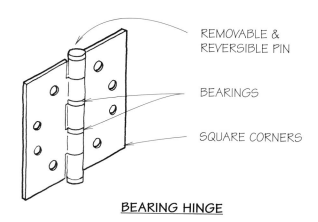

REMOVABLE &
REVERSIBLE PIN

BEARINGS

SQUARE CORNERS

BEARING HINGE

 HINGE TYPES

A door handle is called a lock if it can be secured or a latch if it cannot. The entire operating assembly including the handle, the latch and the locking mechanism is called a lock set or a latch set.

Lock/Latch Set Types

There are only two common lock/latch set types. Each one is available in several grades and with a variety of available functions.

The cylindrical lock set is the most economical, easiest to install, and most common. The highest-quality cylindrical lock sets are used for commercial work. The *mortise lock set*—compared with a cylindrical lock set— is more expensive, more sophisticated and capable of incorporating more locking functions with latching functions. Mortise locks are used mostly in commercial applications, but are also commonly used for residential entry doors.

Lock/Latch Set Function

The function of a latch or lock is described by its operation and how it is locked and unlocked from each side. A passage latch set, for example, is operated by a knob on either side of the door that cannot be locked. There are more than 20 specific functions described by American National Standards Institute (ANSI) for each of the two common lock/latch set types.

Handles

Handles for doors are available in a wide range of styles but may be classified into two basic types, the knob and the lever. The knob is the more prevalent type in North America, but the lever, common in other parts of the world, is easier to operate because it provides more leverage and can be opened without gripping and turning. The lever is therefore required by most accessibility codes. The disadvantage of the lever is that lower-quality levers sometimes tend to sag over time owing to fatigue or wearing of the support spring.

Backset

When ordering handles, the backset must be specified as well as the thickness of the door. The backset is the distance from the edge of the door to the center line of the handle. There are two types: the narrow (2⅜ in.) backset and the deep (2¾ in.) backset. The narrow backset is commonly used in residential construction and is required where the stile of a door is of limited width. The deep backset provides more clearance and is commonly used in commercial construction.

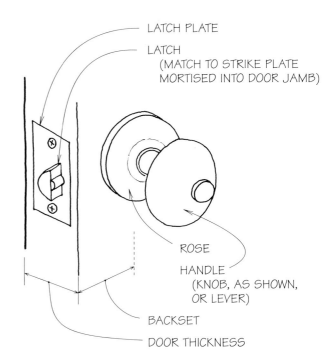

LATCH PLATE

LATCH
(MATCH TO STRIKE PLATE MORTISED INTO DOOR JAMB)

ROSE

HANDLE
(KNOB, AS SHOWN, OR LEVER)

BACKSET

DOOR THICKNESS

LOCK/LATCH SET PARTS

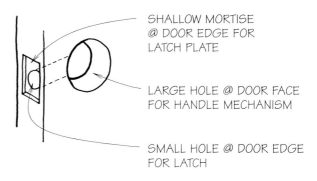

SHALLOW MORTISE @ DOOR EDGE FOR LATCH PLATE

LARGE HOLE @ DOOR FACE FOR HANDLE MECHANISM

SMALL HOLE @ DOOR EDGE FOR LATCH

CYLINDRICAL LOCK

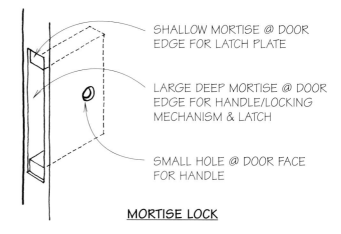

SHALLOW MORTISE @ DOOR EDGE FOR LATCH PLATE

LARGE DEEP MORTISE @ DOOR EDGE FOR HANDLE/LOCKING MECHANISM & LATCH

SMALL HOLE @ DOOR FACE FOR HANDLE

MORTISE LOCK

 DOOR HANDLES

Panic Hardware

In emergency situations in public buildings where a crowd of people may need to exit through a door, panic hardware is required. Panic hardware is almost always used in conjunction with a fire door. On the inside of the door is located a horizontal bar that unlatches the door in response to pressure. On the outside of the door, a surface-mounted thumb latch or lever is the common way to unlatch the door.

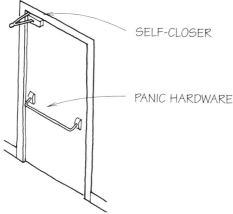

SELF-CLOSER

PANIC HARDWARE

Self-closers

A self-closer mechanically returns a door to the closed position after it has been opened. Self-closers are usually found in public buildings where they are required at all fire-rated corridors and stairwells. They may also be used between a residence and an attached garage. Self-closers fit at the top hinged edge of a door and may be located on either the push or the pull side of the door. Self-closers may be exposed or concealed and are usually matched with the highest-quality hinges.

Flush Bolts and Surface Bolts

These latching devices are used to secure the top and bottom of the inactive side of a pair of (French) doors. Only when the bolts are disengaged can the door be opened. The surface bolt mounts to the face of the door so it is always visible, while the flush bolt fits within the edge of the door and is hidden when both doors are closed.

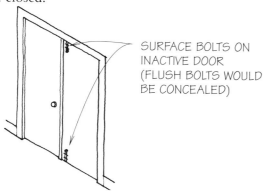

SURFACE BOLTS ON INACTIVE DOOR (FLUSH BOLTS WOULD BE CONCEALED)

Pocket, Bypass and Bifold Door Hardware

Pocket doors, because of their nature, require special hardware. The track and trolley system from which the door hangs should be of high quality because it is virtually impossible to replace if it fails. The double-track system for bypass doors and the single-track system for bifold doors are similar but more easily replaced.

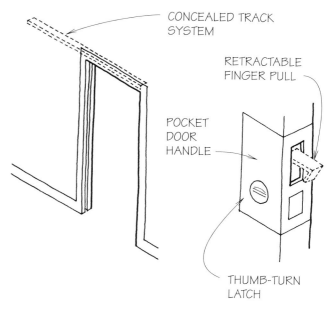

CONCEALED TRACK SYSTEM

RETRACTABLE FINGER PULL

POCKET DOOR HANDLE

THUMB-TURN LATCH

The special handle for a pocket door must not project beyond the surface of the door so that the door can slide into the pocket. This handle assembly typically has a retractable pull and a thumb-turn lock. Bypass handles, also flush with the door surface to allow for doors to pass, are simpler than pocket door handles and are never locked. Bifold handles are usually surface-mounted knobs. It is difficult to match any of these handles with other hardware except with regard to finish surface.

Despite its specialized hardware, a pocket door can get hung up or scratched on wood studs if they warp badly. Some builders prefer to frame a wall containing a pocket door with metal studs, which do not warp.

 MISCELLANEOUS HARDWARE

Floors

2

A floor provides both design challenges and design opportunities, since it is the part of a building that receives the most continuous daily wear—from people (and animals) walking on it, from furniture sitting on and being moved across it, and from spills and other dropped objects. Therefore, it is important to consider the abrasion resistance of a particular type of flooring, as well as its resilience and ease of maintenance.

Every finish-flooring material, no matter what its cost, has some advantages and disadvantages. Beside the factors mentioned above, there are other reasons to select one finish-flooring material over another. Often, the activity that is to occur in a space will strongly suggest a particular type of flooring. For example, the best flooring for a gymnasium is resilient hardwood. But costs must be considered, too, so a gymnasium may have vinyl-tile flooring instead.

The fact that people contact floors through their feet allows the designer to create a mood through textural effects or to provide warmth to be absorbed directly into the body. This, too, will affect flooring choice.

If the use of a space does not give a clear sense of which flooring material to use, consider the factors in the chart below. (This chart provides only average traits for each type, since the range of quality and performance within each category is great.)

Floor Structure

The structural system that supports the finish-floor system must be designed to support all the live loads imposed on the floor by people, furniture and stored items as well as the dead load of the floor system itself. Floors such as dance floors and gymnasium floors work best if they deflect somewhat under a load, while floors made of tile or other brittle materials should not deflect at all. This chapter assumes that the structural support of a finish-floor system has been engineered and appropriately matched to its intended use. The designer should keep in mind that code requirements are minimum standards and are not always adequate to keep a floor from feeling bouncy. For example, if a residential wood floor designed for the standard 40 psf requires 2x10 joists, 2x12 joists will make a significantly more solid floor.

The two materials that provide structural support for floor systems are wood and concrete (with reinforcing steel), which have quite different characteristics when considered as support for various flooring materials.

CHARACTERISTICS	FINISH FLOORING MATERIALS					
	Carpet	Resilient	Wood	Tile	Concrete	Terrazzo
Durability	fair	good	good	excellent	excellent	excellent
Ease of cleaning	fair	excellent	excellent	good	excellent	excellent
Moisture resistance	poor	good	fair	excellent	good	excellent
Resistance to common staining	poor	good	fair	good	good	excellent
Resistance to denting and chipping	excellent	excellent	poor	fair	good	excellent
Resilience	excellent	fair	fair	poor	poor	poor
Traction	excellent	fair	poor	fair	poor	poor
Ability to refinish	no	no	yes	no	yes	yes
Cost	low/medium	medium	medium	high	low	high

Wood structure—A wood floor structure has a series of repetitive spanning members called joists, which are covered with a subfloor, a thin wood skin that forms a base suitable for most finish-flooring materials. The joists may be made of dimension lumber, composite wood I-joists, webbed steel I-joists or trussed wood joists. The subfloor is usually plywood or some other composite panel or individual boards, often tongue-and-groove. The distinguishing characteristic of a wood floor structure is that it is always up off the ground, spanning between supports, and will typically deflect under a load significantly more than a concrete structure.

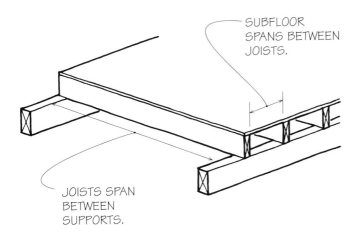

SUBFLOOR SPANS BETWEEN JOISTS.

JOISTS SPAN BETWEEN SUPPORTS.

Concrete structure—Concrete, unlike wood, is not susceptible to decay and therefore can be placed directly on the ground in the form of a slab. When it bears on the ground, a concrete slab will not deflect at all under the imposed load of occupants or furnishings. Even when concrete is used in conjunction with steel to span between supports on upper floors of buildings, it does not usually deflect nearly as much as wood nor does it provide the local resilience of a wood subfloor deflecting between joists.

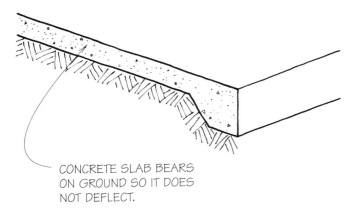

CONCRETE SLAB BEARS ON GROUND SO IT DOES NOT DEFLECT.

Hybrid structures—Wood and concrete may be combined to form a hybrid floor structure for special situations. For example, wood joists may support a concrete subfloor in order to increase mass for passive heating and cooling or for radiant heating (see 59) or to reduce airborne sound transmission. Even though it may deflect the same amount as a pure wood floor structure, such a hybrid structure will not be as lively as wood because of the dampening effect of the concrete mass. Local resilience between joists will also be eliminated.

A lighter-weight alternative to concrete for use over a wood structure is self-leveling gypsum. This material provides most of the advantages of concrete but is about 25% lighter and is much easier to install in a framed building (for its use in radiant-heat systems, see 59). Its primary disadvantage is its susceptibility to scratching and abrasion. For this reason, self-leveling gypsum cannot be exposed like concrete but must be covered with a finish floor.

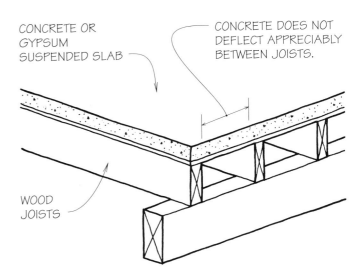

CONCRETE OR GYPSUM SUSPENDED SLAB

CONCRETE DOES NOT DEFLECT APPRECIABLY BETWEEN JOISTS.

WOOD JOISTS

While there are several reasons to place a concrete slab over a wood structure, the only reason to cover concrete with a wood subfloor is to provide nailing for a wood finish floor. Assuming that moisture is controlled, plywood may be attached directly to a concrete slab, taking on most of the characteristics of the slab but providing a good surface for nailing (see 86C). Wood sleepers (screeds) may also be attached to a concrete slab to provide nailing for a finish flooring, such as oak strip flooring, with the capacity to span between sleepers (see 86D). Sleepers also introduce to concrete the local resilience normally provided only by a wood structure.

Subfloor Materials

The smoothness of the subfloor can be critical to the proper installation of certain flooring materials, while it is not so important for others. Carpet on a pad, for example, may be installed over significant imperfections in the subfloor without affecting the quality of the installation, while thin vinyl flooring requires a subfloor that is quite smooth.

Wood and concrete, the same two materials that provide the structural support for floor systems, are also used as the subfloor to which the finish flooring is attached. Both wood and concrete are well matched to the application of most flooring materials but require some heroics to accommodate others.

Wood subfloor—When the subfloor surface is plywood, as it often is, most finish-flooring materials may be applied directly to it. Finish flooring may be applied either with adhesives or nailed (or screwed) to plywood subfloors. For most finish flooring, care must be taken that the quality of the plywood is sufficient to provide a surface free of major defects and to ensure that voids do not occur below the surface ply. Such structural plywood is called combination subfloor-underlayment. To avoid differential deflection between plywood panels, the panel edges should be tongue-and-groove, or should be blocked so that all edges are supported. A small amount of leveling compound between panels will achieve a high degree of smoothness.

Composite wood subfloor materials such as particleboard and hardboard (see Appendix B) that are not structural and are used primarily to adjust the thickness of a subfloor have a tendency to expand with increased moisture content and do not hold nails as well as plywood. These materials are generally less expensive than plywood, however, so they are commonly used in locations where moisture is not a problem and with finish-floor materials that do not require the holding power of nails.

Separate wood boards are less stable and have rougher surfaces than the above-mentioned subflooring materials, so they are generally not recommended for use as a subfloor. They are stiffer than plywood, however, so their use with a heavy finish floor such as mudset tile might be indicated. Wood boards are also adequate for use as a subfloor for certain finish-floor materials, such as wood strip or plank flooring, that have their own stiffness and can straddle any irregularities in the subfloor.

Concrete subfloor—Concrete, like wood, works well as a subfloor for most materials. It is smooth and continuous and, if it has imperfections, can be ground and filled with leveling compound. Compared to wood, however, concrete is less resilient and does not easily receive fasteners. Most finish-flooring materials are therefore glued to concrete subfloors. Wood flooring, which is usually nailed to the subfloor, may be nailed to wood sleepers that are themselves glued or attached with powder-driven fasteners to a concrete subfloor (see 86C & D).

The primary concern with concrete as a subfloor is its tendency when located at or below grade to transmit moisture from the ground. Moisture can break the bond between the concrete and the finish floor and cause blistering, lifting or cupping of the finish floor. If the concrete subfloor is well drained and well protected from sources of moisture, however, it will work well as a subfloor for most flooring materials. The installation of an adequate moisture barrier below a well-drained concrete slab will effectively limit the passage of moisture into the assembly.

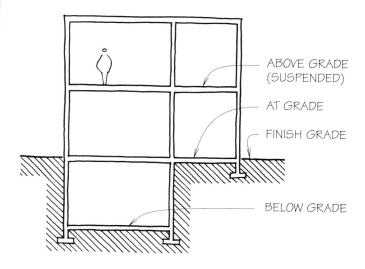

ABOVE GRADE (SUSPENDED)

AT GRADE

FINISH GRADE

BELOW GRADE

Manufacturers of finish-floor materials often prescribe concrete as a suitable subfloor in terms of its location. Concrete located below grade is least suitable, at grade is better, and above grade (suspended) is best because it has virtually no chance of wicking moisture from the ground (see drawing above). In fact, the location of a concrete slab in relation to the ground describes only its potential for absorbing moisture, not its actual moisture content. A slab below grade, if properly detailed and drained, can be as moisture free as a suspended slab in the same building.

Continuity of Subfloor

Whether the subfloor is wood or concrete, care must be taken to provide a surface that is continuous and stable. Any movement in the subfloor has the potential to be transferred to the finish surface in the form of cracks, wrinkles, lumps or other imperfections. In wood subfloors, plywood panels should be staggered and tongue-and-groove or continuously supported at all edges. In concrete subfloors, steel or fiber reinforcement should be incorporated to minimize cracking. In addition, concrete subfloors usually need to be able to move independently of the structure or the earth on which they are supported. Expansion joints at the edges (see 101C) and isolation membranes below the concrete subfloor (see 104C) both allow concrete slabs to move independently.

Situations where a wood floor structure is adjacent to a concrete floor structure should be avoided because the wood system will move more than the concrete with changes in moisture content. When such a situation cannot be avoided, either an expansion joint should be located at the junction or a flexible finish flooring such as carpet should be selected to go over a continuous subfloor.

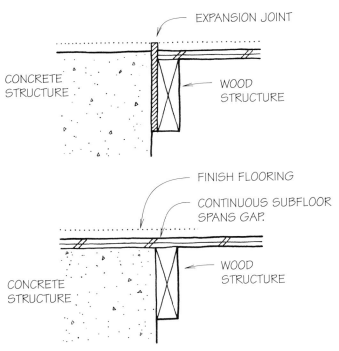

Aligning Adjacent Flooring Materials

Floors are designed so that the finish-floor level (FFL) is consistent even when flooring thicknesses vary. The finish surface of a wood floor adjacent to a vinyl floor, for example, needs to be at the same level, or close to it. Most codes allow no more than a ½-in. difference between adjacent floors.

It is often possible to accommodate small transitions between finish-floor levels by installing a threshold, as shown below.

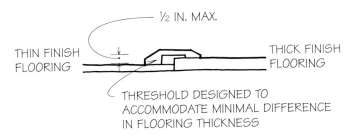

Since it is most economical to construct a wood or concrete subfloor on one level, it may be necessary to manipulate the thickness of a finish-flooring assembly to achieve consistency. In most cases, the overall thickness of a finish-flooring assembly is adjusted by the use of a nonstructural underlayment. By applying an underlayment, the finish level of a thin flooring material may be made flush with a thicker one. Particleboard and hardboard are the most common materials for underlayment because of their low cost. Particleboard can be the source of severe formaldehyde outgassing, however, so specify formaldehyde-free particleboard. Where potential short-term dampness may occur or where wood flooring needs to be nailed, however, plywood is commonly specified as an underlayment.

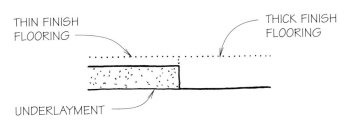

Occasionally, the thickness of a finish-floor assembly will vary so much between adjacent floors that the difference cannot be eliminated by underlayment. In this case, the framing must be adjusted. For example, a thick-bed tile floor adjacent to a vinyl floor could require that subfloors be offset as much as 3 in., as shown below. Such situations must be resolved during the design of the building.

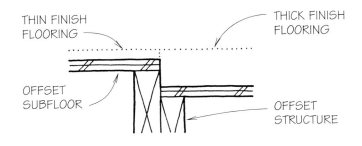

Radiant Heat

Floors are an appropriate location for radiant heating using water (hydronic heat) or electricity and for thermal mass for passive heating and/or cooling. When considering radiant heat, the selection of materials and the integration of the subfloor with finish flooring must be carefully considered.

Concrete is the subfloor of choice for both active radiant and passive floor systems because of its density, its relatively high thermal conductivity and its low cost. Not coincidentally, concrete also makes the best base for tile and other highly conductive finish-flooring materials that are best suited for radiant floors.

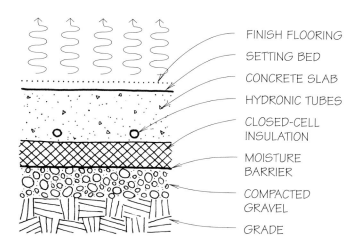

FINISH FLOORING
SETTING BED
CONCRETE SLAB
HYDRONIC TUBES
CLOSED-CELL INSULATION
MOISTURE BARRIER
COMPACTED GRAVEL
GRADE

RADIANT-HEAT SLAB-ON-GRADE

Finish-flooring materials best suited for radiant applications are those that transfer heat best from the slab to the heated space. A concrete slab without any finish flooring works best, but if a finish flooring must be added, dense materials such as tile, stone, terrazzo and most resilient flooring perform well. Less dense materials such as wood are less efficient since they do not conduct heat as well. Insulative flooring materials such as carpet are least effective.

The weight of concrete does not increase the cost of radiant-heat slab-on-grade. But because of the increased structure required to support a concrete or self-leveling gypsum topping slab in the upper stories of buildings, installing radiant floors will cost more (see 56).

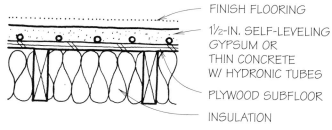

FINISH FLOORING
1½-IN. SELF-LEVELING GYPSUM OR THIN CONCRETE W/ HYDRONIC TUBES
PLYWOOD SUBFLOOR
INSULATION

RADIANT-HEAT SLAB @ UPPER STORY

Alternative systems to reduce weight in upper floors include electric radiant mats and the location of hydronic radiant tubes below the subfloor system. Electric mats may also be used over existing slabs where thickness of assembly needs to be minimal.

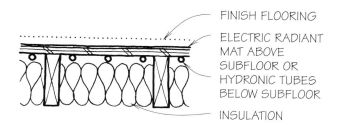

FINISH FLOORING
ELECTRIC RADIANT MAT ABOVE SUBFLOOR OR HYDRONIC TUBES BELOW SUBFLOOR
INSULATION

ALTERNATIVE RADIANT-HEAT SYSTEM @ UPPER STORY

Whenever concrete is used as a thermal mass, either for an active radiant heating system or for passive solar heating (or cooling) it should be insulated from climatic elements and from the earth. Perimeter insulation is required in all cases, and underslab insulation is recommended for slabs in contact with the soil whether underground or at grade.

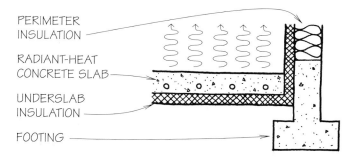

PERIMETER INSULATION
RADIANT-HEAT CONCRETE SLAB
UNDERSLAB INSULATION
FOOTING

TRANSITION TO
OTHER FLOORING
see 67B & C

INSTALLING ROLLED
GOODS
see 66A & B

INSTALLING
CARPET TILE
see 66B

EDGE @ WALL
see 67A

CARPET:
CONSTRUCTION
see 61

TYPES OF FIBER
see 62

PILE CHARACTERISTICS
see 63

BACKING
see 64A

DYEING
see 64B

SIZES
see 65B

PADS
see 65A

Carpet has for centuries been an indicator of the social development of civilizations around the world, from the rugs of the Navaho and the carpets of Persia to the modern carpets developed after the Industrial Revolution. The first wool carpet is believed to have been handwoven in Babylon around 5000 B.C. The first carpet factory in the United States began operation in 1791.

The terms "rug" and "carpet" have been used throughout history more or less interchangeably until the recent advent of the wall-to-wall carpet. Nowadays, "rug" refers specifically to an area rug, which covers only a portion of the floor, typically over another finish flooring such as wood, and is not usually fastened to it. Although rugs have many of the same characteristics as carpets, they are not a permanent part of a building. "Carpet" now refers to soft floor coverings that are attached to the floor, usually covering it entirely. This section deals only with carpet.

The growth of carpet as a major segment of the flooring industry was aided by the development of synthetic fibers to replace expensive natural fibers, by faster and less expensive production techniques and by dyeing methods allowing large inventories and lower prices. These major innovations have combined with other technical advances to make carpeting the most dominant floor covering in use today, covering approximately 70% of all floors in the United States.

Carpet is one of the most common flooring materials not only because of its lower cost, but also because of its numerous other attributes. It is soft and warm underfoot and quiet; it comes in a wide range of colors and textures, can be installed over almost any subfloor, including existing flooring such as wood or resilient flooring, and can be replaced fairly easily. On the negative side, it can be easily damaged by excessive moisture or spills, it tends to trap airborne particulates that contribute to indoor air pollution and it has a short life span relative to other flooring materials. It is also generally unrecyclable (it comprises 3% of the landfill in large urban centers in the United States), and adhesives used in its manufacture outgas at potentially harmful levels. Some carpets have coatings and treatments to meet flammability ratings, to enhance cleaning, to retard soiling and/or to fix colors.

Many characteristics determine the quality of appearance and performance of carpet, including carpet construction, type of fiber, pile characteristics, dyeing method and installation method.

 CARPET

Most carpet is composed of the visible pile, the primary backing, which holds the pile in place, and the secondary bbacking, added for strength. Carpet manufactured today can be either woven, tufted or fusion-bonded. Examples of each type are shown in the drawings below.

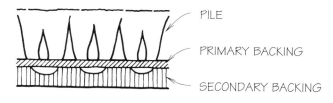

GENERIC CARPET SECTION

Woven Carpet
Produced on mechanized looms in a process very similar to that used to make historic handwoven rugs, woven carpet represents only about 2% of the carpet produced in the United States. In woven carpet, the yarn and backing are interwoven at the same time, creating a single fabric. Until recently, woven carpets were made without the use of adhesives, but modern manufactured woven carpets now sometimes use adhesives to strengthen the weave. There are a number of specific types of woven carpet, each needing its own type of loom. The hallmark of woven carpets is the beautifully complex, intricate patterns of high quality and durability. Woven carpet is primarily used for high-end commercial work and for residential wool carpet.

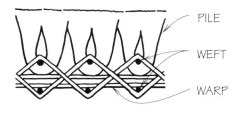

WOVEN CARPET

Tufted Carpet
The majority of carpet sold in the United States is tufted. To make tufted carpet, yarn is sewn through a previously manufactured primary backing and secured in place with a latex coating. This process is from 10

to 25 times faster than the weaving process. Originally limited to solid colors, tufted carpets are now made with computer-controlled machinery in an almost unlimited variety of patterns and textures. The primary backing is usually woven polypropylene, but jute and, less commonly, cotton or kraft cord may sometimes be used. Most tufted carpets have a secondary backing of jute or synthetic fiber to provide additional dimensional stability.

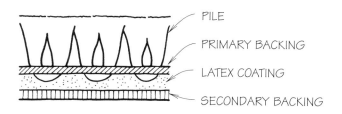

TUFTED CARPET

Fusion-Bonded Carpet
Fusion bonding involves folding yarn back and forth between two parallel backings that have been covered with an adhesive, usually liquid vinyl. The yarn is embedded into the adhesive of both backings, then the sandwiched yarn is cut, producing two pieces of carpet. Less yarn is required to make a quality carpet because the yarn is on the surface of the backing and does not have to pass through it as does the yarn of tufted carpets. The adhesive forms an impermeable barrier to liquids, thus protecting the backing from spills. SB latex adhesive, the source of most outgassing from tufted carpet, is not used in this process.

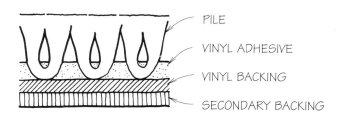

FUSION-BONDED CARPET

 CARPET CONSTRUCTION

Fiber

A primary factor in determining the performance of carpet is the type of fiber used in its construction. Often, poor performance characteristics of a fiber can be compensated for in the construction and pile characteristics of the carpet. For example, carpet fiber with a low resilience will perform best in a dense, short-cut pile. Appearance and performance characteristics must be weighed against cost.

Wool—The original fiber used in all carpet manufacture, wool today accounts for only about 1% to 2% of the market. Its supply is unstable, making its cost high compared with synthetic fibers. Although its initial cost can be high, wool's life-cycle cost is often comparable with synthetic fibers, and its beauty remains the standard to which synthetic fibers aspire.

Wool is a very durable and resilient natural fiber. It is relatively easy to clean and maintain and has natural fire resistance. But wool is vulnerable to moth damage and has low resistance to moisture.

Nylon—Of the carpet manufactured today, about 80% to 90% is made with nylon, either alone or in combination with wool or other synthetic fibers. First developed in the 1930s, nylon fibers substantially lower costs attributed to the use of wool. Recently developed nylon fibers help avoid the shine that is an unfavorable characteristic of earlier nylon fibers. Nylon is economical, very durable and easily maintained; it has excellent crush resistance and can be dyed a wide range of colors.

Acrylic—The synthetic fiber closest in appearance and feel to wool is acrylic. After a short surge into popularity, it is now rarely used. It is economical, easily maintained, has good crush resistance and can be dyed a wide range of colors, but it is only moderately durable.

Polyester—Used primarily in residential applications, polyester is the only carpet fiber that may contain significant recycled content. Clear soda and ketchup bottles are the source of approximately 50% of the polyester currently being made into carpet fiber. Polyester is economical and durable. It is easily maintained, mildew resistant and it holds its color well, but polyester has only fair crush resistance.

Olefin (polypropylene)—Made from natural gas (as opposed to liquid petroleum used for other synthetic fibers), olefin is used primarily in residential applications. Olefin is economical, fairly durable, and especially resistant to moisture and mildew. It has low resilience.

Natural plant fibers—Natural plant fibers such as sisal, jute, coir and cotton are sometimes used as fiber in carpet. Of these, sisal is the most common. It is extremely attractive and durable, but has poor stain and mildew resistance. It should therefore not be used in areas where food stains or moisture are likely. Jute is more common as a backing material (see 64A), but is also used for pile fiber.

Cotton is now available as a commercial carpet material, but it is not common and must be treated with so many chemicals to make it useful for carpet that it can hardly be called a natural material.

Blended fibers—Fibers are often blended to take advantage of the best qualities of each. For example olefin, quite stain resistant and therefore difficult to dye, is often blended with nylon, which is easy to dye. Nylon/polyester, wool/nylon and polypropylene/wool are other common blends. Unfortunately, blends hamper efforts to recycle carpet pile by making pure fiber types impossible to separate.

Yarn

In the spinning process, fibers are transformed into the yarn that makes the exposed pile of the carpet. To do this, the individual fibers are drawn out and twisted together into continuous strands of yarn. For a heavier yarn, multiple strands are twisted

FIBERS SPUN INTO SINGLE STRAND OF YARN.

SINGLE STRANDS OF YARN TWISTED TO FORM MULTIPLE-PLY YARN.

together into 2-, 3- or 4-ply yarns. A tight twist in the yarn is important for the durability of the carpet. Most synthetic yarns used for cut-pile carpets are heat set, a process used to help the yarns retain their twist. By using different colored and textured fibers and yarns, a variety of effects can be created.

A) TYPES OF FIBER

Pile

The pile of a carpet is the thickness of the yarn above the backing. There are numerous variations and combinations of pile type, height and twist that give a carpet its particular texture. The principal distinction between pile types is whether the tufts of yarn are loops or are cut. In woven and tufted carpet, the carpet is constructed with the yarn in loops, which can be either left as loops or cut to make pile. The pile in fusion-bonded carpet is generally cut, but it can also be made in loops.

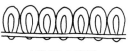

LEVEL LOOP

CUT PILE

The popular Berber carpets, modeled after North African tribal rugs made of handspun wool, have an alternating high and low looped pile. Some carpets combine cut and looped pile for unique textural effects. A very smooth surface may be created by cutting the tufts of yarn eactly even for a plush pile. A rough texture can be achieved with cut pile by using a hard-twisted yarn called *frieze yarn*.

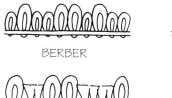

BERBER

PLUSH

CUT AND LOOPED

FRIEZE

Pile density—Pile density is one of the most important factors in determining the performance of a carpet. Pile density is a measure of the compactness of the pile yarn and is listed along with other specifications on most carpet. The pile density may be calculated by the following formula:

$$\text{Pile density (oz./cu. yd.)} = \frac{\text{Face wt.}}{\text{Pile ht. (in.)}}$$

Face weight (pile weight) equals the ounces of yarn (exclusive of backing) per square yard of carpet. Pile height is the pile dimension above the backing.

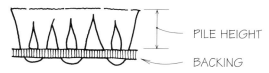

PILE HEIGHT — BACKING

PILE HEIGHT

Tufts per square inch—Another way to compare the quality of carpets is by counting the number of tufts per square inch. The more tufts there are, the better they will contribute to supporting each other, and the more dense and resilient the carpet will be. When the tufts are dense, dirt also tends to remain near the surface of the carpet.

CARPET TYPE	Tufts per sq. in.	Tuft density along length	Tuft density across width
Woven	64	rows = 8	pitch = 216
Tufted	64	stitches = 8	gauge = 1/8

This exercise of calculating tufts per square inch for comparison of carpets is complicated enormously by the terminology and measuring techniques that vary among carpet types. For example, woven and tufted carpets with eight tufts per inch in each direction are described as follows:

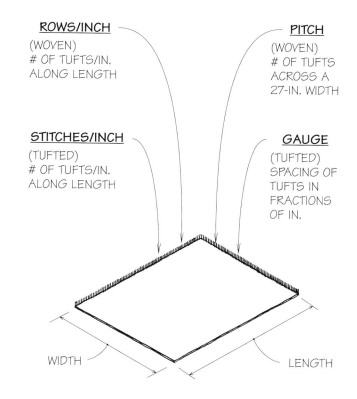

ROWS/INCH
(WOVEN)
OF TUFTS/IN. ALONG LENGTH

PITCH
(WOVEN)
OF TUFTS ACROSS A 27-IN. WIDTH

STITCHES/INCH
(TUFTED)
OF TUFTS/IN. ALONG LENGTH

GAUGE
(TUFTED)
SPACING OF TUFTS IN FRACTIONS OF IN.

WIDTH   LENGTH

A PILE CHARACTERISTICS

Backing provides dimensional stability and depth to carpet.

Primary Backing
Tufted and fusion-bonded carpets rely on a primary backing for their construction. Until recently, jute was the most common backing material. It is dimensionally stable under normal conditions, has the ability to stretch, seams well and accepts adhesive well for glue-down installations, but jute has a tendency to shrink and to stain the carpet face if it gets wet. It is imported primarily from Pakistan, Bangladesh and India and is costly and in unstable supply. Jute has been replaced almost completely by polypropylene. Synthetic backings such as polypropylene are stronger, more waterproof, and less absorbent than jute. Their performance depends to a large extent on whether they are woven or nonwoven. Woven synthetic backings provide stretchability but are heat sensitive, tend to deteriorate in tufted construction and can fray and ravel when cut and stretched. Nonwoven synthetic backings overcome these problems but they have little stretch.

Secondary Backing
For additional stability and strength, a secondary backing is normally attached with a latex coating to the primary backing of the carpet. Usually made of woven polypropylene, the secondary backing occasionally includes an integral cushion to make a much more resilient carpet in a direct glue-down installation (see 66B). Sometimes the secondary backing is merely an extra thick coating of synthetic latex over the primary backing.

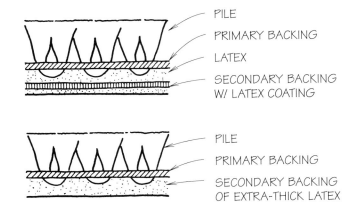

PILE
PRIMARY BACKING
LATEX
SECONDARY BACKING
W/ LATEX COATING

PILE
PRIMARY BACKING
SECONDARY BACKING
OF EXTRA-THICK LATEX

 CARPET BACKING

Whether made of natural or synthetic fibers, carpet relies on pigmented dyes for color. Dyeing methods affect carpet performance and cost. The three general dyeing methods are based on when the process occurs in the carpet manufacturing process, either before spinning, after spinning or after tufting. Certain fibers dye better at particular stages of the manufacturing process.

Before Spinning
Solution dyeing and stock dyeing both occur before spinning. Solution dyeing introduces color into the liquid form of synthetic material prior to its extrusion into fiber. The dye therefore permeates the entire fiber and is long lasting. Stock dyeing introduces color under pressure and heat into the natural or synthetic fiber prior to its being spun into yarn. Stock dyeing (also called vat dyeing) produces uniform color and is generally used to dye wool and wool blends in small batches or nylon in large commercial dye lots.

After Spinning
Dyeing after spinning can be done with two methods: skein dyeing or space dyeing. Skein dyeing (also called

yarn dyeing) introduces color into the yarn prior to constructing the carpet but after the yarn has been wound into manageable-size bundles, called skeins. Skein dyeing produces crisp, uniform colors in the finished carpet. Space dyeing prints yarn with multiple colors at specified distances (or spaces) to give a multi-colored appearance to the finished carpet.

SPACE-DYED YARN

After Tufting
Piece dyeing refers to the processes of dyeing unfinished tufted carpet (or piece) made with undyed yarn. For single colors, a continuous length of carpet is dipped into dye as it moves through the production process. This is called *continuous dyeing*. A similar process is called *beck dyeing*, where the tufted carpet is placed in a beck (a type of vat) and circulated in and out of the dye. For multiple colors, printing allows tremendous variety of pattern at a low cost, often imitating woven patterns but without the durability or subtlety of a true woven carpet.

 DYEING METHODS

A separate pad (also called cushion) is often used under the carpet to provide additional comfort underfoot, reduce the transmission of impact noise and increase the life of the carpet by reducing friction between the carpet and the floor. A few types of carpet come with a pad glued to or integral with the backing, called a cushion back. Most carpet manufacturers will agree that the addition of a pad will increase the life of a carpet's appearance by at least 40% to 100%. It is important to match pad with carpet type: For example, woven carpet requires a relatively smooth and firm pad to minimize flexion of the warp and weft. The three types of carpet pad are felt, rubber and urethane foam. Thickness of all types is usually ½ in. but can range from ¼ in. to ⅝ in.

Felt Pads
Originally made of animal hair, felt pads today are sometimes blends of animal hair and synthetic fiber, but are usually made entirely of synthetic fiber. Some felt padding is made with recycled byproducts of the carpet-making industry. Felt is the least resilient padding, but it is quite durable and has the firmness

that contributes most to extending the life of a carpet. Most felt padding should be used for above-grade installations only, since it has a tendency to mildew when it absorbs significant moisture.

Rubber Pads
A combination of natural and synthetic rubber and fillers, rubber padding is suitable for light to medium traffic. It is occasionally applied as an integral backing to carpets but is also available formed into flat sheets. Sponge rubber is dense, resilient and durable. Foam rubber is similar, but it costs less, and is less dense, less resilient and less durable. Some rubber padding is beginning to be made from ground tire scraps or other recycled rubber sources and bonded with latex.

Urethane Foam Pads
Made from synthetic polymers, urethane foam pads are available in various densities. The foam is sometimes chopped and rebonded into sheets with additives such as paper, vinyl, other foam or wood chips. Urethane foam is extremely dense, very durable and unaffected by moisture.

 CARPET PADS

Rolled Goods
Since the 1930s, wide-width woven carpet has been referred to as *rolled goods* or broadloom carpet. Most commonly produced in 12-ft. wide rolls, it is also available in widths of 13½ ft. to 18 ft. and in hallway widths of 27 in. and 54 in. Carpet is cut from rolls that can be as long as 300 ft., depending on pile height, backing thickness and factory capacity. Rolled goods are the most common carpeting and may be installed by either the stretch-in (see 66A) or glue-down (see 66B) method.

Modular Tiles
Modular carpet tiles are a rapidly growing portion of the carpet industry. They are common in high-traffic commercial spaces where concentrated wear and local spills can be problems. The tiles usually have an integral cushioned back, come in 18-in. squares and are glued down (see 66B). Damaged or worn tiles are easy to replace, so with regular rotation (including the *attic stock,* or extra carpet tiles), wear over the entire floor will be fairly even. Carpet tiles can be used to create patterns, they are easy to install in occupied spaces and there is less waste during installation.

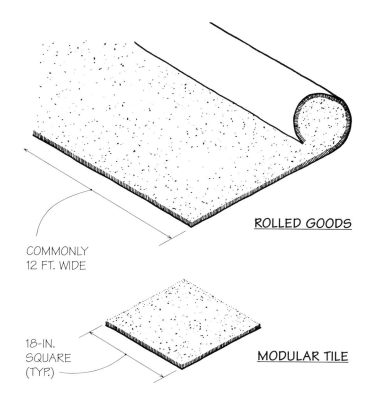

COMMONLY 12 FT. WIDE

ROLLED GOODS

18-IN. SQUARE (TYP.)

MODULAR TILE

 CARPET SIZES & TYPES

PROVIDE CLEARANCE
@ BASE.
see | 67A |

TACKLESS STRIPS
NAILED TO
SUBFLOOR @
PERIMETER
OF ROOM

PAD STAPLED
TO SUBFLOOR

TRANSITIONS TO
OTHER FLOORING
see | 67B |

CARPET STRETCHED IN
W/ POWER STRETCHER &
HOOKED ON TACKLESS STRIPS

Stretch-in installation is the most common method used for residential applications. With the stretch-in method, broadloom carpet is installed loose over a pad and fastened only at the perimeter with tackless strips. The tackless strips are water-resistant plywood strips with two or three rows of rust-resistant pins oriented up and angled away from the center of the room. These strips are nailed to the subfloor at all edges of the room (or glued to a concrete subfloor). The carpet is stretched with a power stretcher before being forced down onto the tackless strips, which hold it in place. Stretch-in installations use no adhesives, produce fewer toxic fumes during installation and are easier to replace than glue-down. The stretch-in installation is the only method that allows rolled goods to be removed and reused. Because the carpet will continue to stretch with use, the stretch-in method works best for areas not exceeding 40 ft. by 60 ft. Carpet that has stretched with use can be restretched in place, but this is uncommon..

When the room is wider than the rolled goods, seams must be made to join the edges of stretched-in carpet. Hot-melt tape is the preferred method for installing seams in over 99% of applications because it is the strongest and least expensive. Occasionally, however, hand sewing is called for because it does not add thickness to the assembly at the seam as does hot-melt tape.

Although strong enough to withstand stretching, seams are the weakest part of a stretched-in carpet assembly. Seams should therefore not be placed in heavy traffic areas, in locations where people change directions or perpendicular to doorways.

Direct Glue-Down Installation

For large areas, broadloom carpet applied by the direct glue-down method rather than the stretch-in method better resists shifting in heavy traffic and supports wheeled traffic better. Unlike stretch-in carpet, damaged areas of glue-down may be cut out and replaced with carpet from the attic stock left over from the installation.

Using this method, carpet with or without an integral pad may be attached directly to the underlayment or subfloor with an adhesive. (Installations without a pad are less forgiving of subfloor irregularities than installations with a pad.) The adhesives used for direct glue-down installations have, until recently, been guilty of emitting more short-term pollutants than the carpet itself. However, low-VOC (volatile organic chemical) products are now available from most manufacturers. Release adhesives can be used to protect the floor underneath from damage during removal and to provide subfloor access.

Double Glue-Down Installation

With the double glue-down method, carpet pad is glued to the subfloor with a release adhesive, then carpet is glued to the pad. This method combines the ease and stability of large-area coverage with the wear and comfort advantages of a separate pad.

Peel-and-Stick Installation

A few manufacturers offer peel-and-stick carpet. It comes with an integral pad and a dry adhesive applied to the back, protected prior to installation with a thin polyethylene film. The dry adhesive is available on carpet tiles and on rolled goods and minimizes pollutants associated with installation adhesives.

Carpet Tiles

To allow for easy rotation and replacement, modular carpet tiles are generally fastened with a release adhesive. The two methods used for installing the tiles are the full-spread and the gridded.

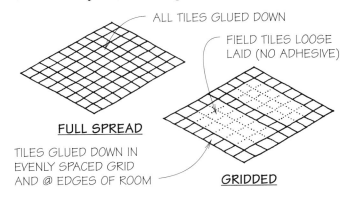

ALL TILES GLUED DOWN

FIELD TILES LOOSE
LAID (NO ADHESIVE)

FULL SPREAD

TILES GLUED DOWN IN
EVENLY SPACED GRID
AND @ EDGES OF ROOM

GRIDDED

(A) STRETCH-IN INSTALLATION
    ROLLED GOODS

(B) GLUE-DOWN INSTALLATION
    ROLLED GOODS & CARPET TILE

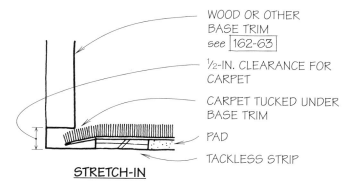

WOOD OR OTHER BASE TRIM see | 162-63 |

½-IN. CLEARANCE FOR CARPET

CARPET TUCKED UNDER BASE TRIM

PAD

TACKLESS STRIP

STRETCH-IN

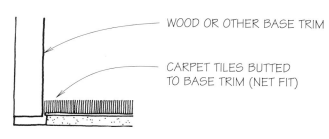

WOOD OR OTHER BASE TRIM

CARPET TILES BUTTED TO BASE TRIM (NET FIT)

CARPET TILE

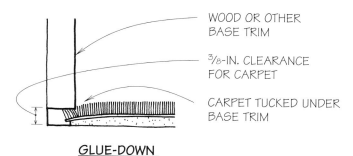

WOOD OR OTHER BASE TRIM

⅜-IN. CLEARANCE FOR CARPET

CARPET TUCKED UNDER BASE TRIM

GLUE-DOWN

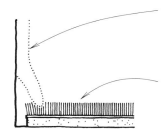

VINYL OR RUBBER BASE APPLIED AFTER CARPET IS INSTALLED.

STRETCH-IN, GLUE-DOWN OR TILE CARPET

VINYL OR RUBBER BASE

A   CARPET @ WALL

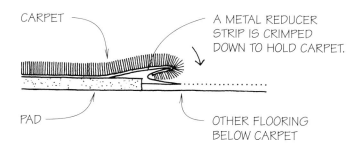

CARPET

A METAL REDUCER STRIP IS CRIMPED DOWN TO HOLD CARPET.

PAD

OTHER FLOORING BELOW CARPET

STRETCH-IN W/ PAD

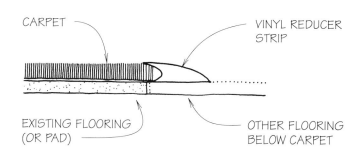

CARPET

VINYL REDUCER STRIP

EXISTING FLOORING (OR PAD)

OTHER FLOORING BELOW CARPET

CARPET ABOVE EXISTING FLOORING

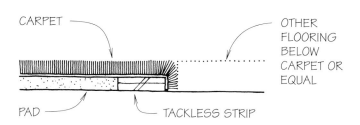

CARPET

OTHER FLOORING BELOW CARPET OR EQUAL

PAD

TACKLESS STRIP

STRETCH-IN OVER PAD

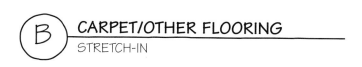

CARPET

OTHER FLOORING FLUSH W/ OR ABOVE CARPET

ADHESIVE

CARPET EVEN W/ OR BELOW OTHER FLOORING

B   CARPET/OTHER FLOORING
STRETCH-IN

C   CARPET/OTHER FLOORING
GLUE-DOWN

FOR MATERIALS
see 69

EDGES @ WALL
see 70A

TRANSITIONS TO
OTHER FLOORING
see 70C

RESILIENT TILE
FLOORING
see 71

RESILIENT SHEET
FLOORING
see 74

Resilient flooring is a class of very thin tile or sheet flooring that is applied to the subfloor with adhesive. Some materials, such as cork or rubber, are truly resilient, while others, such as vinyl tiles, are actually quite hard. Resilient flooring is so thin that the stiffness of the subfloor and floor structure can affect the overall resilience of a floor more than the finish-flooring material itself.

The earliest resilient flooring was cork, used in Portugal in the early 1800s, followed by linoleum, invented in England in the 1860s. Today's many resilient flooring materials include various forms of vinyl, rubber, cork and linoleum, each with its own aesthetic appeal and functional properties. The properties of each resilient flooring material are listed in the chart below, along with general guidelines for cost, size and performance. See individual material descriptions that follow for more information.

RESILIENT FLOORING	RESILIENT FLOORING CHARACTERISTICS					
	Common size	Durability	Ease of care	Moisture resistance	Resilience	Relative cost
Vinyl tile see 72A						
Solid	12 in. sq.	excellent	good	good	poor	high
Composition	12 in. sq.	good	good	good	poor	medium
Rubber tile see 73	18 in. sq.	good	fair	good	good	medium
Cork tile see 72B	12 in. sq.	poor	poor	poor	excellent	high
Vinyl sheets see 74						
Cushioned	12 ft.	fair	good	excellent	excellent	low
Inlaid	6 ft.	good	good	excellent	fair	medium
Solid	6 ft. 7 in.	excellent	excellent	excellent	fair	high
Linoleum sheets see 75		good	fair	fair	good	medium

(A) RESILIENT FLOORING

Sheet vs. tile

Resilient flooring is available in sheet or tile form. Sheet flooring (see 74) has the advantage of minimizing seams to make a floor more resistant to moisture, less likely to collect dirt and easier to clean. It will better protect the subfloor structure, which is especially desirable in a damp location such as a kitchen or bathroom.

Resilient tile flooring (see 71), however, is easier to install and repair than sheet flooring, and colors and sizes of tiles can be easily manipulated to make patterns, such as the classic black-and-white checkerboard floor originally constructed in marble. Making patterns with resilient tiles is so popular that many vinyl tile manufacturers now make narrow strip tiles for borders or other patterns.

Thickness

Most resilient flooring is approximately ⅛ in. thick. Because subtle differences between the thickness of such materials is difficult to describe in fractions of an inch, the thickness of resilient flooring is measured in thousandths of an inch and referred to by the terms "gauge" or "mil." For example, a resilient flooring ⅛ in. thick is 0.125 in. thick, and labeled as 0.125-gauge flooring or 125-mil flooring.

Underlayment

The thinness of resilient flooring with respect to other flooring materials requires that resilient flooring must often be applied to an underlayment to provide extra thickness to the resilient floor assembly.

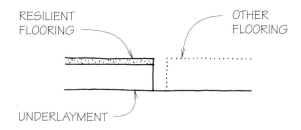

RESILIENT FLOORING

OTHER FLOORING

UNDERLAYMENT

Since it is applied with adhesive, resilient flooring does not require the nail-holding capability of plywood, so particleboard or chipboard underlayment is most commonly used. But where moisture from below may be suspected, a high grade of underlayment plywood would be a better choice.

The thinness of resilient flooring also requires that the subfloor or underlayment be quite smooth and clean before installation. Even small imperfections in the subfloor or underlayment are likely to show through to the finish surface of the floor. Underlayment serves to bridge joints in the subfloor, but it must often be filled between sheets with leveling compound to provide a smooth enough surface for resilient flooring.

Moisture Control

The nonporous nature of most resilient flooring materials that makes them attractive as flooring materials can also cause problems in situations where moisture is likely to accumulate below the floor surface. Moisture trapped below the floor surface can cause the adhesive that binds the flooring to the subfloor or underlayment to fail. It is imperative, therefore, to prevent moisture from entering the assembly. In remodel situations where moisture control is uncertain, a slab should be treated with a material that minimizes vapor emissions before the flooring is applied. A slab can be treated with a penetrating primer or a cementitious underlayment, or it can be covered with fiberglass matting.

Adhesives

Most resilient flooring materials may be attached with a water-soluble, multipurpose latex adhesive. This adhesive contains virtually no volatile solvents that can create health risks for installers. Solvent-based adhesives, which can contain harmful volatile solvents, must occasionally be used in situations where an impervious barrier is needed to prevent water vapor from the subfloor from being trapped below the finish flooring. In this case, good ventilation during installation will diffuse harmful fumes, and the flooring will trap volatile compounds so that their release is slow and virtually undetectable.

Both water-based and solvent-based adhesives are spread evenly across the entire subfloor (or underlayment) and the flooring is applied directly to it. It is important to follow the recommendation of the flooring manufacturer when selecting an adhesive since warranties are typically dependent on installation procedures.

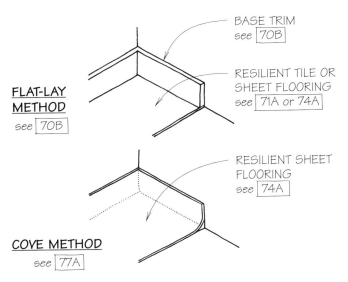

FLAT-LAY
METHOD
see 70B

COVE METHOD
see 77A

BASE TRIM
see 70B

RESILIENT TILE OR
SHEET FLOORING
see 71A or 74A

RESILIENT SHEET
FLOORING
see 74A

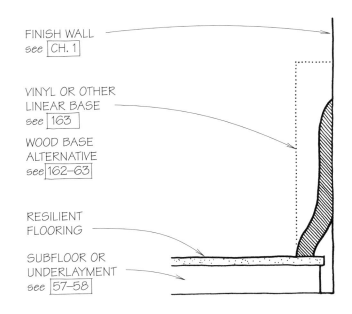

FINISH WALL
see CH. 1

VINYL OR OTHER
LINEAR BASE
see 163

WOOD BASE
ALTERNATIVE
see 162–63

RESILIENT
FLOORING

SUBFLOOR OR
UNDERLAYMENT
see 57–58

Resilient flooring is usually laid flat on the subfloor with its edges trimmed by a vinyl or other linear base. This is called the flat-lay method. An alternative, called the cove method, continues the flooring up the wall for a few inches. The cove method is normally employed with resilient sheet flooring, not tiles.

 EDGES @ WALL

 **BASE TRIM**
FLAT-LAY METHOD

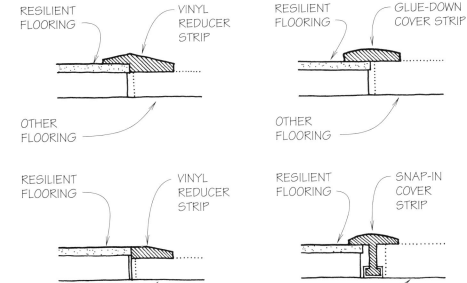

RESILIENT
FLOORING

VINYL
REDUCER
STRIP

OTHER
FLOORING

RESILIENT
FLOORING

VINYL
REDUCER
STRIP

OTHER
FLOORING

**RESILIENT FLOORING
HIGHER THAN OTHER FLOORING**

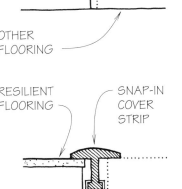

RESILIENT
FLOORING

GLUE-DOWN
COVER STRIP

OTHER
FLOORING

RESILIENT
FLOORING

SNAP-IN
COVER
STRIP

OTHER
FLOORING

**RESILIENT FLOORING
FLUSH W/ OTHER FLOORING**

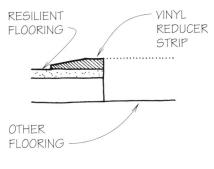

RESILIENT
FLOORING

VINYL
REDUCER
STRIP

OTHER
FLOORING

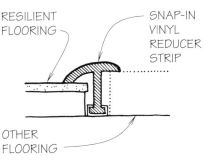

RESILIENT
FLOORING

SNAP-IN
VINYL
REDUCER
STRIP

OTHER
FLOORING

**RESILIENT FLOORING
LOWER THAN OTHER FLOORING**

 TRANSITIONS TO OTHER FLOORING

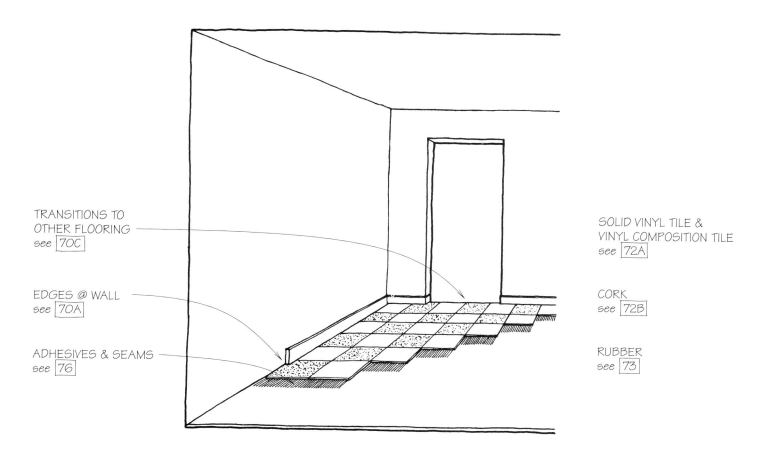

TRANSITIONS TO
OTHER FLOORING
see | 70C |

EDGES @ WALL
see | 70A |

ADHESIVES & SEAMS
see | 76 |

SOLID VINYL TILE &
VINYL COMPOSITION TILE
see | 72A |

CORK
see | 72B |

RUBBER
see | 73 |

Resilient tile flooring is currently available in vinyl, rubber, cork and linoleum. Vinyl is by far the most prevalent, but the other three are becoming more common. Rubber is used in commercial applications because of its textured surface, which provides excellent traction. Cork and linoleum, both quite common earlier in the century, have become popular again. Cork is probably popular despite its higher cost because it is a naturally grown material. Linoleum, more common as a 79-in. wide sheet, is also made of natural materials.

Early petrochemical-based resilient tiles were called asphalt tiles. These tiles contained asphalt as a binder, asbestos, inorganic fillers, pitch and pigments. They tended to be dark in color because of the significant asphalt content. The next generation of synthetic resilient tiles saw vinyl replace the asphalt in what was known as vinyl-asbestos tile. In the late 1960s this tile outsold all other types of resilient floor coverings. Now, with asbestos banned, the prevalent resilient tiles are composed almost entirely of vinyl. Today's vinyl tiles outperform their predecessors in terms of hardness (indentation resistance) and cleanability (nonporous). The continued popularity

of vinyl tile flooring is a result of its durability, ease of maintenance, and relatively low cost relative to other types of flooring.

Because of the number of seams between tiles in a resilient tile floor, there is little point in attempting to seal them against the occasional intrusion of water. The seams in resilient tile floors, therefore, are either not sealed at all or are incidentally sealed with the wax or finish applied to the finished floor. Because the seams between tiles are vulnerable to water, resilient tile flooring (especially over wood subfloors) is not recommended for use in damp locations such as bathrooms.

 RESILIENT TILE FLOORING

The two types of vinyl tile are solid vinyl and vinyl composition. Solid vinyl tile is pure, whereas vinyl composition tile, often referred to as VCT, has additives and fillers added to lower the percentage of polyvinyl chloride. This makes VCT considerably less expensive than solid vinyl tile and only slightly less durable. Solid vinyl tile is rarely specified for residential construction, whereas VCT is common in both commercial and residential applications.

All grades and thicknesses of solid vinyl and vinyl composition tile are largely homogenous, so the wear layer extends fully through the thickness of the material. The surface texture and color of vinyl composition tile can change with wear, however, since it is made with a variety of materials that are mixed together and are not guaranteed to be consistent throughout the depth of the tile. Solid vinyl, being made of pure polyvinyl chloride, will not change texture or color with wear.

By far the most common size of both types of vinyl tile is 12 in. square, although there is some variation among manufacturers. Coordinated feature strips that make borders or otherwise introduce pattern into the floor are available. They range from ¼ in. to 6 in. wide and 24 in. to 36 in. long.

Some vinyl tiles are available with an effective self-stick adhesive for ease of application. Tile thicknesses range from ¹⁄₁₆ in. to ⁵⁄₃₂ in. Commercial-grade tiles are generally ⅛ in. thick.

A SOLID VINYL TILE & VINYL COMPOSITION TILE

Cork flooring, first produced in the United States around the turn of the century, is made from the bark of the cork oak tree, grown primarily in Portugal. The bark, harvested from live trees every 7 to 10 years, is used primarily to make bottle stoppers, but the scrap from this process is shredded, combined with resins and formed into floor tiles.

Early cork flooring was made of pure cork baked under pressure so that the natural resins of the cork flowed and formed a binder between particles. Tiles were sliced from blocks and were sold with no factory finishing. On-site finishing provided durability and resistance to water and staining. Since the late 1940s, manufacturers have used phenolic resin binders that allow the cork to retain its own natural resins, thereby increasing resilience and decreasing porosity of the finished product. This modern cork flooring also has greater tensile qualities so it can be made in thinner gauges than the earlier types.

When compared to other resilient flooring, cork stands out for its excellent resilience and quietness, but it is not as resistant to indentation or staining. Cork is also the least durable of all resilient floorings and usually requires more maintenance.

Cork tile is homogenous, so the wear layer extends the full thickness of the material. Color shades range from light to dark and reflect the color of the material in its natural state. Cork flooring tiles are usually offered in three grades of finish: natural, waxed and coated.

Natural cork—Natural cork is untreated, absorbent cork. Because it is vulnerable to staining and marring, it must be finished with polyurethane or wax after installation.

Waxed cork—Waxed cork has a wax applied with heat at the factory so that the wax penetrates into the cork. It does not require any finishing at the time of installation but must be waxed periodically to maintain its luster and resistance to moisture.

Coated cork—Coated cork has a factory-applied polyurethane or vinyl finish that impregnates the cork and provides increased strength, durability and moisture resistance. Coated cork does not need to be waxed and is relatively easy to maintain.

Most cork flooring is sold in 12-in. square tiles, with smaller tiles available. Cork sheets 36 in. wide are also available. The standard thickness of tiles is ³⁄₁₆ in. for residential floors, ⁵⁄₁₆ in. for commercial applications.

B CORK TILE

Rubber saw its first significant use as a flooring material in the 1920s when natural rubber was "vulcanized" (cured with sulfur and heat) and made into thin sheets. In the mid-1940s synthetic rubber (styrene butadiene rubber or SBR), which is less expensive, more durable and more resistant to oils, replaced the natural material. Rubber had virtually disappeared as a flooring material by the 1960s (replaced by vinyl) when the Pirelli company, the Italian tire manufacturer, introduced the raised disk design in rubber to recapture a significant portion of the resilient flooring market. Recently, rubber recycled from tires has found its way into rubber flooring materials in the form of resilient tiles, mats and interlocking strips.

SBR

SBR tile is thin (about ⅛ in.) and nonporous, and it resembles solid vinyl (see 72A), in that its color is consistent all the way through the tile. It is available primarily in solid colors and usually has a raised-disk design to increase traction (it may also have a smooth surface).

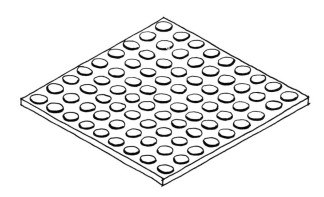

RAISED-DISK RUBBER TILE

SBR is generally available in 12-in., 18-in. and 36-in. square tiles, with 18 in. the most common. It is also available on a limited basis in sheets 36 in. wide. The thickness of SBR varies according to the manufacturer but is generally about ⅛ in., with the top 20% of this being composed of the raised antiskid design (usually circles).

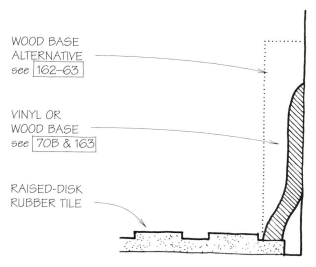

WOOD BASE ALTERNATIVE see 162–63

VINYL OR WOOD BASE see 70B & 163

RAISED-DISK RUBBER TILE

RUBBER TILE @ BASE

NOTE:
TRIM MUST REST ON THINNEST PART OF THE TILE TO AVOID GAPS BETWEEN DISKS.

The raised disks typical of SBR flooring make the application of base trim at the edges of the floor somewhat problematic. Ideally, the base trim should rest on the tile between the raised disks, but this is usually extremely difficult to execute at all edges of a room.

Recycled Rubber

Strips or flakes of recycled automobile and truck tires are bonded to a reinforced rubber backing to provide flooring used for recreational flooring, walkways, entry areas and antifatigue matting.

Recycled rubber is thicker than SBR. Material for walkways is ¼ in. to 1 in. thick, while material for sports activities can be up to 3¼ in. thick.

RECYCLED STRIPS OF TIRE ARE BONDED TOGETHER AND BUFFED TO REVEAL IMPREGNATED NYLON FILAMENTS.

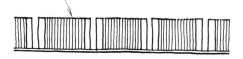

RECYCLED RUBBER MATTING

Ⓐ RUBBER TILE

INSTALLING RESILIENT SHEET FLOORING:

FLAT-LAY METHOD
see | 70B |

TRANSITIONS TO
OTHER FLOORING
see | 70C |

COVED METHOD
see | 77 |

ADHESIVES & SEAMS
see | 76 |

TYPES OF SHEET FLOORING:

LINOLEUM
see | 74 |

VINYL
see | 75 |

The oldest form of resilient sheet flooring is linoleum, first produced commercially in England in the 1860s. Linoleum was practically the only resilient flooring available in sheet form until after World War II, when vinyl was introduced. Vinyl, less expensive and available in a wider variety of surface designs, almost eliminated linoleum from the market. Today, the vast majority of resilient sheet flooring is vinyl, but linoleum is making a comeback because of its natural composition and improving color selection. Vinyl is made of petroleum products and not recyclable or biodegradable, but linoleum is made of naturally occurring biodegradable materials. Linoleum may even be reused in some cases since it does not have to be glued to the subfloor if it covers only a small area.

Cork and rubber, usually sold as tile (see 72B, 73), make up a very small segment of the resilient sheet flooring market.

Linoleum

The wear layer of linoleum is made of natural, biodegradable raw materials such as wood pulp (wood flour), cork, natural pigments, turpentine and linseed oil formed under heat and pressure. This homogenous layer, either a solid color or, more commonly, a blend of several colors swirled together, is applied to a burlap or jute canvas backing.

Compared to other resilient flooring materials, linoleum fares reasonably well with respect to resistance to stains and indentation, quietness and overall durability. The linseed oil has natural

antibacterial properties. But linoleum requires more maintenance than most resilient floors, and it is very sensitive to moisture. With continuous exposure to moisture, the linoleum will become very soft and plastic. It should always be applied, therefore, to a predictably dry subfloor. Linoleum located in sporadically wet locations such as bathrooms should be well sealed and carefully caulked at the edges.

Linoleum has a relatively low-luster surface that performs well in most situations without any finish, but it is more commonly waxed. Linoleum has a good range of colors, but very little pattern choice. The smoothness of the surface makes linoleum suitable for inlaying feature strips.

The thickness of standard linoleum is 0.09 in. with a minimum 0.05-in. wear layer. Thicker battleship linoleum, so-called because it was manufactured to meet the specifications of the U.S. Navy for warship flooring, is 0.125 in. thick (⅛ in.). This gives it a thicker wear layer, and it will better hide subfloor imperfections than the standard-gauge linoleum. Linoleum is generally available in 6-ft. 7-in. (2-meter) wide rolls.

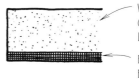

WEAR LAYER OF WOOD PULP,
CORK, PIGMENTS, TURPENTINE &
LINSEED OIL

BURLAP OR JUTE CANVAS
BACKING

<u>LINOLEUM</u>

(A) RESILIENT SHEET FLOORING
LINOLEUM

Vinyl

The primary ingredient in vinyl sheet flooring is polyvinyl chloride (PVC). Also included are pigments, mineral fillers for body, and plasticizers for flexibility. The three types of vinyl sheet flooring are cushioned vinyl, inlaid vinyl and homogenous vinyl, described in detail on the following page.

A paper-thin polyurethane film called a no-wax surface may be applied to the top of residential-grade sheet vinyls. This film provides a lustrous surface that imitates wax and will last for several years. When the surface is worn through, the clear vinyl wear layer continues to protect the colored vinyl below but is not shiny like the polyurethane film. Wax may be applied to achieve a shiny appearance after the no-wax surface is worn through.

Cushioned vinyl—Cushioned vinyl makes up more than 80% of the residential vinyl market and is the least expensive type. Cushioned vinyl is made with a process called rotogravure, in which a spongy vinyl sheet attached to a backing (usually fiberglass) is embossed with a pattern and colored on the exposed upper side. This assembly is coated with a tough, clear vinyl wear layer. The durability and cost of cushioned vinyl are roughly related to the thickness of the wear layer of clear vinyl. When this layer is cut or worn through, the softer, cushioned layer below becomes exposed and the floor can no longer be cleaned.

Cushioned vinyl is more comfortable underfoot, more flexible and easier to install than other vinyls. Because of its relatively thin wear layer, however, cushioned vinyl is generally not as durable as inlaid or homogenous vinyl. Cushioned vinyl is generally available in 12-ft. wide rolls.

Although cushioned vinyl is the most versatile in terms of color and pattern selection, its shiny surface may, despite its utility, be visually objectionable.

Inlaid vinyl—Inlaid vinyl is made of small chips of vinyl with integral color that are bonded to a backing sheet (usually fiberglass). The chips can vary from sand-size granules to pea-size flakes and can be arranged to form patterns or can be distributed randomly. The surface of the colored vinyl chips is coated with a layer of clear vinyl. Like cushioned vinyl, there is usually a surface texture so that small dents on the surface do not show. As with homogenous vinyl, the color and pattern are integral so that the wear layer is continuous throughout most of the depth of the material. Inlaid sheet vinyl is

relatively stiff and more difficult to install than cushioned vinyl. Inlaid vinyl is generally available in 6-ft. wide rolls.

Homogenous vinyl—Homogenous vinyl is made either of a single, solid color continuous throughout the material or of two or more secondary colors mixed in with a dominant color. In all cases the color is homogenous throughout so that the wear layer extends through the full depth of the material. Homogenous vinyl does not have a backing. It generally has a smooth, untextured surface so that denting will be more apparent than on the other types of sheet vinyl. The smoothness of the surface also makes homogenous vinyl the only type of sheet vinyl suitable for the inlay of feature strips or other pattern elements. Homogenous vinyl is the most expensive of sheet vinyls and is primarily used in commercial applications. Homogenous vinyl is generally available in 6-ft. or 6-ft. 7-in. (2-meter) wide rolls.

CLEAR VINYL WEAR LAYER (10–25 MIL)
SPONGY VINYL SHEET EMBOSSED W/ COLOR & TEXTURE (± 100 MIL)
FIBERGLASS BACKING (30 MIL)

CUSHIONED VINYL

CLEAR VINYL WEAR LAYER (4–5 MIL)
INLAID VINYL CHIPS
FIBERGLASS BACKING (30 MIL)

INLAID VINYL

FULL-DEPTH VINYL
SECONDARY COLOR SWIRLED IN (OPTIONAL)

HOMOGENOUS VINYL

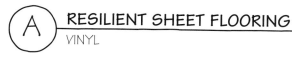

Ⓐ **RESILIENT SHEET FLOORING**
VINYL

Adhesives

Most vinyl sheets have a fiberglass mesh backing that is best attached to the subfloor with a water-soluble, multipurpose latex adhesive. About 10% of inlaid vinyl sheets have a vinyl backing instead of a fiberglass mesh backing. These vinyl sheets are designed to shrink after being applied. A special adhesive designed to be applied just at the edges and seams of these vinyls holds them in place while their shrinking action keeps them taut.

Many homogenous vinyls are applied with a solvent-based release adhesive that allows the vinyl to be removed easily after installation. These adhesives are difficult to use and should be applied only by professionals.

Linoleum, like most sheet vinyls, is usually attached with a water-based latex adhesive. When the area to be covered is small and does not exceed the width of a single sheet, linoleum may be laid dry, without any adhesive.

Seams

Seaming of resilient sheets is required when the roll width is not adequate to cover a floor or when coved corners are made (see 77). The seaming materials and process depend on the type of flooring. When seaming is required, most manufacturers state that sheet flooring can be welded into a continuous watertight unit. The seaming process occurs after the flooring is in place and attached to the subfloor with adhesive.

Solvent-welded seams—Cushioned, inlaid or homogenous vinyl floors may be chemically fused with a solvent forced into the seams with a special applicator. The solvent, similar to the clear solvent used to fuse PVC plumbing pipe, dissolves the two adjacent pieces of vinyl and effectively makes them into one piece. The solvent is extremely hazardous and must be used with plentiful ventilation.

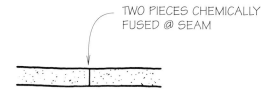

SOLVENT-WELDED SEAM

Heat-welded seams—Homogenous vinyl or linoleum seams may be sealed with a heat-welding process. Heat-welded seams start with a gap of ⅛ in. to 3⁄16 in. between flooring sheets. This gap is filled with a vinyl- or linoleum-type wire that can either match or contrast with the color of the flooring. The wire is melted so that it fills the gap and fuses with the adjacent flooring pieces. The excess melted wire is trimmed with a knife.

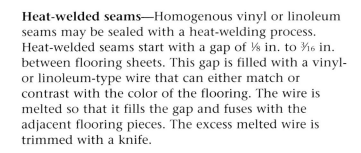

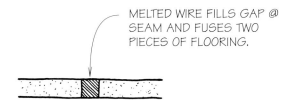

HEAT-WELDED SEAM

Seam sealer—Inlaid vinyl may be joined with a urethane seam sealer that fills the crack between the two sheets of vinyl and is applied with a special applicator. This sealer does not dissolve the vinyl but is a coating that adheres to the edges of it.

Butted seams—Until the very recent development of heat welding for linoleum, there was no system for welding or sealing linoleum seams as there was for sheet vinyl. Instead, linoleum seams were scribed to fit very tightly and relied on time and pressure to allow adjacent edges to merge slowly into a water-resistant whole.

Ⓐ **INSTALLATION OF RESILIENT SHEET FLOORING**
ADHESIVES & SEAMS

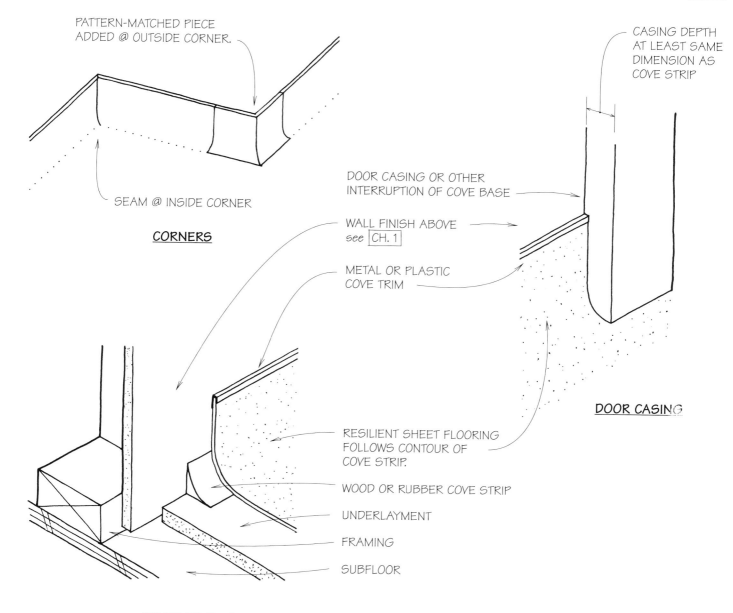

PATTERN-MATCHED PIECE
ADDED @ OUTSIDE CORNER.

SEAM @ INSIDE CORNER

CORNERS

CASING DEPTH
AT LEAST SAME
DIMENSION AS
COVE STRIP

DOOR CASING OR OTHER
INTERRUPTION OF COVE BASE

WALL FINISH ABOVE
see | CH. 1 |

METAL OR PLASTIC
COVE TRIM

DOOR CASING

RESILIENT SHEET FLOORING
FOLLOWS CONTOUR OF
COVE STRIP.

WOOD OR RUBBER COVE STRIP

UNDERLAYMENT

FRAMING

SUBFLOOR

COVED EDGE @ WALL

Resilient sheet flooring is usually installed using the flat-lay method (see 70B). Because of the flexibility of the material, however, many resilient floorings may also be coved at the edges to eliminate the joint between floor and wall. Coved edges are most easily installed with cushioned vinyl because it is more supple than the other sheet vinyls.

To make a coved edge, a wooden or vinyl cove strip is installed at the intersection of floor and wall or other vertical surface, and the resilient flooring is bent to follow the contour of the cove strip and make the transition from horizontal to vertical.

Most cove strips are approximately 1 in. deep, so door casings should be at least the same depth to cover the end of the cove as it meets the casing. Coves at interior corners require a seam at the intersection, but coves on exterior corners require the insertion of an extra piece of flooring to make the joint.

When it is exposed, the top edge of coved flooring is generally trimmed with a vinyl or metal cove cap (see 163C). The cove cap may be eliminated when the flooring terminates at a cabinet toe space or other similar concealed location.

INSTALLATION OF RESILIENT SHEET FLOORING
COVED METHOD

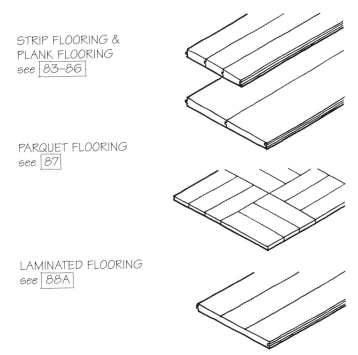

STRIP FLOORING &
PLANK FLOORING
see 83–86

PARQUET FLOORING
see 87

LAMINATED FLOORING
see 88A

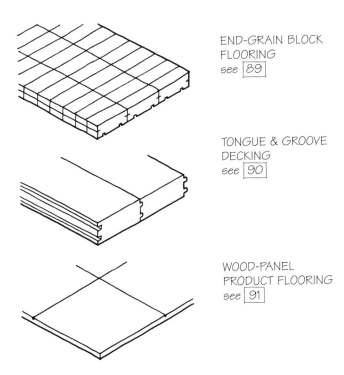

END-GRAIN BLOCK
FLOORING
see 89

TONGUE & GROOVE
DECKING
see 90

WOOD-PANEL
PRODUCT FLOORING
see 91

Wood flooring has been appreciated for centuries for its durability and natural beauty. It is fairly resilient and it is reasonably warm to the touch because of its low thermal conductivity. Wood flooring is relatively easy to maintain and, unlike most flooring, can be refinished to bring back its original luster.

Types of Flooring

Wood flooring can be grouped into two major categories. One is composed of long boards with some structural (spanning) capacity. This category includes strip flooring and plank (or board) flooring and tongue-and-groove decking. When oriented perpendicular to floor joists, flooring in this category will contribute structural stiffness.

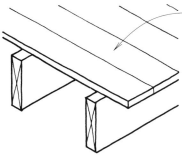

WOOD FLOORING WITH
STRUCTURAL STIFFNESS
CAN SPAN BETWEEN
JOISTS OR SLEEPERS.

The second category includes flooring made of small pieces of wood that have no structural value and are normally glued to the subfloor. Examples are parquet flooring, laminated flooring, end-grain blocks and flooring made of wood-panel products.

Resilience

Although wood flooring itself has some resilience, the floor structure to which it is applied is the real determinant of the system's resilience. Wood flooring of any type applied to a wood subfloor over wood joists is relatively resilient, while wood flooring applied directly to a concrete slab is not.

To provide a resilient floor over a concrete slab, sleepers are attached to the slab. Structural wood flooring can be attached directly to the sleepers, while nonstructural wood flooring is attached to a subfloor spanning across the sleepers. The slight deflection of the subfloor and flooring between the sleepers will provide the resilience.

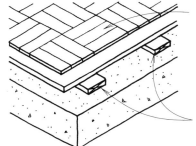

SMALL PIECES OF WOOD
FLOORING WITH NO
STRUCTURAL CAPACITY
REQUIRE SUBFLOOR TO
SPAN BETWEEN JOISTS
OR SLEEPERS.

SLEEPERS FASTENED
TO SLAB

A floating floor with a foam pad will also increase resilience (see 88B). Extra resilience for specialized uses such as sport or dance floors may be achieved with sleepers that have a rubber cushion or metal spring on the bottom.

A WOOD FLOORING

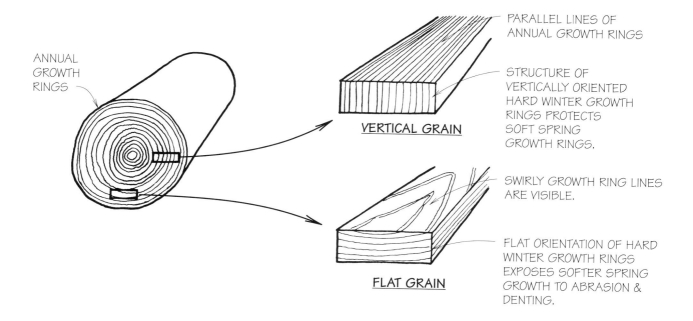

ANNUAL GROWTH RINGS

VERTICAL GRAIN

PARALLEL LINES OF ANNUAL GROWTH RINGS

STRUCTURE OF VERTICALLY ORIENTED HARD WINTER GROWTH RINGS PROTECTS SOFT SPRING GROWTH RINGS.

FLAT GRAIN

SWIRLY GROWTH RING LINES ARE VISIBLE.

FLAT ORIENTATION OF HARD WINTER GROWTH RINGS EXPOSES SOFTER SPRING GROWTH TO ABRASION & DENTING.

Grade

The quality of wood used for a finish floor is extremely important to its overall character and performance. Each flooring type and each species within flooring types has its own grading rules. Most flooring is graded both for appearance and for orientation of the grain. The following table shows species and grades available for strip and plank flooring.

SPECIES	Top grade	Next best	Third best
Oak	clear	select	common
Prefinished oak	prime	standard	tavern
Maple	first	second	third
Most other hardwoods	first	second	third
Fir	C + btr	D + btr	E clear
Pine	select	prime	cabin

Appearance grading classifies flooring according to the absence of defects such as knots, grain irregularities and discoloration. The orientation of grain affects the wood's appearance and strength. The highest quality flooring has a vertical grain, in which the annual growth rings of the tree are oriented perpendicular to the finish surface. In contrast, flat grain, also called plainsawn, has the annual growth rings oriented parallel to the finish surface.

Grain Orientation

Grain orientation is also important because of dimensional changes in wood produced by alterations in moisture content. Vertical-grain strips or planks will expand or contract about half as much as flat-grain flooring of the same species. This difference can be significant in climates with extreme fluctuations in humidity. Only a 25% change in relative humidity, for example, will produce a 5% difference in wood's moisture content. Therefore, a single oak strip-flooring board will expand $1/32$ in. if it is flat grain, but only half that ($1/64$ in.) if it is vertical grain. This dimension, when added to all the strips of flooring across a 10-ft. wide room, will equal $1\frac{3}{8}$ in. for a flat-grain floor but only about $7/8$ in. for a vertical-grain floor.

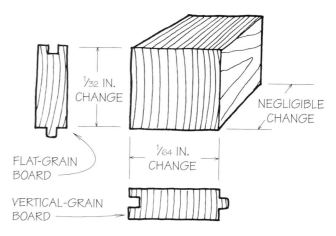

$1/32$ IN. CHANGE

NEGLIGIBLE CHANGE

$1/64$ IN. CHANGE

FLAT-GRAIN BOARD

VERTICAL-GRAIN BOARD

DIMENSIONAL CHANGE IN 2¼-IN. OAK CUBE WHEN SUBJECT TO A 5% CHANGE IN MOISTURE CONTENT

 A GRADE & GRAIN ORIENTATION

Most wood flooring is made of hardwood (predominately oak, sometimes maple and other species) because of its superior hardness and resistance to denting. Softwoods are not nearly as dense as hardwoods, so their resistance to denting from normal wear such as the use of chairs and the impact of high-heel shoes is much lower. In some locations, such as light-duty residential floors, however, softwood flooring is still appropriate and may be chosen for its aesthetic appeal. Historic restorations also often require softwoods for authenticity.

The following chart compares the hardness of the most common hardwoods and softwoods used for flooring.

Species	Hardness (psi*)
Hard maple	1,470
White oak	1,070
Red oak	1,010
Douglas fir	770
Southern yellow pine	610
Douglas fir (end grain)	5,850

*Fiber stress at proportional limit

The hardness of all wood species is related to the orientation of the grain. The vertical orientation of grain in flooring supports loads and wears better than flat-grain orientation (see 79). Moreover, most woods are five to six times as strong in the direction parallel to the grain as they are perpendicular to the grain. Some manufacturers produce softwood end-grain blocks (see 89) that have compressive strengths several times greater than hardwood floors.

The hardness of wood can be enhanced by as much as 50% by impregnating it with acrylic resin. The resin is forced under pressure to saturate thin veneers of porous hardwoods such as oak or ash that are used to make laminated flooring products (see 88A). The resin not only increases hardness but also provides a finish that cannot wear away as do the surface films of traditionally applied finishes.

One characteristic of wood flooring that differentiates it from all other flooring is its tendency to expand and contract with a change in moisture content. It is crucial to allow wood flooring to adjust to the ambient humidity within a finished building before installation so that its moisture content is stabilized. In addition, the structure and subfloor should be detailed to prevent moisture from entering the assembly. Slabs on grade and wood subfloors over crawl spaces are particularly vulnerable and should be detailed with an appropriate moisture barrier, and adequate subsurface drainage should be provided.

Because wood expands and contracts with seasonal changes in humidity, wood flooring must be detailed with this expansion and contraction in mind. Regional climatic differences produce a wide range of responses. For example, strip and plank flooring contractors in some regions recommend leaving a gap between each board, while contractors in other regions require no gap at all.

The specific type of flooring also affects detailing for expansion and contraction caused by change in moisture content. Because the greatest dimensional change in wood occurs across the board, a floor made of parallel boards will expand and contract across a room more than one made of small pieces arranged perpendicular to one another.

In addition to spacing between boards, a gap at the edge of wood flooring is recommended to allow for severe expansion caused by catastrophic flooding, such as a plumbing failure. Because expansion occurs primarily across a board, a large gap is required at the sides parallel to boards, while only a small gap is required at board ends. Wood flooring not made of parallel boards generally has an equal gap at all edges. This safety gap is usually covered with base molding. Wood flooring laid without this gap has been known to force the wall framing off of the structure.

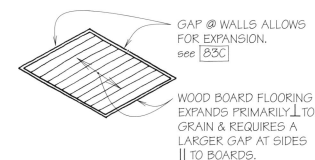

GAP @ WALLS ALLOWS FOR EXPANSION.
see | 83C |

WOOD BOARD FLOORING EXPANDS PRIMARILY ⊥ TO GRAIN & REQUIRES A LARGER GAP AT SIDES || TO BOARDS.

 A   HARDWOOD & SOFTWOOD

 **B**   MOISTURE CONTENT

The two basic wood flooring profiles are tongue-and-groove and square edged. The tongue-and-groove profile found on strip and plank flooring, tongue-and-groove decking and some parquet flooring is designed to align the pieces of flooring and to provide a location for blind nailing (see 81B). The square-edged profile is generally associated with flooring such as end-grain blocks, panel products, and some parquet and plank flooring that is fastened to the subfloor with adhesive.

TONGUE & GROOVE   SQUARE-EDGED

Tongue-and-groove profiles are carefully milled so that when two boards are pushed together, a gap is left at the tongue and the bottom edge of the boards, resulting in a tight fit at the top surface. Some flooring types, particularly hardwood strip and plank flooring, have a tongue-and-groove profile at the ends of boards as well as the sides. This detail, called end matching, helps to keep finished surfaces aligned where boards meet at their ends.

GAPS @ TONGUE & BOTTOM EDGE ALLOW TIGHT JOINT @ FACE.

Since square-edged profiles are not forced into alignment as are tongue-and-groove profiles, they usually have a slight chamfer or bevel at the exposed edge of the flooring board. The bevel allows adjacent boards to be slightly misaligned without causing a ridge or rough spot in the floor.

SQUARE-EDGED BOARD W/ SLIGHT MISALIGNMENT

SLIGHT CHAMFER CONCEALS MISALIGNMENT.

Prefinished flooring (see 83D) also often has a chamfer, since it is not sanded to eliminate minor height variations between boards.

 WOOD FLOORING PROFILES

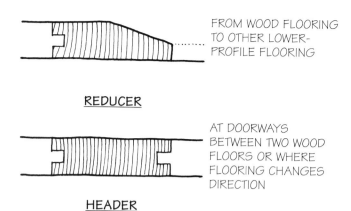

FROM WOOD FLOORING TO OTHER LOWER-PROFILE FLOORING

REDUCER

AT DOORWAYS BETWEEN TWO WOOD FLOORS OR WHERE FLOORING CHANGES DIRECTION

HEADER

Most flooring manufacturers make a number of trim and transitional moldings designed to integrate with their standard flooring. These moldings may be prefinished or unfinished and may attach to the subfloor with mechanical fasteners or adhesives. Transitional pieces such as reducers and stair nosings, which must absorb more severe loading conditions than the body of the floor, often require both mechanical fasteners and adhesives.

 TRANSITIONS

Wood flooring is either site finished or prefinished.

Site Finished
Site-finished floors are sanded and filled after the floor is in place, thus eliminating the minor height variations between boards. The floor is then flooded with a sealer that penetrates the wood and creates a continuous film across the entire floor. The most common site finish is a polyurethane varnish, which gives a very durable surface in three or four coats. Less toxic water-based polyurethane finishes are gaining popularity as they become more durable. Site finishing allows more control over the final appearance than prefinished flooring because staining may be tested and subtly adjusted at the site, and custom work such as feature strips may be integrated into the flooring.

Prefinished Flooring
Prefinished flooring is coated in a clean, controlled environment at the factory. Factory finishes may be similar to those normally applied at the site or may be pressurized or baked-on finishes that cannot be applied on site. Prefinished flooring eliminates the lengthy site-finishing process, eliminates on-site fumes and creates much less mess.

 FINISHES

Wood flooring can be fastened to the subfloor with either mechanical fasteners or adhesives. The type of flooring installed will influence the kind of fastener used . The spanning types of flooring (strip, plank and decking), most of which have tongue-and-groove profiles, are usually attached to the subfloor with mechanical fasteners (see 82). The nonspanning types (parquet, end-grain blocks and panel products), most of which are square-edged, are generally better applied with adhesives.

TONGUE & GROOVE APPLIED W/ NAILS

SQUARE-EDGED BOARD APPLIED W/ ADHESIVE

The type of subfloor must also be considered when selecting a fastening system. Wood subfloors are the most versatile because they readily accept mechanical fasteners or adhesive, while concrete subfloors are not suited to mechanical fasteners. Flooring types designed for mechanical fastening may be matched with concrete subfloors, however, by adding sleepers or plywood to provide a nailing surface (see 86D & 91).

Blind Nailing

Solid wood flooring with a tongue-and-groove profile is designed to be fastened to the subfloor using a method called blind nailing. Strip, plank and the thicker versions of parquet flooring are all usually blind nailed. Special flooring nails placed at an angle through the tongue are concealed by the placement of subsequent floorboards. The nailed tongue secures the groove side of the adjacent board when the two are pushed together. A specialized nailing machine forces the boards together as the nail is driven with one blow of a mallet.

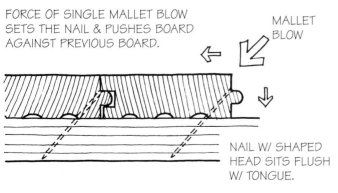

FORCE OF SINGLE MALLET BLOW SETS THE NAIL & PUSHES BOARD AGAINST PREVIOUS BOARD.

MALLET BLOW

NAIL W/ SHAPED HEAD SITS FLUSH W/ TONGUE.

Blind Nailing w/ Pneumatic Staplers—Recently, air-driven equipment has been developed to shoot a staple into the same position as a nail. This pneumatic equipment is faster and less fatiguing for the installer, but since pneumatic staplers do not force the boards together they work best with high-grade flooring material that fits snugly before fastening.

Splines

A spline is a long, slender piece of wood that is set into a groove to effectively make a tongue. A biscuit is a slender, oblong piece of wood that is also set into a groove. The use of splines or biscuit joints between pieces allows square-edged flooring to be blind nailed, concealing the fasteners and helping to maintain the alignment of the flooring. The spline also allows tongue-and-groove flooring to be integrated with square-edged feature strips or transitional pieces.

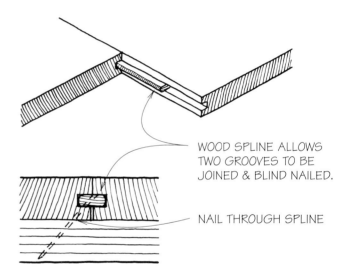

WOOD SPLINE ALLOWS TWO GROOVES TO BE JOINED & BLIND NAILED.

NAIL THROUGH SPLINE

Face Nailing

Face nailing of flooring is generally only found in tongue-and-groove decking, wide-plank flooring that emulates a historic floor, or panel-product flooring. For decking, nails should be hot-dip galvanized to provide the withdrawal resistance necessary for such large flooring members. For historic applications, modern nails with antique heads are available.

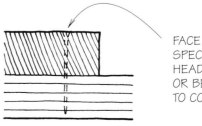

FACE NAILS CAN HAVE SPECIALLY SHAPED HEADS AND BE EXPOSED OR BE SET AND FILLED TO CONCEAL.

 FASTENING WOOD FLOORING
BLIND NAILING & FACE NAILING

Screws

Screws provide a more positive connection of flooring to subfloor than blind nailing but must be installed through the face of the flooring. The use of screws is therefore generally reserved for conditions such as wide-plank floors where their holding power is necessary. Screws are typically countersunk below the surface of the floor and the hole is filled with a hardwood plug. Alternatively, the smaller head trim-head screw can be used (see 158A).

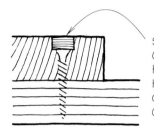

SCREWS CAN BE COUNTERSUNK AND THE HOLE FILLED WITH A HARDWOOD PLUG (W/ GRAIN ⊥ TO FLOORING) OR LEFT EXPOSED.

Adhesives

The use of adhesives to attach wood flooring to the subfloor is usually limited to flooring made of small pieces that fit together precisely without being forced, such as parquet flooring, end-grain blocks, some panel-product flooring and laminated flooring. The traditional cold-tar mastic is inexpensive and works well as an adhesive in most conditions but is toxic and tends to bleed up between pieces of flooring. Other solvent-based adhesives give superior performance and can resist moisture infiltration but are also toxic. Water-based adhesives are much less toxic and will work in most situations but will degrade in moist conditions. It is important to follow the recommendations of the flooring manufacturer when selecting an adhesive because flooring warranties often depend on matching flooring and adhesive.

Alternative Fastening Methods

One of the more common alternative fastening systems is the floating floor (see 88B), which attaches pieces of wood flooring to each other rather than to the building. Floating floors may be used when it is prohibitive to fasten the flooring to the subfloor.

A less common system is self-stick adhesive. Used primarily on parquet tiles (see 87), self-stick adhesive allows the do-it-yourselfer to install wood flooring. Adhesive is factory applied to the back of the flooring and protected during shipping and handling by a plastic sheet. When the flooring is ready to be installed, the plastic sheet is removed and the flooring is adhered to the subfloor.

A FASTENING WOOD FLOORING
SCREWS & ADHESIVES

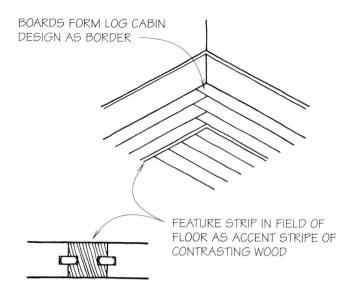

BOARDS FORM LOG CABIN DESIGN AS BORDER

FEATURE STRIP IN FIELD OF FLOOR AS ACCENT STRIPE OF CONTRASTING WOOD

Square-edged moldings such as feature strips may be readily integrated into a site-finished floor with the use of splines or biscuit joints to maintain alignment with the main body of the floor.

B BORDERS & FEATURE STRIPS

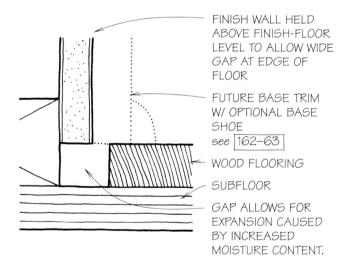

FINISH WALL HELD ABOVE FINISH-FLOOR LEVEL TO ALLOW WIDE GAP AT EDGE OF FLOOR

FUTURE BASE TRIM W/ OPTIONAL BASE SHOE see 162–63

WOOD FLOORING

SUBFLOOR

GAP ALLOWS FOR EXPANSION CAUSED BY INCREASED MOISTURE CONTENT.

The edges of wood flooring must have a gap at the walls (or columns) to allow for the expansion of the flooring caused by moisture changes (see 80B). The required width of this gap varies according to the type of flooring used, but flooring manufacturers generally recommend ½ in. to ¾ in. The gap can be concealed with base trim.

C EDGES @ WALL

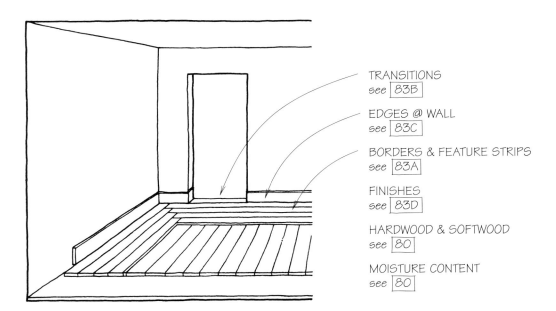

GRADE & GRAIN ORIENTATION
see | 79 |

HARDWOOD FLOORING
see | 85A |

SOFTWOOD FLOORING
see | 85B |

PLYWOOD ON JOISTS
(⊥ TO JOISTS)
see | 86A |

PLYWOOD ON JOISTS
(‖ TO JOISTS)
see | 86B |

PLYWOOD ON SLAB
see | 86C |

SLEEPERS ON SLAB
see | 86D |

TRANSITIONS
see | 83B |

EDGES @ WALL
see | 83C |

BORDERS & FEATURE STRIPS
see | 83A |

FINISHES
see | 83D |

HARDWOOD & SOFTWOOD
see | 80 |

MOISTURE CONTENT
see | 80 |

The earliest wood flooring in America was wide, pine plank flooring. Similar to modern tongue-and-groove decking (see 90), the planks provided both the structural subfloor and the finish flooring. As high-quality lumber became scarce and carpentry more refined, wide structural plank flooring gave way to smaller pieces of finish flooring applied over cruder wood subfloors.

Until the advent of the wall-to-wall carpet after World War II, oak strip flooring was installed in most houses, regardless of their size, and in most public buildings. Peak production of oak flooring occurred in 1956, but carpet's domination of the market almost doomed the hardwood flooring industry. Today, wood flooring is regaining some of its former popularity but is nonetheless used sparingly, since the initial cost of wood is two to three times that of inexpensive carpet. By far the most common wood flooring in use today is the same hardwood strip flooring that has been popular since the late 1800s. This flooring comes in the form of individual random-length boards (strips) that are 2¼ in. wide.

Less common but also available is hardwood plank flooring, which is essentially the same as strip flooring but milled into wider boards. Softwood strip and plank flooring are also available, and both hardwood and softwood are available in laminated versions (see 88A). Most strip and plank flooring is available unfinished or prefinished.

Subfloor
Both strip and plank flooring are almost always blind nailed to a wood subfloor fastened to a wooden structural system (see 80B). Plywood is the most common subfloor because it provides excellent holding power for nails. Although a plywood subfloor alone is capable of supporting floor loads, the spanning ability of the finish flooring also contributes to the overall strength of the floor (see 78). It is best to orient the strip or plank flooring perpendicular to the joists (see 86A). If the flooring is oriented parallel to the joists, blocking should be provided at 24 in. o.c (see 86B), or two layers of ¾-in. (min.) plywood subfloor should be installed in alternating directions.

When applied to a plywood or other wood subfloor, strip flooring is often placed on 15-lb. felt, kraft or resin paper to minimize moisture migration, eliminate squeaks and provide a slick surface for easier installation and a tight fit.

A concrete subfloor may be adapted for strip and plank flooring. Sleepers fastened to the slab (see 86D) at 12-in. o.c. max. provide a nailing surface and also allow the flooring to deflect locally, giving the finish floor some resilience. Plank flooring installed over a concrete slab also requires a layer of plywood on sleepers to provide adequate fastening for screws and the extra nailing required to keep the planks flat (see 86D). Plywood may be installed directly on a concrete slab (see 86C) but won't provide resilience.

 STRIP FLOORING & PLANK FLOORING

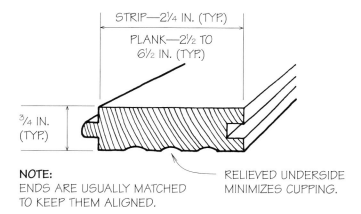

STRIP—2¼ IN. (TYP.)

PLANK—2½ TO 6½ IN. (TYP.)

¾ IN. (TYP.)

NOTE:
ENDS ARE USUALLY MATCHED
TO KEEP THEM ALIGNED.

RELIEVED UNDERSIDE
MINIMIZES CUPPING.

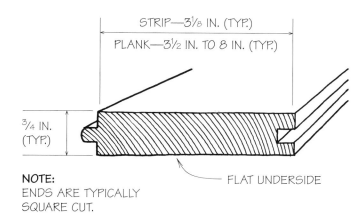

STRIP—3⅛ IN. (TYP.)

PLANK—3½ IN. TO 8 IN. (TYP.)

¾ IN. (TYP.)

NOTE:
ENDS ARE TYPICALLY
SQUARE CUT.

FLAT UNDERSIDE

Hardwood strip flooring—Hardwood strip flooring is most commonly made of red oak, less frequently of white oak or maple, and sometimes of other hardwoods such as beech, birch, cherry, chinquapin, hickory or pecan. The most common strip flooring is 2¼ in. wide and ¾ in. thick, but width can range from ¾ in. to 2¾ in. and thickness from ⁵⁄₁₆ in. to 1 in.

Strip flooring boards are random lengths and usually relieved on the underside to reduce cupping and provide the best contact with the subfloor. Boards are usually end-matched, but occasionally flooring from small mills will be manufactured with square-cut ends, which will produce only some minor unevenness at joints if the wood grain is irregular.

Hardwood plank flooring—Hardwood plank flooring is essentially the same as hardwood strip except that the individual boards are wider. It is available in most of the same species as strip flooring and has a similar profile. Standard nominal widths are 3, 4, 5, 6, and 7 in., but wider planks may be specially ordered.

Because of their extra width, planks are more likely to cup than strips. For this reason, planks 4 in. and wider usually require additional fasteners to keep them flat. These wide planks should have a minimum of two screws located at each end to counteract flexing, bowing and cupping, and along the length of the board at a minimum of 5 ft. o.c. In place of screws, there are specialty nails that imitate the antique nails used to attach traditional plank flooring directly to a wood structure.

Part of the charm of the early plank flooring is the irregular width of the custom-made planks. This is often simulated in modern plank flooring with a random sequence of different width planks (called random width) or with a repeating pattern of different width planks (called variable width).

Softwood strip flooring—Softwood strip flooring is available in fir, pine, hemlock or other custom-milled softwoods. Fir is the finest because of its clear, straight grain and scarcity of knots.

Softwood strip flooring differs from hardwood strip flooring in several minor characteristics. Softwood strips are usually wider—3⅛ in. as opposed to 2¼ in. for hardwood. They are seldom relieved on the underside because softwood does not have the same strength or tendency to cup as hardwood. Softwood strip flooring is rarely end-matched, because the wood tends to chip and tear when milled perpendicular to the grain.

Softwood plank flooring—Used occasionally for historic renovation or to achieve a traditional plank flooring appearance, softwood plank flooring is more common on the East Coast than the West Coast. Tongue-and-groove planks are generally available in widths up to 8 in. Splines or tongue-and-groove edges are recommended to keep edges aligned in boards up to 10 in. wide. Planks over 10 in. wide will almost always cup, and should have square-cut edges to allow each board to twist and cup independent of the adjacent boards.

Because the wider boards have a greater tendency to twist and cup in place, the edges of each board are often beveled or eased so that any minor difference in level between boards will not be apparent. Like hardwood planks, softwood planks require additional fasteners to keep them flat: a minimum of two screws located at each end to counteract flexing, bowing and cupping, and at a minimum of 5 ft. o.c. along the length of the board. Specialty nails that imitate antique nails used traditionally are fairly common, especially in wide, pine plank flooring. Adhesives are sometimes used in conjunction with mechanical fasteners to help hold wide planks flat to the floor.

 HARDWOOD FLOORING

 SOFTWOOD FLOORING

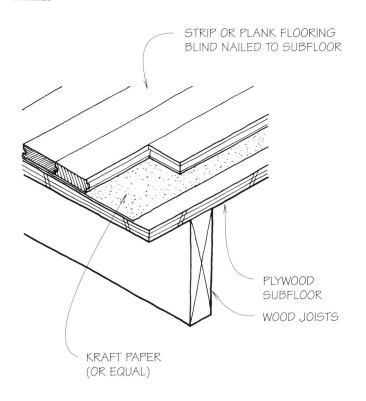

STRIP OR PLANK FLOORING
BLIND NAILED TO SUBFLOOR

PLYWOOD
SUBFLOOR

WOOD JOISTS

KRAFT PAPER
(OR EQUAL)

(A) **PLYWOOD SUBFLOOR ON JOISTS**
FLOORING ⊥ TO JOISTS

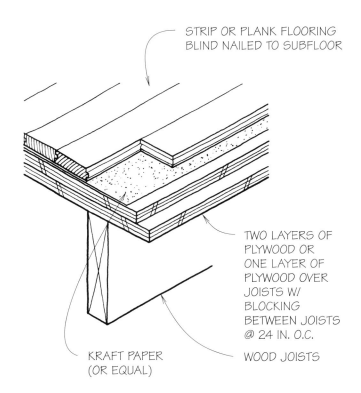

STRIP OR PLANK FLOORING
BLIND NAILED TO SUBFLOOR

TWO LAYERS OF
PLYWOOD OR
ONE LAYER OF
PLYWOOD OVER
JOISTS W/
BLOCKING
BETWEEN JOISTS
@ 24 IN. O.C.

WOOD JOISTS

KRAFT PAPER
(OR EQUAL)

(B) **PLYWOOD SUBFLOOR ON JOISTS**
FLOORING || TO JOISTS

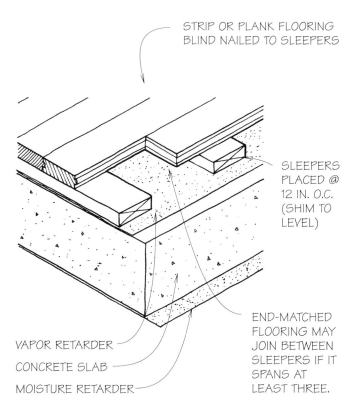

STRIP OR PLANK FLOORING
BLIND NAILED TO SLEEPERS

SLEEPERS
PLACED @
12 IN. O.C.
(SHIM TO
LEVEL)

END-MATCHED
FLOORING MAY
JOIN BETWEEN
SLEEPERS IF IT
SPANS AT
LEAST THREE.

VAPOR RETARDER

CONCRETE SLAB

MOISTURE RETARDER

(C) **SLEEPERS ON SLAB**

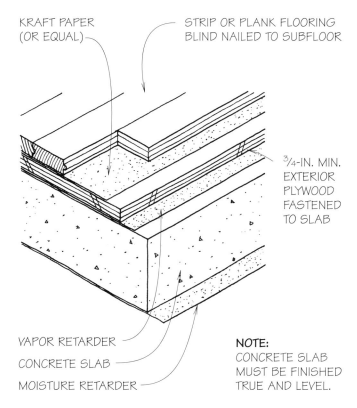

KRAFT PAPER
(OR EQUAL)

STRIP OR PLANK FLOORING
BLIND NAILED TO SUBFLOOR

$^3/_4$-IN. MIN.
EXTERIOR
PLYWOOD
FASTENED
TO SLAB

VAPOR RETARDER

CONCRETE SLAB

MOISTURE RETARDER

NOTE:
CONCRETE SLAB
MUST BE FINISHED
TRUE AND LEVEL.

(D) **PLYWOOD SUBFLOOR ON SLAB**

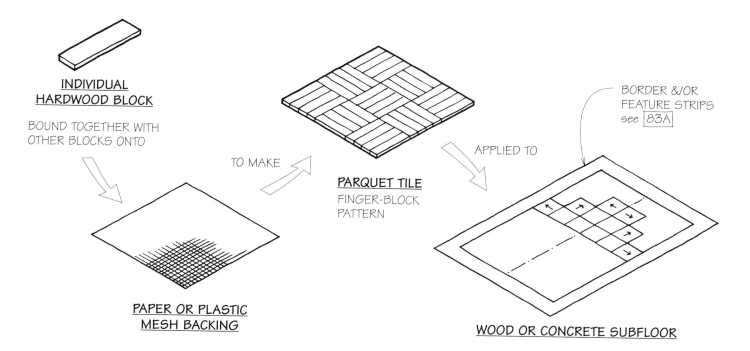

INDIVIDUAL
HARDWOOD BLOCK

BOUND TOGETHER WITH
OTHER BLOCKS ONTO

TO MAKE

PARQUET TILE
FINGER-BLOCK
PATTERN

APPLIED TO

BORDER &/OR
FEATURE STRIPS
see 83A

PAPER OR PLASTIC
MESH BACKING

WOOD OR CONCRETE SUBFLOOR

Early parquet floors were made of many small pieces of exotic hardwoods mixed in intricate geometrical designs. Today's parquet floors are usually much more humble than their ancestors and can be the least expensive of hardwood floors. The pieces that make a modern parquet floor are usually all the same species of hardwood.

Patterns are created by arranging large tiles composed of a number of prearranged pieces (one of the most popular patterns is shown above). The tiles (also called panels) are bound together with a paper or plastic mesh backing, or metal or plastic splines.

Most pattern tiles range in size from 9 in. square to 19 in. square, and occasionally up to 2 ft. square. Tiles are usually ⁵⁄₁₆ in. thick and occasionally ¾ in. thick, but intermediate sizes also exist. Edges of thinner parquet tiles are usually square cut, while thicker tiles often have tongue-and-groove edges on all sides.

Because the smaller pieces arranged in different directions lead to less overall cross-grain expansion, parquet is often a good choice for use where the moisture content of the flooring can be expected to change significantly over time.

Subfloor
Parquet pieces run in more than one direction and are so short that they do not contribute to the stiffness of the floor system. Orientation of the parquet with

regard to the floor structure is therefore not important, and the subfloor must provide all the required structural support. Either a wood or a concrete subfloor can satisfy this requirement, and parquet flooring may be attached directly to either. Concrete slabs, however, often require an underlayment to help compensate for any unevenness.

Layout and Installation
Parquet tiles are usually attached to the subfloor with a bed of adhesive. The webbed backing material allows the individual pieces of wood in a tile to contact the adhesive as the tile is being laid. Where moisture from the subfloor may be a problem, such as on a concrete slab or over a crawl space, an adhesive that can incorporate or act as a vapor retarder should be considered.

Unlike strip or plank flooring, parquet is laid in two directions at once. Laying parquet should start from the middle of a room and work toward the walls so that the geometric design will be centered in the room. Where a border or feature strip is wanted, tile dimensions will affect its width.

Gaps between unfinished parquet tiles, sometimes unavoidable because of an uneven subfloor, may be filled with wood dough made of sawdust from the first floor sanding, as are the gaps in unfinished strip or plank flooring. Prefinished tiles should be carefully laid over a smooth subfloor in order to avoid gaps.

 A PARQUET FLOORING

Laminated flooring is made of three to five thin laminations of wood that are glued together similar to plywood to make flooring that imitates solid strip, plank or parquet flooring. Because the veneers of wood are layered at right angles to one another, laminated wood flooring is more dimensionally stable than solid wood flooring, making it more appropriate for use in areas of great humidity fluctuation and for wide-plank floors, since it has much less tendency to cup and twist. Installation is much easier than for solid wood flooring because the flooring is more consistent and true.

One disadvantage of laminated flooring compared to solid flooring (along with its higher cost) is the thinness of the wear surface, which reduces the amount of sanding and refinishing the flooring can withstand. Although some manufacturers produce a wear surface as thick as ⅙ in., in no case is it as thick as that of solid flooring. To help offset this disadvantage, some manufacturers impregnate the wear layer veneer prior to lamination with acrylic resin, making it more durable and longer lasting.

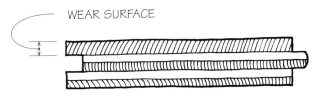

WEAR SURFACE

FIVE-LAMINATION STRIP

Sizes
Thicknesses generally range from ⅜ in. to 9⁄16 in. Strip and plank flooring is available in widths from 2¼ in. to 7 in. Parquet tiles (see 87) are usually about 12 in. square.

Profiles
All edges of strip, plank and parquet laminated flooring are typically matched with a tongue-and-groove joint. The top edges of prefinished laminated flooring are often chamfered, helping to conceal slight misalignments between boards. Recently, however, the trend in manufacturing is to make a square top edge to imitate the look of site-finished flooring.

Fastening
Most laminated flooring is glued to the subfloor (see 82) or installed as a floating floor (see 88B), although some types may be blind nailed (see 81B). Unlike solid wood, laminated flooring may be glued directly to a concrete slab and is suitable for below-grade installations.

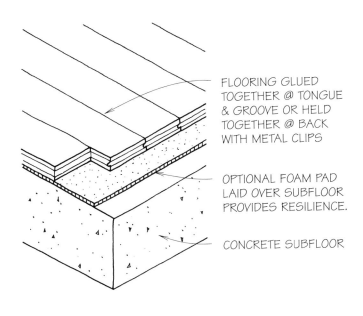

FLOORING GLUED TOGETHER @ TONGUE & GROOVE OR HELD TOGETHER @ BACK WITH METAL CLIPS

OPTIONAL FOAM PAD LAID OVER SUBFLOOR PROVIDES RESILIENCE.

CONCRETE SUBFLOOR

NOTE:
INSTALLATION IS IDENTICAL OVER WOOD SUBFLOOR OR EXISTING FLOORING.

Originally developed for easy installation over a concrete subfloor, the floating floor is composed of strip or parquet flooring that is not fastened to the subfloor but that "floats" above it. Most floating floors are made with laminated flooring, although some solid wood systems are available. Each piece of flooring is connected to its neighbor with glue or metal clips so that the entire assembly expands and contracts as a unit. Gravity and base trim at the walls hold the floor in place. Expansion gaps are located at the walls. For installations over concrete slabs, a foam pad can be placed under the flooring, providing significant resilience.

Floating floors are practical for several reasons. When a resilient wood floor is desired over a concrete subfloor without room for sleepers, a floating floor over a foam pad will provide both resilience and thin profile. When local climatic conditions cause wide swings in humidity between seasons or when wood flooring is desired over a radiant slab, the floating floor will expand and contract without developing gaps between pieces. Floating floors are also quite easy to install relative to most other wood flooring and may be installed by the homeowner.

A **LAMINATED FLOORING**
STRIP, PLANK & PARQUET

B **FLOATING FLOORS**

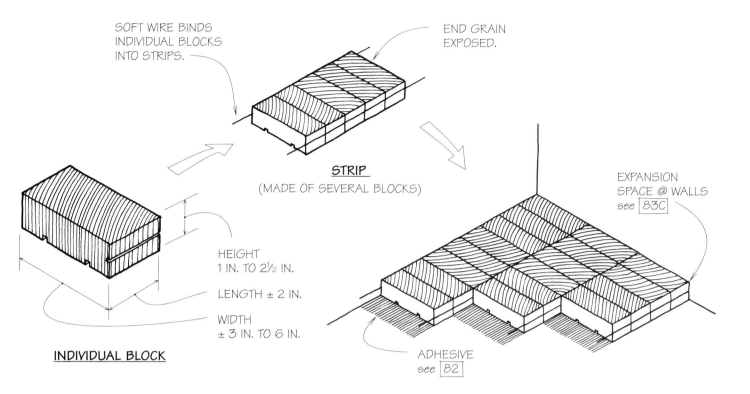

SOFT WIRE BINDS
INDIVIDUAL BLOCKS
INTO STRIPS.

END GRAIN
EXPOSED.

STRIP
(MADE OF SEVERAL BLOCKS)

EXPANSION
SPACE @ WALLS
see │83C│

HEIGHT
1 IN. TO 2½ IN.

LENGTH ± 2 IN.

WIDTH
± 3 IN. TO 6 IN.

INDIVIDUAL BLOCK

ADHESIVE
see │82│

End-grain block flooring is made of small blocks of wood with the end grain exposed. Because the grain of the wood is oriented in the direction most resistant to denting and wear, end-grain block flooring is the most durable of wood flooring materials. It is commonly specified for areas with high traffic or heavy structural loads. It also performs quite well in locations such as museums where partitions are frequently fastened and removed because the orientation of the grain allows small holes to be easily patched.

The individual blocks originate as scrap material, the byproducts of other manufacturing operations, making the environmental impact of end-grain blocks reasonable even though they are made of high-quality, virgin, old-growth wood. The initial material and installation costs of end-grain block flooring are more than for most wood flooring, but life-cycle costs compare favorably because of the exceptional durability of end-grain blocks.

End-grain block flooring is available primarily in fir and hemlock. The flooring comes in random-length, square-edged strips that range in thicknesses from 1 in. to 2½ in. and in widths from 2¾ in. to about 5 in. Soft (aluminum) wire splines forced into kerfs on the sides of each 2-in. long block hold the blocks together in the strips.

Subflooring
End-grain flooring may be installed on plywood or directly on a concrete slab. If installed over a wood joist structure, an adequate subfloor must be provided since the flooring does not contribute structurally (see 78). When end-grain flooring is installed over a concrete slab, the subfloor surface should be smooth, as for parquet flooring (see 87).

Fastening
Like most other wood flooring, end-grain block strips must be acclimatized before they are installed (see 80B). It is also important to detail the subfloor to minimize moisture migration (see 80B) and to detail the installation to allow for expansion and contraction of the flooring (see 83C). The strips are applied to the subfloor with adhesive (see 82).

Finishing
End-grain block flooring is site finished and differs from other wood floors because the exposed end grain is extremely absorbent and will require several times the amount of finish as other wood floors. The advantage of this characteristic is that pigments and protective resins are carried deep into the wood, thus creating a thick layer that does not wear off with abrasion and seldom needs to be refinished.

 END-GRAIN BLOCK FLOORING

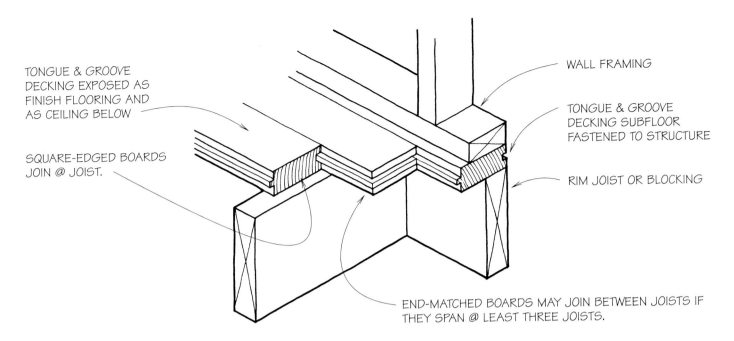

TONGUE & GROOVE
DECKING EXPOSED AS
FINISH FLOORING AND
AS CEILING BELOW

SQUARE-EDGED BOARDS
JOIN @ JOIST.

WALL FRAMING

TONGUE & GROOVE
DECKING SUBFLOOR
FASTENED TO STRUCTURE

RIM JOIST OR BLOCKING

END-MATCHED BOARDS MAY JOIN BETWEEN JOISTS IF
THEY SPAN @ LEAST THREE JOISTS.

Tongue-and-groove decking is structural softwood lumber that can be exposed as finished flooring. Decking is often used on upper floors of a building where it spans across beams or joists, and it can also be exposed as a finished ceiling below.

Commonly made of wood that is of lower quality and with a wider grain than strip or plank flooring, decking tends to expand and contract more with changes in moisture content. Decking is also difficult to lay as tightly as strip or plank flooring because it is less precisely milled and has more internal strength to resist being forced against the previously laid piece as the nails or screws are inserted. Because of these factors, gaps between individual boards are unavoidable and can allow dirt particles to enter and contribute further to an unrefined appearance. Minor cupping and twisting are also likely to occur, producing a less than perfectly smooth surface. A slight chamfer or radius at the edges of individual pieces of decking will make the slight differences in height less apparent.

Decking is ordinarily available in fir, hemlock, pine and cedar, and is milled from 2x6, 2x8, 3x6, and 4x6 nominal solid-sawn lumber. The 3x and 4x decking is

also sometimes built up with parallel grain laminations. The 2x decking has a single tongue-and-groove and is available in a 5-in. or 7-in. width, while the 3x and 4x has a double tongue-and-groove and is also available 5 in. or 7 in. wide.

Fastening
The size and strength of decking make the effectiveness of blind nailing questionable. Even if screws are placed through the tongue instead of nails, the decking will be secured to the structure only at its edges, so cupping and working of the floor are likely to occur.

An effective alternative is to face-nail or screw each piece of decking. Screws will provide a superior method of attachment. Either screws or nails may be exposed at the floor surface or countersunk and plugged (screws) or puttied (nails).

Sequence
Since tongue-and-groove decking is part of the structure, it will generally be installed during the framing of a building. Precautions must therefore be taken to protect the floor from exposure to the elements and job-site abuse.

Finishing
Because of the large gaps and uneven surface inherent in tongue-and-groove decking, the decking is typically treated with a protective finish without filling any of the gaps.

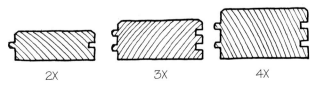

2X   3X   4X

 A   TONGUE & GROOVE DECKING

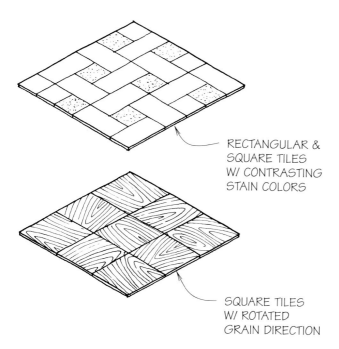

RECTANGULAR &
SQUARE TILES
W/ CONTRASTING
STAIN COLORS

SQUARE TILES
W/ ROTATED
GRAIN DIRECTION

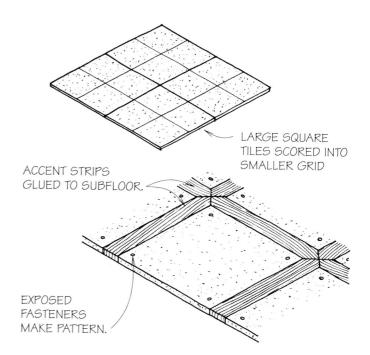

LARGE SQUARE
TILES SCORED INTO
SMALLER GRID

ACCENT STRIPS
GLUED TO SUBFLOOR.

EXPOSED
FASTENERS
MAKE PATTERN.

Wood-panel products are not commonly used for finished flooring, but when selected and detailed carefully, they can produce a durable and handsome floor at low cost. Wood-panel products such as plywood, chipboard, particleboard, fiberboard (MDF or HDF) and hardboard have the most potential for flooring. In terms of durability, less dense panel products such as plywood and chipboard should be considered only for low-traffic areas. The durability of softer panels may be enhanced, however, with the careful selection and application of a finish surface that contributes hardness, such as moisture-cured finishes or polyurethane.

Size
One problem with designing flooring from wood panel products is that the size and shape of the panels (usually 4 ft. by 8 ft.) conveys a message to the user that it is a subfloor rather than a finish floor. There are two strategies for overcoming this problem. First, the panels may be cut into smaller pieces (usually in modular dimensions of 6 in., 8 in., 12 in., 16 in. or 24 in.) that may be arranged in patterns like tiles. Grain patterns in the resulting tiles may be alternated, different colors or species of tiles may be combined, selected pieces may be stained, and other materials may be used as accents or borders, as shown above.

The second strategy for overcoming the look of a subfloor is to score the panel so that it looks like a number of smaller pieces without actually being cut up (drawing top right). Scoring in the field of the panel

should be made to resemble the joint condition between panels. This strategy does not work well for plywood, which has a strong pattern not easily disguised by scoring.

Fastening
Attaching panel products to the subfloor requires careful consideration. Adhesives may be employed exclusively for panel products cut into small tiles but may not provide adequate holding power at the edges of large tiles or full-size panels. Exposed fasteners may prove adequate when used in combination with adhesives. Exposed fasteners should be held back from the edges of panels because of their tendency to tear or split the edge. Concealed fasteners are possible at the edges of most thick panel products with the use of splines or biscuit joints (see 82).

Edges
The edges between panels or between tiles made from panels should be detailed to disguise differences in height between adjacent pieces. This can be accomplished by adding a slight chamfer or radius to the edges. Both of these details will also tend to minimize chipping or splintering of the edge.

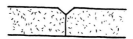

CHAMFER @ EDGES
OF PIECES

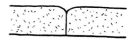

RADIUS @ EDGES
OF PIECES

 WOOD–PANEL PRODUCT FLOORING

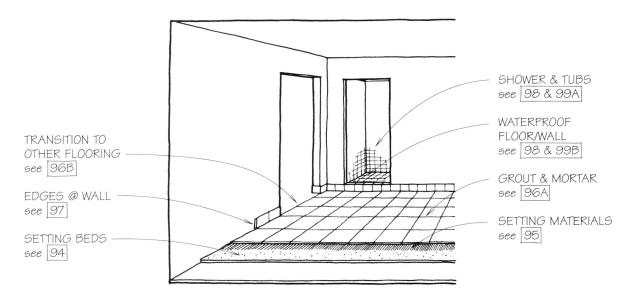

TRANSITION TO
OTHER FLOORING
see 96B

EDGES @ WALL
see 97

SETTING BEDS
see 94

SHOWER & TUBS
see 98 & 99A

WATERPROOF
FLOOR/WALL
see 98 & 99B

GROUT & MORTAR
see 96A

SETTING MATERIALS
see 95

Tile and masonry are the most ancient and among the hardest and most durable of all flooring materials. Tile and masonry are often used in areas of high traffic and heavy use, such as public buildings and residential kitchens and entry halls. Because tile and masonry are brittle and the grout or mortar filling the joints between tiles or masonry units is inflexible, it is important to provide a very stiff subfloor that will not allow the finish flooring to deflect and crack (see 56).

Although there is tremendous variation among tile and masonry floors, they have much in common. Both are composed of pieces arranged in a pattern. The small pieces are bonded to a setting bed with an adhesive (the setting material), and the space between pieces is filled with a cement-based grout or mortar.

To create a durable tile or masonry floor, the performance characteristics of each of the four components—tile or masonry units, setting bed, setting material, and grout or mortar—and must be coordinated with one another, as well as with the subfloor and the structural system.

Ceramic Tile
Tile suitable for use on floors comes in a wide variety of shapes, sizes and qualities (see 25–26 for a description of tile). The smallest mosaic tiles are about 1 in. square and the largest pavers can be up to 24 in. square. Quarry tiles, named and modeled after cut-stone tiles, are the most common and versatile of floor tiles. They are vitreous or semivitreous, unglazed clay tiles available in a variety of shapes, usually about 6 in. square. Other floor tiles are available glazed in a wide variety of colors or unglazed in earth tones. Unglazed floor tiles are usually sealed after installation to minimize staining and increase cleaning ease.

When selecting floor tile, consider the tile's hardness and resistance to impact and scratching or scuffing. The toughness of both the bisque (the body of the tile) and the glaze (if any) contribute to the overall hardness. Most tiles are graded by the American National Standards Institute (ANSI), and theoretically all tiles except those classified as "decorative thin wall tile" should be suitable for use on floors. The amount and type of traffic should also be considered when determining the suitability of a tile.

In addition, tiles specified for damp areas should be scrutinized for both water and skid resistance. Tiles that absorb water equal to 5% or less of their own weight are considered acceptable for use in damp areas. This means that all tiles classified as impervious or vitreous and some tiles classified as semivitreous can be used in such locations. Skid-resistant tiles are usually unglazed and have a ribbed or sanded texture. The grout lines between very small tiles also produce a texture that contributes to skid resistance.

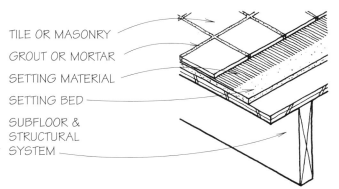

TILE OR MASONRY
GROUT OR MORTAR
SETTING MATERIAL
SETTING BED
SUBFLOOR &
STRUCTURAL
SYSTEM

(A) **TILE & MASONRY FLOORING**
CERAMIC TILE

Brick Masonry

Brick floors are usually made of standard solid bricks or 1-in. thick specially made brick pavers. Standard bricks allow a greater range of color and texture selection than pavers and may be laid dry (without mortar), but they often pose thickness problems when used adjacent to other common flooring systems. Brick pavers are not much thicker than a quarry tile, so their thickness is easier to accommodate. Both materials are durable and relatively economical.

For many practical reasons, it is most common to orient solid bricks flat on the floor with the largest face (the bed face) exposed. If the bricks have been extruded in their manufacture and wire cut, the bed face of the brick is more porous and full of surface imperfections than the other faces, which are compressed and smooth. This roughness of the face of solid bricks can be both an asset (traction) and a liability (cleaning).

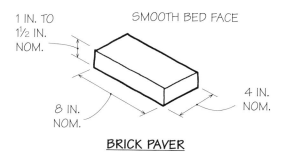

SMOOTH BED FACE

1 IN. TO 1½ IN. NOM.

8 IN. NOM.

4 IN. NOM.

BRICK PAVER

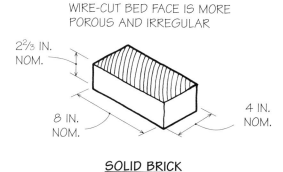

WIRE-CUT BED FACE IS MORE POROUS AND IRREGULAR

2⅔ IN. NOM.

8 IN. NOM.

4 IN. NOM.

SOLID BRICK

Brick sizes vary widely, but the most common brick is 2⅔ in. by 4 in. by 8 in. nominally. Paver bricks are sized to imitate standard bricks (4 in. by 8 in.) but are only about half as thick (1 in. to 1½ in.). Paver bricks are also pressed or molded so their exposed faces are smooth relative to wire-cut standard bricks. Because of their weight, brick floors are usually supported on a concrete slab subfloor.

Marble and Granite

The hardest of all common flooring materials are marble and granite, which are often used in areas with high traffic. Marble, which is somewhat softer than granite, is more common. Both stones are quarried and accurately machine-sliced into uniformly thick slabs that are polished smooth on one side. The standard-size tiles are 12 in. square by ⅜ in. thick. Less common sizes up to 24 in. square and ⅞ in. thick are available. The exposed edges of the tiles are finished with a slight bevel to minimize chipping. Because these edges are so precisely machined, the grout joint between tiles is normally more slender than the common grout joint and may be eliminated altogether (see 96A).

Slate

In strong contrast to marble, slate is one of the least smooth of all floor surfaces, since it is split rather than sliced from the quarried stone. The split slabs of stone are either left in their natural, irregular shapes or cut into tiles, usually 12 in. square. The thickness of slate tiles depends on whether the material is gauged (ground smooth on one side) or ungauged (cleft).

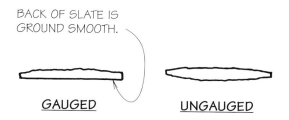

BACK OF SLATE IS GROUND SMOOTH.

GAUGED   **UNGAUGED**

Approximately ¼ in. thick, gauged slate is reasonably uniform in thickness because the back side of the tile has been ground smooth. Gauged slate is available only in a few colors because most slate cannot be ground smooth. Ungauged or cleft slate, available in a wide array of colors, can vary from ⅜ in. to ⅝ in. thick within a single tile because both sides of the tile have been split. Irregularly shaped slate that has not been cut into tiles is always left ungauged.

TILE & MASONRY FLOORING
BRICK & STONE

The setting bed is the material to which the tile or masonry adheres. It can be the subfloor itself or it may consist of other materials added to a subfloor to increase stiffness, improve bonding and/or help to resist moisture penetration.

It is critical for a tile or masonry floor to have an adequately stiff subfloor–setting bed combination to prevent the flooring from cracking. A subfloor assembly with no deflection, such as a concrete slab-on-grade, is best. When a wood floor structure is used, it can be designed to minimize deflection, or a thinbed or thick-bed setting bed can be added to increase stiffness as well as to add other properties desirable for tile or masonry flooring. The size of tile is related to the need for subfloor stiffness. Smaller tiles can better conform to floor deflection, absorbing the curve in the grout joints between tiles better than large tiles.

Subfloor Setting Beds
Often tile or masonry is attached directly to the wood or concrete subfloor without an additional setting bed. Subfloors in moist locations may be coated with a trowel-applied membrane (see 30).

Concrete subfloor—Concrete is the best choice of subfloor for tile, brick and stone. Whether bearing directly on the ground or suspended at an upper floor, a concrete subfloor provides a stable base with less deflection and (usually) less required preparation than a wood subfloor, since the slab itself provides a quality setting bed.

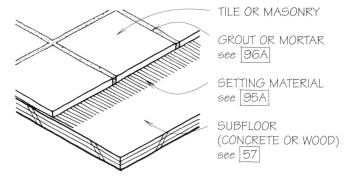

Wood subfloor—When a wood subfloor is used as a setting bed for a tile or masonry finish floor, minimizing deflection is critical. Deflection at midspan of the joists should be limited to $\frac{1}{360}$ of their length. The minimum requirement by most manufacturers is for joists at 16 in. o.c. with ¾-in. tongue-and-groove plywood, but a stiffer system can easily be achieved by decreasing joist spacing and/or increasing subflooring thickness.

Thinbed
If more stiffness, resistance to moisture and better bonding over a wood subfloor are desired, a waterproof cementitious backer board may be used. Since it is reinforced on both sides with fiberglass mesh, backer board may be applied over any subfloor, including existing flooring. Backer board is made in ½-in. and ⁷⁄₁₆-in. thicknesses, commonly 3 ft. by 5 ft.

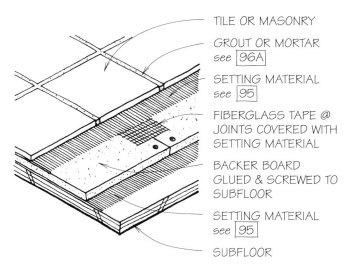

Thick-bed
The most stable and solid addition to a wood subfloor is the traditional reinforced mortar bed—a wire-mesh-reinforced mixture of cement, sand and water (and additive) that is placed on a layer of tar paper. The thickness of the mortar may vary according to the structural system and type and size of flooring to be supported. Usually from 1 in. to about 2¼ in. thick, a mortar setting bed is very strong and can be used to level very uneven wood subfloors. The mortar can be tapered to slope toward a drain such as in a shower or steam room (see 98). Because of the weight of the mortar, the wood structure must be sized accordingly.

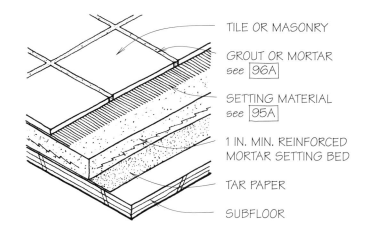

 SETTING BEDS

The most important variables in selecting an appropriate setting material are the flooring material to be set, the kind of use and amount of traffic on the floor, the type of setting bed and the degree of moisture anticipated on the finish floor. The following chart matches setting material with setting beds in common conditions.

DRY	Dry-set mortar	Latex mortar	Organic adhesive	Epoxy
Concrete	✔	✔	✔	✔
Thick-bed mortar	✔	✔	✔	
Backer board	✔	✔		
Plywood				✔
MOIST				
Trowel-applied membrane see 94	✔	✔		
WET				
Concrete	✔	✔		
Thick-bed mortar	✔	✔		

Mudset

Until the late 1940s, all tile and masonry were set directly into a still workable thick-bed of mortar without a separate setting material, or bond coat. The bonding of tile or masonry to the floor occurred because of the adhesive action of the mortar. This method, called the traditional mudset, is rarely used today except for very irregular handmade tile, brick, brick pavers or ungauged slate. The irregular thickness

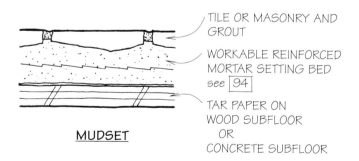

TILE OR MASONRY AND GROUP

WORKABLE REINFORCED MORTAR SETTING BED see 94

TAR PAPER ON WOOD SUBFLOOR OR CONCRETE SUBFLOOR

MUDSET

of these materials requires the depth of a mortar bed rather than a thin setting material to absorb the irregularities of the tile, brick or slate in order to provide a relatively flat finish surface.

Thinset

Today almost all tile flooring and some gauged stone flooring is bonded to the setting bed with a thin (approximately ⅛ in.) layer of setting material. Even when a thick-bed mortar setting bed is used, the tile is adhered to the cured mortar bed with a thin bond coat of setting material. The thinset method saves considerable labor when compared to the mixing and carrying of traditional mudset assemblies, and it produces better bonding.

The two general types of thinset setting materials are adhesives and mortars.

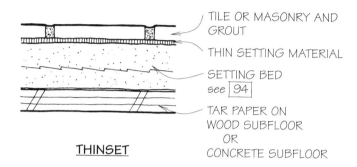

TILE OR MASONRY AND GROUT

THIN SETTING MATERIAL

SETTING BED see 94

TAR PAPER ON WOOD SUBFLOOR OR CONCRETE SUBFLOOR

THINSET

Thinset adhesives—The most commonly used adhesive is organic adhesive, also called mastic. Organic adhesives are generally a bit less expensive and easier to use than thinset mortar, but have inferior bonding and compressive strength and are not as flexible as most thinset mortars. In addition, organic adhesives generally do not perform as well in areas exposed to moisture, since they are susceptible to the growth of bacteria. Organic adhesives are water based and cure by evaporation.

Solvent-based epoxy adhesive is used where a higher bonding and compressive strength is desired, with the ease of use of an adhesive. Epoxy adhesives also tend to perform better than organic adhesives in wet installations.

Thinset mortars—Thinset mortar is a mixture of portland cement, sand, water and additives that provides superior strength and bonding. The three common types of mortar setting material are dry-set mortar, epoxy mortar, and latex/portland cement mortar . Dry-set mortar has excellent water resistance and is used for most applications. The latex additive provides increased flexibility, while the epoxy additive increases bond and compression strength and resistance to chemicals and high temperatures.

 SETTING MATERIALS

Tile and masonry floors are composed of two materials that behave somewhat differently—a predominant surface (tile or masonry) and a joint material (grout or mortar). The joint material is rarely as hard or as impermeable as the material it surrounds. The joint material is also finished below the surface of the tile or masonry, so is more likely to collect dirt and less likely to be easily cleaned. It is important to coordinate the joint material with the type of flooring material.

Unsanded grout is used primarily for absorptive tile and marble when the joint is about 1/16 in. or less.

Sanded grout is used primarily when the joint is wider than 1/16 in.; the sand helps the grout span the wider joint.

Epoxy grout is used when chemical and stain resistance are a priority, or when high temperatures are expected.

Mortar, similar to sanded grout, is used to fill the joints between bricks, brick pavers, slate and other masonry units with imprecise edges. Regular mortar joints are usually 3/8 in. wide.

Where tile floors will unavoidably deflect more than is desirable, there will be a need for the system to have some flexibility in order to eliminate cracking or other types of failure in the surface of the floor. Since the tile units are never flexible, the need for flexibility falls to the grout joint. Flexibility in grout joints can

be achieved by using additives in the grout mixture. Latex or acrylic additives can at the same time increase water and stain resistance. Acid-resistant grout is also available.

When tile or masonry flooring meets other flooring, the primary consideration should be the prevention of chipping at the edge of the tile or masonry flooring. When the tile is slightly above other flooring, a bullnose tile will usually make a durable and aesthetically pleasing transition. A chamfered edge on stone flooring will serve the same purpose.

HIGHER THAN OTHER FLOORING

When the tile or masonry flooring is at the same level as other flooring, a grout joint will normally solve the problem. When the tile or masonry flooring is below other flooring, the tile can usually end either with or without a grout joint, and the other flooring must make the transition.

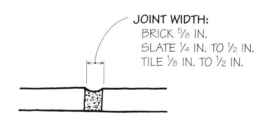

JOINT WIDTH:
BRICK 5/8 IN.
SLATE 1/4 IN. TO 1/2 IN.
TILE 1/8 IN. TO 1/2 IN.

BRICK, SLATE OR TILE JOINT

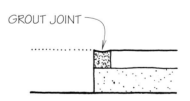

GROUT JOINT

FLUSH W/ OTHER FLOORING

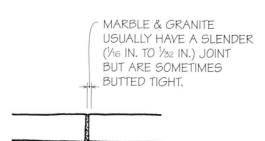

MARBLE & GRANITE USUALLY HAVE A SLENDER (1/16 IN. TO 1/32 IN.) JOINT BUT ARE SOMETIMES BUTTED TIGHT.

GRANITE OR MARBLE JOINT

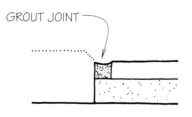

GROUT JOINT

LOWER THAN OTHER FLOORING

 GROUT & MORTAR

 TRANSITION TO OTHER FLOORING

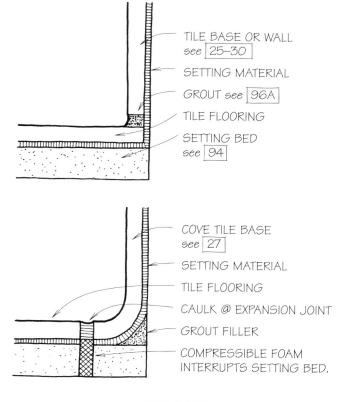
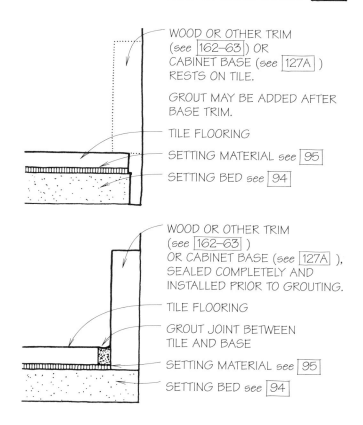

TILE BASE

WOOD OR OTHER BASE

Tile Base or Wall
One of the most common tile details at the transition from flooring to a wall or other vertical surface is to continue the tile up the wall, either as a base or as a wall covering (drawings above left). The advantage of a tile base (or tile wall) is that the tile-and-grout surface is continuous, providing a fairly watertight joint that is easy to clean. Masonry flooring at a tile or masonry wall may be detailed similarly, but cove trim pieces to make the transition gentle are not available.

Wood or Other Base
It is often desirable to surround tile or masonry floors with wood, vinyl or other linear base trim. The most common approach is to add the trim to cover the gap between floor and wall after the floor is grouted (top drawing, right). One problem with this method is that the bottom edge of the trim rests on the tile (or masonry) and spans over the grout joints, which are recessed slightly below the surface of the floor. These small gaps at the grout joints provide pockets for dust to collect or moisture to penetrate.

An alternative and superior detail is to install the base trim (or cabinet) before the floor is grouted and then grout all the voids between floor and wall (bottom

drawing, right). This requires that any wood that contacts grout must first be totally sealed and the wall protected during the grouting process.

Expansion Joints
When the area of a tile or masonry floor exceeds 16 ft. to 24 ft. square, room should be provided at its perimeter for the independent expansion and contraction of the setting bed and flooring. A common method of providing for this movement is a ¼-in. gap between setting bed and flooring and the wall. This gap is concealed with base trim(top drawing, right). Where this detail is inappropriate, a caulked joint replacing a grout joint between tiles and continuous through the setting bed may be employed (bottom drawing, left).

Expansion joints are also required in the field of a tile or masonry floor when the overall dimensions of the floor exceed 24 ft. to 36 ft. in any direction. These joints should be ¼ in. to ½ in. wide, should extend through the setting bed and should replace a grout line. In multiroom installations, expansion joints may be conveniently hidden under door thresholds. Expansion joints in tile or masonry floors applied to concrete slabs should follow control joints in the slab.

 EDGES @ WALL

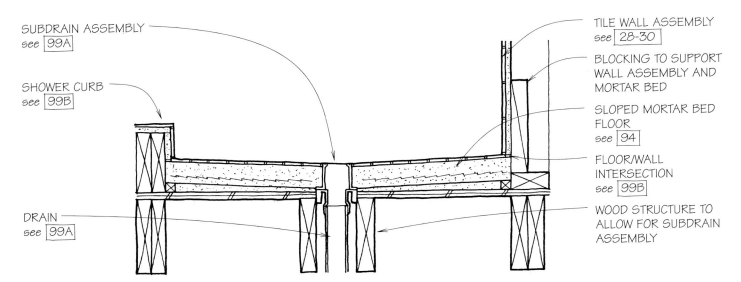

SUBDRAIN ASSEMBLY
see 99A

SHOWER CURB
see 99B

DRAIN
see 99A

TILE WALL ASSEMBLY
see 28-30

BLOCKING TO SUPPORT
WALL ASSEMBLY AND
MORTAR BED

SLOPED MORTAR BED
FLOOR
see 94

FLOOR/WALL
INTERSECTION
see 99B

WOOD STRUCTURE TO
ALLOW FOR SUBDRAIN
ASSEMBLY

Because a shower, tub or steam room is subjected to considerable moisture, the floor assembly must be carefully selected. Tile should be rated for moist use, and masonry should preferably be nonabsorptive and properly sealed. Grout may have additives to prevent moisture penetration and be resistant to mildew and bacteria growth. The setting material should be able to retain its bond strength when moist or wet, and the setting bed and/or structure should be well protected with a waterproof membrane.

In addition to including the proper materials, the wet floors must be properly detailed and sloped to allow water to drain. Because the slopes usually approach a floor drain from several directions, the resulting floor surface generally resembles a shallow, inverted pyramid. For this reason, when wet floors are tiled, the setting bed is always a mortar thick-bed assembly (see 94), which can be readily shaped with the necessary slope to provide drainage. Floor tiles should be small (usually mosaic tile) to conform to the shape of the mortar bed. The mortar setting bed can be placed over either a concrete slab or wood subfloor and should slope down to the subdrain at approximately ¼ in. per ft., to the surrounding walls (drawing above).

Waterproof Membrane
A waterproof membrane between subfloor and mortar bed protects the subfloor from moisture. This membrane, typically called a shower pan, has traditionally been made of soldered metal, either galvanized steel, copper or lead. Recently, however, chlorinated polyethylene (CPE) sheets have superseded metal pans because they are less expensive to install, are flexible and do not degrade over time.

At the lowest point of the pan, the drain is both glued and mechanically clamped to the membrane. At inside corners, the CPE membrane is folded from a single sheet. At outside corners, a separate piece of membrane is chemically welded to the shower pan to make a watertight container open only at the drain. The membrane should be continuous to 3 in. (min.) above the overflow waterline of a tiled tub, or 9 in. above a shower subfloor.

At the top edge of the shower pan, the waterproof membrane of the wall should lap over the top edge of the shower pan by about 5 in., and if possible the two membranes should be sealed with caulk or chemically welded to form a seal. Details of this intersection with the wall depend on whether the wall setting bed is gypsum wallboard, plywood, backer board, or mortar thick-bed (see 28).

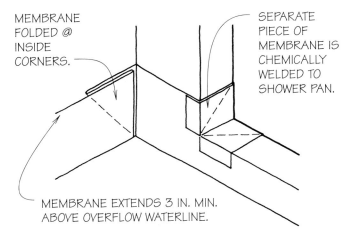

MEMBRANE
FOLDED @
INSIDE
CORNERS.

SEPARATE
PIECE OF
MEMBRANE IS
CHEMICALLY
WELDED TO
SHOWER PAN.

MEMBRANE EXTENDS 3 IN. MIN.
ABOVE OVERFLOW WATERLINE.

SHOWER PAN CORNERS

A SHOWER & TUB FLOORS

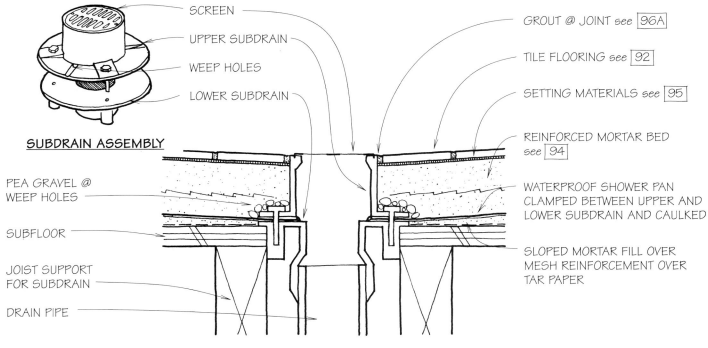

SCREEN

UPPER SUBDRAIN

WEEP HOLES

LOWER SUBDRAIN

SUBDRAIN ASSEMBLY

GROUT @ JOINT see 96A

TILE FLOORING see 92

SETTING MATERIALS see 95

REINFORCED MORTAR BED see 94

PEA GRAVEL @ WEEP HOLES

SUBFLOOR

JOIST SUPPORT FOR SUBDRAIN

DRAIN PIPE

WATERPROOF SHOWER PAN CLAMPED BETWEEN UPPER AND LOWER SUBDRAIN AND CAULKED

SLOPED MORTAR FILL OVER MESH REINFORCEMENT OVER TAR PAPER

Ⓐ TUB/SHOWER FLOOR @ DRAIN

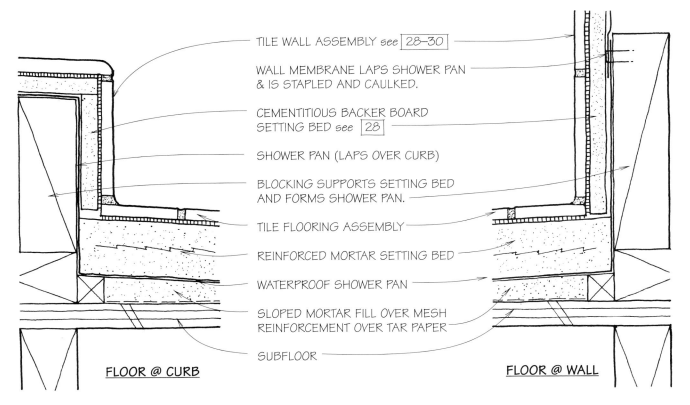

TILE WALL ASSEMBLY see 28-30

WALL MEMBRANE LAPS SHOWER PAN & IS STAPLED AND CAULKED.

CEMENTITIOUS BACKER BOARD SETTING BED see 28

SHOWER PAN (LAPS OVER CURB)

BLOCKING SUPPORTS SETTING BED AND FORMS SHOWER PAN.

TILE FLOORING ASSEMBLY

REINFORCED MORTAR SETTING BED

WATERPROOF SHOWER PAN

SLOPED MORTAR FILL OVER MESH REINFORCEMENT OVER TAR PAPER

SUBFLOOR

FLOOR @ CURB

FLOOR @ WALL

Ⓑ TUB/SHOWER FLOOR @ CURB & WALL

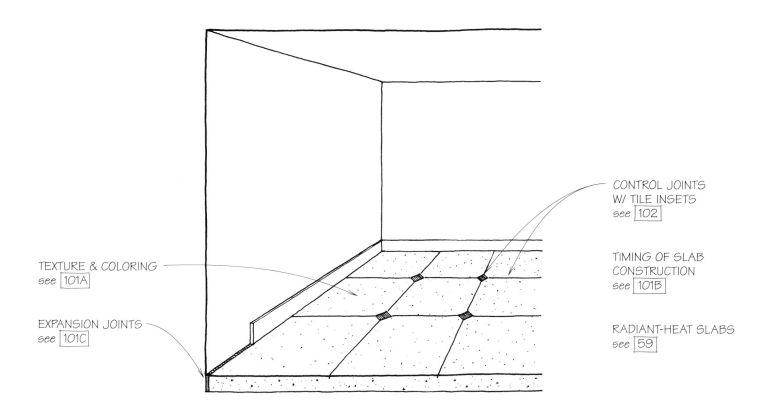

TEXTURE & COLORING
see 101A

EXPANSION JOINTS
see 101C

CONTROL JOINTS
W/ TILE INSETS
see 102

TIMING OF SLAB
CONSTRUCTION
see 101B

RADIANT-HEAT SLABS
see 59

From the time of ancient Rome, concrete has proven to be an economical and durable flooring material. In modern buildings, concrete is usually employed as a subfloor for other types of flooring. But concrete can also be used effectively as a finish floor. Despite its reputation as a functional, industrial material, concrete has many attributes that can make it attractive as a finish surface.

A concrete floor is relatively inexpensive, because exposing the concrete surface eliminates the need for finish-flooring materials. A finished concrete surface is very durable and easy to maintain. The combination of its mass and high conductivity relative to other flooring makes concrete an excellent medium for radiant heat (see 59) and passive heating and cooling.

A finished concrete floor can be beautiful too. An expanse of undifferentiated grey concrete can be transformed with minimal expense by adding color by a variety of methods (see 101A), by cutting or casting required control joints in carefully designed geometric patterns (see 101A) and by using accents of a different material, usually ceramic or stone tile.

Although concrete construction is common and the construction process straightforward, there are many potential pitfalls in the placing and finishing of a concrete floor. Since proper execution is critical to a successful concrete finish floor, only experienced labor should be employed.

Composition
Concrete is composed of portland cement, sand and gravel aggregate in the approximate proportion of 1:2:3. Water is added in various proportions depending on the weather, the type(s) of additive(s) and the stiffness required. The more cement (and the less water) added to the mix, the higher the strength of the concrete. Depending on the structural requirements, reinforcing in the form of glass fibers, woven wire mesh or steel rebar may be placed in the slab.

At a weight of 150 lb. per cu. ft., standard concrete is a relatively heavy material to be supported on the upper floors of a building. Lighter aggregates can lower the density of the concrete, but will also lessen its strength and hardness and increase its porosity.

 CONCRETE FLOORING

Pigmenting Concrete

Concrete may be pigmented with integral color in any of three ways:

Integral color—Pigment may be added to the wet concrete while it is being mixed and before it is placed on the floor. Compared to the other two methods, integral color tends to be duller, with more pastel hues. It is also the most expensive method but leaves less room for error or unexpected problems.

Dusted-on color—Dusting on pigment is also called broadcasting. Powdered pigment is spread over the surface of fresh concrete and worked in as the concrete is finished. Dusted-on pigment provides a more intense color than the other methods.

Dyes and stains—Added to finished and cured concrete, dyes and stains are less uniform than the other methods. The colors can be richer, and they tend to emphasize the variation inherent in the surface of the concrete. Some methods (especially using a dark color) will minimize this variation.

Paint

Concrete may also be finished with specially formulated paint, which simply coats the concrete with a color. The color obtained with paint leaves less room for guesswork, but the rich variation contributed by the concrete itself will be missing from the finished floor. Surface durability may be extended with epoxy-based paint. Nonskid texture may also be achieved by adding sand to some paints.

Surface Texture

Although concrete can be finished with a variety of textures, such as the brushed high-traction sidewalk, an interior concrete floor is usually worked to a smooth surface to facilitate cleaning and polishing. But smoothness does not necessarily mean a completely uniform appearance. The surface of finished concrete should be expected to show the variation in texture and color that are inherent in the composition of the material and the finishing process. Hardened concrete may also be machine-ground like terrazzo (see 103), which exposes the aggregate.

 COLORING & TEXTURE

When possible, slabs that are to be exposed should be placed and finished late in the construction process. This allows the finishing of the slab to occur after it is protected from the weather and after many of the subcontractors who must walk and work on the surface have completed their tasks.

When concrete is used as a structural slab-on-grade or as a suspended floor, it is not possible to delay placing it because it supports walls. In this instance, the slab should be protected from the wear and abuse typical of a construction site with a temporary material such as plywood placed over it. Slabs that must be placed early in construction should be protected from the weather as best as possible.

Concrete slabs, whether a slab-on-grade or a nonstructural topping slab, usually have expansion joints at the walls to allow for movement of the slab independent from the walls and columns. The most

common expansion joint is an asphalt-impregnated soundboard about ½ in. thick, but rigid insulation can also be used when the insulating value is required. Base trim conceals the expansion joint material.

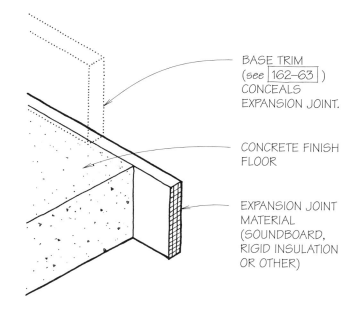

BASE TRIM
(see | 162–63 |)
CONCEALS
EXPANSION JOINT.

CONCRETE FINISH
FLOOR

EXPANSION JOINT
MATERIAL
(SOUNDBOARD,
RIGID INSULATION
OR OTHER)

 TIMING OF SLAB CONSTRUCTION   EXPANSION JOINTS

FINISH CONCRETE
CONTROL JOINT
ALIGN GROUT JOINT W/ CONTROL JOINT SO THAT POTENTIAL CRACKING OCCURS @ GROUT, NOT @ TILE.

CONCRETE SLAB
WOOD OR FOAM FORM PROVIDES SPACE FOR TILE ASSEMBLY.

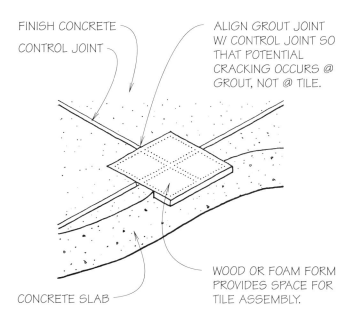

TILE INSET IN SLAB

The field of a concrete floor should have control joints cast or cut into the surface to direct the cracking that often occurs because of expansion and contraction. The control joints should be placed at locations most likely to crack, such as the diagonal radiating from an inside corner.

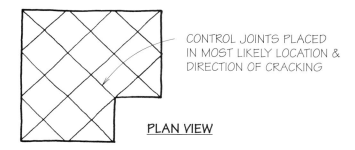

CONTROL JOINTS PLACED IN MOST LIKELY LOCATION & DIRECTION OF CRACKING

PLAN VIEW

Because the concrete is thinnest where the control joint is made, cracking will tend to occur along these lines.

CONTROL JOINT
CONCRETE SLAB
INDUCED CRACK

The recommended spacing of control joints depends on the type of subfloor, the mix of the concrete and the type of reinforcement (if any) used. A rule of

CONTROL JOINT
TILE SET ON MOUND OF MORTAR BEFORE CONCRETE IS PLACED.

CONCRETE TOPPING SLAB
ANY CRACKING OF SLAB WILL NOT CRACK MORTAR OR TILE.
SUBFLOOR

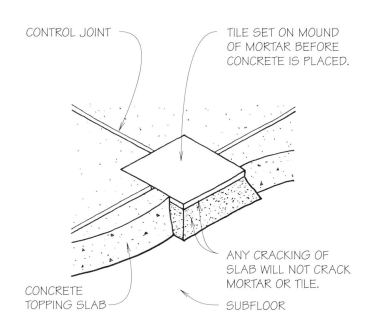

TILE INSET IN TOPPING SLAB

thumb is to space control joints so that they surround no more than 150 sq. ft. of slab area. With careful layout and placement, the control joints can become decorative elements in an otherwise monolithic floor surface.

Using ceramic or stone tiles at the intersections of control joints can effectively transform a simple, inexpensive concrete floor into an elegant pattern of strategically placed detail. To prevent the potential cracking at the control joints from telegraphing through and breaking the tiles, the tiles should be isolated from the slab with an isolation membrane or with mounds of mortar.

One method of inserting tiles in the slab is to form the space where the tiles are to be located with a wood or foam block that is placed while the concrete is finished (drawing, top left). After the slab has cured, the form is removed and the tile assembly is installed. A tiny isolation member or an elastic setting material will minimize the potential for tile cracks.

Another method when using a topping slab over a concrete or wood subfloor is to set tile on mounds of mortar at the height of the finish floor (drawing, top right). The tile (or a temporary material used in place of the tile) will provide a reference point for leveling the concrete as it is being placed.

 CONTROL JOINTS

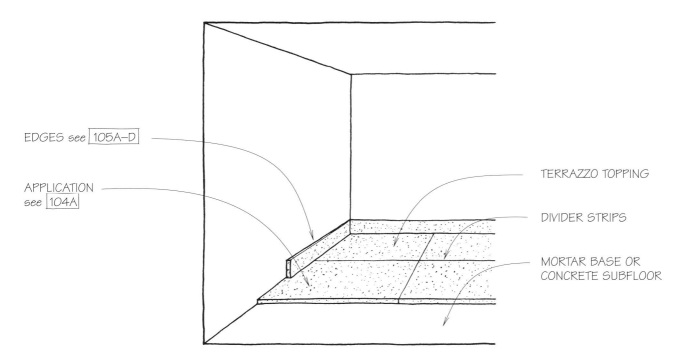

EDGES see 105A–D

APPLICATION see 104A

TERRAZZO TOPPING

DIVIDER STRIPS

MORTAR BASE OR CONCRETE SUBFLOOR

Terrazzo floors have their origins in 15th-century Venice, inspired by earlier Roman marble mosaic floors. Terrazzo has been in continuous use since its invention because of its beauty, its extreme durability and its ease of maintenance. High initial cost relative to other flooring limits the use of terrazzo primarily to public buildings, where its resistance to wear can make it worth the expense. Today, terrazzo is available not only in the traditional forms, but also in precast tiles that are laid like marble with a minimal 1/16-in. grout line (see 93 & 96A).

Composition
Composed of a thin, stone-chip topping adhered to a mortar base or concrete slab, a terrazzo floor is divided into sections by thin divider strips that help to control cracking.

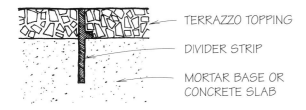

TERRAZZO TOPPING

DIVIDER STRIP

MORTAR BASE OR CONCRETE SLAB

Terrazzo topping—Traditional terrazzo is composed of a graded marble or onyx aggregate (70% or more) in a cement matrix, and is usually ½ in. to ⅝ in. thick (see 104B & C). Its durability arises primarily from the extreme hardness of the stone aggregate. Color is often added to the cement matrix in order to highlight the stone aggregate, which itself is a mix of colors and sizes. Traditional terrazzo can be applied to a concrete or wood subfloor.

A thinset terrazzo made with an epoxy or polyester matrix can be as thin as ¼ in. Thinset terrazzo can be applied only to a concrete subfloor (see 104D).

Divider strips—A terrazzo floor is divided into sections by strips, usually brass, zinc or plastic. The divider strips create weakened vertical planes, inducing unavoidable cracking to occur at these locations. The strips also create patterns and allow different colors of terrazzo to be placed side by side. On concrete slabs, divider strips should be located at any location likely to crack because of structural movement, particularly at control joints and at the intersection of the floor and walls. Maximum spacing of divider strips ranges from 4 ft. to 15 ft. o.c., depending on the type of terrazzo system employed.

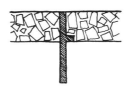

STANDARD DIVIDER STRIP EXTENDS INTO SLAB OR MORTAR BED.

THINSET DIVIDER STRIP SITS ON TOP OF SLAB.

 TERRAZZO FLOORING

The most durable terrazzo floors are installed over a mortar base. The mortar base adds strength and helps to isolate the terrazzo topping from the structure and minimize cracking. The mortar base can be applied directly to a concrete slab, or over a thin sand cushion, further isolating the terrazzo from the structure. Over a wood subfloor, a mortar base provides stiffness and a cementitious surface to which the terrazzo topping can adhere. A mortar base installed over a sand cushion or wood structure needs reinforcement, but no reinforcement is required when the mortar is directly on a concrete slab.

To apply the terrazzo, a thin (¼ in. to ⅝ in.) mixture of terrazzo is placed on the mortar base or concrete subfloor and is compressed with a roller to force out excess water and cement. The compressed wet surface is troweled flat and even with the tops of the divider strips. The cured terrazzo is machine ground to achieve a smooth, polished finish. A clear sealer is applied to prevent the cement matrix from staining or absorbing moisture (the marble or granite aggregate is not porous and will not absorb the sealer).

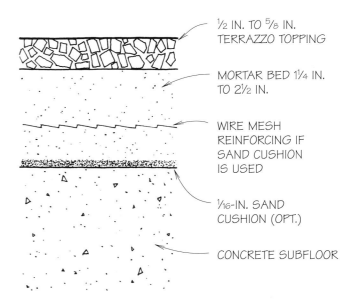

½ IN. TO ⅝ IN. TERRAZZO TOPPING

MORTAR BED 1¼ IN. TO 2½ IN.

WIRE MESH REINFORCING IF SAND CUSHION IS USED

1/16-IN. SAND CUSHION (OPT.)

CONCRETE SUBFLOOR

NOTE:
TERRAZZO TOPPING CAN ALSO BE APPLIED DIRECTLY TO REINFORCED CONCRETE SLAB WITHOUT MORTAR BED.

(A) **TERRAZZO**
APPLICATION

(B) **TERRAZZO ON MORTAR**
CONCRETE SUBFLOOR

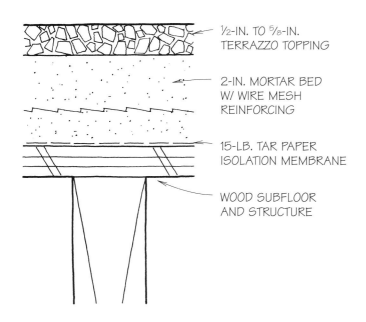

½-IN. TO ⅝-IN. TERRAZZO TOPPING

2-IN. MORTAR BED W/ WIRE MESH REINFORCING

15-LB. TAR PAPER ISOLATION MEMBRANE

WOOD SUBFLOOR AND STRUCTURE

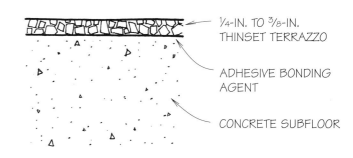

¼-IN. TO ⅜-IN. THINSET TERRAZZO

ADHESIVE BONDING AGENT

CONCRETE SUBFLOOR

NOTES:
1. THINSET TERRAZZO CAN ONLY BE APPLIED DIRECTLY TO A CONCRETE SLAB.
2. DIVIDER STRIPS MAY BE LOCATED UP TO 15 FT. O.C.

(C) **TERRAZZO ON MORTAR**
WOOD SUBFLOOR

(D) **THINSET TERRAZZO**
CONCRETE SUBFLOOR

The edges of terrazzo at a wall may be trimmed with any base material, but are most often finished with a terrazzo base. Base is available precast, or it may be poured in place with the same material used for the body of the floor. It is difficult to grind the top edge of poured-in-place base because of the proximity of finish wall materials. A metal base cap is usually used to eliminate the need for grinding the base top. A divider strip should be located between the main floor and the flush precast or poured base.

Where terrazzo meets other flooring it is best if the two materials are flush. A terrazzo divider strip (see 103) can serve as a transition between the two surfaces. If the terrazzo is not flush with the adjacent flooring, its edge may be treated similar to that of tile or masonry (see 96).

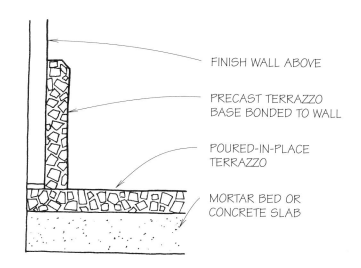

FINISH WALL ABOVE

PRECAST TERRAZZO BASE BONDED TO WALL

POURED-IN-PLACE TERRAZZO

MORTAR BED OR CONCRETE SLAB

Ⓐ TERRAZZO EDGES
FINISHING OPTIONS

Ⓑ PRECAST BASE

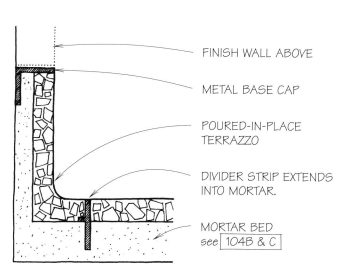

FINISH WALL ABOVE

METAL BASE CAP

POURED-IN-PLACE TERRAZZO

DIVIDER STRIP EXTENDS INTO MORTAR.

MORTAR BED
see 104B & C

NOTE:
DETAIL @ TOP OF BASE CAN BE AS SHOWN IN 105D.

Ⓒ POURED-IN-PLACE BASE
OVER MORTAR BED

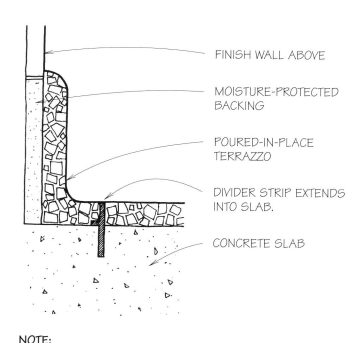

FINISH WALL ABOVE

MOISTURE-PROTECTED BACKING

POURED-IN-PLACE TERRAZZO

DIVIDER STRIP EXTENDS INTO SLAB.

CONCRETE SLAB

NOTE:
DETAIL @ TOP OF BASE CAN BE AS SHOWN IN 105C.

Ⓓ POURED-IN-PLACE BASE
ON CONCRETE SLAB

Cabinets & Countertops

3

U ntil this century, cabinets were largely considered to be furniture, finished on all sides and movable within a room. Most of these early cabinets were made of solid wood with wood tops. Only with the advent of interior plumbing in the late 19th century did cabinets begin to be built integral with the building.

These new built-in cabinets continued to be made of wood, but the tops needed to be water resistant, so impervious surfaces such as tile became the standard. Countertops have evolved to the point that most are now made of continuous synthetic sheets. Modern cabinets continue to be built of wood products, particularly composite sheet materials such as plywood and particleboard rather than the many small pieces of solid wood from which their hand-crafted predecessors were built.

The new composite and synthetic materials have simplified the construction of cabinets and have made them stronger, more durable and more economical. And despite the significant shift toward more monolithic materials for both cabinets and countertops, traditional cabinet styles are still quite affordable and common.

Standards for Dimensions

Nearly universal acceptance of cabinets as a built-in part of the building has led to some standards for the height and depth of various cabinets (see the chart below). These dimensions are based on ergonomic considerations that are standard throughout the cabinet industry and the country. Accessibility standards for wheelchair-bound people have recently been accepted also. Except for these accessibility standards, cabinet dimensions are not governed by codes; nevertheless, cabinet shops will follow these standards unless directed otherwise.

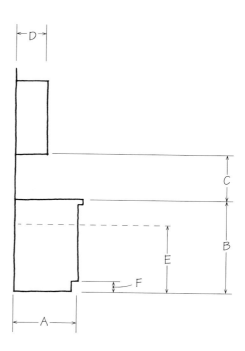

STANDARD CABINET DIMENSIONS

A	24 in.	base cabinet depth
B	36 in. 32-34 in. 29-30 in. 26-28 in.	kitchen vanity desktop typing
C	18 in. 30 in. 30 in.	standard over sink over cooktop
D	12 in.	wall cabinet depth
E	24-28 in.	under-desk space
F	4 in.	toe space

Cabinet Quality Standards

The quality of cabinets in the United States is clearly defined by the Architectural Woodwork Institute (AWI). In the AWI Quality Standards, the materials, joinery and finish quality of cabinets are spelled out in detail. There are three grades described for custom-manufactured cabinets that are made to order in small- to medium-size cabinet shops: Premium, Custom and Economy. Premium is the highest grade, reserved for only the finest cabinets. Premium-grade cabinets are extremely expensive and not often specified. Custom is the most common grade of cabinet, and is made of excellent materials durably joined. Custom grade is specified for the vast majority of all cabinet work, both commercial and residential. Economy is the lowest grade, used for only utilitarian and some residential cabinets. A separate Modular grade is described in the AWI standards for mass-produced modular cabinets. The quality of the Modular grade is virtually the same as Custom grade for custom-manufactured cabinets.

The AWI standards take into account whether the cabinets are to have an opaque finish (paint grade), a transparent finish (stain grade) or are made with plastic-laminate material. The standards also distinguish between parts of a cabinet that are concealed, semi-exposed or exposed (shown in the drawing above) and specify a minimum grade of material for each of these surface classifications.

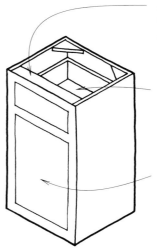

CONCEALED SURFACES ARE NOT VISIBLE AFTER THE CABINET IS INSTALLED, EVEN IF THE CABINET IS OPEN (BACKS, TOPS, ENDS).

SEMI-EXPOSED SURFACES ARE VISIBLE ONLY WHEN INSTALLED CABINET IS OPEN (DRAWERS, CASE SIDES & BOTTOMS).

EXPOSED SURFACES ARE VISIBLE WHEN INSTALLED CABINET IS CLOSED.

A consequence of the AWI Quality Standards is that the designer may control the construction quality of cabinets by the mention of a grade. Cabinet designers are thus free to concentrate on proportion, shape, material selection and other details that make a visible difference in the appearance of the cabinet.

Modern cabinet design includes many possibilities, from a traditional paneled style to a smooth-faced box. Aside from its proportions, the appearance of a cabinet depends mostly on a few simple design decisions, which are described in general on 109-111.

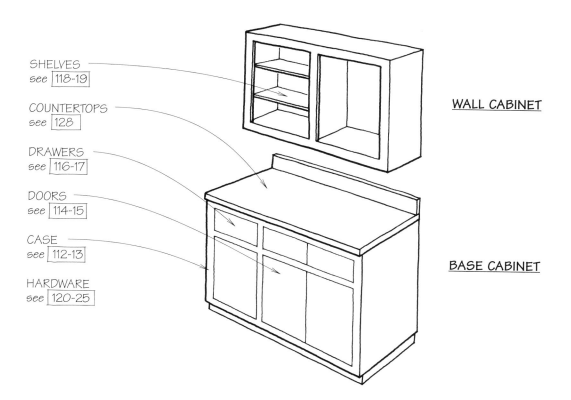

SHELVES
see | 118-19 |

COUNTERTOPS
see | 128 |

DRAWERS
see | 116-17 |

DOORS
see | 114-15 |

CASE
see | 112-13 |

HARDWARE
see | 120-25 |

WALL CABINET

BASE CABINET

Frameless vs. Face-Frame Cabinets

The body, or case, of a cabinet is a simple box. It usually has a single functional face into which doors, drawers and shelves are fitted. As shown in the drawing below, this functional face of the case may either consist of the simple edge of the box (frameless) or have a frame attached to it (face-frame). These two cabinet types are discussed below in terms of their appearance and in the cabinet case section (see 112-13) in terms of their functional details.

The *frameless* cabinet (also called a European cabinet), is the type used for virtually all commercial cabinetry. It is less flexible than the face-frame cabinet in terms of the style of the cabinet and the arrangement of its parts. The doors and drawers of a frameless cabinet are usually adjacent to each other with only a small (⅛-in.) gap between.

The *face-frame* cabinet has a frame that is usually exposed, allowing the designer to control the amount of space between doors and drawers and other openings by means of adjusting the frame width. The frame also allows compositional flexibility because it can support doors and drawers independent of the sides of the cabinet case.

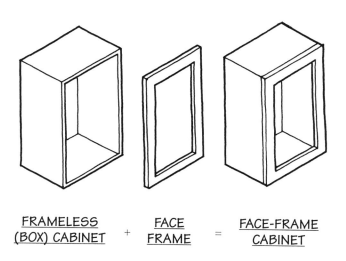

FRAMELESS
(BOX) CABINET   +   FACE
FRAME   =   FACE-FRAME
CABINET

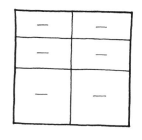

FRAMELESS

FACE-FRAME

CABINETS

Custom vs. Modular

A decision that can significantly affect the appearance of a set of cabinets is whether the cabinets are custom made in a local shop or mass-produced as modular units. The difference between the two is that custom cabinets are tailor made to fit a particular location, while modular cabinets for the same location would not necessarily fit exactly and might require a spacer or leave a gap. Modular cabinets are made of several segments (modules), while custom cabinets may be made in one single large piece. Modular cabinets are often chosen because custom-made cabinets are not available locally.

When there is a practical choice between the two, the custom cabinet will afford considerably more design control, but modular cabinets offer assured quality control and greater potential for remodeling and/or re-use in another location.

Door/Drawer Style

Given that most of the exposed surface of a cabinet consists of doors or drawer fronts, the style of these elements contributes significantly to the appearance of a cabinet. There are two basic styles of door and drawer front:

Single-piece doors and drawer fronts are made with a single piece of panel product such as plywood, particleboard or fiberboard, with a veneer surface of wood, plastic laminate or melamine. Small to medium-size drawer fronts are sometimes made from a single piece of solid lumber. Single-piece doors and drawers, therefore, have a smooth appearance and a clean, uncluttered look.

Frame-and-panel doors and drawer fronts are built up from several pieces. The simplest are made from a four-sided frame around a central panel. The panel is usually made of wood, but can also be made of other materials such as glass or metal. Wood panels are either flat or raised, and can be made of solid wood, plywood or fiberboard, depending on whether they are to be painted or stained. This style of door and drawer front is more traditional, dating to the days before panel products made single-piece doors possible.

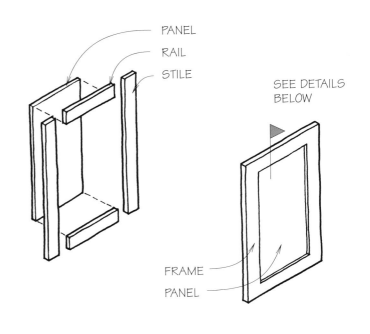

PANEL
RAIL
STILE

SEE DETAILS BELOW

FRAME
PANEL

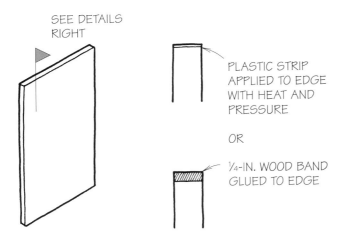

SEE DETAILS RIGHT

PLASTIC STRIP APPLIED TO EDGE WITH HEAT AND PRESSURE

OR

¼-IN. WOOD BAND GLUED TO EDGE

SINGLE-PIECE DOOR

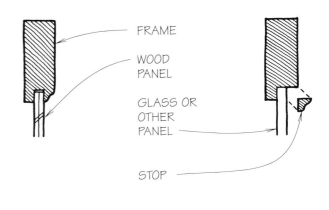

FRAME
WOOD PANEL
GLASS OR OTHER PANEL
STOP

FRAME-AND-PANEL DOOR

Door/Drawer Edge

The relationship of the doors and drawers to the face of the cabinet is also quite significant in determining the overall appearance of the cabinet. The three basic door/drawer edge conditions are discussed below in terms of their appearance and in the cabinet door section (see 114-15) in terms of their functional details.

Overlay—In an overlay cabinet, doors and drawers fully overlap the face of the cabinet. There are two variations:

The *flush overlay* detail, shown below, creates the cleanest, least complicated-looking cabinet because the doors and drawers are set only about ⅛ in. from each other and virtually cover the entire face of the cabinet. A flush overlay detail may be used on either face-frame or frameless cabinets.

The *reveal overlay* detail, shown below, exposes the cabinet case and emphasizes the full thickness of the doors and drawer fronts, which are visible at their edges. This detail can be used only with face-frame cabinets.

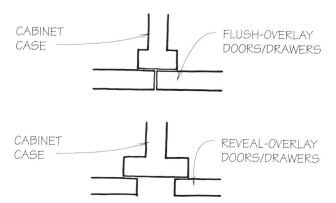

Lip—Doors and drawers with lipped edges are rabbeted on the back side and only project half of their thickness beyond the face of the cabinet. This detail, which is practical only in face-frame cabinets, is often employed, along with a frame-and-panel door, to create a traditional look.

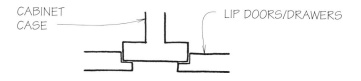

Inset—Doors and drawers with inset edges have their finished faces flush with the face of face-frame cabinets. This is the most traditional of door types but can be the most expensive because the doors and drawers must be precisely adjusted to control the gap exposed between door and cabinet case. Inset frame-and-panel doors complement the clean planar quality of the cabinet face.

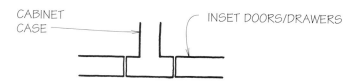

Surface Finishes

The three standard finishes for cabinets are paint, stain and plastic laminate. The final finish affects the materials, the cost and even the style of the cabinets.

Paint-grade cabinets are normally made of relatively inexpensive hardwood and/or hardwood plywood that accepts paint evenly, such as birch, alder or poplar. This makes paint-grade cabinets less expensive than *stain-grade cabinets*, which are normally made of finer grained and more expensive woods such as oak, maple, cherry, mahogany and fir. The higher cost of stain-grade cabinets is also a result of the increased labor involved in matching wood grain and color, the requirement for concealed nailing and the fact that manufacturing mistakes often require remaking the cabinet rather than repairing it. The cost of both paint-grade and stain-grade cabinets must ultimately include the cost of the protective finish itself, and bids for this work can vary considerably.

Plastic-laminated particleboard cabinets are limited in design because of the panel materials inherent to their construction. Single-piece doors and drawer faces are standard, as are frameless cases. The cost of plastic laminated cabinets, however, is not increased by the requirement for an additional protective finish as is the cost of paint- or stain-grade cabinets.

 CABINETS

Cabinet cases are usually made of ¾-in. thick plywood, particleboard or fiberboard (see Appendix B) for descriptions of these materials). How a cabinet is made and what it is made from depends primarily on whether the cabinet case is to be frameless or face-frame. Cabinet-case details also depend on whether the surface will be concealed or exposed (see 111), what materials the cabinet will abut and whether the cabinet is to have a painted, transparent or plastic-laminate finish (see 111).

The principal difference between the cases of these two types of cabinet is that the frameless cabinet is a simple box while the face-frame cabinet has an additional layer in the form of a frame that is attached to the face of the cabinet.

Frameless Cabinets
Frameless cabinets are made as a series of boxes one or two doors wide that are ganged together on site to make a composite whole. Because they do not have a face frame to make them rigid, frameless cabinets invariably have a back. The raw front edges of the case are normally trimmed with plastic edge-banding material and are concealed behind flush overlay doors or drawers.

The frameless cabinet has been developed into a modular system that is standardized worldwide. This modular system is based on a 32-mm increment that is primarily evident in the holes drilled in the melamine-coated particleboard case sides. These holes support standardized shelf, drawer and door hardware. The principal advantages of this system are that it can be easily adjusted with standardized hardware to fit a number of door, drawer and shelf configurations and that it can be easily remodeled with no modification of the cabinet case by changing the cabinet doors and drawer fronts.

Face-Frame Cabinets
The face frame adds rigidity to the case, which frameless cabinets must acquire by having a back. The face frame also adds considerable design flexibility not available with the frameless cabinet. Face-frame cabinets may be made in long sections incorporating several pairs of doors or several stacks of drawers. The presence of a face frame allows considerably more design flexibility than does the frameless cabinet, both for the appearance of the cabinet (see 109) and for its functional details. The face frame may be used to support drawers or other elements in a design that does not align all elements vertically (see 109).

In wall cabinets, the face frame can be detailed to cover the gap at the end of adjustable shelves (see 119B) and to conceal thin-profile light fixtures under the bottom shelf (see 113B). In both wall and base cabinets, the face frame may be cleanly detailed to scribe to walls, ceilings or other elements to which the cabinet is attached (see 127B).

Base and Wall Cabinets
Base cabinets are deeper and more accessible than wall cabinets, so they are often designed with drawers, bins, slide-out shelves or other storage alternatives. Wall cabinets are usually restricted to shelving because their height makes drawers, bins and other storage alternatives hard to reach. The interior of a wall cabinet is more visible when open than a base cabinet, so wall cabinets ordinarily have backs whether frameless or face-frame. Base cabinets usually only have backs when required for rigidity, as with a frameless case, or to limit infestation by insects or rodents.

(A) CABINET CASES

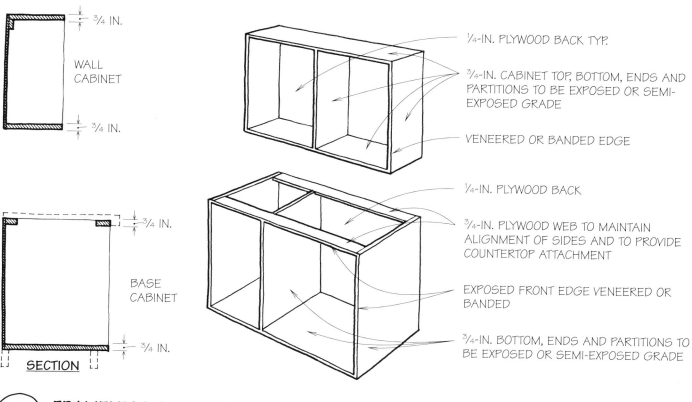

¾ IN.

WALL
CABINET

¾ IN.

¾ IN.

BASE
CABINET

¾ IN.

SECTION

¼-IN. PLYWOOD BACK TYP.

¾-IN. CABINET TOP, BOTTOM, ENDS AND
PARTITIONS TO BE EXPOSED OR SEMI-
EXPOSED GRADE

VENEERED OR BANDED EDGE

¼-IN. PLYWOOD BACK

¾-IN. PLYWOOD WEB TO MAINTAIN
ALIGNMENT OF SIDES AND TO PROVIDE
COUNTERTOP ATTACHMENT

EXPOSED FRONT EDGE VENEERED OR
BANDED

¾-IN. BOTTOM, ENDS AND PARTITIONS TO
BE EXPOSED OR SEMI-EXPOSED GRADE

 A FRAMELESS CABINET CASES

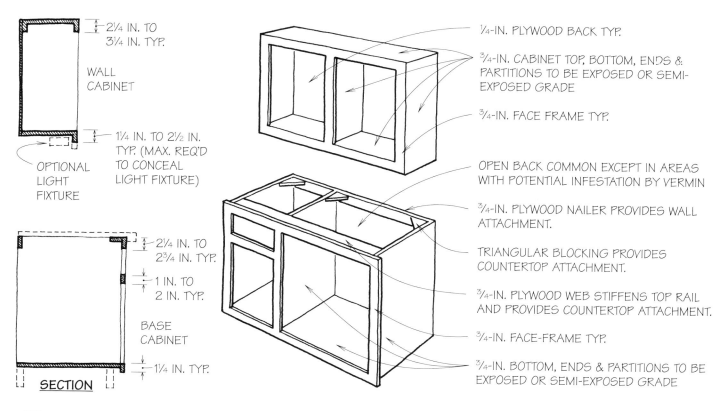

2¼ IN. TO
3¼ IN. TYP.

WALL
CABINET

1¼ IN. TO 2½ IN.
TYP. (MAX. REQ'D
TO CONCEAL
LIGHT FIXTURE)

OPTIONAL
LIGHT
FIXTURE

2¼ IN. TO
2¾ IN. TYP.

1 IN. TO
2 IN. TYP.

BASE
CABINET

1¼ IN. TYP.

SECTION

¼-IN. PLYWOOD BACK TYP.

¾-IN. CABINET TOP, BOTTOM, ENDS &
PARTITIONS TO BE EXPOSED OR SEMI-
EXPOSED GRADE

¾-IN. FACE FRAME TYP.

OPEN BACK COMMON EXCEPT IN AREAS
WITH POTENTIAL INFESTATION BY VERMIN

¾-IN. PLYWOOD NAILER PROVIDES WALL
ATTACHMENT.

TRIANGULAR BLOCKING PROVIDES
COUNTERTOP ATTACHMENT.

¾-IN. PLYWOOD WEB STIFFENS TOP RAIL
AND PROVIDES COUNTERTOP ATTACHMENT.

¾-IN. FACE-FRAME TYP.

¾-IN. BOTTOM, ENDS & PARTITIONS TO BE
EXPOSED OR SEMI-EXPOSED GRADE

 B FACE-FRAME CABINET CASES

Cabinet doors may be constructed of either a single piece or an assembly of several pieces around a central panel. Both types of doors may be used with either frameless or face-frame cabinet cases (see 109 & 112) and may have any of the three edge conditions (see 111). The selection of a door is therefore based not so much on its relationship to the cabinet case as it is with aesthetics and economics.

Single-Piece Doors

These doors are usually made of ¾-in. thick particleboard, medium-density fiberboard (MDF) or plywood (MDP) (see Appendix B). Particleboard and fiberboard doors are usually laminated with a high-pressure laminate or low-pressure melamine. Melamine costs less but is also less durable and more limited in color selection. The choice of a material for single-piece doors should be related to both the use of the cabinets and to the finish.

The edges of single-piece doors, because they are exposed, must usually be banded for appearance with either a machine-applied plastic veneer or a solid (⅛-in. to ¼-in.) hardwood glued under pressure. Particleboard or plywood single-piece doors also require edge banding for durability, whereas MDF doors do not. Because of the need for edge banding, single-piece doors rarely have a lipped edge unless they are made of MDF and are to have an opaque finish.

A variation of the typical single-piece cabinet door is made of several pieces of edge-glued solid lumber. Such a door may warp if not carefully manufactured, so a horizontal stiffener affixed to the back of the door may be required.

Frame-and-Panel Doors

Frame-and-panel doors are generally made of hardwood stiles and rails with matching panels. The stiles and rails are profiled to include a groove at the inner edge designed to hold the panel in place and are glued together under pressure. The profile of the stiles and rails is variable and should be coordinated with the panels.

The wood panel is slightly undersized to allow room for expansion and contraction and is not glued to the frame. The panel is usually either a ¼-in. thick plywood panel or a raised, solid-wood panel. Raised panels may be manufactured with any of several sections. Glass is often substituted for a panel.

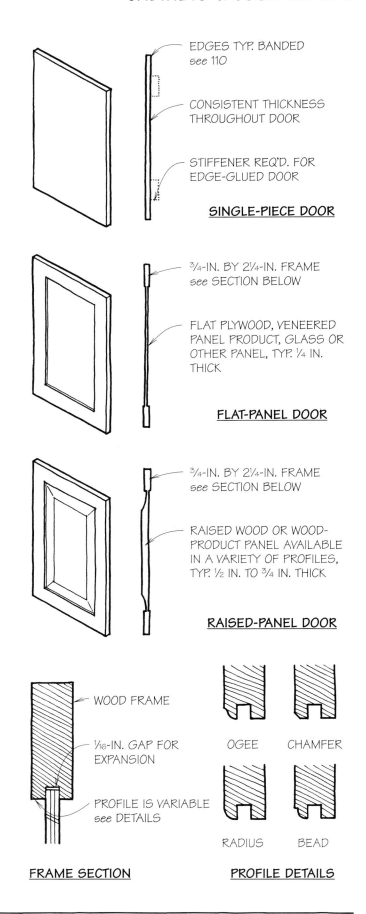

EDGES TYP. BANDED
see 110

CONSISTENT THICKNESS
THROUGHOUT DOOR

STIFFENER REQ'D. FOR
EDGE-GLUED DOOR

SINGLE-PIECE DOOR

¾-IN. BY 2¼-IN. FRAME
see SECTION BELOW

FLAT PLYWOOD, VENEERED
PANEL PRODUCT, GLASS OR
OTHER PANEL, TYP. ¼ IN.
THICK

FLAT-PANEL DOOR

¾-IN. BY 2¼-IN. FRAME
see SECTION BELOW

RAISED WOOD OR WOOD-
PRODUCT PANEL AVAILABLE
IN A VARIETY OF PROFILES,
TYP. ½ IN. TO ¾ IN. THICK

RAISED-PANEL DOOR

WOOD FRAME

1⁄16-IN. GAP FOR
EXPANSION

PROFILE IS VARIABLE
see DETAILS

OGEE   CHAMFER

RADIUS   BEAD

FRAME SECTION   **PROFILE DETAILS**

CABINET DOORS
SINGLE-PIECE VS. FRAME-AND-PANEL

Both single-piece and frame-and-panel doors may be made with any of the three edge conditions—overlay, lip or inset. These edges are discussed on 111 with regard to their appearance and below concerning their functional differences. Coordinating door edge with cabinet case type, hardware (see 122-23) and finish is important.

CASE TYPE	DOOR EDGE			
	Flush overlay	Reveal overlay	Lip	Inset
Frameless	✔			
Face-frame	✔	✔	✔	✔

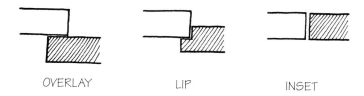

OVERLAY   LIP   INSET

Overlay

There are two variations of the overlay edge condition (see 111). Flush-overlay doors and drawers have only very small (⅛-in.) gaps between them so that the overall surface of the cabinet is quite planar or flush. Reveal-overlay doors and drawers have wide (usually 1-in. to 2-in.) gaps between them, revealing the edge of the door and the face frame of the cabinet.

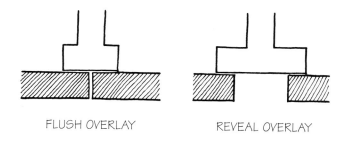

FLUSH OVERLAY   REVEAL OVERLAY

Flush-overlay doors are used in high-quality residential or commercial cabinets. Both high-pressure laminate and clear-stained plywood are commonly used materials. Flush-overlay doors are usually mounted with concealed hinges (see 122-23), which allow for adjustment so that the gaps between doors can be made consistent.

Reveal-overlay doors have two principal advantages. The first is that the doors are sufficiently distant from one another so that little adjustment is required to make them appear precisely trimmed relative to the other doors. The second advantage is the potential for integrating pulls within the edge of the door. As shown below, the space between doors and drawers provides enough room to grasp the edge of the door, eliminating the need for face-mounted pulls.

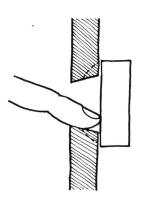

Lip

The lip door is most common and practical for panel doors. This is because the edge of panel doors is made of solid material that is strong even when reduced to ⅜-in. thickness by the rabbet that forms the lip of the door. Single-piece doors made with a lip edge are not banded and are usually made of painted MDF. Lip doors are never used with frameless cabinets.

The principal advantage of the lip door is that it minimizes the need for fitting adjustment while providing a relatively smooth (planar) appearance to the face of the cabinet. Fitting is minimal because, like the reveal-overlay door, the lip door covers the gap between cabinet and door while remaining sufficiently distant from other doors that it doesn't require precise alignment. Lip doors and drawers require pull hardware.

Inset

The inset door edge is practical for both frame-and-panel doors and single-piece doors. Fitting inset doors to a cabinet requires much greater care and craft than installing lip or overlay doors does; therefore, this edge condition is usually reserved for the finest cabinets. Inset doors and drawers require pull hardware.

SIDE/BACK JOINT
see 117

FRONT/SIDE JOINT
see 117

EDGES DETAILED LIKE
DOOR EDGES
see 115

DRAWER FRONT MATERIAL
TYP. MATCHES DOOR
MATERIAL.

BOTTOM JOINTS
see 117

DRAWER-GUIDE
HARDWARE
see 121

The cabinet drawer may be thought of as a simple box attached to the back of a small cabinet door. Functionally, it is the box and its supporting hardware that are most important, but visually it is the drawer front that draws our attention and relates to the rest of the cabinet. Whatever the size or style of the drawer, its front may be designed to match the door style and to fit into the face of the cabinet in the same way as the doors (see 114-15). Because drawers are smaller than doors, however, it may be impossible to make frame-and-panel drawer fronts with the same components used for doors. For this reason, single-piece drawer fronts are frequently paired with frame-and-panel doors in the same cabinet, as shown below.

Materials

The materials that are used to make drawers vary considerably and are related primarily to the quality and type of cabinet but also to the size and use of the drawer. Drawer components are specified by AWI whose standards have been adapted by most professional cabinet makers.

Sides are ½-in. thick lumber or panel-product material. Backs are required to be ½ in. thick but many shops use ¾-in. thick backs because the thicker material receives fasteners with less chance of a blowout. Bottoms are specified to be ¼-in. panel product (usually plywood) but should be ½ in. thick for drawers over 30 in. wide or those destined to carry heavy loads. Drawer fronts should be ¾-in. thick lumber or panel product.

Hardware

The most critical decision for the proper operation of a drawer is the selection of appropriate guide hardware. Heavy-duty guides are rated for the amount of weight they will carry. Full-extension guides allow the drawer to be pulled out so that its entire area is exposed beyond the face of the cabinet. Light-duty guides remain concealed when the drawer is open and are adequate for most residential drawers. Drawer hardware is discussed in detail in the cabinet hardware section (see 120-21 & 125).

SINGLE-PIECE
DRAWERS

OVER

FRAME-AND-PANEL
DOORS

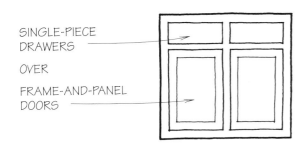

CABINET DRAWERS

Joints between sides and back of a drawer are rarely stressed structurally. Joints at the edges of the drawer bottom are only minimally stressed unless loads are excessive. Joints between the front and the sides of the drawer can be the most critical for the longevity of the drawer because the impact of closing the drawer against the face of the cabinet can stress these joints considerably. These joints are also visible when the drawer is open, so aesthetic qualities must be considered in addition to strength.

There are two fundamentally different ways of making the side/front joint. The first is to make the drawer front out of two pieces, a subfront and a finish front. This method is used almost exclusively for commercial cabinets. The second method is to make the drawer front out of one piece that is attached directly to the drawer sides. This method is common in residential cabinet construction. There are several good details (see drawing top right) that mechanically lock the pieces together.

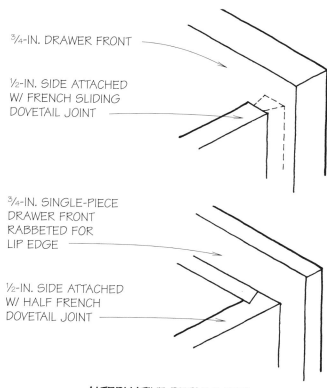

¾-IN. DRAWER FRONT

½-IN. SIDE ATTACHED W/ FRENCH SLIDING DOVETAIL JOINT

¾-IN. SINGLE-PIECE DRAWER FRONT RABBETED FOR LIP EDGE

½-IN. SIDE ATTACHED W/ HALF FRENCH DOVETAIL JOINT

ALTERNATIVE DETAILS FOR SINGLE-PIECE DRAWER FRONT

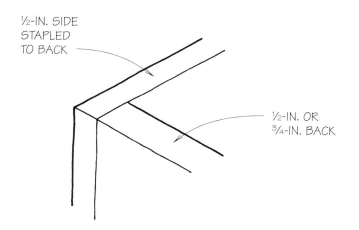

½-IN. SIDE STAPLED TO BACK

½-IN. OR ¾-IN. BACK

TYPICAL BACK/SIDE JOINT

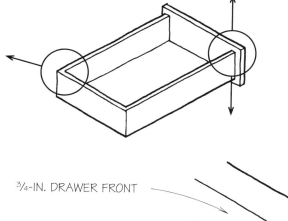

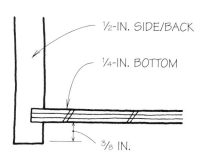

½-IN. SIDE/BACK

¼-IN. BOTTOM

⅜ IN.

TYPICAL BOTTOM JOINT

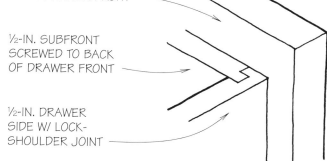

¾-IN. DRAWER FRONT

½-IN. SUBFRONT SCREWED TO BACK OF DRAWER FRONT

½-IN. DRAWER SIDE W/ LOCK-SHOULDER JOINT

TWO-PIECE DRAWER FRONT

A DRAWER JOINERY

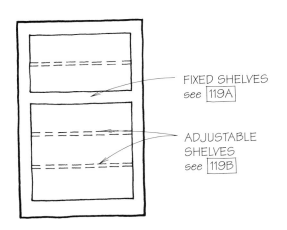

FIXED SHELVES
see 119A

ADJUSTABLE SHELVES
see 119B

Shelves are perhaps the simplest of all cabinet elements. Most cabinet shelves are made adjustable for convenience. Fixed shelves, however, are not entirely uncommon for single-purpose uses such as wine racks, equipment storage, or as design elements.

Solid wood shelves are strong but are often the most expensive. For economy and dimensional stability, shelves are most commonly made of panel products such as plywood for transparent finishes and particleboard or fiberboard for painted or melamine-coated finishes. Plywood shelves usually have an edge band of matching wood to cover the laminations exposed at the front edge of the shelf. Painted fiberboard shelves need only to be sanded at the edge as a preparation for the paint. If fiberboard or particleboard shelves are melamine coated, however, the exposed front edge must be veneered, usually with a PVC edging.

BANDED

SANDED

VENEERED

Sizing Shelves

Shelves must be designed to carry loads without deflecting excessively. The AWI suggests the following as minimum standards:

MATERIAL	Thickness	Max. span
Solid lumber	¾ in.	36 in.
	1¹⁄₁₆ in.	48 in.
Veneer core plywood	¾ in.	36 in.
	1 in.	48 in.
Fiberboard or plywood	¾ in.	32 in.
	1 in.	42 in.

These guidelines are sufficient for normal bookshelves and kitchen use. Shelves expected to carry heavier than normal loads should be either shorter or thicker than the minimums in the chart. Another way to strengthen shelves is to band the shelf at the front with lumber deeper than the shelf is thick.

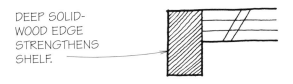

DEEP SOLID-WOOD EDGE STRENGTHENS SHELF.

Glass shelves are often used to support small items on display. The transparency of glass shelves gives them a delicate look and allows a single-source light to illuminate an entire cabinet of shelves. Glass is usually ground to eliminate sharp edges. Regular float glass commonly used for windows is the most common material, with longer spans and heavier loads requiring thicker glass, as shown in the chart below.

Glass thickness	Max. span
³⁄₁₆ in.	18 in.
¼ in.	48 in.

Fixed shelves are set into dadoes at their ends for support. The front ends of the dadoes are covered with either a face frame or, on a frameless cabinet, the edge banding.

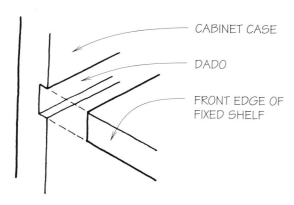

CABINET CASE

DADO

FRONT EDGE OF FIXED SHELF

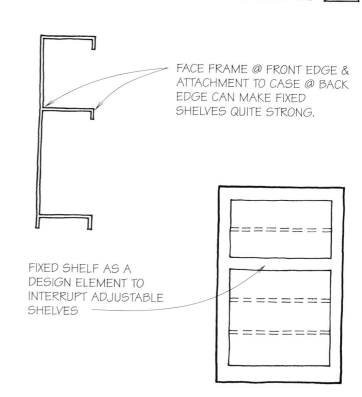

FACE FRAME @ FRONT EDGE & ATTACHMENT TO CASE @ BACK EDGE CAN MAKE FIXED SHELVES QUITE STRONG.

FIXED SHELF AS A DESIGN ELEMENT TO INTERRUPT ADJUSTABLE SHELVES

If the cabinet is a face-frame cabinet, the fixed shelf can be a design element for dividing a shelf opening while adding rigidity to the cabinet. Fixed shelves may also be attached to the back of the cabinet to make them less likely to deflect.

 FIXED SHELVES

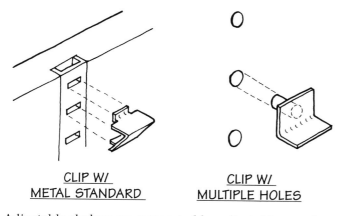

CLIP W/ METAL STANDARD

CLIP W/ MULTIPLE HOLES

Adjustable shelves are supported by adjustable metal clips set into the cabinet sides. These clips may be set either into continuous metal standards that are dadoed into the cabinet sides or into multiple holes drilled into the cabinet ends. The holes are generally spaced 1¼ in. (32mm) apart (see 112 for a discussion of the modular 32mm system).

To allow for shelf removal and adjustment, there must be a slight gap between the end of the shelf and the side of the cabinet case. This gap may be covered with a cabinet door or a face frame, but it will be exposed if it is in a frameless cabinet without a door.

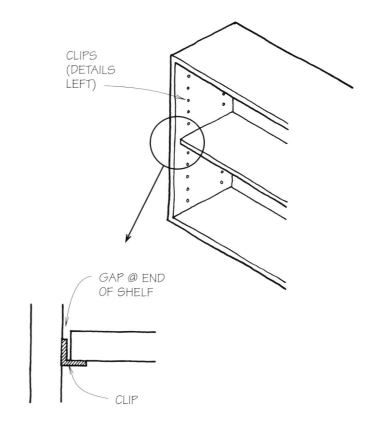

CLIPS (DETAILS LEFT)

GAP @ END OF SHELF

CLIP

 ADJUSTABLE SHELVES

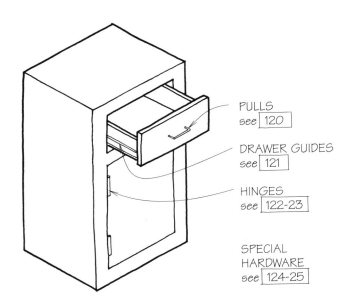

A variation of the surface-mounted pull is the routed-in pull. This pull is set into the thickness of the door or drawer so that its profile is much closer to flush than a typical surface-mounted pull. Because of the depth required, routed-in pulls are normally used only in conjunction with single-piece (not panel) doors. They may be self-contained and set into the central portion of the door or drawer, or they may be located along the full length of the top edge of doors or drawers in base cabinets.

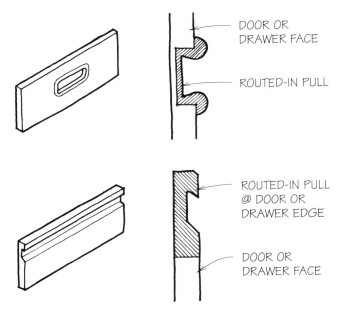

A very important component of the overall quality of a cabinet is the hardware. Because pulls are touched, they are usually the most prominent hardware, but in terms of durability, the most critical are the hinges and drawer guides, because they allow movement of the cabinet parts. Hinges may also play a significant role in the appearance of a cabinet.

Pulls have a significant impact on the appearance of a cabinet. The two basic pulls are surface-mounted (those mounted on the face of the drawer or door) and edge (those incorporated into the edge of the door or drawer).

Surface-Mounted Pulls

By far the most common type, the surface-mounted pull works on every kind of cabinet door and drawer. Surface-mounted pulls are typically made of metal in a loop design through which several fingers may be passed. The pulls are commonly screwed through the back to the face of the door or drawer, as shown below. Wood and plastic loop pulls are also available, as are knobs made of of metal, wood or plastic.

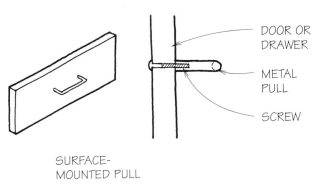

Edge Pulls

Edge pulls give cabinets a clean, uncluttered appearance. They can be used only on reveal-overlay doors and drawers because there is a space required between each door and drawer (reveal) for the full ¾-in. space required to allow a hand to grasp the edge of the door or drawer comfortably.

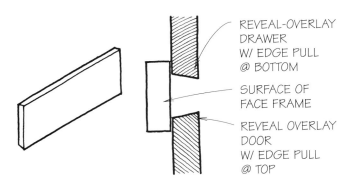

Wall cabinet doors are occasionally designed to open without any pulls by merely projecting the lower edge of the door below the lowest shelf of the cabinet.

Drawers used to be set into furniture on wooden guides. The best quality guides were hardwood, waxed for ease of operation. Modern guides are made of metal and are designed for smooth operation and ease of installation. Many are epoxy-coated with plastic rollers, while others are bare or plated metal with ball bearings. Most metal guides allow the drawer to operate so smoothly and with so little friction that a small hump is built in to keep the drawer seated in the closed position.

Unlike hinges, drawer guides do not have to be matched to the cabinet type. Any drawer guide will work with any drawer type. All guides will also mount in face-frame or frameless cabinets, although a shim strip is usually required with side-mount guides in face-frame cabinets.

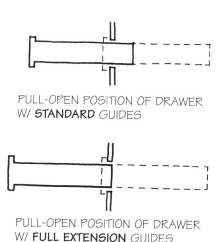

PULL-OPEN POSITION OF DRAWER
W/ **STANDARD** GUIDES

PULL-OPEN POSITION OF DRAWER
W/ **FULL EXTENSION** GUIDES

Side vs. bottom mount—Until very recently, there was a simple choice between side- or bottom-mount drawer hardware. Bottom-mount hardware was used extensively for light-duty situations, and side-mount for medium-duty, heavy-duty and full-extension drawers. With the introduction of epoxy-coated, medium-duty side-mount guides, light-duty bottom-mount guides have all but disappeared. They are still worth consideration, however, since they are totally concealed and do not consume drawer width.

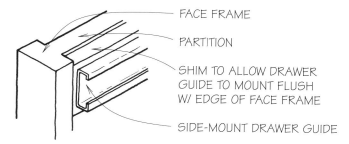

FACE FRAME

PARTITION

SHIM TO ALLOW DRAWER GUIDE TO MOUNT FLUSH W/ EDGE OF FACE FRAME

SIDE-MOUNT DRAWER GUIDE

Characteristics of Drawer Guides

The principal differences among drawer guides are their capacity, their extension and both their appearance when the drawer is open and their method of attachment.

Capacity—Drawer guides must be strong enough to handle the loads placed in the drawers and durable enough to withstand thousands of uses. Guides are rated for the weight they will carry. The expected use of the drawer should be matched to guide capacity. Light-duty guides are rated to carry approximately 25 lb. to 35 lb., medium-duty guides are rated at 75 lb. and heavy-duty guides are rated for up to 250 lb.

Extension—Standard guides allow the drawer to open only 80% of its depth. This extension is similar to that of traditional drawers on wooden guides and does not usually cause problems in reaching items at the back of the drawer. To allow a drawer to be fully pulled out, full-extension guides are available. These guides are especially useful for file drawers, where stored material needs to be lifted out vertically. One problem with full-extension guides is that, because of the inclusion of a third element to allow for the longer extension, the drawers tend to wobble from side to side more than drawers on standard guides do.

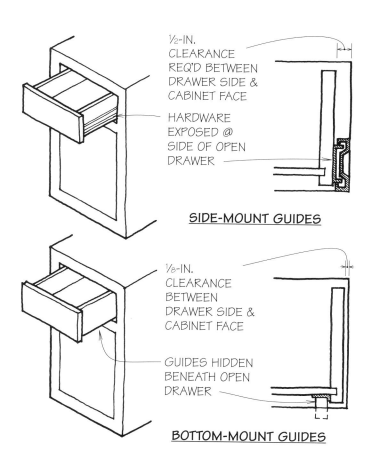

½-IN. CLEARANCE REQ'D BETWEEN DRAWER SIDE & CABINET FACE

HARDWARE EXPOSED @ SIDE OF OPEN DRAWER

SIDE-MOUNT GUIDES

⅛-IN. CLEARANCE BETWEEN DRAWER SIDE & CABINET FACE

GUIDES HIDDEN BENEATH OPEN DRAWER

BOTTOM-MOUNT GUIDES

(A) CABINET HARDWARE
DRAWER GUIDES

The earliest metal cabinet hinges were wrought-iron strap hinges for inset doors. These simple hinges were mounted flat on the surface of the cabinet. By comparison, modern cabinet hinges are extremely varied and complex. Cabinet hinges will now close the doors themselves, can be completely concealed and can be adjusted in three directions for alignment.

Opening and Closing the Door

The following functional characteristics should be carefully considered when selecting hinges.

Self-closing hinge—This modern feature of cabinet hinges spring-closes the cabinet door when it is within 28° from being closed. When it is open beyond 30°, the self-closer does not function, allowing the door to be left open. The self-closing feature eliminates the need for catches (described below). Most cabinet hinges are available with the self-closing feature.

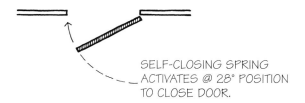

SELF-CLOSING SPRING ACTIVATES @ 28° POSITION TO CLOSE DOOR.

Catches—Catches hold in a closed position cabinet doors that are not self-closing. Catches have two components, one mounted on the door and one mounted on the cabinet case. These components, locked together when the cabinet door is closed, are usually of the friction type or the magnetic type.

Touch latch—This is a special category of catch that allows a cabinet door to be opened by applying pressure to the face of the door. The pressure releases a spring-loaded mechanism that pops the door open sufficiently to grab the edge. When the door is closed, it must be pushed in, thus reloading the spring mechanism. Touch latches eliminate the need for pulls and can be mounted on any type of door.

Adjustability

The amount of adjustability built into a hinge design is usually only important to the cabinetmaker, not the user or owner of the hinge. Adjustability is especially important for cabinet doors that must align precisely for appearance, such as flush-overlay or inset doors. Some hinges have full adjustment in three dimensions (concealed), some in two dimensions (knife) and some have no adjustment at all (butt).

Door Swing

Until the recent introduction of the concealed hinge, all cabinet door hinges allowed cabinet doors to open fully (180°).

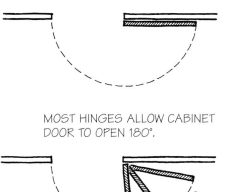

MOST HINGES ALLOW CABINET DOOR TO OPEN 180°.

STANDARD CONCEALED HINGE OPENS 95° TO 125°.

MOST EXPENSIVE CONCEALED HINGE OPENS 170°.

Because of their complexity, most concealed hinges open only from 95° to 125° (some open to 170°). Until people get used to this limited door swing, cabinet doors with concealed hinges will be overstressed by being forced beyond their designed limits.

The chart below lists the most common cabinet hinges in relation to their functional characteristics. The functions of these hinges are described on this page, and the hinges themselves are described on the next page.

HINGE TYPE	FUNCTION		
	Self-closing option	Door swing	Adjustability
Face-mount	yes	180°	no
Knife	yes	180°	2-way
Concealed	yes	95° 125° 170°	3-way
Wraparound	yes	180°	1-way
Butt	no	180°	no

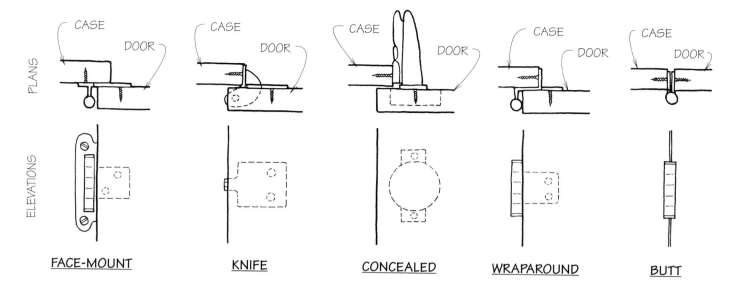

PLANS					
ELEVATIONS					
FACE-MOUNT	**KNIFE**	**CONCEALED**	**WRAPAROUND**	**BUTT**

There are many types of cabinet hinge, each one being unique and having distinct functional capabilities. These hinges must fit the door edge (see chart below)

| HINGE TYPE | DOOR EDGE | | | |
	Flush overlay	Reveal overlay	Lipped	Inset
Face-mount		✔	✔	
Knife	✔	✔	✔	
Concealed	✔	✔		✔
Wraparound		✔	✔	
Butt				✔

and must be sized to carry the door's weight over thousands of operations. Cabinet door hinges not only support the door's weight but also keep it aligned with the cabinet face. Very tall doors require more hinges. The chart below specifies hinge requirements according to door height and weight.

No. of hinges	2	3	4
Max. height of door	36 in.	66 in.	80 in.
Max. weight of door	15 lb.	30 lb.	45 lb.

Selection of Hinges

The hinge types listed below are commonly used in residential and commercial cabinets. The first three are most prevalent, but all are readily available through hardware distributors. The selection of exposed hinge types is often limited by the availability of finishes.

Face-mount—One leaf of the face-mount hinge attaches to the face of the cabinet case, usually with two screws, while the other is attached to the rear of the cabinet door. These hinges were extremely popular until the advent of the concealed hinge.

Knife—Only a small pivot point between the two leaves of the knife hinge is visible in a kerf at the edge of the cabinet door.

Concealed—Concealed hinges are fully concealed when the door is closed. In addition to full concealment, a primary advantage of this type is built-in adjustability in three dimensions. The most recent editions include a feature that allows doors to be unclipped from the cabinet without tools. Disadvantages of the concealed hinge include its complexity, which makes operation somewhat sloppy and failure more likely, and the fact that most versions do not allow doors to open more than 125°. A more expensive and complicated version allows 170° of swing, but only with even more sloppiness than in the standard concealed hinge.

Wraparound—Both leaves of the wraparound hinge are concealed in the gap between door and cabinet, and only the barrel of the hinge is exposed.

Butt—Butt hinges are attached to mortises in cabinet and door so that only the barrel of the hinge is exposed. Butt hinges are appropriate only for inset doors. They are not adjustable (except by shimming or slight shifting in screw holes), thus making precise fitting of doors difficult and time-consuming.

(A) **CABINET HARDWARE**
HINGE TYPES

Specialized hardware for particular situations can add convenience to and enhance the appearance of cabinets. Most specialized hardware requires extra clearance and therefore comes with some loss in available cabinet volume. Many types of may require a door edge that is different from the rest of the cabinet doors in a particular installation (see 115).

Most mechanisms discussed below are made of metal but may also be simplified and custom-made entirely of wood, thus saving hardware costs and space but making operation more delicate. Following is a discussion of the most useful and commonly requested specialized hardware.

Sliding Doors

Sliding doors in cabinets are guided by tracks at both top and bottom of the door opening. The principal advantage of sliding cabinet doors is that they do not swing into the room. The disadvantages are that the system requires two doors side by side, only one of which may be open at a time, and that the track hardware can be unsightly and make it more difficult to clean the bottom shelf.

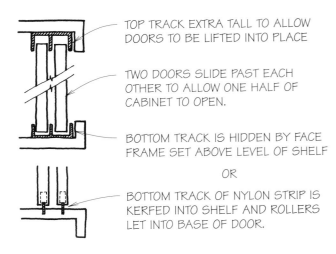

TOP TRACK EXTRA TALL TO ALLOW DOORS TO BE LIFTED INTO PLACE

TWO DOORS SLIDE PAST EACH OTHER TO ALLOW ONE HALF OF CABINET TO OPEN.

BOTTOM TRACK IS HIDDEN BY FACE FRAME SET ABOVE LEVEL OF SHELF

OR

BOTTOM TRACK OF NYLON STRIP IS KERFED INTO SHELF AND ROLLERS LET INTO BASE OF DOOR.

Pocket Doors

Also called a flipper door, a pocket door opens by pivoting outward, then sliding into the cabinet. This feature requires that pocket doors have an inset edge detail. These doors are commonly used at countertop level in kitchens for appliance garage doors or to conceal the electronic equipment in TV or stereo cabinets. The hardware may be mounted to make the door rotate up or to the side. For a cleaner appearance, the open door should fit fully into the cabinet. The primary disadvantage of the pocket door is that it takes up space inside of the cabinet, limiting room for the equipment it is designed to conceal.

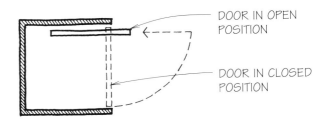

DOOR IN OPEN POSITION

DOOR IN CLOSED POSITION

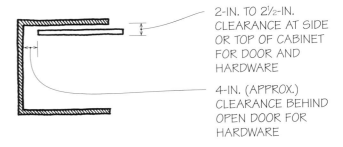

2-IN. TO 2½-IN. CLEARANCE AT SIDE OR TOP OF CABINET FOR DOOR AND HARDWARE

4-IN. (APPROX.) CLEARANCE BEHIND OPEN DOOR FOR HARDWARE

Tambour Door

Like the pocket door, the tambour door is most frequently used on appliance garages or TV/stereo cabinets. The door consists of a series of ½-in. wide slats joined together on a flexible backing that rolls into the cabinet as for a roll-top desk. Space for the door is required at both the top and back of the cabinet.

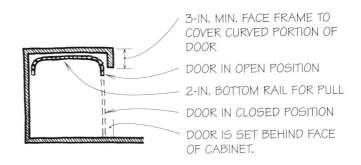

3-IN. MIN. FACE FRAME TO COVER CURVED PORTION OF DOOR

DOOR IN OPEN POSITION

2-IN. BOTTOM RAIL FOR PULL

DOOR IN CLOSED POSITION

DOOR IS SET BEHIND FACE OF CABINET.

Tambour doors do not require specialized hardware, and are generally custom-made in the cabinet shop. The ends of the slats project at both sides of the cabinets into curved dadoes, which hold them in place and guide their operation. Aside from being difficult to match with other doors, the principal disadvantage of the tambour door is the space it requires inside the cabinet, especially at the top.

(A) SPECIALIZED HARDWARE

DOORS

Specialized shelving units are available for particular situations, such as corners or where roll-out shelves are desired.

Lazy Susan Shelf

Mounted in the inside corner of a base cabinet, the lazy susan shelf rotates on a central spine to make stored items more accessible. The lazy susan is most appropriate when two cabinet partitions are located approximately 12 in. to 16 in. from the inside corner of the cabinet.

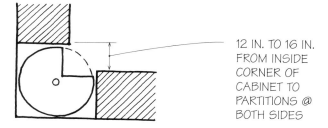

12 IN. TO 16 IN. FROM INSIDE CORNER OF CABINET TO PARTITIONS @ BOTH SIDES

The cabinet door on a lazy susan can be independent of the rotating shelf mechanism or integral with it. If independent, a bifold door or a simple hinged door allows the lazy susan door to match the other cabinet doors and lie flat against the cabinet when open. If other cabinet doors in the installation are inset, an

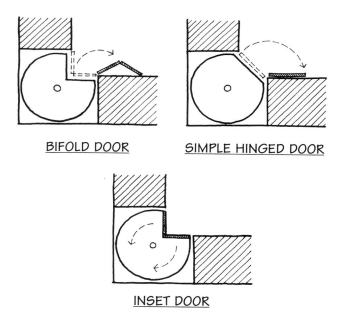

BIFOLD DOOR   **SIMPLE HINGED DOOR**

INSET DOOR

inset door would be used. The drawback of an inset door is that when items fall off the shelves, the entire assembly is more likely to jam as the rotating doors force items against the cabinet walls. Lazy susan shelves are available in coated wire, plastic or metal, or they can be made of plywood in the shop.

Quarter-Turn Shelf

An alternative to the lazy susan, the quarter-turn shelf opens in only one direction and rotates only 90°, compared to 360° for the lazy susan. The quarter-turn is most appropriate where one cabinet partition is from 15 in. to 24 in. from the corner and another partition is at the corner.

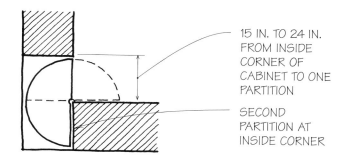

15 IN. TO 24 IN. FROM INSIDE CORNER OF CABINET TO ONE PARTITION

SECOND PARTITION AT INSIDE CORNER

The quarter-turn shelf has the advantage over the lazy susan in that it is easy to install a drawer above the mechanism. A disadvantage to the quarter-turn shelf is that half the shelf remains behind the face of the cabinet when the shelves are rotated.

Roll-Out Shelf

Essentially a drawer with no front and low sides, a roll-out shelf is usually mounted behind a cabinet door. Roll-out shelves are commonly used to store large items because they provide the ease of access of a drawer without the visual complexity of a bank of drawers. Very wide and flexible roll-out shelves can be hidden behind a pair of cabinet doors.

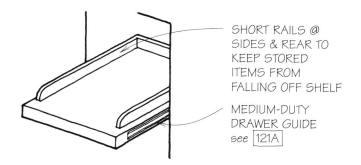

SHORT RAILS @ SIDES & REAR TO KEEP STORED ITEMS FROM FALLING OFF SHELF

MEDIUM-DUTY DRAWER GUIDE see 121A

The disadvantage of a roll-out shelf is that two motions—opening the cabinet door and pulling out the shelf—are required to reach an item. A drawer could accomplish the same task with only one motion; on the other hand, items stored at the front of a roll-out shelf can be reached easily by merely opening the cabinet door. Another disadvantage is its expense; it costs as much as a drawer and a door combined.

A **SPECIALIZED HARDWARE**
SHELVES

BLOCKING @ TOP & BOTTOM OF WALL CABINETS

CABINET/WALL (OR CEILING) CONNECTION
see 127B

CABINET/FLOOR CONNECTION
see 127A

FINISHED WALL SURFACE

WALL CABINETS ATTACHED TO BLOCKING THROUGH BACK OF CABINET

WIRES FOR UNDER-CABINET LIGHTING STUBBED ABOVE BOTTOM SHELF

BASE CABINETS ATTACHED TO STUDS THROUGH NAILER

TOE KICK ATTACHED TO BASE CABINET TO FLOOR
see 127A

How finishes are applied to cabinets and how cabinets connect to the structure and to each other affects not only the design of the cabinet but the overall quality of the building. Understanding the principles of cabinet installation will help the cabinet designer, the cabinetmaker and the building contractor communicate effectively to produce a high-quality installation.

Preparation for installing cabinets begins before finish materials are applied to the walls. Blocking should be installed at critical locations to support cabinets, especially wall cabinets. Wires for cabinet lights and plugs should be stubbed out at appropriate locations. Stud locations should be marked on finish wall surfaces to facilitate attaching base cabinets.

Cabinets are usually installed after walls are finished and painted. This minimizes the difficulty of painting the edge between cabinet and wall.

Finish floors may be installed either before or after cabinets. The sequence depends on the type of floor and the detail at the base of the cabinet. In general, it is easiest to finish the flooring before installing the cabinets. When it becomes necessary to install cabinets before flooring, the installation of the toe kick alone (without cabinet case) will usually solve the sequencing problem and save the cabinet from being damaged by floor installation (see 127A).

When cabinets are ganged together, such as when modular cabinets are connected or when custom cabinets meet in a corner, two approaches provide adequate solutions. The more common is simply to screw the cabinets together and allow the seam to be exposed. This method is effective because the edges of cabinets are always true and can be made plumb. An alternative approach is to cover the seam between the cabinet sections with a small trim strip.

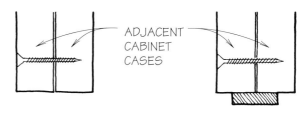

ADJACENT CABINET CASES

EXPOSED SEAM   **TRIMMED SEAM**

The manufacturers of built-in appliances such as ranges, dishwashers, ovens and trash compactors specify the size of openings required in cabinets and provide trim packages to cover the gap between cabinet and appliance. Freestanding appliances such as refrigerators and ranges are generally located adjacent to a cabinet that is left unfinished at the end.

 CABINET INSTALLATION

Base cabinets are usually built with a separate toe kick attached to the bottom of the case. This toe kick supports the case above the floor and provides a toe space. The case/kick assembly is generally attached to the floor diagonally through the face of the toe kick. The toe kick will later be covered with base trim (see 162-63) or coved flooring (see 77).

The toe kick alone can be installed first. This allows floors such as tile and coved resilient flooring—best installed with toe kick in place—to be installed before base cabinets. A long single-piece toe kick, installed independently, can also be used to align a series of frameless cabinets.

An alternative to the toe kick is the projecting countertop, which provides the same amount of space for toes while not making the cabinet appear to be floating above the floor. The projecting countertop does limit access to the top drawer somewhat, but this can be overcome with full extension drawer guides.

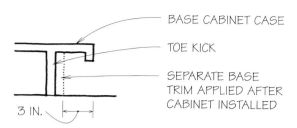

BASE CABINET CASE
TOE KICK
SEPARATE BASE TRIM APPLIED AFTER CABINET INSTALLED
3 IN.

STANDARD TOE SPACE

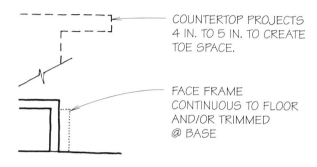

COUNTERTOP PROJECTS 4 IN. TO 5 IN. TO CREATE TOE SPACE.
FACE FRAME CONTINUOUS TO FLOOR AND/OR TRIMMED @ BASE

PROJECTING COUNTERTOP

 A   CABINET/FLOOR CONNECTION

Wherever any cabinet meets a wall or ceiling, there is the possibility of a significant gap caused by irregularities in the wall surface. There are several strategies to minimize this potential gap.

For paint-grade cabinets, the joint between cabinet and wall may simply be caulked. For stain-grade cabinets, the gap may be covered with a small piece of trim applied to the surface of the cabinet. The thinness of the trim will allow it to conform to most irregularities in the wall. Another strategy for stain-grade cabinets is to scribe the vertical edge of the cabinet so that it conforms to the irregularities of the wall. This method is more time-consuming but provides a cleaner, more finished appearance.

For frameless cabinets, a reveal strip set behind the face of the cabinet gives a trimmed appearance while allowing the cabinet to be independent of the wall surface. The reveal strip can be caulked or scribed to the wall depending on finishes.

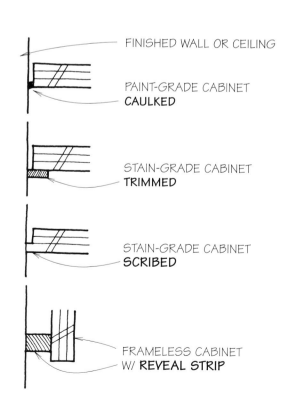

FINISHED WALL OR CEILING
PAINT-GRADE CABINET **CAULKED**
STAIN-GRADE CABINET **TRIMMED**
STAIN-GRADE CABINET **SCRIBED**
FRAMELESS CABINET W/ **REVEAL STRIP**

 B   CABINET/WALL OR CEILING CONNECTION

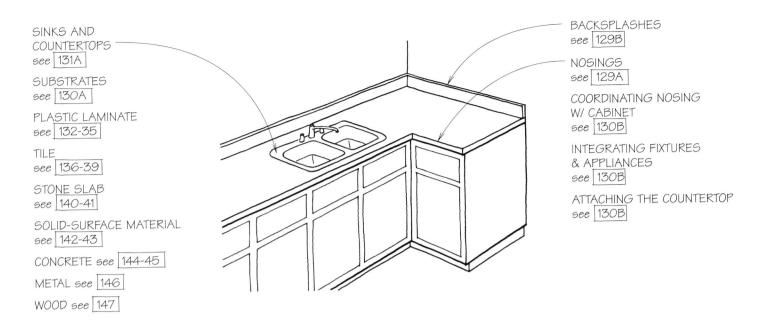

SINKS AND
COUNTERTOPS
see 131A

SUBSTRATES
see 130A

PLASTIC LAMINATE
see 132-35

TILE
see 136-39

STONE SLAB
see 140-41

SOLID-SURFACE MATERIAL
see 142-43

CONCRETE see 144-45

METAL see 146

WOOD see 147

BACKSPLASHES
see 129B

NOSINGS
see 129A

COORDINATING NOSING
W/ CABINET
see 130B

INTEGRATING FIXTURES
& APPLIANCES
see 130B

ATTACHING THE COUNTERTOP
see 130B

Commonly found in both residential and commercial construction, countertops require careful material selection and detailing to provide a functional and beautiful work surface. The kitchen countertop is the most difficult to design because it is frequently exposed to moisture, heat and bacteria, and it must accommodate sinks and appliances. Bathroom and laundry counters must be resistant to moisture, and desktop surfaces designed for comfort.

Although the countertop in a finished installation appears to be integral with the base cabinets, it is usually made of a different material and is typically built separately, often spanning multiple cabinet units. A countertop assembly is made of a number of components: the countertop surface, which is often attached to a structural substrate, the nosing at the front edge of the countertop and the backsplash against the wall. Although all these components are often made of the same material, there is an opportunity to combine different materials to take advantage of the best qualities of each. The table below compares various countertop materials in terms of function, cost and appearance.

Although countertops are usually supported by base cabinets, which are installed first, they can also rest on wall brackets, be supported by legs, or span between base cabinets.

	Plastic laminate	Ceramic tile	Stone tile	Stone slab	Solid surface	Stainless steel	Wood	Concrete
Ease of cleaning	excellent	poor	poor	excellent	excellent	excellent	fair	good
Resistance to water	excellent	fair	fair	excellent	excellent	excellent	poor	good
Resistance to staining	good	fair	fair	fair	good	excellent	poor	fair
Resistance to scratches	fair	good	excellent	excellent	good	good	poor	fair
Resistance to heat	poor	excellent	excellent	excellent	excellent	excellent	poor	good
Appearance of seams	fair	excellent	excellent	fair	good	good	good	excellent
Cost	low	medium	med/high	high	high	high	medium	low

A COUNTERTOPS
INTRODUCTION

Countertop nosing is the outer edge of a countertop. Nosing typically extends 1½ in.beyond the face of the cabinet, typically 1½ in., for aesthetic reasons and to prevent spills from dripping down the cabinet face. Nosings are sometimes as thin as the countertop itself, but more often they are thickened for strength and aesthetic reasons. Monolithic countertop materials can be exposed at the edge to make a simple nosing but are often thickened by attaching a strip of material the same or similar to the underside of the nosing. Countertops made of thin material laminated to a substrate usually require a nosing to cover the exposed edges of the surface material and the substrate. The nosing can be the same material as the countertop surface wrapped over the edge of the substrate, or of another material, commonly vinyl, metal or wood, applied to the substrate.

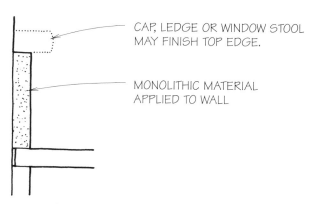

MONOLITHIC APPLIED BACKSPLASH

CAP, LEDGE OR WINDOW STOOL MAY FINISH TOP EDGE.

MONOLITHIC MATERIAL APPLIED TO WALL

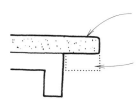

MONOLITHIC COUNTERTOP EXPOSED AT EDGE TO FORM SIMPLE NOSING

A THICKER PROFILE MAY BE OBTAINED BY LAMINATING AN ADDITIONAL STRIP OF MATERIAL.

MONOLITHIC NOSINGS

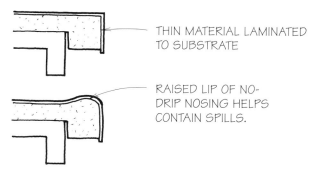

THIN MATERIAL LAMINATED TO SUBSTRATE

RAISED LIP OF NO-DRIP NOSING HELPS CONTAIN SPILLS.

WRAPPED NOSINGS

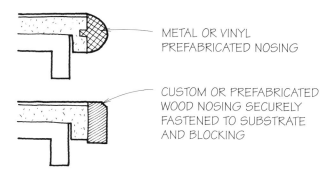

METAL OR VINYL PREFABRICATED NOSING

CUSTOM OR PREFABRICATED WOOD NOSING SECURELY FASTENED TO SUBSTRATE AND BLOCKING

APPLIED NOSINGS

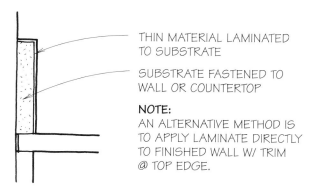

THIN MATERIAL LAMINATED TO SUBSTRATE

SUBSTRATE FASTENED TO WALL OR COUNTERTOP

NOTE:
AN ALTERNATIVE METHOD IS TO APPLY LAMINATE DIRECTLY TO FINISHED WALL W/ TRIM @ TOP EDGE.

LAMINATED APPLIED BACKSPLASH

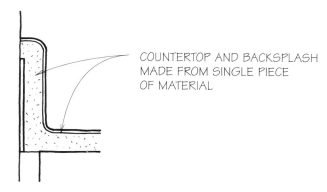

COUNTERTOP AND BACKSPLASH MADE FROM SINGLE PIECE OF MATERIAL

INTEGRAL BACKSPLASH

The joint between the back of the countertop and the wall is usually covered with a backsplash, which also serves to protect the finish wall surface from the occasional splash or abrasion. The selection of backsplash material should be carefully coordinated with countertop and wall materials to provide tight joints with the countertop and the wall. To be merely functional, the backsplash needs to extend up the wall just a few inches, but it is often extended higher for aesthetic reasons. With careful detailing, the backsplash can be integrated with a ledge or window stool.

 A NOSINGS

 B BACKSPLASHES

Although a few monolithic finish materials are inherently strong and capable of spanning between partitions of base cabinets, most surfaces require a rigid substrate for support. The rigid substrate for a countertop is typically ¾-in. solid sheet material, either plywood or particleboard, depending on the type of finish surface. In addition, cementitious backer board or a cement mortar bed is sometimes used in combination with a rigid substrate.

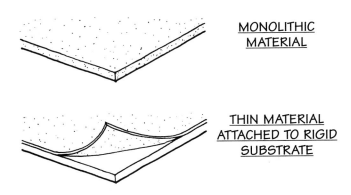

MONOLITHIC MATERIAL

THIN MATERIAL ATTACHED TO RIGID SUBSTRATE

Plywood is the strongest composite wood product and the most resistant to deterioration resulting from moisture penetration, but it lacks a surface sufficiently smooth for some countertop materials.

Particleboard and *MDF* are very smooth substrate surfaces and are required for the application of finishes such as high-pressure decorative laminate (see 132-35). Neither performs very well when exposed to moisture, so careful detailing and waterproofing are essential.

Often, countertop design dictates joining two or more sections of substrate together. A reinforcing plate centered on the joint and fastened to both sections from below will provide a tight, lasting joint. Alternatively, a spline or biscuits can be used to join the two sections.

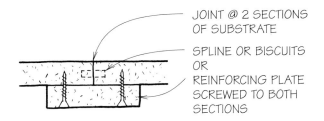

JOINT @ 2 SECTIONS OF SUBSTRATE

SPLINE OR BISCUITS OR

REINFORCING PLATE SCREWED TO BOTH SECTIONS

JOINING TWO SECTIONS OF SUBSTRATE

Attaching the Countertop

A prefinished countertop such as postformed plastic laminate (see 133A) must be attached with screws through the cabinet case from below. Although the substrate alone is sometimes fastened to the cabinet case from above, it too is best attached from below. This maintains a smooth substrate top and allows for easier replacement.

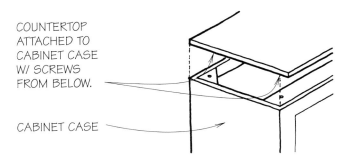

COUNTERTOP ATTACHED TO CABINET CASE W/ SCREWS FROM BELOW.

CABINET CASE

Coordinating Nosing w/ Cabinet

Cabinet dimensions should be coordinated with the nosing (see 130A). Nosing thickness will dictate drawer and door height in a frameless cabinet. On a face-frame cabinet, nosing thickness will affect the exposed dimension of the face-frame top rail.

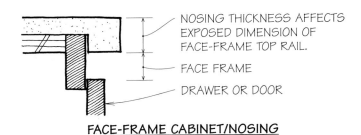

NOSING THICKNESS AFFECTS EXPOSED DIMENSION OF FACE-FRAME TOP RAIL.

FACE FRAME

DRAWER OR DOOR

FACE-FRAME CABINET/NOSING

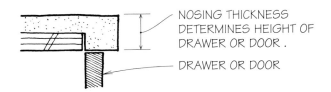

NOSING THICKNESS DETERMINES HEIGHT OF DRAWER OR DOOR .

DRAWER OR DOOR

FRAMELESS CABINET/NOSING

Integrating Fixtures and Appliances

Freestanding countertops are often designed to accommodate sinks, cutting boards and appliances and usually terminate where they are to be inserted. Appliances are accommodated by stopping the countertop flush with the end of the cabinet. The countertop and backsplash should have a finished edge adjacent to the appliance.

(A) SUBSTRATES

(B) COUNTERTOP/CABINET DETAILS

Sinks are available in many sizes and a range of materials, including cast iron, enameled steel, stainless steel, ceramic, plastic and composites (solid surface). There are several types of sink installations, each associated with particular materials.

Drop-in Sinks

Drop-in sinks are the most common and least expensive option. A hole for the sink is cut out of the countertop and the sink is dropped in. A bead of silicone sealant under the edge of the rim provides protection against water penetration. Because the sink projects above the counter, liquid cannot flow into the sink, making cleaning the countertop more difficult. Drop-in installations are performed in two possible ways.

Self-rimming—By far the most common drop-in sink, the self-rimming sink has an integral rim that rests on the countertop. The joint between sink and countertop is generally protected by a sealant. Self-rimming sinks made of heavy materials such as enameled cast iron are held in place by gravity, while lighter materials such as stainless steel require clips on the underside of the countertop to hold the sink down tight.

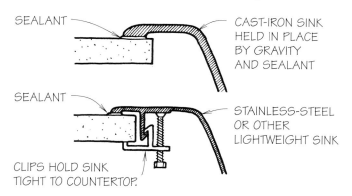

SELF-RIMMING SINKS

Separate rim—A separate stainless-steel rim covers the joint between sink and countertop. A separate-rim sink must be sealed at both the joint between countertop and tim, and the joint between rim and sink. Stainless-steel rims are generally used with cast-iron and enameled steel sinks.

SEPARATE-RIM SINK

Flush-Mount Sinks

Specifically designed for use with tile countertops, the flush-mount sink rests on the tile setting bed, allowing the tile surface and the top of the sink to be flush. A grout joint fills the gap between tile and sink.

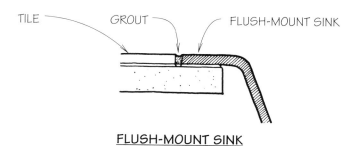

FLUSH-MOUNT SINK

Undermount Sinks

The undermount sink is mounted from under the countertop. This arrangement requires that the edge of the countertop opening be finished. An undermount sink can be supported by clips, by the substrate or by a separate frame built within the cabinet case. It is important to consider the ease of removing the sink, should it need to be replaced.

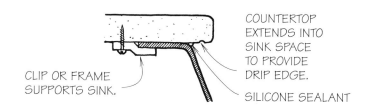

UNDERMOUNT SINK

Integral Sinks

If the sink and countertop are made of the same material, they may be joined to make an integral unit. Solid surface material (see 142-43) and metal (see 146) are commonly used to make integral installations. Integral sinks perform best because they eliminate the joint between sink and countertop, providing watertightness and exceptional cleaning ease.

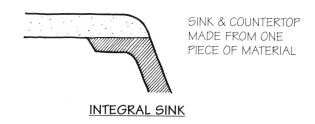

INTEGRAL SINK

 SINKS & COUNTERTOPS

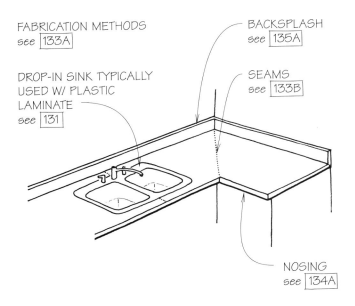

FABRICATION METHODS
see 133A

DROP-IN SINK TYPICALLY
USED W/ PLASTIC
LAMINATE
see 131

BACKSPLASH
see 135A

SEAMS
see 133B

NOSING
see 134A

High-pressure decorative laminate, more commonly called plastic laminate, is the most common countertop surface. It is available in a multitude of colors and patterns, and it is inexpensive and easy to install. Although very easy to maintain, plastic laminate has a low resistance to scratches and heat, and will wear out with heavy use.

Plastic laminate consists of a phenolic backing, a color and pattern sheet covering the backing, and a clear protective coating of melamine resin. The phenolic backing is layered kraft paper saturated with phenolic resin and bonded under high pressure.

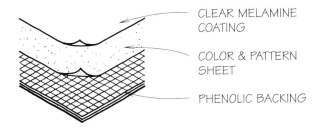

CLEAR MELAMINE
COATING

COLOR & PATTERN
SHEET

PHENOLIC BACKING

STANDARD PLASTIC LAMINATE

Whenever the edge of standard plastic laminate is exposed, the dark brown kraft-paper core is visible and often detracts from its appearance, especially in light-colored laminates. Deep scratches will also expose the paper core.

A plastic laminate that is a solid color throughout its depth combats these problems. This type of laminate consists of many sheets of colored paper coated with melamine resin but without phenolic backing, producing a more brittle plastic laminate that costs three times as much as standard plastic laminate.

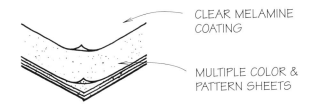

CLEAR MELAMINE
COATING

MULTIPLE COLOR &
PATTERN SHEETS

COLOR-INTEGRAL PLASTIC LAMINATE

Sizes and Grades
Plastic laminate is available in widths of 24 in., 30 in., 36 in., 48 in. and 60 in. and in lengths of 60 in., 72 in., 96 in., 120 in. and 144 in., depending on the pattern, color and manufacturer.

Plastic laminate is available in three grades:

Horizontal or standard grade—About $1/16$ in. thick (.050 in.), standard grade is the most common. It can be bent to approximately a 6-in. radius.

Vertical grade—About half the thickness (.028 in. typ., also .030 in., .032 in.) and much less expensive than standard grade, vertical-grade plastic laminate is used for facing cabinet cases and doors and drawers, and sometimes for backsplashes. It is fairly brittle.

Postforming grade—Used exclusively for postformed installations (see 133A), postforming-grade plastic laminate is slightly thinner than standard grade (.042 in.). The fibers in the phenolic backing run in only one direction to allow for easier forming.

Substrates
The two common substrates for plastic laminate are $3/4$-in. thick particleboard or medium-density fiberboard (MDF). Plywood, although it still appears occasionally, is unacceptable because it lacks uniformity, making flush seams in the plastic laminate difficult to achieve. In addition, defects in the plywood core can transmit through the surface of the plastic laminate, eventually causing cracks.

To maintain a flat countertop on unsupported areas over 6 sq. ft., a thin sheet of laminate, called a balancing sheet, is attached to the bottom of the substrate.

PLASTIC LAMINATE COUNTERTOPS

There are two methods of fabricating a plastic laminate countertop. The self-edged method uses separate pieces to form the horizontal surface, the nosing and the backsplash. The postformed method uses a single piece of laminate extending from the nosing to the backsplash. (For nosing details, see 130.)

Self-Edged Countertops

Consisting of several separate pieces, self-edged plastic laminate can be applied to a substrate in the field or in the shop. Oversized pieces of laminate are attached to the substrate and are trimmed flush with a router (see 134A). Seams between pieces are susceptible to water penetration. If standard plastic laminate is self-edged, the dark paper core is exposed at the edges. The self-edged method is inherently more flexible than other methods but is becoming less prevalent.

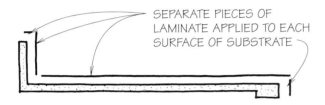

SEPARATE PIECES OF LAMINATE APPLIED TO EACH SURFACE OF SUBSTRATE

SELF-EDGED COUNTERTOP

Postformed Countertops

Postforming is a specialized process in which the substrate assembly, application of the laminate and forming of the curves are performed by a custom fabricator on an assembly line. Postforming-grade laminate, which bends to a tight radius, is molded to a substrate with heat to form a countertop that is seamless from backsplash to nosing (see 134B). The resulting long sections are cut in the shop or in the field, leaving an exposed end that is covered by an end cap (see 134D). Postformed countertops provide excellent water resistance and are becoming the most common low-cost installation method.

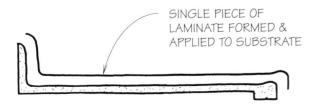

SINGLE PIECE OF LAMINATE FORMED & APPLIED TO SUBSTRATE

POSTFORMED COUNTERTOP

A — FABRICATION METHODS
PLASTIC LAMINATE COUNTERTOPS

The number of seams in a plastic-laminate countertop should be minimized. To reduce seam length in a self-edged installation, many installers prefer to locate the seam at the sink. The drawback to this approach is that the area around the sink has the most potential to experience standing water. When a seam is required at a corner, it can be either mitered or butted.

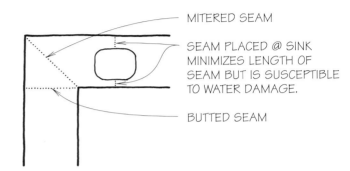

MITERED SEAM

SEAM PLACED @ SINK MINIMIZES LENGTH OF SEAM BUT IS SUSCEPTIBLE TO WATER DAMAGE.

BUTTED SEAM

SEAM PLACEMENT

When two sections of postformed countertop need to be joined at a corner, the sections are mitered (usually in the shop), glued in the field and pulled together tightly with joint connectors let into the underside of the substrate.

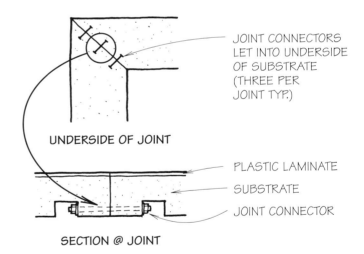

JOINT CONNECTORS LET INTO UNDERSIDE OF SUBSTRATE (THREE PER JOINT TYP.)

UNDERSIDE OF JOINT

PLASTIC LAMINATE
SUBSTRATE
JOINT CONNECTOR

SECTION @ JOINT

SEAM @ POSTFORMED COUNTERTOP

Adhesives

Plastic laminate is typically bonded to the substrate with contact cement. The most common type is solvent-based cement, which emits highly toxic fumes during installation. Epoxy adhesive is used primarily for bonding plastic laminate to impervious substrates such as steel.

B — SEAMS
PLASTIC LAMINATE COUNTERTOPS

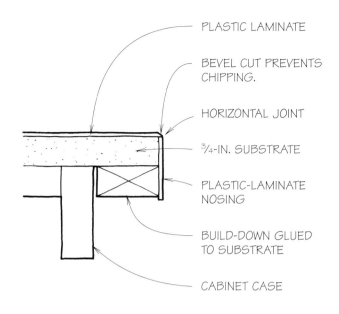

PLASTIC LAMINATE

BEVEL CUT PREVENTS CHIPPING.

HORIZONTAL JOINT

¾-IN. SUBSTRATE

PLASTIC-LAMINATE NOSING

BUILD-DOWN GLUED TO SUBSTRATE

CABINET CASE

NOTE:
PREFABRICATED NOSING IS AVAILABLE IN PLASTIC LAMINATE, WOOD, VINYL & SOLID PLASTIC.

 A **SELF-EDGED NOSING**
PLASTIC LAMINATE COUNTERTOP

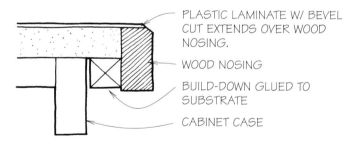

PLASTIC LAMINATE W/ BEVEL CUT EXTENDS OVER WOOD NOSING.

WOOD NOSING

BUILD-DOWN GLUED TO SUBSTRATE

CABINET CASE

PLASTIC LAMINATE OVER WOOD NOSING

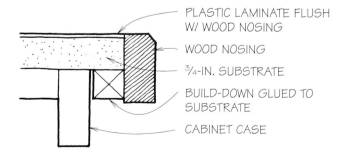

PLASTIC LAMINATE FLUSH W/ WOOD NOSING

WOOD NOSING

¾-IN. SUBSTRATE

BUILD-DOWN GLUED TO SUBSTRATE

CABINET CASE

PLASTIC LAMINATE FLUSH W/ WOOD NOSING

 **C** **WOOD NOSING**
PLASTIC LAMINATE COUNTERTOP

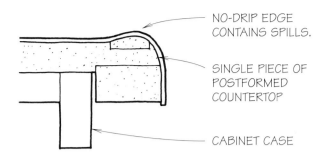

NO-DRIP EDGE CONTAINS SPILLS.

SINGLE PIECE OF POSTFORMED COUNTERTOP

CABINET CASE

NO-DRIP NOSING

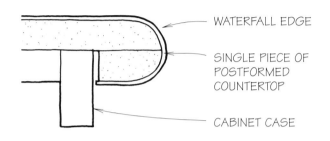

WATERFALL EDGE

SINGLE PIECE OF POSTFORMED COUNTERTOP

CABINET CASE

WATERFALL NOSING

 B **POSTFORMED NOSING**
PLASTIC LAMINATE COUNTERTOP

SELF-EDGED SIDESPLASH IS GLUED & SCREWED TO END IN FIELD SIMILAR TO 135A.

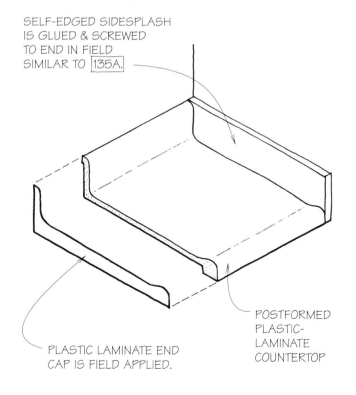

PLASTIC LAMINATE END CAP IS FIELD APPLIED.

POSTFORMED PLASTIC-LAMINATE COUNTERTOP

 D **POSTFORMED ENDS**
PLASTIC LAMINATE COUNTERTOP

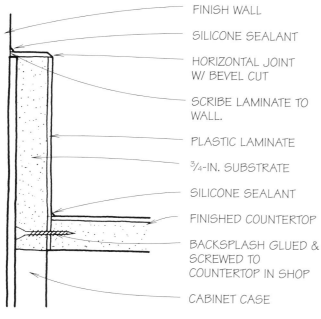

FINISH WALL

SILICONE SEALANT

HORIZONTAL JOINT
W/ BEVEL CUT

SCRIBE LAMINATE TO
WALL.

PLASTIC LAMINATE

¾-IN. SUBSTRATE

SILICONE SEALANT

FINISHED COUNTERTOP

BACKSPLASH GLUED &
SCREWED TO
COUNTERTOP IN SHOP

CABINET CASE

NOTE:
IF MOVEMENT OCCURS, COUNTERTOP & BACKSPLASH
MOVE TOGETHER AND A TIGHT JOINT IS MAINTAINED.

(A) **SHOP-APPLIED BACKSPLASH**
SELF-EDGED

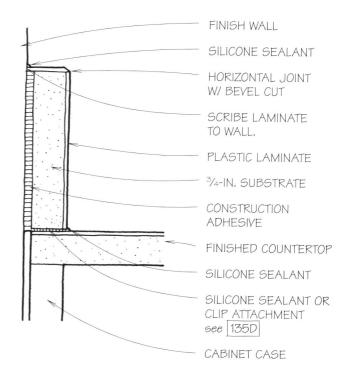

FINISH WALL

SILICONE SEALANT

HORIZONTAL JOINT
W/ BEVEL CUT

SCRIBE LAMINATE
TO WALL.

PLASTIC LAMINATE

¾-IN. SUBSTRATE

CONSTRUCTION
ADHESIVE

FINISHED COUNTERTOP

SILICONE SEALANT

SILICONE SEALANT OR
CLIP ATTACHMENT
see | 135D |

CABINET CASE

(B) **FIELD-APPLIED BACKSPLASH**
SELF-EDGED

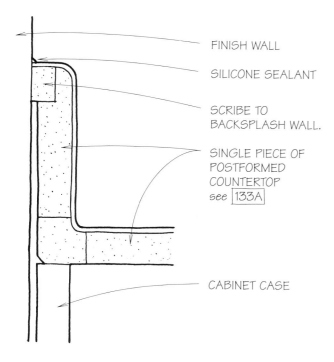

FINISH WALL

SILICONE SEALANT

SCRIBE TO
BACKSPLASH WALL.

SINGLE PIECE OF
POSTFORMED
COUNTERTOP
see | 133A |

CABINET CASE

(C) **POSTFORMED BACKSPLASH**

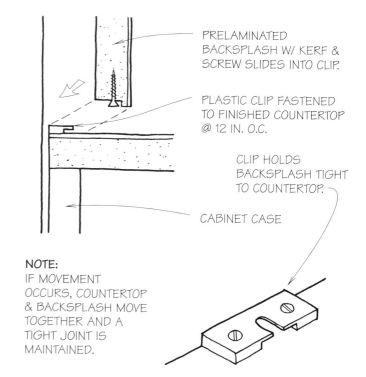

PRELAMINATED
BACKSPLASH W/ KERF &
SCREW SLIDES INTO CLIP.

PLASTIC CLIP FASTENED
TO FINISHED COUNTERTOP
@ 12 IN. O.C.

CLIP HOLDS
BACKSPLASH TIGHT
TO COUNTERTOP.

CABINET CASE

NOTE:
IF MOVEMENT
OCCURS, COUNTERTOP
& BACKSPLASH MOVE
TOGETHER AND A
TIGHT JOINT IS
MAINTAINED.

(D) **FIELD-APPLIED BACKSPLASH**
CLIP ATTACHMENT

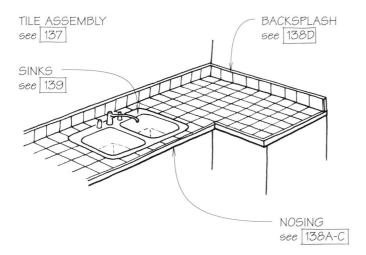

TILE ASSEMBLY see 137

SINKS see 139

BACKSPLASH see 138D

NOSING see 138A-C

A large, continuous piece of tile would make an excellent countertop, but that is not the nature of tile, which instead must be applied in many small pieces with grout joints between. These grout joints make a tile countertop difficult to clean and provide many places for water to enter the assembly. Tile is often avoided in kitchens, where staining of grout joints is more likely and the hard surface is likely to damage fragile dishes and cookware, or to be damaged itself. Nevertheless, tile is not uncommon as a countertop material. Renowned for its beauty, tile is even more popular for backsplashes where performance is not as critical.

Types of Tile
Stone and ceramic are the most common types of tiles used for countertop applications.

Stone tile—Tile is available in a variety of stone materials (see 140-41). For countertops in damp locations, the use of porous stones such as slate and limestone is generally avoided.

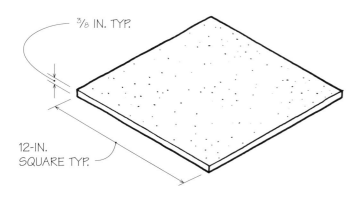

STONE TILE

The most common size of stone tile used for countertops is ⅜ in. thick and 12 in. square. Larger sizes are available in many stone materials. Stone tile trim shapes are not available, so special pieces must be cut on site.

Ceramic tile—For countertops in damp locations such as kitchens and baths, ceramic tile should preferably be impervious or vitreous and is generally glazed. Unglazed tile that is more absorptive should be reserved for countertops that receive little or no contact with moisture. Darker-colored glazes such as cobalt blue and black and glossy glazes are more susceptible to scratching and less durable than light-colored and matte glazes.

Ceramic tiles typically range in thickness from ¼ in. to ⅜ in. Many trim shapes are commonly available (see 26-27). Special trim tiles called V-cap tiles can form a no-drip nosing. V-cap tiles are mitered at the inside and outside corners. Quarter-round tiles are frequently used for undermount sink installations (see 139C). Special quarter-round tiles are also available for inside corners.

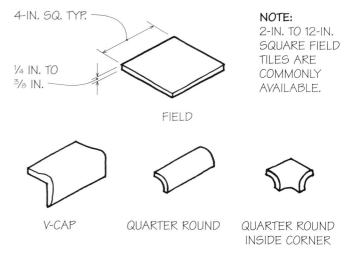

FIELD

NOTE: 2-IN. TO 12-IN. SQUARE FIELD TILES ARE COMMONLY AVAILABLE.

V-CAP QUARTER ROUND QUARTER ROUND INSIDE CORNER

CERAMIC TILE

Tile Modules
The careful coordination of countertop size with tile module is recommended to avoid having to cut tile. This is especially true for islands and peninsulas where the tile borders three or more edges. In addition, the placement of sinks should be coordinated with the tile module. Special attention should be paid to stone tile countertops because of the large tile size and lack of trim shapes. For ceramic tile countertops, the range of sizes and availability of trim shapes allows for easier coordination of countertop to tile module.

 TILE COUNTERTOPS

Setting Beds

The two types of setting beds for tile are the traditional thick-bed method and the more common thinbed method. The thick-bed method is more durable, but it is more labor intensive and costly.

Thick-bed—With the thick-bed method, a portland cement/mortar setting bed that is ¾ in. to 1 in. thick is usually floated over a 15-lb. tar-paper curing membrane stapled to ¾-in. exterior plywood and reinforced with 1-in. wire mesh. Weak spots such as interior corners and the area around the sink and at other cutouts may need to be further reinforced similar to concrete countertops (see 144).

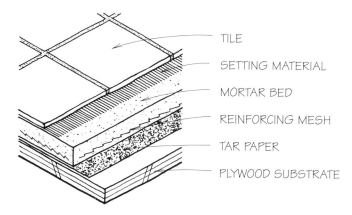

TILE
SETTING MATERIAL
MORTAR BED
REINFORCING MESH
TAR PAPER
PLYWOOD SUBSTRATE

THICK-BED ASSEMBLY

Thinbed—With the thinbed method, ¼-in. to ¾-in. cementitious backer board is laminated with thinset adhesive and fastened with screws to a ¾-in. plywood substrate. Joints between sheets of backer board should be covered with fiberglass-mesh tape and filled with thinset adhesive to prevent any movement in the substrate from telegraphing through the joints and cracking the tile.

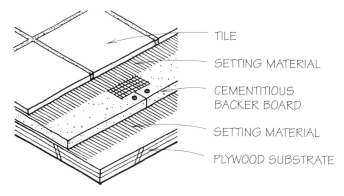

TILE
SETTING MATERIAL
CEMENTITIOUS BACKER BOARD
SETTING MATERIAL
PLYWOOD SUBSTRATE

THINBED ASSEMBLY
W/ CEMENTITIOUS BACKER BOARD

TILE COUNTERTOP ASSEMBLY

A less desirable but sometimes acceptable installation method for countertops that receive light use is to adhere the tiles directly to plywood. Because plywood will expand and contract with changes in moisture content, it should be avoided in countertops that might get wet, and the plywood should be sealed completely with a penetrating sealer prior to setting the tile.

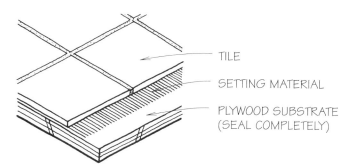

TILE
SETTING MATERIAL
PLYWOOD SUBSTRATE (SEAL COMPLETELY)

THINBED ASSEMBLY W/ PLYWOOD

Setting Materials

Tiles are usually adhered to the setting bed with a thin (approximately ⅛ in.) layer of setting material. The most commonly used setting material for countertops is thinset portland-cement mortar. The three common types of thinset mortar are dry-set mortar, latex mortar and epoxy mortar. Dry-set mortar has excellent water resistance, while latex mortar provides increased flexibility. Epoxy mortar has increased bond strength and is the recommended setting material for use on a plywood setting bed. Organic adhesive, also called mastic, is the least expensive and easiest-to-use setting material, but it is not recommended for damp or wet installations since it tends to lose its bond strength when it is constantly exposed to moisture.

Grout

It is important to use the right grout for countertops since the surface is horizontal and may be exposed to water, food and liquids capable of staining. Cement grout is the most common, and most commercially available cement grouts contain additives to improve hardness and stain resistance. Epoxy grout is very stain resistant, although it is more expensive and difficult to apply. Caution must be exercised when using colored grouts, as the color will sometimes bleed and stain the tile.

Sealer

A penetrating sealer should be used to protect tile after it has been grouted. If cement grout is used, it is best to wait 28 days after grouting to allow the grout to cure completely before applying the sealer.

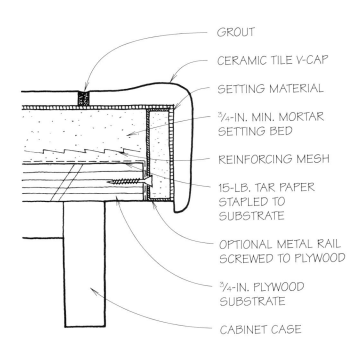

GROUT

CERAMIC TILE V-CAP

SETTING MATERIAL

¾-IN. MIN. MORTAR SETTING BED

REINFORCING MESH

15-LB. TAR PAPER STAPLED TO SUBSTRATE

OPTIONAL METAL RAIL SCREWED TO PLYWOOD

¾-IN. PLYWOOD SUBSTRATE

CABINET CASE

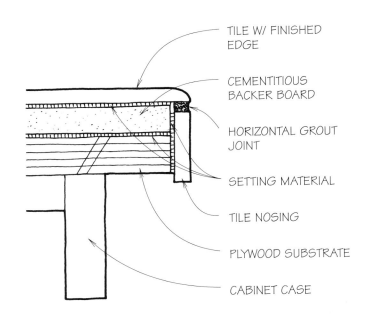

TILE W/ FINISHED EDGE

CEMENTITIOUS BACKER BOARD

HORIZONTAL GROUT JOINT

SETTING MATERIAL

TILE NOSING

PLYWOOD SUBSTRATE

CABINET CASE

 A THICK-BED TILE NOSING
TILE COUNTERTOP

B THINBED TILE NOSING
TILE COUNTERTOP

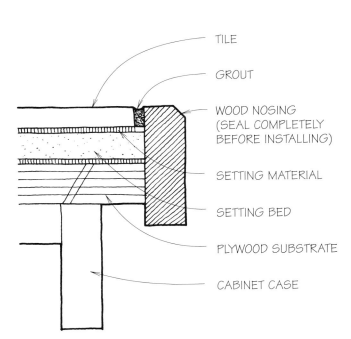

TILE

GROUT

WOOD NOSING (SEAL COMPLETELY BEFORE INSTALLING)

SETTING MATERIAL

SETTING BED

PLYWOOD SUBSTRATE

CABINET CASE

 **C** WOOD NOSING
TILE COUNTERTOP

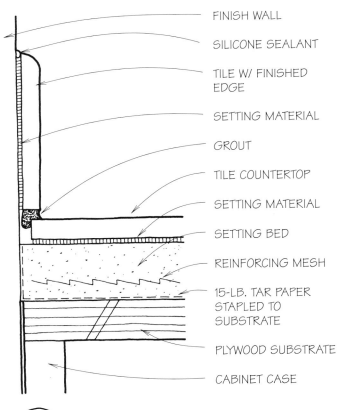

FINISH WALL

SILICONE SEALANT

TILE W/ FINISHED EDGE

SETTING MATERIAL

GROUT

TILE COUNTERTOP

SETTING MATERIAL

SETTING BED

REINFORCING MESH

15-LB. TAR PAPER STAPLED TO SUBSTRATE

PLYWOOD SUBSTRATE

CABINET CASE

 **D** TILE BACKSPLASH
TILE COUNTERTOP

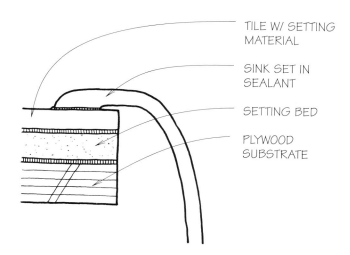

TILE W/ SETTING MATERIAL

SINK SET IN SEALANT

SETTING BED

PLYWOOD SUBSTRATE

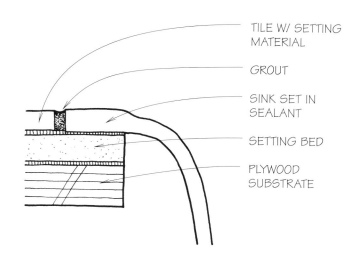

TILE W/ SETTING MATERIAL

GROUT

SINK SET IN SEALANT

SETTING BED

PLYWOOD SUBSTRATE

The most common sink in a tile countertop is a self-rimming sink. Because of the grout joints and the irregularity of stone tiles, however, it is difficult to achieve a perfect seal at the joint between the sink rim and the countertop.

 A **SELF-RIMMING SINK**
TILE COUNTERTOP

 **B** **FLUSH-MOUNT SINK**
TILE COUNTERTOP

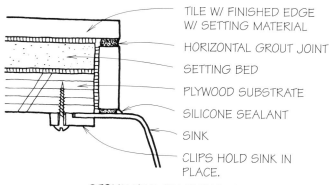

TILE W/ FINISHED EDGE W/ SETTING MATERIAL

HORIZONTAL GROUT JOINT

SETTING BED

PLYWOOD SUBSTRATE

SILICONE SEALANT

SINK

CLIPS HOLD SINK IN PLACE.

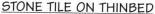
STONE TILE ON THINBED

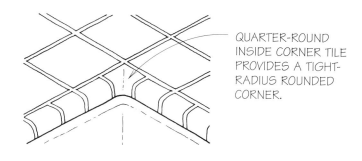

QUARTER-ROUND INSIDE CORNER TILE PROVIDES A TIGHT-RADIUS ROUNDED CORNER.

CERAMIC TILE CORNER @ UNDERMOUNT SINK

Undermount sinks in tile countertops are more costly to install and finish than other sink types but produce a better-performing sink and countertop assembly. It is important to consider the shape of the sink in relation to the inside corners. Stone tile requires square inside corners, and many types of ceramic tile are available with special quarter-round inside corner tiles, which provide a rounded corner with a tight radius. Undermounted round or oval sinks are very difficult to accommodate in a tile countertop.

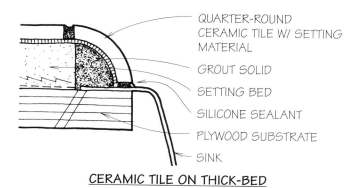

QUARTER-ROUND CERAMIC TILE W/ SETTING MATERIAL

GROUT SOLID

SETTING BED

SILICONE SEALANT

PLYWOOD SUBSTRATE

SINK

CERAMIC TILE ON THICK-BED

 C **UNDERMOUNT SINK**
TILE COUNTERTOP

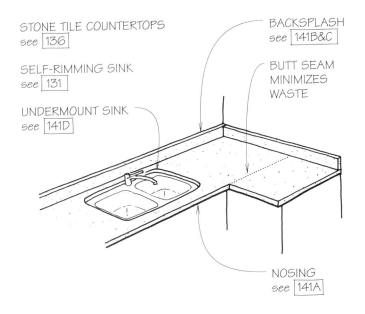

STONE TILE COUNTERTOPS
see 136

SELF-RIMMING SINK
see 131

UNDERMOUNT SINK
see 141D

BACKSPLASH
see 141B&C

BUTT SEAM
MINIMIZES
WASTE

NOSING
see 141A

Stone is desirable for countertops because of its beauty and resistance to water, scratching and heat. Stone slabs for countertops are available in many colors and patterns; each piece is unique. When compared to stone tiles (see 137), stone slabs provide a more continuous surface, but are more expensive than tiles.

Types of Stone

The types of stone most frequently used as countertops are granite, marble, slate and limestone.

Granite—The best-performing and most expensive stone is granite. Most common granites are flecked with minerals, while others have veining similar to marble. Granite is available in many colors and is either honed until it is smooth or highly polished. It is dense and hard and has high resistance to scratches, heat and moisture but is susceptible to staining.

Marble—Any stone that is capable of taking a polish (except granite) is considered to be marble. Marble is soft, somewhat porous, chips fairly easily and shows wear. In addition, contact with acidic foods can wreck its surface quickly. It is expensive but generally costs less than granite. Because of its smooth surface and ability to dissipate heat quickly, marble is often used for pastry countertops.

Slate—Slate provides a rougher and more porous surface than granite or marble since it is split rather than sliced. It is less expensive and is available in many colors. Gauged slate is most common for countertops since its surface is honed fairly smooth.

Limestone—Like granite and marble, limestone is sliced and can be honed smooth, but it is a soft and porous sedimentary stone and is too absorbent to use in damp locations. It is generally quite light in color.

Stone Slab Applications

There is little consistency in stone slab sizes. Slabs range from ¾ in. to 1¼ in. thick, 3 ft. to 6 ft. wide, and 5 ft. to 10 ft. long, depending on the particular stones and where they are quarried. Stone is heavy, with a ¾-in. thick slab of granite weighing about 12 lb. per sq. ft.

Substrate under stone slabs—Stone slabs ¾ in. thick can usually span between the supports of base cabinets, but to lessen the chance of excessive deflection that may cause cracking, they should be applied over a rigid substrate such as plywood. Thicker slabs can be installed without a rigid substrate.

Setting material—Gravity and adhesives will hold most stone slabs in place. An epoxy thinset mortar (see 137) is recommended to attach the stone slab to a plywood substrate, but silicone adhesive can also be used.

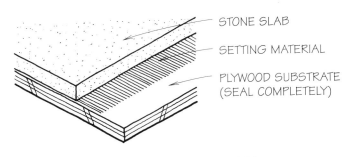

STONE SLAB

SETTING MATERIAL

PLYWOOD SUBSTRATE
(SEAL COMPLETELY)

STONE SLAB ASSEMBLY

Seams—When the size of the countertop requires more than one piece of stone, a seam is made with epoxy that has been colored to match the stone. To reduce waste, seams are always square butt joints.

Protective finish—The faces of stone slabs should be treated with a penetrating sealer prior to installation. Light-colored slabs should be treated on the backs as well to prevent any staining agents from migrating from the bottom of the stone to the surface.

STONE SLAB COUNTERTOPS

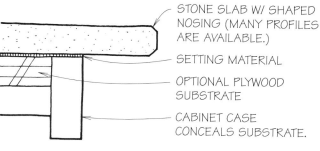

SLAB EDGE NOSING

STONE SLAB W/ SHAPED NOSING (MANY PROFILES ARE AVAILABLE.)
SETTING MATERIAL
OPTIONAL PLYWOOD SUBSTRATE
CABINET CASE CONCEALS SUBSTRATE.

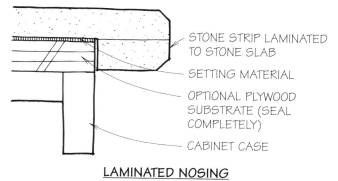

LAMINATED NOSING

STONE STRIP LAMINATED TO STONE SLAB
SETTING MATERIAL
OPTIONAL PLYWOOD SUBSTRATE (SEAL COMPLETELY)
CABINET CASE

A · NOSING
STONE SLAB COUNTERTOP

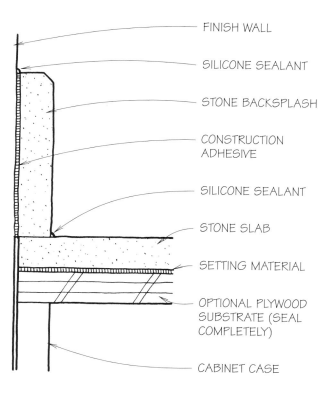

FINISH WALL
SILICONE SEALANT
STONE BACKSPLASH
CONSTRUCTION ADHESIVE
SILICONE SEALANT
STONE SLAB
SETTING MATERIAL
OPTIONAL PLYWOOD SUBSTRATE (SEAL COMPLETELY)
CABINET CASE

B · BACKSPLASH ON WALL
STONE SLAB COUNTERTOP

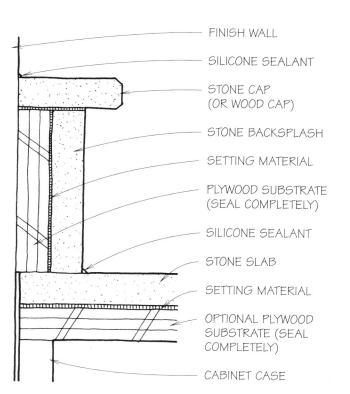

FINISH WALL
SILICONE SEALANT
STONE CAP (OR WOOD CAP)
STONE BACKSPLASH
SETTING MATERIAL
PLYWOOD SUBSTRATE (SEAL COMPLETELY)
SILICONE SEALANT
STONE SLAB
SETTING MATERIAL
OPTIONAL PLYWOOD SUBSTRATE (SEAL COMPLETELY)
CABINET CASE

C · BACKSPLASH W/ SUBSTRATE
STONE SLAB COUNTERTOP

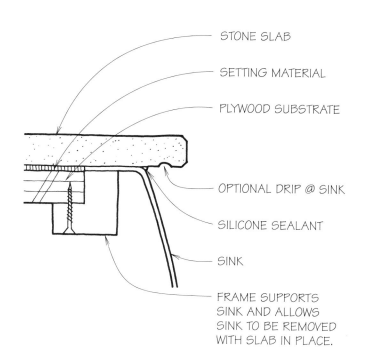

STONE SLAB
SETTING MATERIAL
PLYWOOD SUBSTRATE
OPTIONAL DRIP @ SINK
SILICONE SEALANT
SINK
FRAME SUPPORTS SINK AND ALLOWS SINK TO BE REMOVED WITH SLAB IN PLACE.

D · UNDERMOUNT SINK
STONE SLAB COUNTERTOP

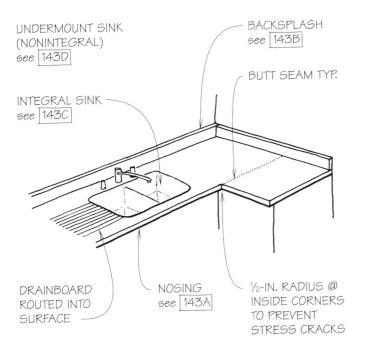

UNDERMOUNT SINK
(NONINTEGRAL)
see 143D

INTEGRAL SINK
see 143C

BACKSPLASH
see 143B

BUTT SEAM TYP.

DRAINBOARD
ROUTED INTO
SURFACE

NOSING
see 143A

½-IN. RADIUS @
INSIDE CORNERS
TO PREVENT
STRESS CRACKS

A fairly recent development in countertop materials, solid-surface material has achieved tremendous popularity. It is a monolithic, nonporous synthetic material that is composed of minerals blended with acrylic resin, and each manufacturer has subtle compositional variations.

Solid-surface material is quite resistant to stains from food and chemicals, scratches, heat and bacteria. Because color and pattern are consistent through the material, most scratches and burns can be easily sanded out and polished. In addition, solid-surface materials can be cut and shaped fairly easily, making custom features such as an integral drainboard or an inset cutting board possible. Most versions are capable of being seamed inconspicuously (except in a few patterns).

A wide range of colors and patterns is available. Heavy wear tends to be more apparent on the darker colors. As expected for a high-performance work surface, solid-surface material is usually very expensive.

Available Sizes

Solid-surface material is typically available in sheet form. Thicknesses range from ¼ in. for vertical surfaces (such as backsplashes) to ½ in. and ¾ in. for horizontal surfaces. Sheets are available up to 30 in. by 12 ft., depending on the manufacturer, thickness, color and pattern. Some manufacturers offer one-piece solid-surface vanity tops with integral sinks and integral coved backsplashes.

Installation

Most manufacturers recommend that the solid-surface countertop be installed directly on the cabinet case without the use of a substrate. Solid-surface material absorbs heat very quickly and a substrate would prevent the heat from dissipating, which could cause stress cracks in the surface.

The weight of the solid-surface material combined with drops of silicone adhesive every 10 in. to 12 in. hold the countertop in place. Cut-outs and inside corners should be made with a slight (³⁄₁₆-in. to ½-in.) radius to prevent stress cracks.

Seams—If the size or shape of the countertop requires two pieces of solid-surface material to be joined, the pieces should be butted in order to minimize material waste. Seams should be supported by cabinet framing. Manufacturers provide special epoxy adhesives and directions for joining pieces to achieve an inconspicuous joint.

Because of the ease of joining solid-surface material, individual components can be fabricated and joined in a shop. Special nosings with inlays, coved backsplashes and integral sinks are all fairly common. Seaming together pieces from different manufacturers is not recommended.

Sinks—Sinks made from solid-surface material are readily available from most manufacturers. Undermounted solid-surface sinks are joined to the countertop from below with the manufacturer's special epoxy adhesive (see 143D). Bevel-mounted solid-surface sinks are dropped into a precise cutout in the countertop and joined with the manufacturer's special epoxy adhesive (see 143C).

If a sink made from a different material is to be mounted under the counter, a frame may be built within the cabinet case to support the weight of the sink completely when it is filled with water and/or dishes (see 143D). As an alternative, a few manufacturers provide special fittings that allow the sink to be fastened directly to the underside of the solid-surface countertop with special fittings.

SOLID-SURFACE COUNTERTOPS

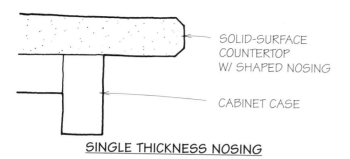

SOLID-SURFACE
COUNTERTOP
W/ SHAPED NOSING

CABINET CASE

SINGLE THICKNESS NOSING

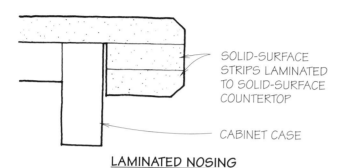

SOLID-SURFACE
STRIPS LAMINATED
TO SOLID-SURFACE
COUNTERTOP

CABINET CASE

LAMINATED NOSING

 A **NOSING**
SOLID-SURFACE COUNTERTOP

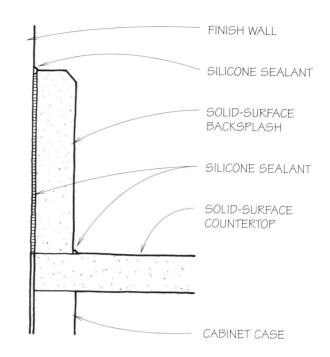

FINISH WALL

SILICONE SEALANT

SOLID-SURFACE
BACKSPLASH

SILICONE SEALANT

SOLID-SURFACE
COUNTERTOP

CABINET CASE

 **B** **BACKSPLASH**
SOLID-SURFACE COUNTERTOP

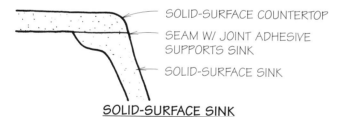

SOLID-SURFACE COUNTERTOP
SEAM W/ JOINT ADHESIVE
SUPPORTS SINK
SOLID-SURFACE SINK

SOLID-SURFACE SINK

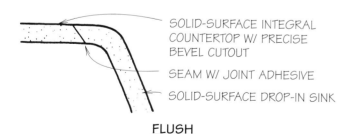

SOLID-SURFACE INTEGRAL
COUNTERTOP W/ PRECISE
BEVEL CUTOUT
SEAM W/ JOINT ADHESIVE
SOLID-SURFACE DROP-IN SINK

FLUSH

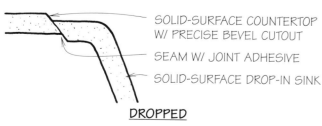

SOLID-SURFACE COUNTERTOP
W/ PRECISE BEVEL CUTOUT
SEAM W/ JOINT ADHESIVE
SOLID-SURFACE DROP-IN SINK

DROPPED

 **C** **INTEGRAL SINK**
SOLID-SURFACE COUNTERTOP

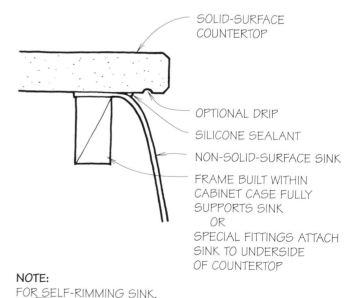

SOLID-SURFACE
COUNTERTOP

OPTIONAL DRIP

SILICONE SEALANT

NON-SOLID-SURFACE SINK

FRAME BUILT WITHIN
CABINET CASE FULLY
SUPPORTS SINK
       OR
SPECIAL FITTINGS ATTACH
SINK TO UNDERSIDE
OF COUNTERTOP

NOTE:
FOR SELF-RIMMING SINK,
see 131

 D **UNDERMOUNT SINKS**
SOLID-SURFACE COUNTERTOP

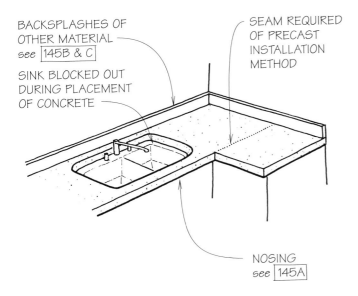

BACKSPLASHES OF OTHER MATERIAL see 145B & C

SINK BLOCKED OUT DURING PLACEMENT OF CONCRETE

SEAM REQUIRED OF PRECAST INSTALLATION METHOD

NOSING see 145A

Substrate

The substrate should be ¾-in. exterior-grade plywood. All surfaces to be in contact with the concrete should be covered with 6-mil polyethylene or moisture barrier to prevent moisture migration to adjacent materials during casting and curing.

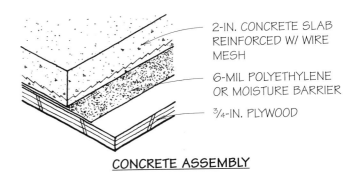

2-IN. CONCRETE SLAB REINFORCED W/ WIRE MESH

6-MIL POLYETHYLENE OR MOISTURE BARRIER

¾-IN. PLYWOOD

CONCRETE ASSEMBLY

Not ordinarily thought of as a countertop material, concrete makes an inexpensive, durable and beautiful countertop work surface. It is a monolithic material made from common raw materials, and is fairly resistant to stains, scratches and heat.

The assembly of materials for a concrete countertop is very similar to a thickbed tile assembly, only without the tile and with concrete substituted for the mortar bed (see 137). The concrete, made of cement, sand, aggregate and water, should be mixed rich (approximately six sacks of cement per cubic yard of concrete) to increase the compressive strength. The aggregate should be small, such as pea gravel. In addition, a strengthening additive should be included in the mix. The slab should generally be about 2 in. thick, and it should be reinforced with wire mesh. Extra reinforcement should be provided at weak spots such as inside corners and around cutouts such as sinks. This is best accomplished with #3 (⅜-in.) rebar.

Installation

Concrete countertops can either be cast-in-place or precast. Regardless of where the countertop is made, formwork must be built to support and shape the nosing and any other projections or cutouts.

Cast-in-place—A cast-in-place installation has numerous advantages. It results in a monolithic surface free of seams and eliminates the difficult task of moving a heavy slab of concrete. In addition, the countertop is supported evenly without shims since the concrete conforms to any irregularities in the cabinets that support it. The countertop also will conform to a preinstalled backsplash (145B).

One disadvantage of cast-in-place concrete is that the process tends to slop concrete where it isn't wanted, so extreme care must be taken to protect cabinets and other finish surfaces. In addition, some sealer manufacturers recommend that the cured concrete surface be washed with muriatic acid and then rinsed with water prior to finishing. This is difficult to accomplish while in place, so the sealer used should not require a muriatic acid cleanup.

Precast—The major advantage of precasting the countertop outside the finished space is that it is less important to control the mess associated with casting and finishing the concrete carefully. Other than this advantage, precasting is not recommended. Maneuvering an extremely heavy slab can be awkward at best. Larger or more complex shapes may require the countertop to be cast in more than one section, requiring one or more seams, which could detract from the appearance of the countertop and make it less desirable as a work surface.

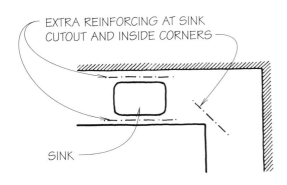

EXTRA REINFORCING AT SINK CUTOUT AND INSIDE CORNERS

SINK

REINFORCING DIAGRAM

A CONCRETE COUNTERTOPS

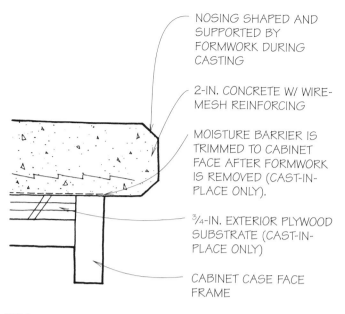

NOSING SHAPED AND SUPPORTED BY FORMWORK DURING CASTING

2-IN. CONCRETE W/ WIRE-MESH REINFORCING

MOISTURE BARRIER IS TRIMMED TO CABINET FACE AFTER FORMWORK IS REMOVED (CAST-IN-PLACE ONLY).

¾-IN. EXTERIOR PLYWOOD SUBSTRATE (CAST-IN-PLACE ONLY)

CABINET CASE FACE FRAME

NOTE:
FOR CAST-IN-PLACE, THE FACE FRAME, SHOWN ABOVE, CONCEALS THE SUBSTRATE. IN A FRAMELESS CABINET, THE SUBSTRATE IS INTEGRAL AND BANDED.

 A NOSING
CAST-IN-PLACE & PRECAST

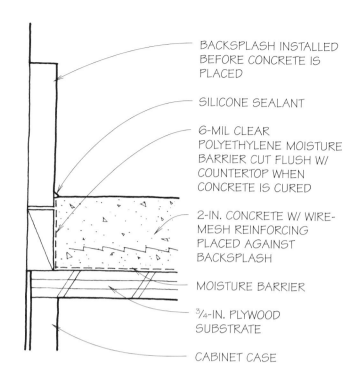

BACKSPLASH INSTALLED BEFORE CONCRETE IS PLACED

SILICONE SEALANT

6-MIL CLEAR POLYETHYLENE MOISTURE BARRIER CUT FLUSH W/ COUNTERTOP WHEN CONCRETE IS CURED

2-IN. CONCRETE W/ WIRE-MESH REINFORCING PLACED AGAINST BACKSPLASH

MOISTURE BARRIER

¾-IN. PLYWOOD SUBSTRATE

CABINET CASE

 B BACKSPLASH
CAST-IN-PLACE COUNTERTOP

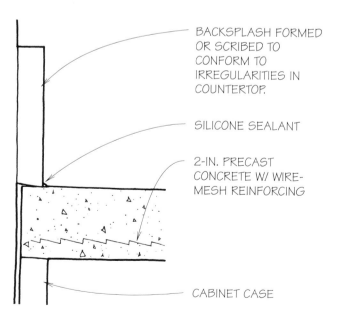

BACKSPLASH FORMED OR SCRIBED TO CONFORM TO IRREGULARITIES IN COUNTERTOP.

SILICONE SEALANT

2-IN. PRECAST CONCRETE W/ WIRE-MESH REINFORCING

CABINET CASE

Producing a successful concrete countertop requires experience, skilled execution and the proper tools. Although the natural color of concrete can be quite appealing, the addition of a different color is often desired. The use of colored aggregates can produce subtle variations, and white cement can be used to produce a unique effect. In addition, pigment can be added to the material (see 101A). Regardless of the coloring method, a test sample should be made before casting a countertop.

Many surface textures and effects can be obtained by using different finishing techniques. For example, different types of floats used to finish the concrete will produce different results. After the concrete has cured, its texture and appearance can be further manipulated by grinding or sanding the surface.

When all other finishing is complete, a sealer should be applied to protect the porous surface. A floor wax may also be used to provide a protective build-up. Surfaces to be used for food preparation should be sealed with nontoxic finishes.

 **C** BACKSPLASH
PRECAST COUNTERTOP

 D FINISHING CONCRETE

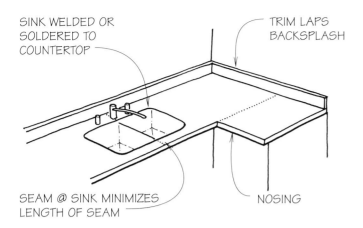

Varieties of Metal Countertops

Combining a beautiful appearance with a superior performance, three kinds of sheet-metal are commonly used for countertops.

Stainless steel—Stainless steel is strong, durable, stain and heat resistant, and is used particularly where sanitation is a principal concern. It is fairly expensive, and when shaped and seamed must be fabricated by a skilled sheet metal shop, so labor costs are fairly high.

Galvanized steel—Steel with a zinc coating to prevent corrosion, called galvanized steel, is less durable than stainless steel, and the zinc coating makes it unsuitable for surfaces used for food preparation.

Copper—Compared with stainless and galvanized steel, copper is the softest and most expensive metal countertop, but it performs very well and is beautiful.

Sizes

Stainless or galvanized steel countertops should be 16-ga. or thicker. Thinner gauges will dent easily. Maximum sheet size is 60 in. by 44 in. Copper should be 32 oz. or 48 oz. Maximum sheet size is typically 36 in. by 120 in.

Substrate

A metal countertop's dent resistance is partially dependent on the density of the substrate. Plywood ¾ in. thick is typical, but MDF is superior if moisture is controlled.

Fabrication and Installation

Metal countertops are usually fabricated in a shop, and can be formed by bending and fusing together pieces to make a seamless surface in nearly any shape. Seams are welded or soldered and ground smooth. The metal countertop is typically attached to the substrate with a tile-setting material (see 137). Large or intricate metal countertops can be installed premounted to the substrate.

Sinks—Ideally, a metal sink is fabricated from the same material as its countertop so that it becomes integral with the countertop. A prefabricated stainless-steel countertop can be welded to a stainless steel sink for economy.

Nosing—The nosing is usually made by bending the metal. Bent metal is strong, so the nosing doesn't need to be fully supported. Other nosing materials can be used for appearance and to reduce the fabrication cost.

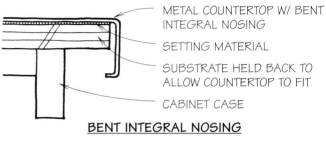

BENT INTEGRAL NOSING

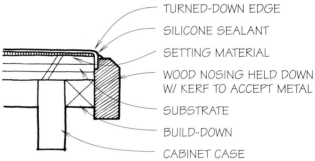

APPLIED WOOD NOSING

Backsplash—In wet locations, the backsplash can be made integral with the countertop similar to plastic laminate (see 135A & B). Backsplashes of other materials such as wood will save considerable fabrication costs.

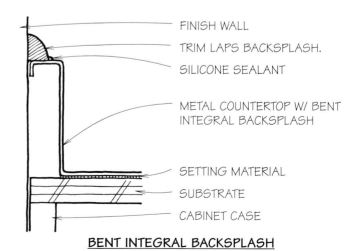

BENT INTEGRAL BACKSPLASH

 METAL COUNTERTOPS

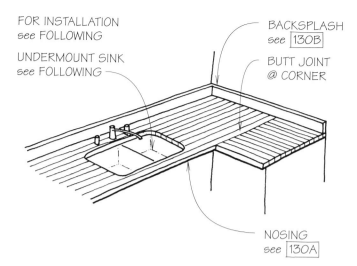

FOR INSTALLATION
see FOLLOWING

UNDERMOUNT SINK
see FOLLOWING

BACKSPLASH
see 130B

BUTT JOINT
@ CORNER

NOSING
see 130A

When installed and maintained properly, wood is a beautiful and functional countertop. Wood is the only surface that is suitable for cutting food. Although scars and stains are inevitable, they can enhance rather than detract from the appearance of the countertop.

Face-laminated wood countertops are generally referred to as butcher block. Although traditional butcher block was several inches thick, today's butcher block is almost exclusively 1¼ in. to 1½ in. thick. Maple is the preferred species because of its dense grain. Wood is susceptible to bacterial contamination so more care is required in its use and maintenance than for other countertop materials.

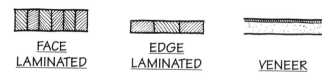

FACE
LAMINATED

EDGE
LAMINATED

VENEER

Countertops used for surfaces free from moisture and knives can be made of almost any wood product, generally edge-laminated solid sawn boards, a veneer on a core of plywood, or occasionally MDF (see Appendix B). Most wood countertops other than butcher block are made from ¾-in. thick material that is capable of spanning the cabinet frame without requiring a substrate.

Finish

It is important that both sides of a solid wood countertop be finished, preferably prior to installation, to prevent cupping. Butcher-block countertops may be finished with mineral oil, olive oil or vegetable oil. The oil should be reapplied as required. Countertops not used for food preparation may be finished any number of ways (see Appendix A). Hardwood plywood and MDF are often painted.

Installation

Depending on the species and orientation of the grain, a wood countertop can contract and expand up to ⅛ in. per foot. A standard 2-ft. deep countertop can change in dimension up to ¼ in., so the installation must allow for this movement. Typically, the back of the countertop is fastened tight and the front is fastened with screws that pass through elongated holes. This allows the nosing edge of the assembly to move as the wood expands and contracts.

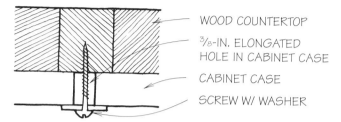

WOOD COUNTERTOP

⅜-IN. ELONGATED
HOLE IN CABINET CASE

CABINET CASE

SCREW W/ WASHER

This method is not effective for L-shaped and U-shaped wood countertops where nosing movement would create gaps between countertop sections. To overcome this problem, each section may be installed with the front fastened tight while the back is held away from the wall and screwed through elongated holes. A backsplash covers the gap at the wall. A sliding joint at the corner allows independent movement of the two countertop sections while keeping them aligned.

Sinks—If a sink has to be installed in a wood countertop, an undermount sink (131) should be used, as a self-rimming sink tends to trap water at the sink edge. An undermount sink with the countertop extended slightly over the sink space will help prevent this problem. A kerf at the underside of the wood around the sink will prevent water from migrating to the joint between countertop and sink.

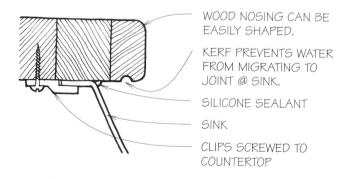

WOOD NOSING CAN BE
EASILY SHAPED.

KERF PREVENTS WATER
FROM MIGRATING TO
JOINT @ SINK.

SILICONE SEALANT

SINK

CLIPS SCREWED TO
COUNTERTOP

Nosings—Wood nosing can be shaped in many ways. A kerf made on the underside will help prevent spills from running down the cabinet face.

 WOOD COUNTERTOPS

Trim

4

SOLID WOOD TRIM
see 150-51

ALTERNATIVES TO
SOLID WOOD TRIM
see 152 & 153A

FINISHES
see 153B

DOOR & WINDOW TRIM
see 159-61

BASE TRIM
see 162-63

OTHER TRIM TYPES
see 164-65

TRIM APPLICATION:

COVERING GAPS &
MEETING ADJACENT
EDGES
see 154

ALIGNING PARALLEL
PIECES & SPLICING TRIM
see 155

ENDING TRIM
see 157

TURNING CORNERS
WITH TRIM
see 156

TRIM FASTENERS
see 158

T rim, one of the very last things to be added to a building under construction, has the primary function of covering gaps between loosely fitting parts, such as between window and wall and between wall and floor.

Trim can also protect the building from abrasion where furniture or people are likely to bump into it. Baseboards, for example, protect walls from shoes, chairs and other things moving at the level of the floor, while door casings keep walls from being damaged as people and objects pass through the doorway.

Trim, called molding when it is cut into specific shapes, also contributes significantly to the character of an interior space. There is an obvious difference between a door trimmed in the most minimal fashion and one trimmed with a full complement of ornate period moldings.

Coordinating trim with the scale of a room, with the other surface materials and with the architectural features of a building is an important aspect of interior detailing.

Wood molding was once made by hand with planes that held uniquely shaped blades. With the development of the molding machine in the late 19th century, trim started to be mass-produced, and the use of intricately shaped pieces increased significantly. The earliest trim was made of the finest-grained wood available, both for its beauty and to facilitate manufacture and installation. Today, such fine-grained wood is scarce, so alternatives, including composite wood products and nonwood products, have been developed (see 152). Some of these alternatives are virtually indistinguishable from traditional wood molding when painted, but no modern alternative can match its predecessors when treated with a clear, natural finish.

This chapter describes primarily the principles and particular details that apply to solid wood moldings. Most of these principles and details also apply to alternative moldings made of MDF, and many apply to plastic moldings.

Trim Profiles

The simplest trim is made from unprofiled boards, rectangular in shape and milled to a smooth surface on all four sides. These boards are typically available in 1x2, 1x3, 1x4, 1x5, 1x6, 1x8, 1x10 and 1x12 sizes (nominally), depending on the species.

When boards are milled into more complex shapes with combinations of curved and straight surfaces, they are known as moldings. Wood moldings are characterized by their profiles, or cross-sectional shapes. Available profiles vary from region to region, but most can be milled from a 1-in. (nominal) board.

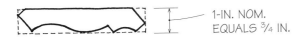

1-IN. NOM.
EQUALS ¾ IN.

The moldings shown on 151 represent a sample of typical stock wood profiles.

Many of the larger profiles have a relieved back designed to minimize cupping by reducing the thickness of the trim. The relieved back also allows the trim to span over irregularities in the wall and helps the installer fit the edges of the trim tight against the adjacent materials.

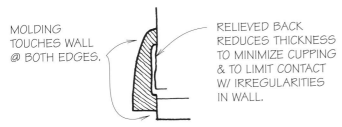

MOLDING TOUCHES WALL @ BOTH EDGES.

RELIEVED BACK REDUCES THICKNESS TO MINIMIZE CUPPING & TO LIMIT CONTACT W/ IRREGULARITIES IN WALL.

MOLDING W/ RELIEVED BACK

Typical Species

Standard, off-the-shelf profiled wood molding is made primarily of lengths of softwood—namely fir, pine or hemlock—and some hardwood, primarily oak and some white hardwoods such as alder, birch or poplar. Unprofiled boards are generally available in the same species as profiled moldings.

Finger-jointed molding made of inexpensive short lengths of clear softwood (usually pine) joined at the ends with interlocking, glued joints is also available in some profiles for trim that is to be painted (see 153B). Finger-jointed pine boards with a clear wood veneer are also available in some species for stain-grade trim (see 153B).

FINGER-JOINTED TRIM

Moisture Content

Like all lumber products, wood trim changes dimensions with a change in moisture content (see 156). To minimize the effects of this, trim is dried to 7% to 10% moisture content, depending on the location of manufacture and time of year. As a precaution, however, trim should be stored inside at the (heated) job site for several days before installation.

Custom Milling

Custom milling to achieve a special profile or to use an unusual species of wood is more expensive than using standard moldings but is not uncommon. Special profiles may be milled from any species of wood, but when the trim is to be painted, species that have consistent grain and are easily machined, such as pine or poplar, are preferred. When the trim is to have a transparent finish, it is not uncommon to custom mill more unusual species such as mahogany, redwood, maple or katsura to showcase their features or to match cabinetry. Most trim carpenters mill some simple special-purpose moldings on site with a table saw and/or router at little additional cost.

Building Up Trim

Because elaborate trim profiles can be nearly impossible to make from a single piece of wood, complex profiles have traditionally been built up of several smaller pieces of standard trim. The smaller pieces are also more flexible so that they will conform to irregularities in the adjacent surfaces more readily than a single large piece. Since standard trim profiles are milled from less expensive small-dimension stock, building up trim is generally less expensive than custom milling a larger intricate molding from a single piece.

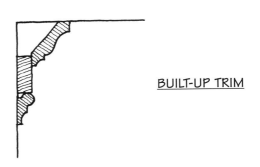

BUILT-UP TRIM

(A) SOLID WOOD TRIM

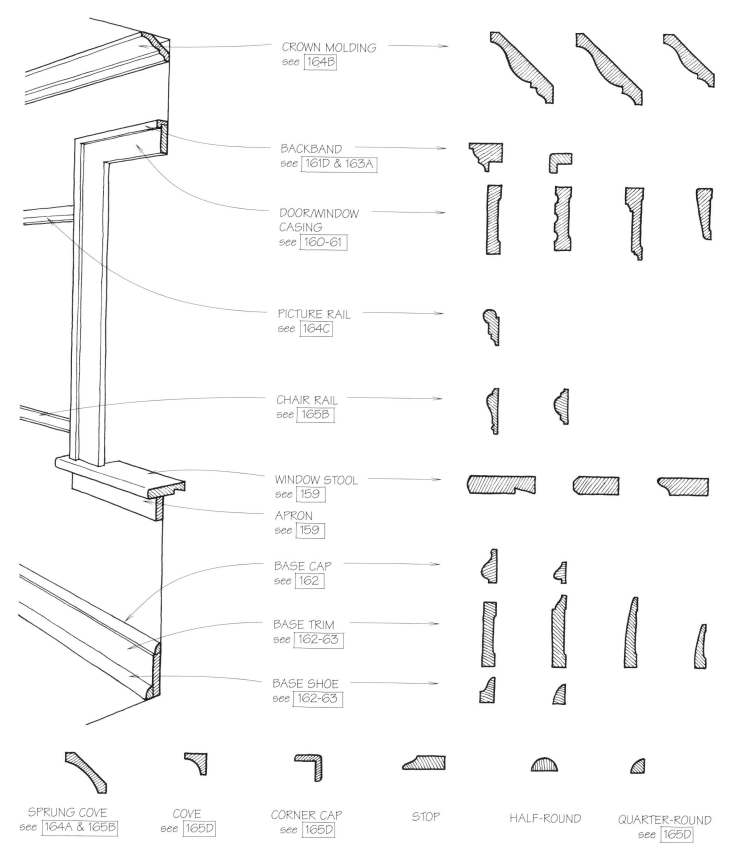

CROWN MOLDING
see 164B

BACKBAND
see 161D & 163A

DOOR/WINDOW
CASING
see 160-61

PICTURE RAIL
see 164C

CHAIR RAIL
see 165B

WINDOW STOOL
see 159

APRON
see 159

BASE CAP
see 162

BASE TRIM
see 162-63

BASE SHOE
see 162-63

SPRUNG COVE
see 164A & 165B

COVE
see 165D

CORNER CAP
see 165D

STOP

HALF-ROUND

QUARTER-ROUND
see 165D

 MOLDING PROFILES

There are several alternatives to solid wood trim that are appropriate if the work is to be painted. The choice of profiles tends to be somewhat more limited for these alternatives than for standard wood trim, but most material types have a sufficient selection of trim for all standard conditions.

Medium-Density Fiberboard (MDF)

MDF is a dense, recombined wood product that is relatively inexpensive and is easily cut, sanded, shaped and attached to the building with normal woodworking tools (see Appendix B). For use as trim, MDF is available in sheets that can be custom cut and/or shaped at the site, precut rectangular sections (boards) and a limited number of shaped profiles similar to the common wood trim profiles (see 151A).

Because of its appearance as a raw material, MDF trim is typically painted, and many premanufactured profiles are available primed. MDF used as trim has the drawback that changes in moisture content will affect the length of the pieces more than the same change would affect solid wood. Therefore, using it in buildings without air conditioning and in regions with significant seasonal humidity swings may not be appropriate. Given its low cost relative to other trim, its availability and its similarities to solid wood, however, MDF seems the most likely of the current alternatives to displace solid wood as the principal material for the painted trim market.

Plastic Moldings

Made of petroleum products, plastic trim has a density similar to pine. It can be cut, sanded, shaped and attached to the building with normal woodworking tools. However, plastic molding is more consistent than wood since it does not have the irregularities of grain. Plastic molding also does not absorb moisture so is not subject to dimensional changes.

Plastic molding is less expensive than hardwood molding but more expensive than finger-jointed pine. Plastic is also not generally available in the same shapes as board, so built-up trims (see 150) must usually be combined with MDF or wood.

The most common plastic moldings are made of fiber-reinforced polyester or extruded polystyrene. Both are available in standard profiles for typical trim tasks such as base, casing, chair rail and crown mold. They are typically manufactured with a primed coating or prefinished with an ersatz wood grain pattern. Plastic

corner blocks are available for virtually all conditions and thus allow the inexperienced homeowner to apply the molding without having to make anything but square cuts (see 156).

A slightly more dense plastic molding is made of polyurethane. Many profiles made of this material are modeled after traditional wood profiles. In addition, there are elaborate ornamental molded profiles with sculptural repeating forms that would originally have been made of cast plaster or of several built-up pieces of wood. Because the plastic material is dimensionally stable, these complex shapes can be and are often quite wide. Some patterns are also made in a flexible molding that is able to conform to inside or outside curves with a radius as small as 2 ft., depending on the pattern.

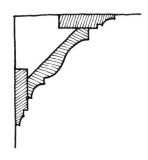 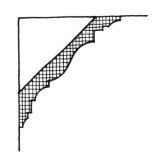

BUILT-UP WOOD CROWN MOLDING   SINGLE-PIECE PLASTIC CROWN MOLDING

Plaster Moldings

Fiber-reinforced gypsum-plaster moldings that are either extruded (drawn) or cast are available. Many of these moldings are modeled after historic plaster castings that were used to make elaborate ceilings. Because they are relatively soft and brittle, the use of modern plaster moldings is generally limited to ceilings and other areas of a building that do not receive abuse.

Vinyl and Rubber Molding

Vinyl and rubber molding are thin (approximately ⅛ in. thick) and are manufactured in long rolls. The materials are supple and durable and are available in a variety of colors. Vinyl and rubber moldings are attached to the wall with adhesives rather than fasteners. Used extensively in commercial work, these materials are available only as base molding (see 163C).

 ALTERNATIVES TO SOLID WOOD TRIM

One of the most common alternatives to using wood trim is to eliminate the trim altogether by using gypsum wallboard (GWB). With the aid of metal or plastic edge trim (see 9A), GWB makes a clean edge against the window or door. This economical approach is most commonly employed at windows or exterior doors where the GWB wraps the corner of the opening and dies into, or butts into, the window or door jamb, eliminating both jamb extender and wood trim.

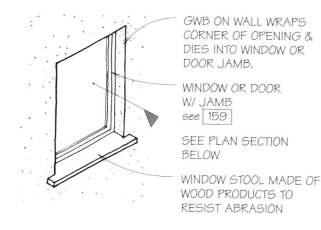

GWB ON WALL WRAPS CORNER OF OPENING & DIES INTO WINDOW OR DOOR JAMB.

WINDOW OR DOOR W/ JAMB
see 159

SEE PLAN SECTION BELOW

WINDOW STOOL MADE OF WOOD PRODUCTS TO RESIST ABRASION

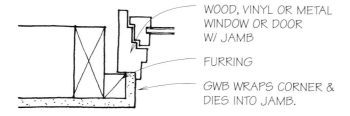

WOOD, VINYL OR METAL WINDOW OR DOOR W/ JAMB

FURRING

GWB WRAPS CORNER & DIES INTO JAMB.

PLAN SECTION

When a wood jamb (or jamb extender) extends the full thickness of the wall, such as for an interior wood door, GWB may still be used in place of trim and may butt or lap the jamb.

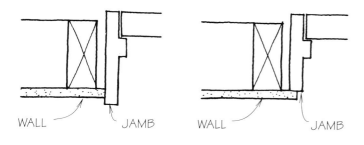

WALL   JAMB   WALL   JAMB

GWB BUTTS JAMB   GWB LAPS JAMB

A — THE NO-TRIM ALTERNATIVE
@ WINDOWS & DOORS

The decision of whether trim is to be painted with an opaque finish or to have a transparent natural finish such as a stain should be made before trim materials are selected. Each choice has cost implications and will make a significant impact on the appearance of the interior. Painted trim is generally more easily matched with other components of an interior space such as doors, windows and cabinets. However, stained wood can take abuse better than painted wood because a scratched or chipped surface does not show as much and dents tend to blend with and may even complement the exposed natural grain. Stained trim can also be changed to painted while the reverse is not true.

For painted work, the options for materials are considerably greater than for stained work since the trim will be coated with an opaque film. This means that low-cost moldings made of finger-joined pine, MDF or plastic may be used. The cost of labor to install painted trim is also less than for stained work, since the painting (and caulking) cover a lack of refinement in the trim and its installation. Substantial gaps can be filled with a quality caulk that is applied with a caulk gun and smoothed with a wet finger. Fasteners used to attach the trim are also easily concealed when the work is painted. In fact, modern caulking and filling compounds that accept paint well are an important component of quality painted trim.

The savings realized in the cost of material and the installation of painted trim will likely be eroded somewhat by the application of the paint itself. A high-quality paint job generally requires three coats— a primer and two finish coats (with caulk applied between the primer and first finish coat). A stain job can normally be completed in two coats. Finishing painted trim is likely to cost about 50% more than finishing stained trim.

Trim that is finished with a stain or other transparent coating must be fastened to the finish wall more carefully than paint-grade trim. There are fewer choices for materials, and the material specified is usually an expensive clear grade of wood. In addition, the installation cost is greater since the cracks and gaps that can be easily filled with caulk in painted work are not acceptable for work intended for a clear finish. Even nail or staple holes (see 158), easily filled and concealed in paint-grade work, must in stain-grade trim be either strategically located or filled with material that is carefully color-matched to the wood.

B — FINISHES
PAINT VS. STAIN

Understanding the general principles of how trim is applied and how it performs under various conditions will help the designer select moldings and design details so that the entire assembly of trim in a room or building can be logical, durable and beautiful.

Covering Gaps

Given that the primary objective of trim is to conceal gaps between the edges of adjacent materials, a simple overlapping of the trim onto the material is the most direct way to accomplish this task.

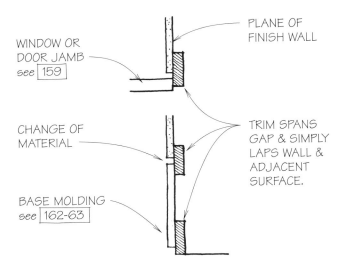

PLANE OF FINISH WALL

WINDOW OR DOOR JAMB see | 159 |

CHANGE OF MATERIAL

TRIM SPANS GAP & SIMPLY LAPS WALL & ADJACENT SURFACE.

BASE MOLDING see | 162-63 |

Most trim will be applied to the finished surface of an interior wall, so it is sensible to use this plane as a reference point.

Meeting Adjacent Surfaces

The gaps between materials that must be covered by trim are, for the most part, quite long and are adjacent to materials that have less than perfectly regular surfaces. The use of a reasonably thin trim piece that will bend to conform to the irregularities of the adjacent surface is often required to make a tight joint.

When a single piece of trim is expected to bend in both directions to conform to irregularities, a molding such as quarter-round that is thin in both directions works best.

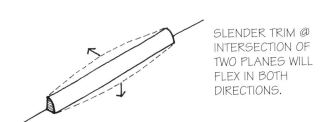

SLENDER TRIM @ INTERSECTION OF TWO PLANES WILL FLEX IN BOTH DIRECTIONS.

Sanitary molding, a thin, inexpensive molding with one curved corner, and other moldings of similar size are usually sufficiently supple in both directions to achieve the desired fit (see also 162).

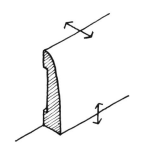

SANITARY MOLDING OR OTHER THIN BASE CONFORMS TO IRREGULARITIES IN WALL & FLOOR.

When a wider molding, such as a tall baseboard, is specified, it must often be accompanied by a smaller piece such as a base shoe or base cap that will bend to conform to the irregularities of the floor (see also 162).

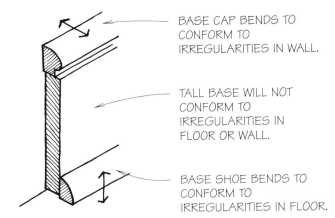

BASE CAP BENDS TO CONFORM TO IRREGULARITIES IN WALL.

TALL BASE WILL NOT CONFORM TO IRREGULARITIES IN FLOOR OR WALL.

BASE SHOE BENDS TO CONFORM TO IRREGULARITIES IN FLOOR.

If wide moldings are desired without having to build up with thin pieces that bend, a single-piece wide molding can be scribed to the material it trims. Scribing involves planing the edge of the molding so that it conforms to the contours of the material adjacent to it. The labor of scribing can sometimes be more expensive than the addition of a thin trim piece such as that discussed above.

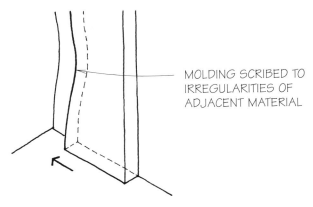

MOLDING SCRIBED TO IRREGULARITIES OF ADJACENT MATERIAL

 COVERING CAPS & MEETING ADJACENT SURFACES

Aligning Parallel Pieces

The perfect alignment of trim edges to the edges of window or door jambs or to other molding is very difficult. This is because the existing window and door edges are rarely perfect, and the internal strength of the trim pieces makes them difficult to bend.

It is most common and practical to offset the two edges to create a reveal. The reveal makes a shadow line that for all practical purposes aligns the two edges without having to make the alignment perfect. Slight variations in alignment will not be perceptible because of the offset between the two edges. The reveal is used extensively in trim detailing.

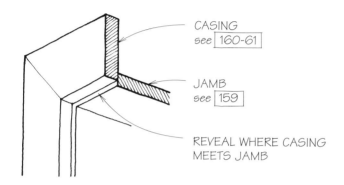

CASING
see 160-61

JAMB
see 159

REVEAL WHERE CASING MEETS JAMB

When it is necessary to align a piece of trim flush with another material, the trim may first be glued and nailed to hold it in place. The joint can then be planed and sanded smooth to make the edges perfectly flush. The nail or screw holes can be filled and the surface painted. For stained or clear finish trim, the exposed fasteners may be eliminated with a spline or biscuit joint that locks the pieces together internally like a tongue-and-groove detail.

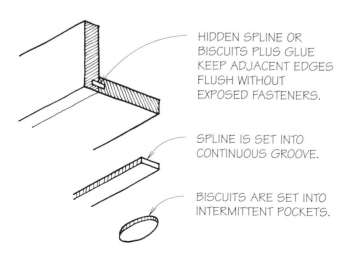

HIDDEN SPLINE OR BISCUITS PLUS GLUE KEEP ADJACENT EDGES FLUSH WITHOUT EXPOSED FASTENERS.

SPLINE IS SET INTO CONTINUOUS GROOVE.

BISCUITS ARE SET INTO INTERMITTENT POCKETS.

A ALIGNING PARALLEL PIECES

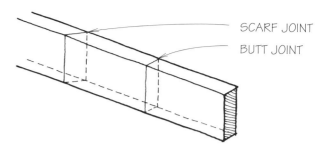

SCARF JOINT

BUTT JOINT

Trim must be spliced if a single piece cannot be found to extend the full length of a long wall. The scarf joint, which joins the ends of trim with a sloping lap-joint, has traditionally been considered the best detail for this situation, especially for stain-grade trim.

Any slight change in the length of the trim will slide the lapped pieces across one another but will not cause a crack in the joint. The scarf joint is not used as much today because it is slow and troublesome compared to the simple butt joint. The butt joint may be considered as good a joint as the scarf joint, especially for painted work, which will show a crack in the paint if the trim moves, whatever the joint used.

B SPLICING TRIM

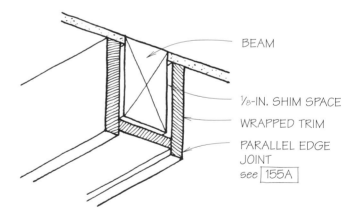

BEAM

⅛-IN. SHIM SPACE

WRAPPED TRIM

PARALLEL EDGE JOINT
see 155A

Structural members such as columns and beams are frequently wrapped (or boxed) with finish material to improve their appearance. Wrapping can be accomplished with virtually any material, but it is most frequently done with gypsum wallboard or wood trim, as shown above.

A ⅛-in. shim space is required between structure and finish because the structural member can be expected to be irregular, and this space will usually be sufficient to span the irregularities of the member.

C WRAPPING COLUMNS & BEAMS

It is very common for trim to turn a corner. The corner can be an inside corner, an outside corner or a flat corner. Following are the basic joints that can be employed to make these corners:

Miter joint—The miter joint is common because of its versatility. The two pieces of trim that make a corner are cut at 45°, which allows moldings of any profile to make corners of any type.

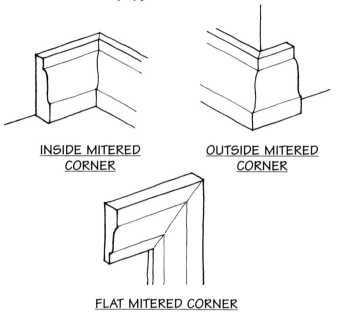

INSIDE MITERED CORNER

OUTSIDE MITERED CORNER

FLAT MITERED CORNER

The only disadvantage of the miter joint is that dimensional changes across the width of the trim caused by variations in moisture content can create a gap at the miter. This phenomenon is especially likely to occur with wider or thicker molding pieces but is often disregarded when choosing them.

Butt joint—The simplest of corner joints, the butt joint is useful only for simple trim pieces of rectangular section. Common for inside or flat corners, the butt joint at the flat corner has the disadvantage of showing end grain, which does not paint or stain well.

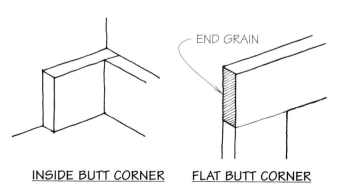

END GRAIN

INSIDE BUTT CORNER   FLAT BUTT CORNER

Coped joint—The coped joint is superior to the mitered joint for profiled molding at inside corners. This joint is made by cutting (coping) the end of the second molding piece to match the profile of the piece applied first. The coped cut incorporates a backcut so that only the exposed edge of the coped piece touches the first piece of molding. When the second piece is pushed up against the first, a tight joint that is unlikely to open with changes in the wood's moisture content is made. If a gap does appear, it will be consistent at all points.

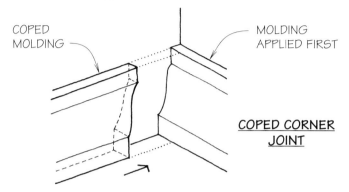

COPED MOLDING

MOLDING APPLIED FIRST

COPED CORNER JOINT

Block joint—The block joint is a simple, versatile joint that, like the miter joint, allows trim of any profile to make corners of any type. The pieces of trim butt against a thick block (called a plinth block when at the base of door trim—see 163A) to create a reveal. The disadvantage of the joint is that the block requires its own means of attachment.

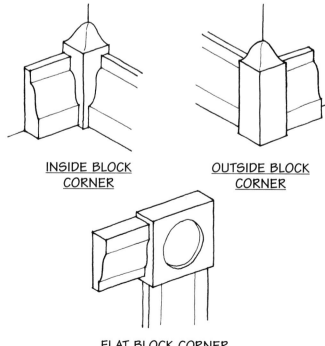

INSIDE BLOCK CORNER

OUTSIDE BLOCK CORNER

FLAT BLOCK CORNER

(A) TURNING CORNERS WITH TRIM

Each piece of trim must end somehow. If it does not turn a corner, it can either die into another material, such as a floor or another piece of trim, or it can simply stop. Knowing a few principles about conditions at the end of a piece of trim is useful in designing an overall trim package.

Trim Dies into Another Material

One of the simplest ways for a piece of trim to end is for it to die (butt) into the surface of another material that is perpendicular to its length. This condition has the effect of capping the end of the trim piece with the surface into which it dies. Nothing further need be added to the assembly to make it appear finished.

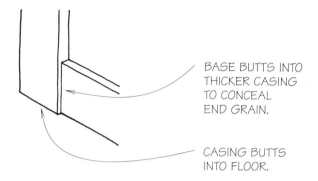

BASE BUTTS INTO THICKER CASING TO CONCEAL END GRAIN.

CASING BUTTS INTO FLOOR.

Trim Terminates

Occasionally, it is desirable or necessary to end a piece of trim without butting against another material or turning a corner. This condition frequently occurs at window and door trim.

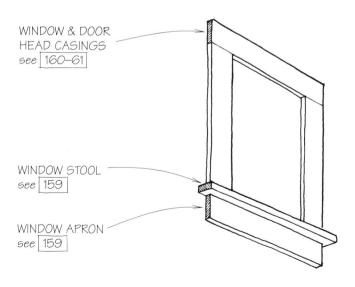

WINDOW & DOOR HEAD CASINGS see 160–61

WINDOW STOOL see 159

WINDOW APRON see 159

There are three basic approaches that can be taken to terminate trim:

Square-cut—The trim can simply be square-cut to length and left with the end grain exposed. This works fine in many cases, especially if the trim has a simple profile or is a simple board. The square-cut detail has the disadvantages that the end grain does not paint or stain well and that trim profiles with relieved backs will show the gap at the back of the piece.

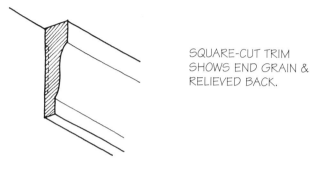

SQUARE-CUT TRIM SHOWS END GRAIN & RELIEVED BACK.

Coped—Moldings with shaped profiles can be coped so that the end of the molding matches the cross-sectional profile. This detail has the same disadvantages as the square-cut detail described above.

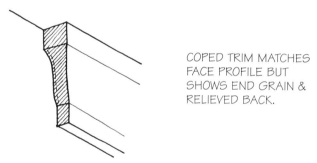

COPED TRIM MATCHES FACE PROFILE BUT SHOWS END GRAIN & RELIEVED BACK.

Mitered & returned—Trim can be mitered and returned to the wall (or other surface) with a small piece of the same trim glued in place. This approach, although somewhat more involved, has the advantages of eliminating the end grain while also ending the molding with the same profile as its cross section.

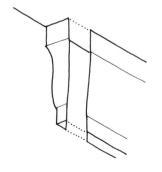

MITERED & RETURNED TRIM MATCHES FACE PROFILE, HIDES END GRAIN & HIDES RELIEVED BACK.

 ENDING TRIM

Pneumatic Nailers

Until the advent of the pneumatic nailers (air guns) in the 1970s, virtually all trim was fastened by hand with finish nails. Finish nails, which have very small heads, are driven to the surface of the wood trim with a finish hammer and then below the surface with a few hammer blows to a nail set. This method is still used, but trim applied by professionals is now almost always fastened with pneumatic equipment.

The advantages of the pneumatic nailer are so numerous and compelling that it is almost impossible for finish carpenters to compete for work without one. Primary among these advantages is the speed with which the fastener is set to its finished position. This operation takes only a fraction of the time taken to drive and set a finish nail by hand. The operation also takes only one hand, freeing the other hand to hold the trim accurately in place. Finally, the single blow with which the air gun sets the nail below the surface also applies force to the trim piece, which tends to make the trim fit tighter to the wall than it would with the multiple blows of a hammer. This single pneumatic blow is sharp and crisp and allows some pieces to be joined that could not be easily joined with a hammer.

An air gun can also be used with staples. If both the nail and the staple are sized to have sufficient holding power for the materials on which they are used, the main difference between the two is the shape of the hole that they leave on the surface of the trim.

O   FINISH NAIL HOLE

▭   FINISH STAPLE HOLE

For painted work, the shape of the holes to be filled makes little difference because a good painter can make them disappear even to the critical eye. For clear-finished work, however, the fastener holes can be seen through the transparent finish and can detract from the overall appearance. Staple holes have the advantage of being long and thin so that, if oriented in the direction of the grain, can blend better with the natural surface of stained woods.

Screws

In addition to nails and staples, screws are sometimes used to attach trim. Trim-head screws are used to attach trim to steel studs. They are also advantageous for locations that require more holding power than a nail or staple can deliver. Trim-head screws have heads only slightly larger than the heads on pneumatically driven finish nails and are installed with a square driver. The screws are self-tapping, and some will create their own pilot holes in light steel framing as they are being installed. This type of fastener tends to split solid wood trim, especially hardwood, so predrilling of molding may be recommended.

Adhesives

Adhesives are used, usually in conjunction with other fasteners, to increase the bond between trim and the material to which it is fastened. Adhesives are especially useful where two pieces of trim must remain flush (see 155). Adhesives are also sometimes used by themselves for very small pieces of trim that would probably be split by a nail or staple.

Filling Fastener Holes

Filling holes in trim that is to be painted is reasonably straightforward. There are many fillers available that can be matched to the materials, applied, sanded and covered with paint. For stained trim, however, the job of filling holes is much more critical because the filled hole will remain visible after the trim is finished. Matching the color of the wood is the most difficult part of filling stained work. The darker the stain, the less critical this task becomes, whereas for very light stains or clear finishes, the color of the wood must be matched almost exactly for the fastener holes to disappear into the finished work. Over time, clear finished wood usually changes color, so that even though the filler color matches the wood at the time of installation, it probably will not match the finished trim in a year or two.

Premixed fillers with colors supposedly matched to specific species are available, but they rarely match exactly because of the variety within each species and, in some cases, within a single piece of trim. These premixed fillers are often adequate for dark stained work, however. The best way to match trim color with filler is to custom-mix the filler at the site with the aid of a palette of colors. This is done for the best clear finish work, often after the trim has been finished and has had a year or more to change color.

TRIM FASTENERS

Doors and windows have basic functional components, as shown below (door components are like windows except that a door replaces the window sash and doesn't have a stool or apron).

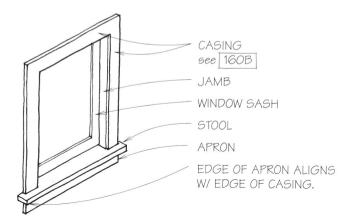

Jambs

Key among door and window components is the jamb. The side jambs and the head jamb (often simply called the head) of a window or door hold the operational elements—the door or the window sash—in place. The edge of the jamb is lapped by trim, called casing (see 160–61), which spans the gap between jamb and finish wall. Windows today are provided with a range of trim packages from which to choose. It is also possible to select trim casings, stools and aprons separately.

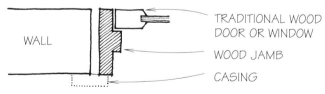

Some jambs are made the same way today as they have been for centuries. For example, interior door jambs are usually made of a single piece of wood that extends the full thickness of the wall and has trim on both sides of the wall lapping the jamb.

Jamb extenders—Most modern wood windows and exterior doors have jambs that do not extend through walls that are framed with materials thicker than 2x4s. To trim these windows and doors with wood, extenders must be added to the jamb. Modern metal

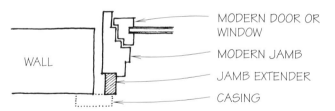

and vinyl windows require wood jamb extenders if wood casing is to the used.

Stools & Aprons

Wood windows traditionally have been trimmed inside with a wood stool and apron as a complement to the exterior sloped sill. The stool protects against water penetration at its outer edge and provides a wide level surface inside. A trim piece called an apron covers the gap between stool and finish wall surface. The simplest apron can be an unprofiled board. Elaborate aprons may be built up of several pieces.

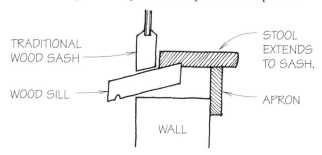

The sill of a modern window is not sloped but is usually the same as the side and head jambs. And instead of a stool, these windows are often trimmed at the bottom with a jamb extender and casing that are identical to the jamb extenders and casing on the rest of the window, thus making picture-frame casing (see 160A).

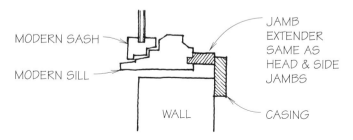

Alternatively, a shallow stool with an apron may trim the modern window base. This detail provides a wider surface and allows a variety of casing types to be used (see 160-61). A stool and apron can also be used when there is no head or side casing and gypsum wallboard wraps the corner and butts the jamb (see 153A).

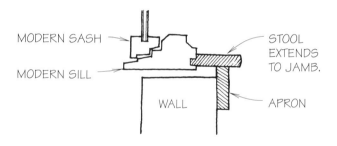

DOOR & WINDOW TRIM
JAMBS, STOOLS & APRONS

MITERED JOINT
see 160C

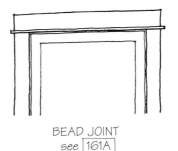

BEAD JOINT
see 161A

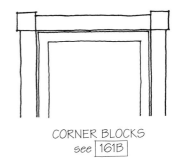

CORNER BLOCKS
see 161B

A MITERED JOINT IS OFTEN
USED @ BASE OF WINDOW
WITHOUT STOOL. THIS IS CALLED
PICTURE-FRAME CASING.
see 159

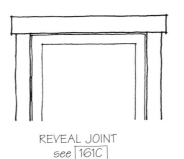

REVEAL JOINT
see 161C

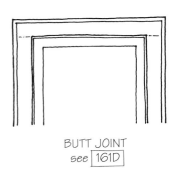

BUTT JOINT
see 161D

 A **DOOR & WINDOW CASING**
JOINT TYPES

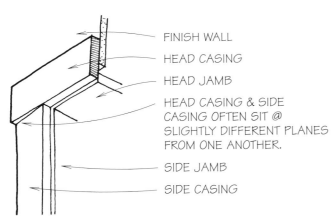

FINISH WALL

HEAD CASING

HEAD JAMB

HEAD CASING & SIDE
CASING OFTEN SIT @
SLIGHTLY DIFFERENT PLANES
FROM ONE ANOTHER.

SIDE JAMB

SIDE CASING

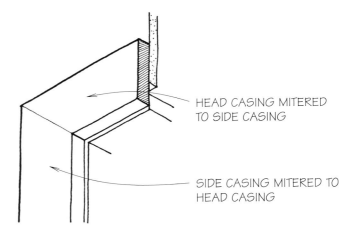

HEAD CASING MITERED
TO SIDE CASING

SIDE CASING MITERED TO
HEAD CASING

The gap between jamb or jamb extender and wall is covered with trim that is called casing. There are several types of window and door casing, and they are differentiated primarily by the way the head and side casing meet. Because casings straddle the gap between the jamb and the often irregular surfaces of the wall, the head casing and side casing often sit at slightly different planes from each other. Most of the corner joints have therefore been developed to provide a reveal, allowing the unavoidable slight misalignment to go unperceived.

One of the most common corner joints, the mitered joint has the advantage of simplicity, but it does not make a reveal, so misaligned casings will be perceptible. In addition, the joint is useful only for narrow (3 in. or less) casings; dimensional changes across wider moldings will open the joint. When a jamb extender is used in place of a stool, the miter joint is usually used at the bottom corners to allow the casing to wrap around the base of the window. This trim arrangement is commonly called picture-frame casing (see 160A).

 B **DOOR & WINDOW CASING**
DESIGN STRATEGIES

 C **MITERED JOINT**
@ DOOR & WINDOW CASING

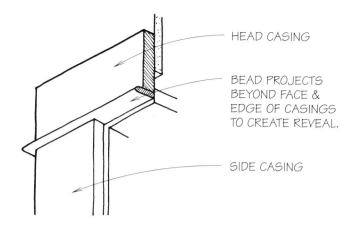

HEAD CASING

BEAD PROJECTS BEYOND FACE & EDGE OF CASINGS TO CREATE REVEAL.

SIDE CASING

The insertion of a thin but extra-deep trim piece—a bead—below the head casing creates a reveal that allows a slight misalignment between side and head casings. Another advantage of this treatment is that if the head jamb is recessed from the wall plane the bead can be trimmed at its ends so that the central portion of the bead can rest firmly against the head jamb. The joint was popularized in Victorian buildings.

A   BEAD JOINT
@ DOOR & WINDOW CASING

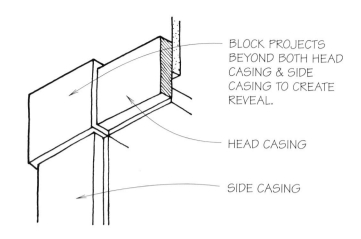

BLOCK PROJECTS BEYOND BOTH HEAD CASING & SIDE CASING TO CREATE REVEAL.

HEAD CASING

SIDE CASING

Inserting at the corners blocks that are thicker than the casings creates a reveal that allows both side and head casings to assume a slightly different plane from that of the wall. Popular in Victorian buildings, the joint was also used at the base of door casing where the casing meets the base trim.

B   CORNER-BLOCK JOINT
@ DOOR & WINDOW CASING

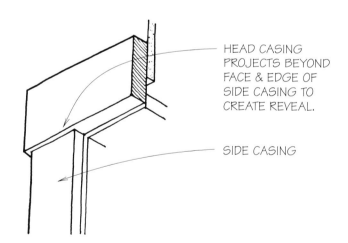

HEAD CASING PROJECTS BEYOND FACE & EDGE OF SIDE CASING TO CREATE REVEAL.

SIDE CASING

Similar to the bead joint, the reveal joint allows the side casings to be slightly misaligned from the plane of the wall. The reveal itself is created by using a head casing thicker than the side casings. A disadvantage of this system compared to the bead joint is that a jamb behind the plane of the wall cannot be so easily accommodated. The reveal joint came into common usage during the Craftsman period in the early 1900s.

C   REVEAL JOINT
@ DOOR & WINDOW CASING

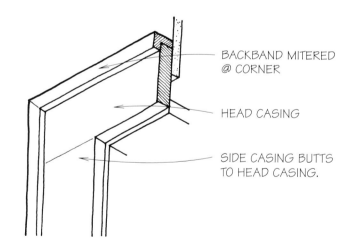

BACKBAND MITERED @ CORNER

HEAD CASING

SIDE CASING BUTTS TO HEAD CASING.

Simplest of all casing joints, the butt joint works only for square-edged casings of identical thickness and does not allow misaligned casings. The butt joint is often used in conjunction with a backband that covers the end grain of the head casing. The backband also adds visual complexity to the casing and can provide a reveal for base or other moldings that may die into the casing.

D   BUTT JOINT
@ DOOR & WINDOW CASING

The transition between wall and floor is usually trimmed with a base molding designed to form a neat edge against both surfaces.

- FINISHED WALL
- BASE MOLDING FORMS A NEAT EDGE AGAINST WALL & FLOOR.
- FINISH FLOORING

Base trim not only covers the gap between wall and floor but can also protect the wall from marks caused by shoes and furniture. Residences usually have a wood base molding, while commercial buildings often employ a vinyl or rubber base trim.

Base trim in wood and other materials is available in many profiles. Base trims tend to have a slender or sloped top edge to ease the task of installing them against an uneven wall and to minimize places for dust to accumulate.

The finish materials of the walls and the floor are important to consider when selecting base moldings. Carpet, for example, has different requirements for meeting a base trim than does wood flooring.

- WOOD BASE HELD UP FROM SUBFLOOR ⅜ IN. TO ½ IN. TO ALLOW CARPET TO TUCK UNDER.
- NO BASE SHOE REQUIRED

Wood Base Trim

Wood base is available not only in a number of profiles but also in many different sizes. Smaller profiles such as sanitary base or quarter round are common because they are narrow enough to conform to irregularities in both wall and floor (see 154) and therefore can be applied as a single piece (drawing top right). Taller bases may be built up of several pieces and usually require a base shoe to conform to flooring contours (drawing middle right). An independent base cap may also be required to conform to irregularities in the wall.

One variation of the standard wood base is the flush base molding, which looks simple but which can be expensive to install because of the required blocking and edge detailing of wall material (drawing bottom right).

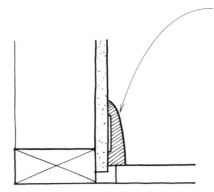

SMALLER PROFILES SUCH AS SANITARY BASE

NOTE:
SMALLER PROFILES SUCH AS SANITARY BASE CAN CONFORM TO WALL & FLOOR IRREGULARITIES.
see 154

SMALL BASE

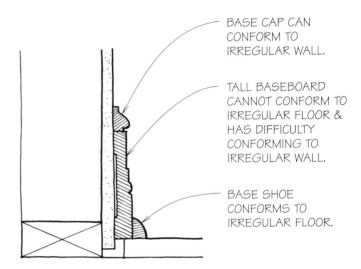

- BASE CAP CAN CONFORM TO IRREGULAR WALL.
- TALL BASEBOARD CANNOT CONFORM TO IRREGULAR FLOOR & HAS DIFFICULTY CONFORMING TO IRREGULAR WALL.
- BASE SHOE CONFORMS TO IRREGULAR FLOOR.

TALL BASE W/ BASE SHOE

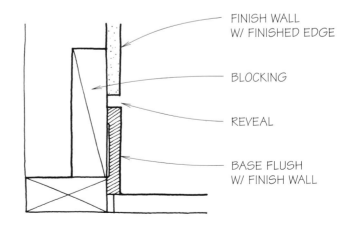

- FINISH WALL W/ FINISHED EDGE
- BLOCKING
- REVEAL
- BASE FLUSH W/ FINISH WALL

FLUSH BASE

 A BASE TRIM

Base molding is typically applied to the surface of the finish wall, and it butts into the edge of the door casing. Coordination of base molding with door casing should ensure that the face of the base molding does not project beyond the door casing. Although the base and door trims shown below have rectangular profiles, moldings of other profiles may be used.

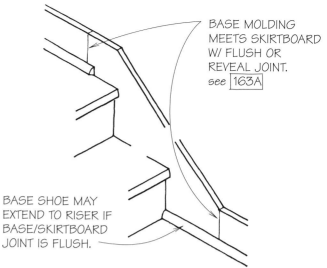

BASE MOLDING MEETS SKIRTBOARD W/ FLUSH OR REVEAL JOINT.
see | 163A |

BASE SHOE MAY EXTEND TO RISER IF BASE/SKIRTBOARD JOINT IS FLUSH.

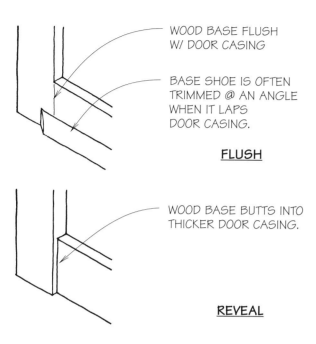

WOOD BASE FLUSH W/ DOOR CASING

BASE SHOE IS OFTEN TRIMMED @ AN ANGLE WHEN IT LAPS DOOR CASING.

FLUSH

WOOD BASE BUTTS INTO THICKER DOOR CASING.

REVEAL

DOOR CASING & BASE BOTH BUTT INTO THICKER PLINTH BLOCK.

PLINTH BLOCK

BASE BUTTS INTO THICKER BACKBAND.

BACKBAND

To make a neat connection between base trim and a stair skirtboard, the base trim should match the thickness of the skirtboard. The base shoe will then continue over the flush joint to the first riser. If the skirtboard is thicker than the baseboard, the baseboard can meet the skirtboard with a reveal joint (see 163A) but a base shoe (if any) will not continue to the stair riser.

(B) **BASE TRIM @ STAIR**

Common in commercial work, vinyl or rubber base molding is inexpensive, available in a number of colors and easily applied with adhesive. It easily conforms to wall and floor irregularities. Standard heights are 2½ in., 4 in. and 6 in. Three typical profiles (shown below) can be matched with specific flooring types.

Manufactured outside corners are commonly used, but inside corners are usually coped. Vinyl and rubber base moldings are narrow enough to die into door casings.

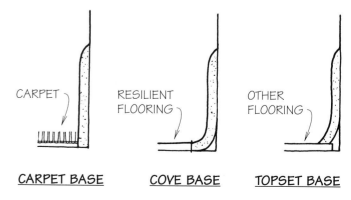

CARPET

RESILIENT FLOORING

OTHER FLOORING

CARPET BASE   **COVE BASE**   **TOPSET BASE**

(A) **BASE TRIM @ DOOR CASING**

(C) **VINYL OR RUBBER BASE MOLDING**

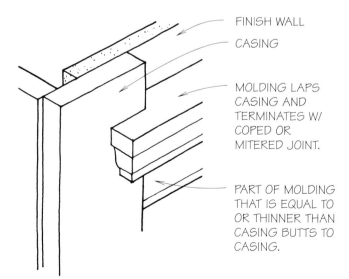

CROWN MOLDING
see 164B

PICTURE RAIL
see 164C

PLATE RAIL
see 165A

CHAIR RAIL
see 165B

WAINSCOT CAP
see 165C

CORNER MOLDING
see 165D

There are several specialized types of traditional moldings that can be used functionally and decoratively. Many of these moldings are applied continuously around a room and often require backing or blocking, so it is important to plan for such moldings before wall finishes are in place.

Some of these moldings (especially plate rails, chair rails and wainscot caps) commonly terminate at door or window casings. If the molding is thinner than the casing, it can simply butt into the casing, leaving a reveal (see 163A) If the molding is thicker than the casing, however, it must be terminated independently of the edge of the casing. This is commonly done with a coped or mitered end (see below and 157). An alternative is to add a backband to the casing and butt the molding to the backband (see 163A).

Located at the intersection of a wall and ceiling, the crown (or sprung cove) molding makes a transition between these two planes. Crown molding typically circumscribes a room and is fastened to both wall and ceiling, so some blocking in the ceiling is usually required. Crown molding can be built up of several pieces to be quite elaborate. Crown molding can also be made with plaster (see 14D).

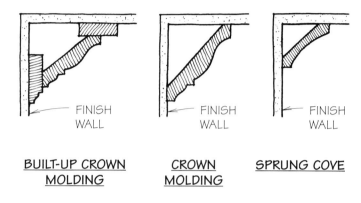

FINISH WALL | FINISH WALL | FINISH WALL

BUILT-UP CROWN MOLDING | CROWN MOLDING | SPRUNG COVE

(B) CROWN MOLDING

Historically, picture rail has been used as a continuous strip around a room from which to hang pictures. Although the picture rail is not always used for hanging pictures today, its use has persisted because it provides a trim high on the wall that acts as an accent strip or a logical place to change paint colors. The picture rail is usually set either just below the heads of doors and windows where it dies into the side casings or just below the ceiling plane where it can flow around the room without interfering with other trim.

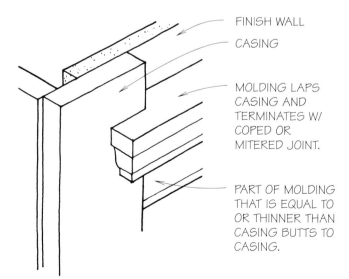

FINISH WALL

CASING

MOLDING LAPS CASING AND TERMINATES W/ COPED OR MITERED JOINT.

PART OF MOLDING THAT IS EQUAL TO OR THINNER THAN CASING BUTTS TO CASING.

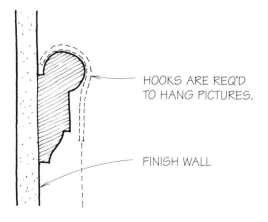

HOOKS ARE REQ'D TO HANG PICTURES.

FINISH WALL

(A) SPECIALIZED MOLDINGS
INTRODUCTION

(C) PICTURE RAIL

The plate rail was developed to display plates and other objects approximately at eye level. It is usually built up of several pieces of molding and was used frequently in Craftsman-style houses. The plate rail is not common today.

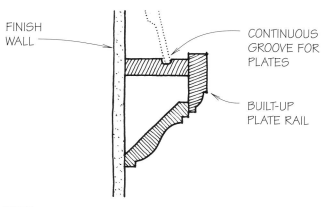

NOTE:
AN ALTERNATIVE IS TO SUPPORT A CONTINUOUS SHELF WITH INDIVIDUAL BRACKETS.

 PLATE RAIL

The wainscot cap covers the gap between the top of the wainscot (see 40-41) and the wall above. If the wainscot is flush with the wall, the wainscot cap can be very simple and, indeed, identical to a chair rail (see 165B). If the wainscot is applied to the surface of the wall, the cap must accommodate the difference between the planes of the wainscot and the wall above. In this case, the wainscot cap frequently builds out beyond the door (or window) casing and is detailed to lap the casing.

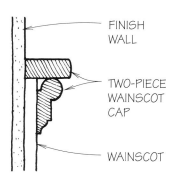
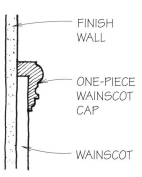

 WAINSCOT CAP

A horizontal molding set about 3 ft. above the floor, a chair rail has historically performed two functions. First, it protected the relatively soft plaster surface of the wall from abrasion by chairs placed against it. Second, some types of chair rail were fitted with pegs on which chairs were hung while the floor was swept. The modern chair rail rarely has pegs, but rather acts as a visual divider of the height of the wall. The wall surface below the chair rail is often finished differently from the wall above, making the chair rail effectively into an inexpensive wainscot cap (see 165C).

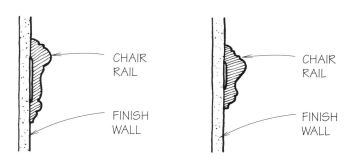

 CHAIR RAIL

Several moldings are available primarily to trim corners.

Corner cap—The corner cap is designed to trim outside corners with a single piece of molding. It is generally used in a vertical application, such as where the board paneling on two walls meet. The thin profile of the corner cap allows it to butt to other moldings leaving a reveal.

Cove—Cove molding is commonly used to trim inside corners and in combination with other moldings to make built-up profiles.

Quarter-round—Like cove molding, quarter-round molding is used to trim inside corners. Quarter-round is also often used in place of a base shoe (see 162).

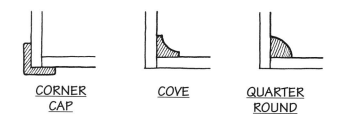

CORNER CAP   COVE   QUARTER ROUND

 CORNER MOLDINGS

Stairs

5

The stair originated at least 2,500 years ago as a practical means to ascend from one level to another. The evolution of the simple notched log or climbing pole, one of the earliest types of stair, has followed fascinating paths shaped by available technology and the use of the stair. Today's stairs are arranged in many configurations and incorporate many details as well as a number of practical safety features that have been developed over the years.

The stairway, because of its spatial and dynamic qualities, is frequently placed in a prominent part of the building and receives much attention by the designer and/or the builder. The prominence and complexity of the stair, as well as safety requirements, make it necessary to understand the structure and materials of stairbuilding, as well as how stairs are configured and dimensioned.

Stair Configuration

The straight stair (shown below) is the most common stairway and the most economical to build. Sections can be combined with a landing, a small intermediate platform between primary floor levels, to make the most common stair configurations.

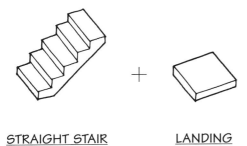

STRAIGHT STAIR   +   LANDING

Landings are usually employed to allow a stairway to change directions. For example, two straight-stair sections can be combined with a landing to form an L-shaped or a U-shaped stairway. Landings must be structurally supported, and can provide support for the straight-stair sections that are combined with them.

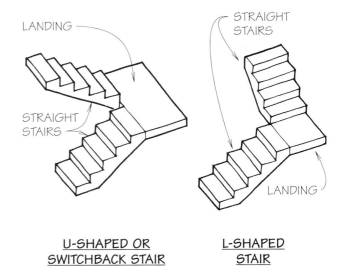

LANDING — STRAIGHT STAIRS

STRAIGHT STAIRS

LANDING

U-SHAPED OR SWITCHBACK STAIR

L-SHAPED STAIR

Spiral stairs (drawing below left) are unique because of their structure and their efficient use of floor area, but their use is limited by codes (see 173). The space-saver stair (drawing below right) provides the most efficient use of floor area of any stair configuration. This stairway, which includes a separate stairway for each foot, is not discussed further because it is not allowed by code as an egress stair.

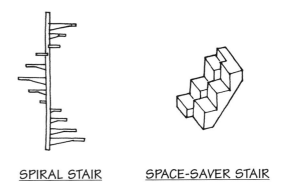

SPIRAL STAIR   SPACE-SAVER STAIR

Since the straight stair is the basis for most stair configurations, the discussion in this chapter will focus on straight stairs. The principles for straight stairs may be interpreted to extend to curved stairs, which are similar but more difficult and costly to build.

Building codes ensure stair safety by specifying stair dimensions (see 168B) and location and design of handrails (see 181A). In multiple-story public buildings, stairs serve as emergency exits. Codes require that emergency lighting be provided, that the walls around the stair be fire-rated and that stair materials be rated for flame and smoke spread (see Appendix C). Because there is more danger of falling on a stairway than on a level floor, and injuries are likely to be more severe, stair design should extend beyond the minimum code requirements.

Traction, lighting and a concern for the safety of children, the elderly and the disabled are areas that deserve special consideration. Traction on stairways is extremely important. Some finish materials inherently provide good traction, while others need to be augmented with slip-resistant strips (see 175B).

Lighting stairways is more important than lighting other circulation spaces. Also useful is lighting that differentiates the treads from the risers on stairs where treads and risers are made of the same material.

Children's safety is important in the design of stairways, and particularly banisters, (see 181-86) to minimize the risk of children climbing on them and falling off. Open-riser stairs should also be used with caution, since it is possible for a child to fall through the stair.

Older people may have difficulty negotiating stairs and deserve special consideration. Safety features for the elderly include stairways that are not as steep, handrails that extend farther than required and visual contrasts that distinguish the treads.

<u>ACCEPTABLE</u>   <u>NOT ACCEPTABLE</u>

The Americans with Disabilities Act (ADA) has specific regulations for stairs. One example is the nosing section illustrated below, designed to allow a person with the use of only one leg to climb stairs without catching the trailing foot on the nosing.

Ⓐ STAIR SAFETY

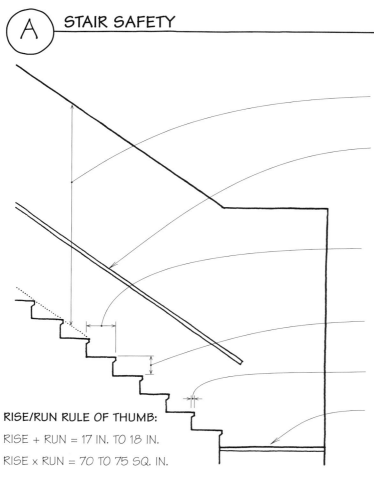

RISE/RUN RULE OF THUMB:

RISE + RUN = 17 IN. TO 18 IN.

RISE × RUN = 70 TO 75 SQ. IN.

HEADROOM: MIN. HEADROOM FROM NOSING TO CEILING OR OTHER STRUCTURE IS 6 FT. 8 IN. (RESIDENTIAL CODES MAY ALLOW 6 FT. 6 IN.)

HANDRAIL: STAIRWAYS WITH THREE OR MORE RISERS REQ. A HANDRAIL ON EACH SIDE OF STAIR. (RESIDENTIAL STAIRS REQ. A HANDRAIL ON ONE SIDE ONLY).

STAIR WIDTH: 36-IN. MIN. TO 44 IN. CLEAR WIDTH (DEPENDING ON USE) IS REQ'D FROM FINISH WALL TO FINISH WALL.

TREAD: 11-IN. MIN. RUN (RESIDENTIAL CODES ALLOW 9-IN. MIN. RUN.)

WINDER: A WEDGE-SHAPED TREAD WITH SPECIAL CODE REQUIREMENTS.

RISER: 4 IN. MIN. TO 7 IN. MAX. RISE (RESIDENTIAL CODES ALLOW 8 IN. MAX. RISE.)

NOSING: 1 IN. TO 1½ IN. REQ'D. SEE 168A FOR SPECIAL ADA REQUIREMENTS.

LANDING: CODES REQUIRE LANDINGS TO BE AS DEEP AS THE STAIRWAY IS WIDE. A LANDING IN A STAIRWAY IS REQ'D AT LEAST EVERY 12 FT. VERTICALLY IF THERE IS NO INTERMEDIATE FLOOR.

Ⓑ STAIR DIMENSIONS
CODE REQUIREMENTS

STRUCTURAL WOOD OR STEEL STRINGERS OR CAST-CONCRETE STAIR SPANS BETWEEN FLOORS AND/OR LANDINGS.

FREE-SPANNING
(WOOD/STEEL/CONCRETE)

STRUCTURAL COMBINATION OF TREADS & RISERS SPANS BETWEEN WALLS.

SUPPORTED BY WALLS
(WOOD/STEEL/CONCRETE)

STAIR FOLLOWS GRADE.

ON GRADE
(CONCRETE)

CEILING STRUCTURE SUPPORTS STAIR.

STRUCTURAL HANDRAIL SUPPORTS STAIR.

SUPPORTED FROM ABOVE
(WOOD/STEEL)

STRUCTURAL TREADS CANTILEVER FROM WALL.

CANTILEVERED
(WOOD/STEEL/CONCRETE)

TREADS CANTILEVER FROM CENTER SUPPORT.

SPIRAL
(WOOD/STEEL)

WOOD STRUCTURE see 170   HYBRID STRUCTURE see 172B   SPIRAL STAIRS see 173

STEEL STRUCTURE see 171   TREAD STRUCTURE see 172C   FINISH MATERIALS see 174

CONCRETE STRUCTURE see 172A

The details of a stairway depend to a large extent on its structural system. For example, a simple, straight stair supported by walls on both sides will be finished differently from a cantilevered stair, even if both are made from the same materials. When the structure surface of the stairway is exposed, an understanding of structural principles, in combination with knowing the properties of the stair materials, becomes especially important.

The general types of stairways are shown above. Some can be combined, such as supporting one side of a stairway with a wall and the other side with a carriage or stringer.

Three basic materials (wood, steel and reinforced concrete) are used in the construction of stairs. Each stair structure requires particular materials, as listed under the drawing titles above. Also influencing the choice of stair materials is the primary structural system of the building in which the stairway will be built, as well as cost and code requirements. Most residential stairways are made of wood, while commercial, institutional and industrial stairs are commonly made of steel or concrete.

Stairway structural materials are frequently covered with a finish surface (see 174), and sometimes materials are combined to make a hybrid stairway structural (see 172B).

 STAIR STRUCTURE

Wood stairs have a long history, and their use has been extremely widespread in both masonry and wood-framed buildings for several centuries. Compared to concrete and steel, wood is lightweight and easy to shape on site. These characteristics, along with a relatively low cost, make wood the most common material for a stair structure. Today, wood stairs are usually found in lightweight wood-frame construction, including most residential and some commercial and institutional buildings.

Common Site-Built Stair

The most common wood stairway, the site-built stair, is made of two or more 2x carriages (also called stringers) that are nailed with spacers to the wall framing and supported by the floor with a ledger or blocking. This structural assembly is usually framed during the early phase of construction and has temporary treads that serve as a construction stair.

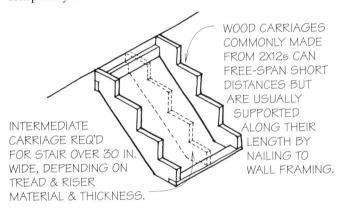

INTERMEDIATE CARRIAGE REQ'D FOR STAIR OVER 30 IN. WIDE, DEPENDING ON TREAD & RISER MATERIAL & THICKNESS.

WOOD CARRIAGES COMMONLY MADE FROM 2X12s CAN FREE-SPAN SHORT DISTANCES BUT ARE USUALLY SUPPORTED ALONG THEIR LENGTH BY NAILING TO WALL FRAMING.

Toward the end of construction, the temporary treads are typically replaced with solid wood finish treads and risers (see 176B). Alternatively, the temporary treads are replaced with plywood subtreads and subrisers (see 177A) that are later covered with a finish material.

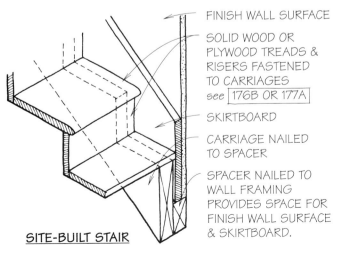

FINISH WALL SURFACE

SOLID WOOD OR PLYWOOD TREADS & RISERS FASTENED TO CARRIAGES see 176B OR 177A

SKIRTBOARD

CARRIAGE NAILED TO SPACER

SPACER NAILED TO WALL FRAMING PROVIDES SPACE FOR FINISH WALL SURFACE & SKIRTBOARD.

SITE-BUILT STAIR

Custom Site-Built Stair

Wood, because it is warm, beautiful and easily shaped, is often employed in the design of custom site-built stairways. Exposed wood, free-spanning stringers and open-riser treads are common, and wood can be laminated or carved to make curves and unique shapes. Custom site-built stairs are not used for construction traffic, which requires a temporary stair.

EXPOSED WOOD FREE-SPANNING STRINGER

WOOD TREADS W/ OPEN RISERS

CUSTOM OPEN-RISER STAIR

Shop-Built Stair

Wood may also be made into a shop-built stairway, which is installed near the end of the construction process. The most common shop-built stair is a straight-run section similar in appearance to a site-built wood stair but combining structure and finish into one assembly (see 177B). The shop-built stair sometimes can be less costly than a common site-built stair made with comparable materials. A shop-built stair is a more solid assembly with fewer opportunities for gaps or checking to occur. A disadvantage is that a temporary stair is required to accommodate workers during construction. Spiral stair kits, most commonly steel (see 173A), are also available in wood.

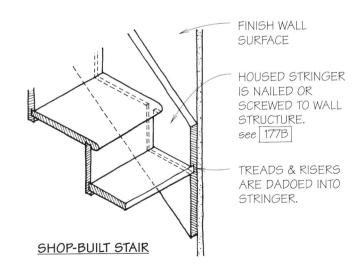

FINISH WALL SURFACE

HOUSED STRINGER IS NAILED OR SCREWED TO WALL STRUCTURE. see 177B

TREADS & RISERS ARE DADOED INTO STRINGER.

SHOP-BUILT STAIR

(A) WOOD STAIR STRUCTURE

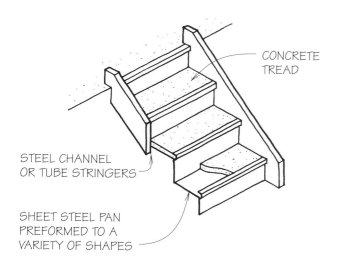

CONCRETE TREAD

STEEL CHANNEL OR TUBE STRINGERS

SHEET STEEL PAN PREFORMED TO A VARIETY OF SHAPES

Steel stairs are relatively new to stairbuilding, having been in existence only since the advent of steel-frame construction in the late 1800s. Today, steel stairs are usually found in steel-framed commercial and institutional buildings.

Compared to concrete and wood, steel is very strong for its weight. It is also extremely durable. Steel transmits sound and resonates more than other materials, however, so it is often combined with concrete treads, which add mass to reduce sound transmission. Steel may also be covered with a finish material such as rubber or carpet to absorb sound.

The most common steel stair has channel or tubing stringers (also called jacks) and preformed tread and riser sections. For ease of construction, the tread and riser sections are welded to metal clips that have been welded into position on the stringers.

The underside of this metal stair may be exposed or covered with a soffit. In some exposed stairs, the pan is welded directly to the stringers for a look that's cleaner than metal clips.

Steel stairways are sometimes site-built but are more frequently built in the controlled environment of a shop. Tread and riser sections may be ordered from metal stair manufacturers but more often are made of standard sheet steel (16 ga. to 12 ga.) and formed to order by a local sheet metal shop or a steel fabricator.

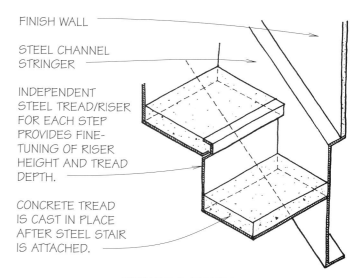

FINISH WALL

STEEL CHANNEL STRINGER

INDEPENDENT STEEL TREAD/RISER FOR EACH STEP PROVIDES FINE-TUNING OF RISER HEIGHT AND TREAD DEPTH.

CONCRETE TREAD IS CAST IN PLACE AFTER STEEL STAIR IS ATTACHED.

TREADS & RISERS

The strength of the standard steel stair usually allows it to be self-supporting (depending on width and overall rise) so that it does not rely on the structure of the wall. This means that even though it is immediately adjacent to the wall, the stair structure can be free-spanning and independent of the wall finish. Even if attached to the wall, it is the stair stringer that provides structure for the stair.

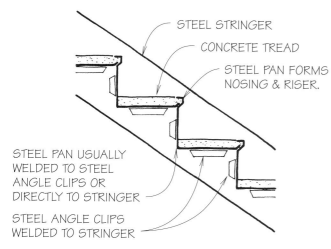

STEEL STRINGER

CONCRETE TREAD

STEEL PAN FORMS NOSING & RISER.

STEEL PAN USUALLY WELDED TO STEEL ANGLE CLIPS OR DIRECTLY TO STRINGER

STEEL ANGLE CLIPS WELDED TO STRINGER

STEEL STAIR W/ CLIPS

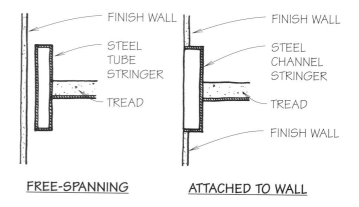

FINISH WALL

STEEL TUBE STRINGER

TREAD

FINISH WALL

STEEL CHANNEL STRINGER

TREAD

FINISH WALL

FREE-SPANNING   **ATTACHED TO WALL**

A **STEEL STAIR STRUCTURE**

Concrete can be formed to almost any shape, so concrete stairways of virtually every configuration and structural type are possible. By far the most frequent is the straight-run concrete stair. Because of the weight of the material, concrete stairs are almost always custom built on site, but precast stairways are occasionally installed. Concrete is most often used for stairways in masonry or concrete constructions.

The strength and reasonable cost of reinforced concrete make the material ideal for durable utilitarian stairs, and the fire resistance of concrete makes it the material of choice for fire-rated exit-stair assemblies. Unlike wood and steel, concrete is not subject to deterioration by moisture. This suggests its use wherever a stairway must be placed directly on grade, such as at a grade change between concrete slabs. The minimal deflection in a reinforced concrete stair also makes it ideal as a base for tile, stone and terrazzo finish materials.

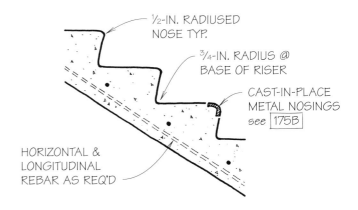

Concrete may be covered with a finish material, but most often it is left unfinished. Since concrete in interior applications is generally finished to a relatively smooth surface for cleaning ease, a slip-resistant surface is usually needed for the tread on concrete stairs (see 175B). With heavy or rough traffic, the nosings of concrete stairs can deteriorate. Special metal nosing plates with slip-resistant surfaces can be cast into the stairs to strengthen the nosing (see 175B).

 CONCRETE STAIR STRUCTURE

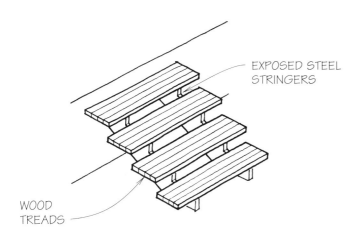

Wood, steel and concrete may be combined to make a hybrid stair structure that features the materials in contrast with one another and takes advantage of the efficiency of each material. For example, steel can be elegant when combined with wood, especially when the steel is used for structural components that might be cumbersome in wood.

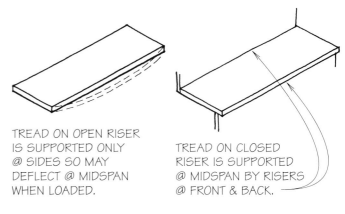

While the stair structure supports the entire stairway and the weight of all the people using it, the individual tread must act locally to support the weight of the person or persons standing on it. Each tread may act independently to span between supports, or it may act in combination with a riser. Stairs made of independent treads without a riser are called open-riser stairs, while those that include a riser are called closed-riser stairs. As shown above, treads on open-riser stairs must be stronger than closed-riser treads because they are not strengthened by risers. Open-riser stairs are not allowed as access stairs in public buildings, so their use is limited.

 HYBRID STAIR STRUCTURE

 TREAD STRUCTURE
OPEN RISERS VS. CLOSED RISERS

Because of its geometry, the spiral stair is in a category by itself. Its structure is singular and its spatial considerations and code restrictions are unique.

Structure and Materials

In the structure of a spiral stair, all treads are cantilevered from a central support (newel) that is usually made of steel because it needs to be stiff and strong. The central support is braced at each floor by the landing and concentrates the weight of the entire stair on one spot at its base.

The most common spiral tread is also made of steel and can be left exposed or be covered with hardwood or plywood and a thin finish material such as carpet. Handrails for spiral stairs are a continuous curve (helix) and are most commonly made of metal and/or wood. Balusters are usually metal.

The spiral stair is an assembly of curved and tapered parts that must be finely crafted and structured to cantilever from the central support. Consequently, the parts for spiral stairs are typically manufactured in the controlled environment of a factory or shop. The parts are sometimes preassembled but more often are assembled at the site.

Spatial Requirements

Spiral stairs provide a vertical connection between floors that uses less floor area than the most efficient standard stair. As a trade-off for efficiency, however, the spiral stair gives up some flexibility of floor plan because the top and bottom step must always be in approximate vertical alignment. This feature does not always complement a floor plan, and the same is not true of standard stairs made of straight sections, with or without intermediate landings.

Code Restrictions

The spiral stair makes more efficient use of floor area than a standard stair, but it is less easily negotiated, especially in an emergency. Consequently, building codes allow the installation of a spiral stair only in residential construction and only to serve a limited floor area (400 sq. ft. or less by UBC standards). This restriction on use allows the dimensional limits of a spiral stair to be less stringent than the limits required of straight-run stairs. For example, the pie-shape tread of the spiral stair would not be allowed if it were a winder in a standard stair.

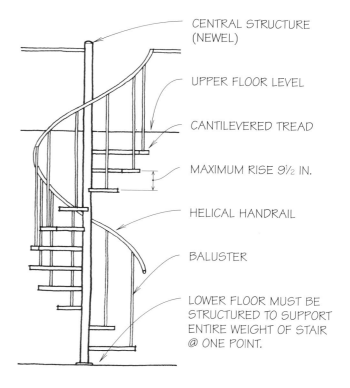

CENTRAL STRUCTURE (NEWEL)

UPPER FLOOR LEVEL

CANTILEVERED TREAD

MAXIMUM RISE 9½ IN.

HELICAL HANDRAIL

BALUSTER

LOWER FLOOR MUST BE STRUCTURED TO SUPPORT ENTIRE WEIGHT OF STAIR @ ONE POINT.

ELEVATION

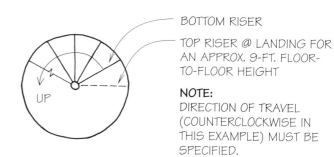

BOTTOM RISER

TOP RISER @ LANDING FOR AN APPROX. 9-FT. FLOOR-TO-FLOOR HEIGHT

NOTE:
DIRECTION OF TRAVEL (COUNTERCLOCKWISE IN THIS EXAMPLE) MUST BE SPECIFIED.

UP

PLAN

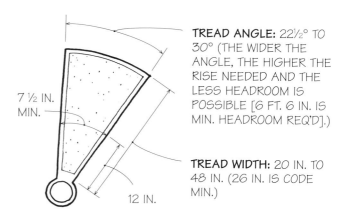

TREAD ANGLE: 22½° TO 30° (THE WIDER THE ANGLE, THE HIGHER THE RISE NEEDED AND THE LESS HEADROOM IS POSSIBLE [6 FT. 6 IN. IS MIN. HEADROOM REQ'D].)

TREAD WIDTH: 20 IN. TO 48 IN. (26 IN. IS CODE MIN.)

7 ½ IN. MIN.

12 IN.

TREAD

SPIRAL STAIRS

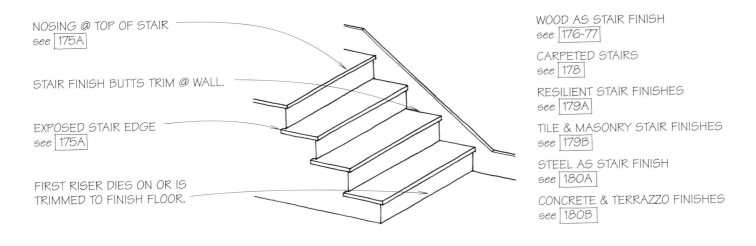

NOSING @ TOP OF STAIR
see 175A

STAIR FINISH BUTTS TRIM @ WALL.

EXPOSED STAIR EDGE
see 175A

FIRST RISER DIES ON OR IS
TRIMMED TO FINISH FLOOR.

WOOD AS STAIR FINISH
see 176-77

CARPETED STAIRS
see 178

RESILIENT STAIR FINISHES
see 179A

TILE & MASONRY STAIR FINISHES
see 179B

STEEL AS STAIR FINISH
see 180A

CONCRETE & TERRAZZO FINISHES
see 180B

The selection of a finish material for a stair has a significant impact on its overall appearance, and can also improve its durability and traction. Material selection depends on the characteristics of the finish choices, on the characteristics of the stair type and structure, on the needs of the people who will use the stair, on code requirements and, often, on cost.

Common Materials

Wood, steel and concrete—the materials from which stair structures are made—can also be finish materials. In addition, most types of flooring materials can become stair finishes. Common stair finishes in homes are warm, soft materials such as wood and carpet. In public buildings where use is much more intensive, harder and more durable materials, such as concrete, vinyl and stone, prevail.

Coordinating Finish with Stairway Type

In terms of design, a straight-run stairway with closed risers and a finished stringer or curb (see 182–84) will provide the most flexibility in selecting a finish material and will be the least expensive to finish. Some common materials such as carpet or vinyl are difficult to apply to stairs with intricate detailing, such as an open baluster without a curb (see 185).

Coordinating Finish with Structure

Coordinating finish materials with the stair's basic structure is critical to how the finish material attaches. For example, finish materials (such as carpet) that are attached to stairs with mechanical fasteners work best with a wood stair structure, which can readily accept such fasteners. Materials that require stiffness for structural support, such as tile, are best attached to a rigid concrete stair. Some materials, such as vinyl and rubber, require a crisp edge at the nosing of the stair, so using them is difficult with concrete, which generally has a rounded nosing.

Durability

Steel and concrete finishes are quite durable. Adding a very hard finish material such as ceramic tile or masonry to a stair will also provide exceptional durability. Softer materials such as wood or carpet are not as durable. Wood is generally reserved for residential stairs or public stairs with minimal use. Carpet is very common on residential stairs and is also used frequently for public stairways, because it provides good traction, is quiet and is easily replaced.

Cost

The initial cost of a finish material for a stairway is not usually the most important consideration for selecting one kind of stairway over another. The amount of material used to build a stairway is minimal compared with what is used for the entire building, and coordination of stair materials with adjacent floor materials can often be more important than the cost of the stairway materials. Durability, which relates to long-term costs, appearance and traction, is usually more important than initial cost.

Only in multiple-flight stairways for public or multiple-residence buildings does the initial cost of finish materials become a major consideration. In these cases, long-term durability and fire resistance also play roles in material selection. Exposing the primary stair structure (commonly concrete) without the addition of a finish material is often the choice for such stairs.

STAIR FINISH MATERIALS
INTRODUCTION

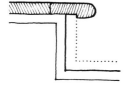

TOP NOSING SAME AS FLOOR

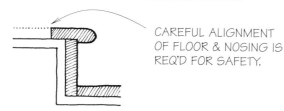

CAREFUL ALIGNMENT OF FLOOR & NOSING IS REQ'D FOR SAFETY.

TOP NOSING SAME AS STAIR

A stair finish material must be carefully detailed where it meets the flooring, both at the top and bottom of the stairway, and where it meets the wall or trim at the side of the stairway. The nosing at the top of the stair can generally be made of the same material as the flooring itself (top drawing above) or it can be made of the same material that is used for the stair treads or

nosings (bottom drawing left). The riser at the base of the stairway can create a neat edge by simply dying on top of the finish flooring.

The edge of the finish treads and risers at the side of the stairway can usually be a very simple butt joint, as shown below. However, ends of treads and risers at an open banister without a curb must be detailed carefully since they are exposed.

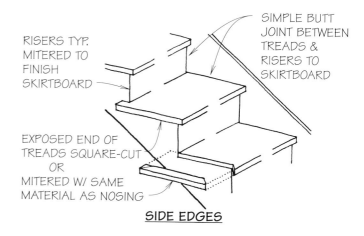

RISERS TYP. MITERED TO FINISH SKIRTBOARD

SIMPLE BUTT JOINT BETWEEN TREADS & RISERS TO SKIRTBOARD

EXPOSED END OF TREADS SQUARE-CUT OR MITERED W/ SAME MATERIAL AS NOSING

SIDE EDGES

 A DETAILS @ STAIR EDGES

STEEL NOSING W/ SLIP-RESISTANT RIDGES CAST INTO CONCRETE STAIR

ANCHOR

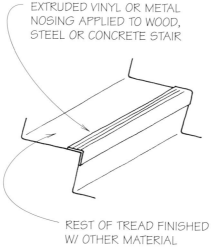

EXTRUDED VINYL OR METAL NOSING APPLIED TO WOOD, STEEL OR CONCRETE STAIR

REST OF TREAD FINISHED W/ OTHER MATERIAL

ABRASIVE TAPE EPOXIED TO SURFACE OF WOOD, STEEL OR CONCRETE STAIR

Traction is especially important on high-use public stairs or stairs used by elderly or disabled persons. Carpet is commonly used because it is inherently slip-resistant (see 178). For a harder, more durable and more easily cleaned surface, vinyl and rubber treads are manufactured with raised patterns to produce a textured, slip-resistant surface (see 179A).

Traction may also be gained on stairs by applying slip-resistant strips to the treads. For example, slip-resistant metal strips may be cast into the surface of concrete treads, metal or vinyl nosings may be mechanically fastened to wood or abrasive tape can be epoxied to the surface of concrete, steel or wood.

 B PROVIDING TRACTION

Finished wood treads may be applied to the structure in one of three ways. The first two methods are used on site-built stairs, and the last is a technique employed to make shop-built stairs.

Wood Fastened Directly to Carriage

Solid wood treads and risers, available in fir, pine, oak and many other hardwoods, can span between carriage supports (approximately 30 in.) on their own without subtreads or subrisers. The wood treads and risers are nailed or screwed and glued to the carriages and fit flush to a finish skirtboard that has been previously applied to the wall or curb at the side of the stairway (see 176B for this detail).

Nail holes in the treads and risers may be filled and recessed. Screw holes may be plugged similar to wood flooring (see 81).

Premium-quality vertical-grain lumber of the dimension required for treads is becoming scarce, so treads composed of a number of edge-glued boards are now common.

Wood Applied over Subtreads

Smaller-dimension wood flooring such as parquet (see 87) or strip (see 84), which does not have the structural capacity to span between carriages, may be applied as a veneer to plywood subtreads that support the nonstructural finish material. This assembly will typically require a special nosing. This type of wood stair will likely become more common as vertical-grain, solid wood treads become less available and more expensive. See 177A for this detail.

Treads & Risers Housed in Stringers

Both high-quality hardwood stairs and lower-cost softwood versions that are designed to be covered with a finish material can be prefabricated in a shop with a housed stringer assembly. One advantage of the housed stringer is that joints between treads, riser and finish stringer will not open up with shrinkage or other minor movement in the structure. See 177B for this detail.

 WOOD AS STAIR FINISH

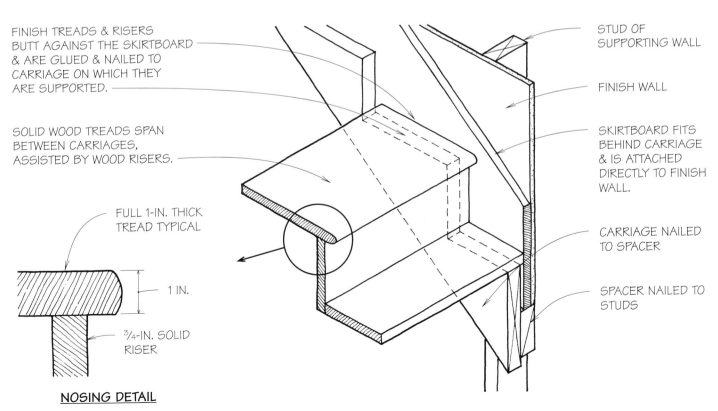

FINISH TREADS & RISERS BUTT AGAINST THE SKIRTBOARD & ARE GLUED & NAILED TO CARRIAGE ON WHICH THEY ARE SUPPORTED.

SOLID WOOD TREADS SPAN BETWEEN CARRIAGES, ASSISTED BY WOOD RISERS.

FULL 1-IN. THICK TREAD TYPICAL

1 IN.

¾-IN. SOLID RISER

NOSING DETAIL

STUD OF SUPPORTING WALL

FINISH WALL

SKIRTBOARD FITS BEHIND CARRIAGE & IS ATTACHED DIRECTLY TO FINISH WALL.

CARRIAGE NAILED TO SPACER

SPACER NAILED TO STUDS

B **SITE-BUILT WOOD STAIR**
FINISH TREADS & RISERS FASTENED TO CARRIAGE

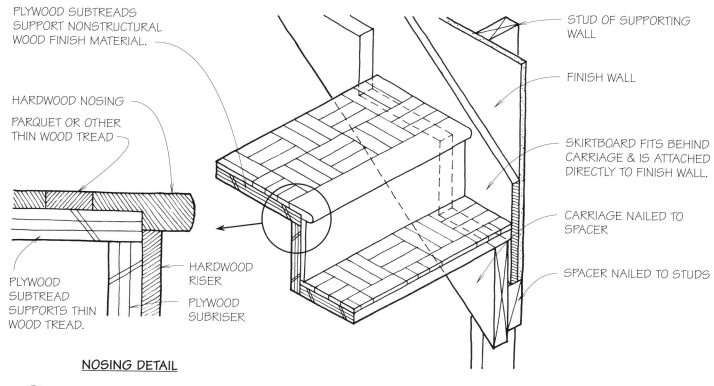

PLYWOOD SUBTREADS SUPPORT NONSTRUCTURAL WOOD FINISH MATERIAL.

HARDWOOD NOSING

PARQUET OR OTHER THIN WOOD TREAD

PLYWOOD SUBTREAD SUPPORTS THIN WOOD TREAD.

HARDWOOD RISER

PLYWOOD SUBRISER

STUD OF SUPPORTING WALL

FINISH WALL

SKIRTBOARD FITS BEHIND CARRIAGE & IS ATTACHED DIRECTLY TO FINISH WALL.

CARRIAGE NAILED TO SPACER

SPACER NAILED TO STUDS

NOSING DETAIL

 SITE-BUILT WOOD STAIR
FINISH TREADS & RISERS APPLIED TO SUBTREADS AND SUBRISERS

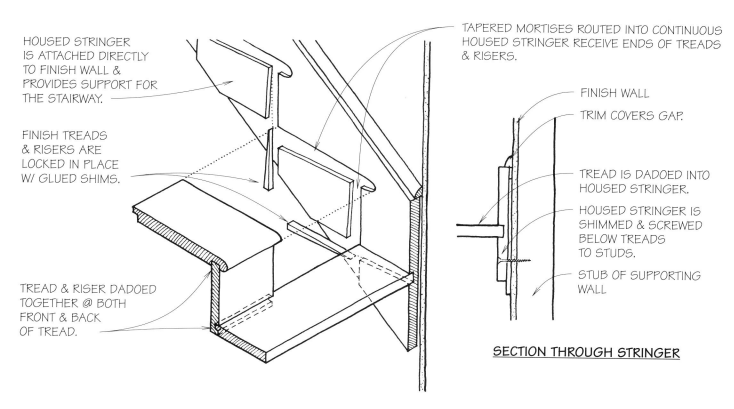

HOUSED STRINGER IS ATTACHED DIRECTLY TO FINISH WALL & PROVIDES SUPPORT FOR THE STAIRWAY.

FINISH TREADS & RISERS ARE LOCKED IN PLACE W/ GLUED SHIMS.

TREAD & RISER DADOED TOGETHER @ BOTH FRONT & BACK OF TREAD.

TAPERED MORTISES ROUTED INTO CONTINUOUS HOUSED STRINGER RECEIVE ENDS OF TREADS & RISERS.

FINISH WALL

TRIM COVERS GAP.

TREAD IS DADOED INTO HOUSED STRINGER.

HOUSED STRINGER IS SHIMMED & SCREWED BELOW TREADS TO STUDS.

STUB OF SUPPORTING WALL

SECTION THROUGH STRINGER

 SHOP-BUILT WOOD STAIR
TREADS & RISERS HOUSED IN STRINGERS

Applying Carpet to Stairs

Carpet can be applied to a wood, steel or concrete stair structure. Installers tend to prefer wood because it is easy to fasten tackless strips to wood (see 66A). Regardless of the stair structure, a carpet that is forgiving as it bends over the stair nosing is preferred (see 63).

Most types of carpet can be glued to steel or concrete stairways (see 66B). The direct glue-down method best attaches the carpet to the substrate, but the double glue-down method and glued down tackless strips with a pad provide a cushion to prolong carpet life.

Methods for Applying Carpet to Wood Stairs

Following are the two methods of applying carpet to wood stairways:

Cap-and-band method—This method, also known as "Hollywood" or "Colonial," is the more difficult and costly of the two (drawing top right). One piece of carpet covers the tread and its nosing, and a separate piece covers the riser above. The carpet backing must be flexible enough to obtain a tight fit at the nosing, and the pile must be deep enough to hide the staples that attach the carpet edges under the nosing and at the top of the riser.

Waterfall method—This technique is easier and less expensive than the cap-and-band method. The carpet simply falls from the edge of the nosing to the next tread, eliminating the articulation of the nosing (drawings bottom right).

An alternative to carpeting the entire stairway is to carpet only the central portion of the stairs where people walk (drawing below). This is analogous to the runner carpet in a hallway and allows a carpeted stair to be gracefully combined with a curbless open baluster (see 185). The cost of such a stairway is rather high since it has all the work of a wood stair plus the added expense of the carpet.

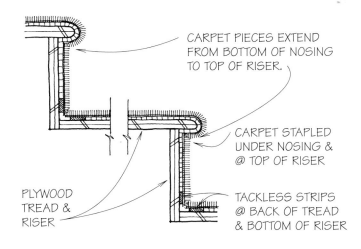

CARPET PIECES EXTEND FROM BOTTOM OF NOSING TO TOP OF RISER.

CARPET STAPLED UNDER NOSING & @ TOP OF RISER

TACKLESS STRIPS @ BACK OF TREAD & BOTTOM OF RISER

PLYWOOD TREAD & RISER

CAP & BAND

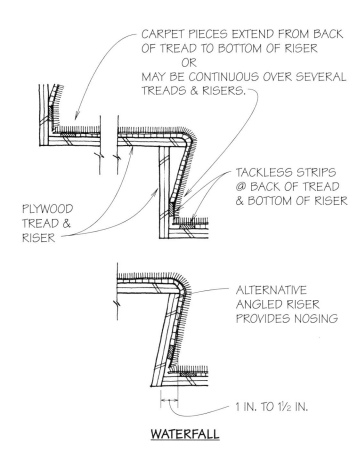

CARPET PIECES EXTEND FROM BACK OF TREAD TO BOTTOM OF RISER
OR
MAY BE CONTINUOUS OVER SEVERAL TREADS & RISERS.

TACKLESS STRIPS @ BACK OF TREAD & BOTTOM OF RISER

PLYWOOD TREAD & RISER

ALTERNATIVE ANGLED RISER PROVIDES NOSING

1 IN. TO 1½ IN.

WATERFALL

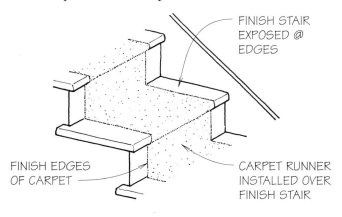

FINISH STAIR EXPOSED @ EDGES

FINISH EDGES OF CARPET

CARPET RUNNER INSTALLED OVER FINISH STAIR

 CARPETED STAIR

Some resilient floor materials, namely extruded vinyl and rubber, are also made as stair treads and risers in a variety of colors and textures. Vinyl or rubber treads and risers may be attached to a wood, steel or concrete stair structure with adhesives specified by the manufacturer.

Resilient treads and risers are made as separate components. This allows treads to be used separately on open-riser stairs and allows treads and risers to be trimmed independently to fit a range of rise/run combinations. Treads and risers must be cut to width on site to fit between stringers.

The tread usually has a raised or etched slip-resistant pattern or an abrasive surface near the nose, while the rear of the tread is smooth (top drawing). The smooth portion can be trimmed on site to fit the tread depth. Risers usually have a smooth surface with a cove base that laps the rear of the tread. The top of the riser is lapped and trimmed by the nosing of the tread. An alternative detail is to have a separate, textured nosing piece that slides under a flat tread (bottom drawing).

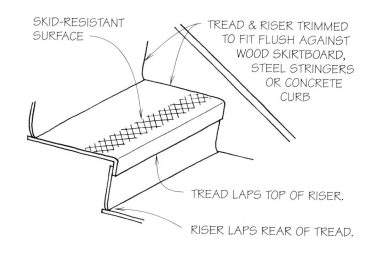

SKID-RESISTANT SURFACE

TREAD & RISER TRIMMED TO FIT FLUSH AGAINST WOOD SKIRTBOARD, STEEL STRINGERS OR CONCRETE CURB

TREAD LAPS TOP OF RISER.

RISER LAPS REAR OF TREAD.

LINOLEUM, SHEET VINYL, VINYL TILE, CORK TILE OR RUBBER FLOORING

VINYL OR RUBBER NOSING

ALTERNATIVE DETAIL

A   **RESILIENT STAIR FINISHES**

As with tile and masonry floors, tile and masonry used on stairs require a stiff structure in order to limit cracking of the tiles, masonry or grout. Tile and masonry are therefore generally applied to a concrete or steel stair structure. It is possible to tile open-riser stairs, but the treads must be extremely stiff, such as those provided by a steel-pan tread filled with concrete (see 171).

Some stone materials are capable of spanning an open riser stair in a single piece. Marble, granite and other dense quarried stone can be custom manufactured for such applications but are extremely expensive.

Because they are brittle, tile and masonry stairs are not very resistant to severe abuse concentrated at the nosing. Tile and masonry stairs should be avoided, therefore, in locations where hand trucks, skateboards and other wheeled objects may chip the nosings.

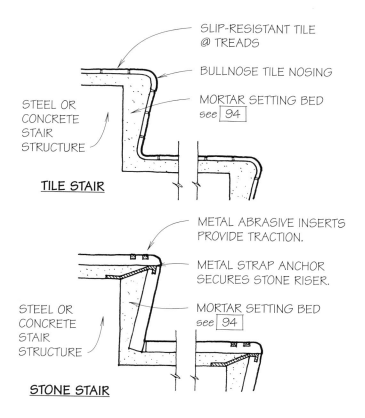

SLIP-RESISTANT TILE @ TREADS

BULLNOSE TILE NOSING

MORTAR SETTING BED see | 94 |

STEEL OR CONCRETE STAIR STRUCTURE

TILE STAIR

METAL ABRASIVE INSERTS PROVIDE TRACTION.

METAL STRAP ANCHOR SECURES STONE RISER.

MORTAR SETTING BED see | 94 |

STEEL OR CONCRETE STAIR STRUCTURE

STONE STAIR

B   **TILE & MASONRY STAIR FINISHES**

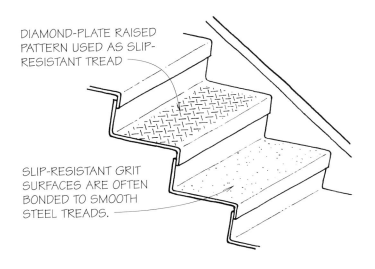

DIAMOND-PLATE RAISED PATTERN USED AS SLIP-RESISTANT TREAD

SLIP-RESISTANT GRIT SURFACES ARE OFTEN BONDED TO SMOOTH STEEL TREADS.

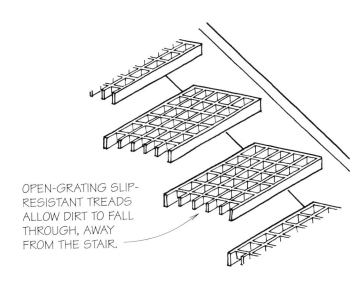

OPEN-GRATING SLIP-RESISTANT TREADS ALLOW DIRT TO FALL THROUGH, AWAY FROM THE STAIR.

Steel stairs are made from sheet steel, which is very smooth and slippery. Manufacturers of steel stairs therefore modify sheet steel to produce slip-resistant treads. These treads may have either raised patterns or a grit surface that is bonded to the steel (drawing left). Another steel-tread version is an open-riser stair with an open gridwork at the treads (drawing right).

 STEEL AS A FINISH STAIR

Concrete
Like concrete for floors (see 100A), concrete as a stair finish not only is inexpensive and durable, but it can also be quite beautiful with the addition of color, texture or decorative tiles set into the surface. In addition, a concrete stair structure can be cast into many shapes. The principal drawback of concrete as a stair finish is that it can chip at edges such as the nosing. Cast-in-place metal nosings can prevent chipping (see 175B).

Terrazzo
Terrazzo, which makes an extremely durable floor (see 103), can also be applied to a concrete or steel stair structure. Terrazzo as a stair finish is available precast (top drawing) or can be cast in place (bottom drawing). Precast terrazzo, which combines tread and riser into one piece, is reinforced and can be engineered to span between supports located at the ends. Thinset terrazzo (see 104D), the most economical and common terrazzo flooring, is not practical for stairs because it is not as thick as the abrasive inserts that are set into the terrazzo treads.

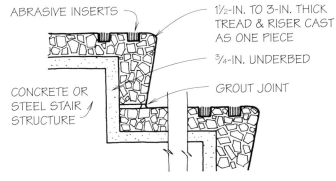

ABRASIVE INSERTS

1½-IN. TO 3-IN. THICK TREAD & RISER CAST AS ONE PIECE

¾-IN. UNDERBED

GROUT JOINT

CONCRETE OR STEEL STAIR STRUCTURE

PRECAST TERRAZZO

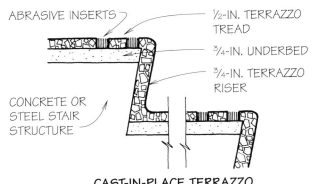

ABRASIVE INSERTS

½-IN. TERRAZZO TREAD

¾-IN. UNDERBED

¾-IN. TERRAZZO RISER

CONCRETE OR STEEL STAIR STRUCTURE

CAST-IN-PLACE TERRAZZO

 CONCRETE & TERRAZZO STAIR FINISHES

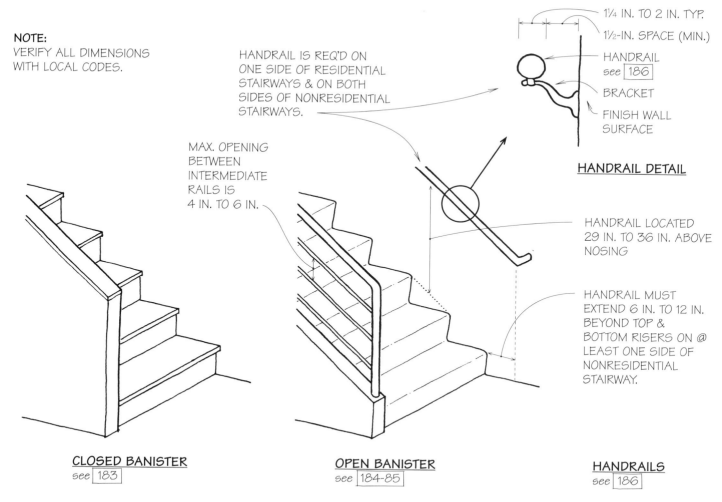

NOTE:
VERIFY ALL DIMENSIONS
WITH LOCAL CODES.

HANDRAIL IS REQ'D ON
ONE SIDE OF RESIDENTIAL
STAIRWAYS & ON BOTH
SIDES OF NONRESIDENTIAL
STAIRWAYS.

MAX. OPENING
BETWEEN
INTERMEDIATE
RAILS IS
4 IN. TO 6 IN.

1¼ IN. TO 2 IN. TYP.

1½-IN. SPACE (MIN.)

HANDRAIL
see | 186 |

BRACKET

FINISH WALL
SURFACE

HANDRAIL DETAIL

HANDRAIL LOCATED
29 IN. TO 36 IN. ABOVE
NOSING

HANDRAIL MUST
EXTEND 6 IN. TO 12 IN.
BEYOND TOP &
BOTTOM RISERS ON @
LEAST ONE SIDE OF
NONRESIDENTIAL
STAIRWAY.

CLOSED BANISTER
see | 183 |

OPEN BANISTER
see | 184-85 |

HANDRAILS
see | 186 |

The banister is the assembly at the open side(s) of a stairway. It is typically composed of structural support elements, intermediate rails, a handrail and trim. The primary purpose of a banister is to minimize the risk of people falling down or off stairways, but a banister can also contribute significantly to the beauty of a stair.

Selecting a banister material depends primarily on the material of the stair structure. A wood banister, for example, is most readily integrated with a wood stair (see 169), and a steel banister is easily welded to a steel stair (see 171), bolted to a wood stair or cast into or anchored to a concrete stair (see 172A). Although banister assemblies are typically made from wood and/or metal, almost any material can be used, including concrete, panel products, glass, plastic, wire, rope and fabric.

Closed vs. Open Banisters
The simplest banisters are closed with no openings (see 183), and are usually built like the adjacent and surrounding walls. More complicated than the closed

banister is the open banister (see 184-85), which is made of numerous parts that are usually decorative but that also contribute to the support of the assembly.

Banister & Handrail Codes
To prevent people from falling off any open side of a stair, banisters are generally required to extend the full length of the stair and to be as tall as the required handrail. To prevent people from falling through the assembly, local building codes typically specify the maximum opening allowed between intermediate rails to be 4 in. to 6 in.

The handrail provides a continuous bar that can be grasped while a person is ascending or descending a stairway. A handrail may be attached to a wall or incorporated into a banister. Codes specify the location of handrails, the height above the stair nosing and the dimensions of the handrail to accommodate grasping (see above right and 186).

  BANISTERS & HANDRAILS

Banister Structure

The design of a banister depends a great deal on its structure, which must be sufficient to resist lateral loads applied by people leaning on or falling against it. The structure of a closed banister is generally the least complicated because the studs of a typical wall, when connected to the stairway, provide a strong cantilever, as shown below.

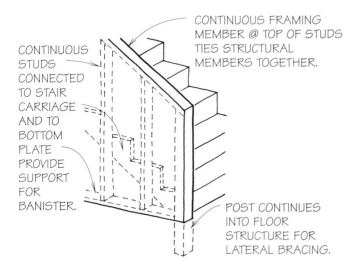

CONTINUOUS STUDS CONNECTED TO STAIR CARRIAGE AND TO BOTTOM PLATE PROVIDE SUPPORT FOR BANISTER.

CONTINUOUS FRAMING MEMBER @ TOP OF STUDS TIES STRUCTURAL MEMBERS TOGETHER.

POST CONTINUES INTO FLOOR STRUCTURE FOR LATERAL BRACING.

The structural support of an open banister can be much more complicated (and expensive) than the closed banister. The open banister often depends on structural connections that must be finely crafted because they are exposed. In both wood and steel construction, the open banister is typically supported by either vertically oriented intermediate rails, called balusters (drawing below left), or by intermittent posts, called newel posts (drawing below right). A combination of these two types of structure is also common.

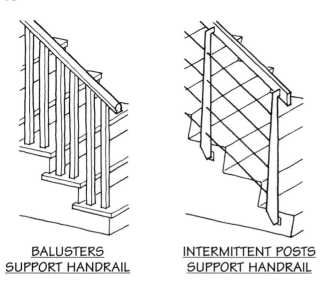

BALUSTERS SUPPORT HANDRAIL

INTERMITTENT POSTS SUPPORT HANDRAIL

When newel posts are used for support, the intermediate rails of an open banister are not structural and can be oriented in any direction (horizontal rails are not recommended where children are likely to climb on them).

When balusters alone are used for support, each baluster must be connected to the stair structure so that all are able to resist lateral loads collectively. This is relatively easy to achieve with steel balusters welded to a steel stair (see 171) or with wood balusters lagged to the side of a free-spanning wood stringer, as shown below.

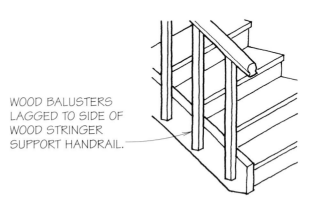

WOOD BALUSTERS LAGGED TO SIDE OF WOOD STRINGER SUPPORT HANDRAIL.

Projecting wood balusters from the wood treads of a traditional open baluster wood stair (see 185) is technically more difficult.

Curbed vs. Curbless Stairs

Open banisters can be made with a curb or without a curb. The use of a curb allows the edge of the treads to be simply butted to the curb. An open banister without a curb requires that the edge of the treads at the open side be finished, a more painstaking and expensive treatment.

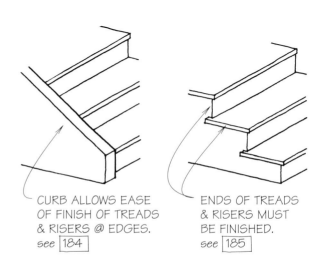

CURB ALLOWS EASE OF FINISH OF TREADS & RISERS @ EDGES. see 184

ENDS OF TREADS & RISERS MUST BE FINISHED. see 185

 BANISTER STRUCTURE & CURB

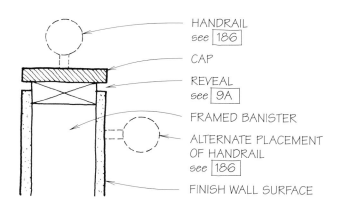

HANDRAIL
see | 186 |

CAP

REVEAL
see | 9A |

FRAMED BANISTER

ALTERNATE PLACEMENT
OF HANDRAIL
see | 186 |

FINISH WALL SURFACE

SECTION @ TOP OF FRAMED BANISTER

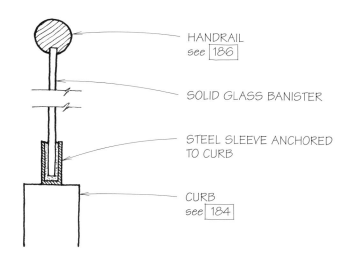

HANDRAIL
see | 186 |

SOLID GLASS BANISTER

STEEL SLEEVE ANCHORED
TO CURB

CURB
see | 184 |

SECTION @ GLASS BANISTER

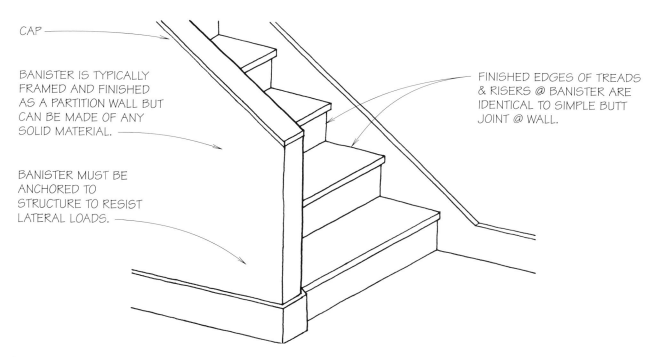

CAP

BANISTER IS TYPICALLY
FRAMED AND FINISHED
AS A PARTITION WALL BUT
CAN BE MADE OF ANY
SOLID MATERIAL.

BANISTER MUST BE
ANCHORED TO
STRUCTURE TO RESIST
LATERAL LOADS.

FINISHED EDGES OF TREADS
& RISERS @ BANISTER ARE
IDENTICAL TO SIMPLE BUTT
JOINT @ WALL.

Usually less expensive than an open banister, a simple closed banister without any openings is typically made of the same material and in the same way as a common partition wall, which is built of light wood framing for residential construction and wood or light metal framing for commercial work. Concrete stairs sometimes have a cast-concrete closed banister. The economy of the closed banister is augmented by the fact that the handrail may be simply attached to the banister in the same way as it would be to any wall.

Less common and more expensive, a closed banister can be made of solid sheet materials including metal, wood panel products or glass. Handrail attachment to this type of banister is often more difficult than for the simple partition-wall banister. Closed-banister assemblies with glass panels are available as manufactured components (drawing top right).

 CLOSED BANISTER

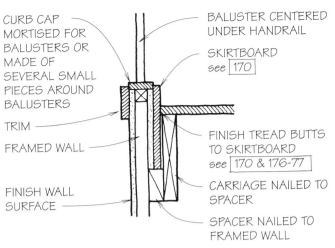

CURB CAP MORTISED FOR BALUSTERS OR MADE OF SEVERAL SMALL PIECES AROUND BALUSTERS

BALUSTER CENTERED UNDER HANDRAIL

SKIRTBOARD see 170

TRIM

FRAMED WALL

FINISH TREAD BUTTS TO SKIRTBOARD see 170 & 176-77

CARRIAGE NAILED TO SPACER

FINISH WALL SURFACE

SPACER NAILED TO FRAMED WALL

SECTION @ WOOD CURB

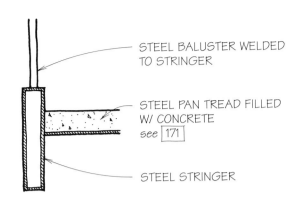

STEEL BALUSTER WELDED TO STRINGER

STEEL PAN TREAD FILLED W/ CONCRETE see 171

STEEL STRINGER

SECTION @ STEEL STRINGER

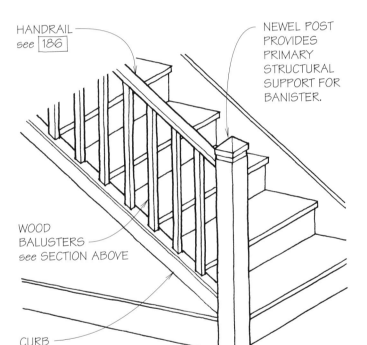

HANDRAIL see 186

NEWEL POST PROVIDES PRIMARY STRUCTURAL SUPPORT FOR BANISTER.

WOOD BALUSTERS see SECTION ABOVE

CURB see SECTION ABOVE

WOOD BANISTER

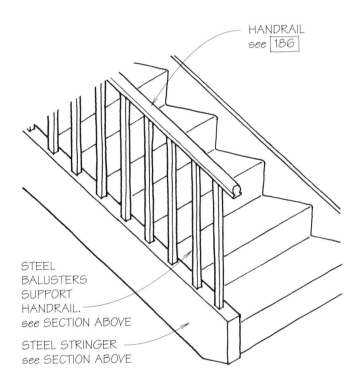

HANDRAIL see 186

STEEL BALUSTERS SUPPORT HANDRAIL. see SECTION ABOVE

STEEL STRINGER see SECTION ABOVE

STEEL BANISTER

The use of a curb with an open banister allows the edge of the treads and risers to be butted to the curb in the same way as they are against a finish skirtboard at a wall. An additional advantage of the curb is that it allows the balusters to be independent of the treads so that each baluster is identical.

Wood—In a wood stair with a curb, newel posts usually provide the primary structural support for the banister. The handrail must be sized to span between

newel posts, and wood balusters are attached to the bottom of the handrail and to the top of the curb. Alternatively, intermediate rails parallel to the handrail may span between newel posts, or other intermediate materials may be supported by the curb, newel posts and/or handrail.

Steel—In a steel stair, the stringer itself forms the curb. Steel balusters are typically welded to the stringer and collectively support the handrail.

OPEN BANISTER W/ CURB

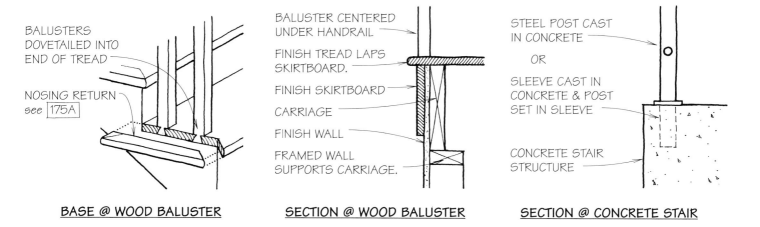

BALUSTERS
DOVETAILED INTO
END OF TREAD

NOSING RETURN
see │175A│

BALUSTER CENTERED
UNDER HANDRAIL

FINISH TREAD LAPS
SKIRTBOARD.

FINISH SKIRTBOARD

CARRIAGE

FINISH WALL

FRAMED WALL
SUPPORTS CARRIAGE.

STEEL POST CAST
IN CONCRETE

OR

SLEEVE CAST IN
CONCRETE & POST
SET IN SLEEVE

CONCRETE STAIR
STRUCTURE

BASE @ WOOD BALUSTER   **SECTION @ WOOD BALUSTER**   **SECTION @ CONCRETE STAIR**

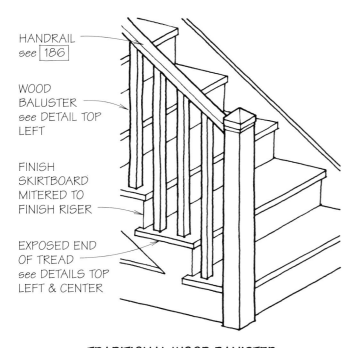

HANDRAIL
see │186│

WOOD
BALUSTER
see DETAIL TOP
LEFT

FINISH
SKIRTBOARD
MITERED TO
FINISH RISER

EXPOSED END
OF TREAD
see DETAILS TOP
LEFT & CENTER

TRADITIONAL WOOD BANISTER

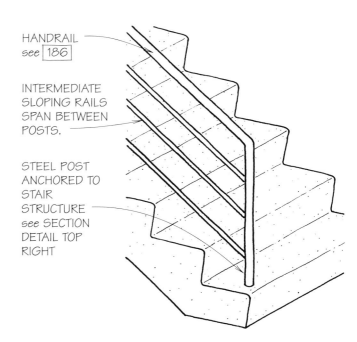

HANDRAIL
see │186│

INTERMEDIATE
SLOPING RAILS
SPAN BETWEEN
POSTS.

STEEL POST
ANCHORED TO
STAIR
STRUCTURE
see SECTION
DETAIL TOP
RIGHT

STEEL BANISTER ON CONCRETE STAIR

The open banister without a curb is the most technically difficult and expensive banister if made of wood in conjunction with a wood stair. It is quite simple and inexpensive if made of steel in conjunction with a concrete stair.

Wood—In the traditional wood banister, wood balusters are carefully joined to wood treads, providing both structural support of the handrail and protection from falling through. The ends of the treads are exposed and must be finished. Newel posts may also provide primary structural support for the handrail, while the balusters contribute little or only partial support. In any case, the connection of balusters and/or newel posts

to the stairs must be finely crafted for both structural and aesthetic purposes (drawing top left).

The tops of the balusters typically fit into a dado on the bottom of the handrail and are spaced with blocks between them.

Steel—When made of steel on concrete stairs, the open curbless banister generally has structural posts that are cast into the concrete with intermediate rails that run parallel to the handrail. This is a common combination because the concrete stairs are most easily cast without a curb, and the steel banister is strong, durable and simple to construct.

 OPEN BANISTER WITHOUT CURB

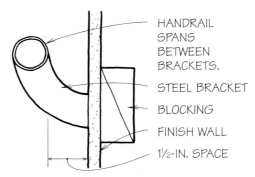

**STANDARD ROUND WOOD
HANDRAIL ON BRACKET**

- HANDRAIL SPANS BETWEEN BRACKETS.
- METAL BRACKET
- BLOCKING
- FINISH WALL
- 1½-IN. SPACE

**STANDARD TUBE STEEL
HANDRAIL ON BRACKET**

- HANDRAIL SPANS BETWEEN BRACKETS.
- STEEL BRACKET
- BLOCKING
- FINISH WALL
- 1½-IN. SPACE

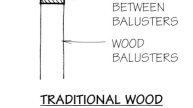

**TRADITIONAL WOOD
HANDRAIL ON BANISTER**

- HANDRAIL
- SPACER BETWEEN BALUSTERS
- WOOD BALUSTERS

Handrails provide stability and security for everyone using a stairway, including the young, the old, the blind and the infirm. Handrails run parallel to the stair and are either attached to a wall with brackets or incorporated into the top of a banister. They are typically made of hardwood or metal (usually steel) and are available in numerous manufactured shapes with accessories that allow for a variety of designs.

The height of the handrail is specified by code. Most codes fall within the range of 29 in. to 36 in. above the nosing of the stairs. If the handrail is against a wall, a 1½-in. space is required between the handrail and the wall.

The most important design feature of a handrail is its ability to be grasped, especially in an emergency. The 1¼-in. to 2-in. round rail is the most effective and common shape, as it allows the thumb and fingers to curl around and under the rail.

On most nonresidential stairways, the handrail must extend 6 in. to 12 in. beyond the first and last risers. This extension provides the person using a stairway the opportunity to grasp the handrail while on the floor (or landing) before or after using the stairway. In addition, the handrail often must be designed to return to the wall at the end or be shaped at the end in a way that will not snag clothing.

The handrail must often change direction to follow the stairway, or rise to meet a guardrail or newel post. These transitions in the direction or height of the rail are most often made of simple pieces designed to be used with standard wood or metal handrails. Transitions may also be made of highly decorative components such as the gooseneck and volute (bottom drawing), also available as manufactured items.

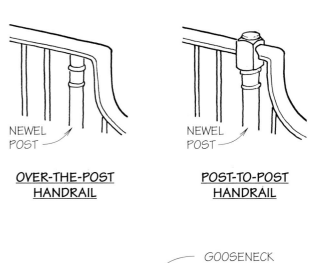

**OVER-THE-POST
HANDRAIL**

NEWEL POST

**POST-TO-POST
HANDRAIL**

NEWEL POST

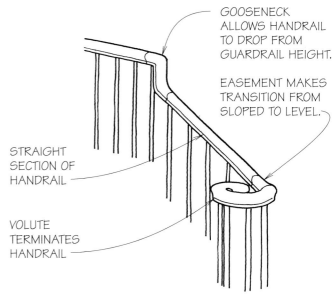

- GOOSENECK ALLOWS HANDRAIL TO DROP FROM GUARDRAIL HEIGHT.
- EASEMENT MAKES TRANSITION FROM SLOPED TO LEVEL.
- STRAIGHT SECTION OF HANDRAIL
- VOLUTE TERMINATES HANDRAIL

TRADITIONAL HANDRAIL

HANDRAILS

APPENDICES

APPENDIX A

PAINTS & COATINGS

There is an impressive array of paints and coatings for treating floors, walls, ceilings, cabinets and trim. While most of these materials have been designed to protect surfaces such as wood, plaster and masonry from dirt and deterioration, they have the added benefit of providing a relatively inexpensive decorative finish. Finishes may be opaque, translucent or transparent, and they may range from matte (which conceals the texture of the substrate) to glossy (which reveals texture). Color distribution may range from consistent across a surface to richly variegated.

Many different effects can be achieved with paints and coatings, depending upon how the medium is applied. Possible application techniques include spraying, rolling, brushing, stippling, sponging, rag-rolling, spattering, dragging and combing. Brushes, rollers and sprayers are the most common tools, but other applicators for various decorative effects include such objects as cheesecloth, paper, plastic, chamois, sponges and feathers. However, the method of application may be limited by the type of finish selected. The type of finish itself may be dictated by the substrate to which it is applied.

Components of Finishes

Vehicle is the term used to describe the liquid medium in which color and additives are suspended. The vehicle typically consists of a binder and a solvent, or thinner. Binders (which may consist of oils, alkyds, latex, oleoresins, phenols, synthetic rubber or urethane) determine the quality and durability of the finish. The amount and type of binder also determine whether the coating will have a matte or gloss finish. Thinners (such as water, turpentine, alcohol and mineral spirits) regulate a coating's workability, which is determined by how smooth and thick a coating is. While the thinner evaporates or oxidizes as the coating dries, the binder remains behind and holds the coating to the surface. Coatings may vary greatly depending upon the proportion of binder to thinner. While there are additives to increase the viscosity of coatings (see below), only thinners will dilute them.

Coloring agents may be derived from mineral or vegetable sources or from synthetic compounds. The finishes they produce range from opaque to transparent. Paint contains a white pigment that is sometimes called the *body*. Lead carbonate was formerly the most common body but is now illegal. Today, zinc oxide is used in low-quality paints, while higher-grade paints use titanium dioxide. The white body provides the opacity in all paints, with other pigments being added for color. *Pigments* consist of very small particles of coloring agents suspended in a medium and are used in coatings ranging from opaque to translucent. *Dyes* completely dissolve in liquid and, as a result, they are able to penetrate porous surfaces and are often used to give color to stains.

Many color options (generally derived from synthetics) are available in premixed paints. Color can also be added to a basic white paint with artist's oil or acrylic paints, but care must be taken not to mix oil- and water-based media.

Additives perform a wide variety of functions. For example, dryers are frequently added to reduce evaporation/oxidation time. Antisettling agents are used in many premixed paints to hold the pigment in suspension. Fungicides, biocides and preservatives are used to prevent growth of foreign organic substances, both in the can and after the coating has been applied. Thixotropic agents are used to create nondrip emulsions. Antiskinning agents, used in quick-drying paints, prevent the growth of a skin on the surface of the coating while it is in the can. Fire retardants reduce the flammability of coatings. Extenders are inexpensive materials used to increase bulk, thereby reducing overall cost. Thickeners reduce application time, because they allow a surface to be coated more thoroughly in fewer applications. Many other additives are used for various conditions; some may contain or consist of highly toxic materials such as heavy metal compounds, coal tar or xylene.

Types of Finishes

Paint is the most common coating material and provides an opaque surface that may be flat (matte), satin, semigloss or glossy. Oil-based paints create an impermeable surface, while water-based paints such as latex and whitewash are capable of "breathing."

Stains are used to add color to woods. They penetrate the wood and result in a translucent finish through which the wood grain is visible. The principal medium may be water, oil, spirits or wax; color is provided by dyes. A stained surface is not impermeable to water, and a sealer is required where possible water damage is unacceptable.

Varnish creates a transparent finish that may be matte, satin or glossy. It may be based on spirits (shellac), water (acrylic varnish) or oil (polyurethane varnish). Finely ground pigments may be added for color.

Washes and *glazes* are translucent coatings applied over an undercoat of paint. They consist of pigments suspended in clear vehicles.

Waxes (such as beeswax, paraffin and carnauba wax) and *oils* (such as tung, linseed and teak) may be applied separately or mixed together. Neither is impermeable, but all may be applied over a waterproof sealer if necessary.

Primers are used to increase surface adherence between a porous substrate and the finish coating. They may be specially formulated products or simply a thinned-down version of the finish coat. Primers are not very durable and require the addition of a finish coating.

Fillers are opaque finishes that are used to create a smooth surface for irregular materials such as

masonry, concrete and some woods. Fillers require the addition of a finish coating.

Sealers create an impermeable surface on the substrate. They may be opaque or transparent and sometimes serve as the finish coat.

The chart below shows which finishes are appropriate for which substrate.

TYPE OF FINISH	SUBSTRATE				
	Wood	GWB & Plaster	Tile & Stone	CMU & Concrete	Metal
Paint	✔	✔	✔	✔	✔
Stain	✔				
Varnish	✔				
Wash/ glaze	✔	✔		✔	
Wax/oil	✔		✔	✔	
Primer	✔	✔			✔
Filler	✔			✔	
Sealer	✔		✔	✔	

Environmental Concerns

Many coatings contain highly toxic materials that may pose health and environmental hazards during manufacture, application, disposal and building occupancy. To gauge the toxicity of a coating, you may request the Material Safety Data Sheets (MSDS) from the manufacturer. Precautions should be taken during application to avoid inhaling or absorbing coatings through the skin. Indoor air quality may be compromised by outgassing, especially during the first few days after a coating is applied.

APPENDIX B
COMPOSITE PANELS

The materials listed here are found in the assemblies described in every chapter of this book. Most are made of wood fibers that are glued together in various ways. The two broad classifications of composite panels are plywood and composition board.

Plywood

Plywood is commonly used for wall and ceiling panels, subfloor, cabinets and countertop substrate. The panels are made of thin layers or plies of wood that are peeled from large logs and glued together under heat and pressure. The plies are stacked so that the grain of each ply is perpendicular to the grain of the ply above or below it. This produces a dimensionally stable sheet that is resistant to warping, tearing and splitting. Plywood has the strength to span in both directions but is stronger parallel to its long edge because the grain of the plies on the two outer surfaces, where the stresses are greatest, runs in the same direction.

Plywood sheets of the same thickness do not always have the same number of plies. The greater the number of plies in a sheet, generally the stronger and more stable the assemblage. The quality of the plies and whether they are made of hardwood or softwood is important in determining the stiffness of the sheets, their resistance to impact and the smoothness of their surfaces.

Used as a substrate for nonstructural material, plywood is not as smooth as most composition boards but is more resistant to water. It is the best substrate for materials such as some metals or thick-bed and thinbed tile installations that do not require a perfectly smooth surface.

Composition Board

Dwindling forest reserves combined with wood technology research have given rise to the production of new composition sheet goods. Because composition boards are made from much smaller pieces of wood than plywood, they do not require large trees for their manufacture and are generally less expensive than plywood. But attention must be paid to the resins used in their manufacture, since some of these products produce enough outgassing to be a source of indoor air pollution. The primary types of composition board are hardboard, fiberboard, particleboard and oriented-strand board.

Hardboard, or high-density fiberboard (HDF)—HDF is made of very small wood fibers that are bonded either naturally, using a wet process, or with synthetic resins, using a dry process. Hardboard has a very smooth and hard face on one side and a screen-textured face on the other side. Hardboard can be standard (untempered) or tempered. Tempered hardboard is standard hardboard that has been subjected to a curing treatment, which increases its stiffness, hardness and density.

Hardboard sheets are usually quite thin (⅛ in. to ¼ in.) and are used frequently for interior paneling, often with a decorative surface applied (melamine, paper overlay or paint). Hardboard can be oil-treated and coated with plastic for use in wet areas such as showers. Unfinished hardboard can be also be cut into tiles and coated to make a handsome and durable finish floor. It is also occasionally used in cabinets or as a subfloor.

Fiberboard—As with hardboard, medium-density fiberboard (MDF) panels are made with wood fibers that are bonded together under heat and pressure, usually using a urea-formaldehyde resin adhesive. The bonding resin typically emits toxic fumes, but formaldehyde-free MDF is available. Standard fiberboard is water-resistant but not waterproof. A moisture-resistant MDF is made with phenolic resin for use where significant moisture is expected.

Because of the manufacturing process, MDF is usually more dense near the surface than at the core. This dense surface is sanded very smooth during manufacture, but the relative porosity of the core makes the finishing of cut panel edges difficult. A high-density fiberboard with a core more consistent with surface density is available for conditions where cut edges are to be finished.

MDF is commonly used for cabinets, countertops, paneling and trim. Compared to hardboard, it is less dense and thicker, with available thicknesses ranging from $\frac{5}{16}$ in. to $1\frac{3}{8}$ in. Compared to particleboard (see below), it is more dense and about 50% more expensive for comparable thicknesses.

Particleboard—Particleboard, also known as chipboard, is made of wood waste particles of various sizes that are bonded together under heat and pressure, usually using a urea-formaldehyde resin adhesive in a dry process similar to fiberboard. Finer particles are usually located in the surface layers, with coarser particles in the core. Particleboard is available in various densities, with the higher densities resulting in a less porous, smoother surface. Both sides are usually sanded.

Particleboard is not waterproof but is available in a moisture-resistant version. Fire-resistant particleboard is also available. Particleboard is often used as a substrate for plastic laminate countertops, as a core for decorative finish panels and as underlayment for floors. Its thickness ranges from $\frac{1}{8}$ in. to $1\frac{1}{8}$ in., and it weighs about twice as much as plywood. It is less dense and less expensive than fiberboard of the same thickness.

Oriented-strand board—Oriented-strand board (OSB), also known as wafer board or flake board, is composed of strands or flakes of wood (about $\frac{1}{32}$ in. by $\frac{1}{2}$ in. by $3\frac{1}{2}$ in.) that are bonded together using a waterproof binder (phenolic resin adhesive plus a little wax) under heat and pressure. The strands are oriented in layers perpendicular to each other so that they give structural rigidity in both directions. OSB is generally available with a textured surface showing the size of the strands on one side and on the other side the appearance of the resin pressed against a fine screen. It

is also available with strand texture on both sides or a sanded surface on one side. OSB is occasionally used as underlayment and also has potential for paneling walls or ceilings. It is typically available $\frac{1}{4}$ in. or $\frac{7}{16}$ in. thick. It is a relatively inexpensive material with density even lower than that of particleboard.

Less common composition boards include soundboard, recycled newspaper board, strawboard and cement backer board.

Soundboard—A soft, very low-density board made of small wood fibers that adhere loosely to one another, soundboard (also called building board), because of its low density, has acoustical dampening qualities. Soundboard has a very limited strength and is usually available no thinner than $\frac{1}{2}$ in. thick. It is commonly seen in ceilings as interlocking tiles or in suspended ceiling assemblies. Although uncommon as a finish wall material, soundboard can be applied over gypsum wallboard or other backing material for use as tackboard.

Recycled newspaper board—A low-density board, ideal for acoustical applications and for tack surfaces, recycled newspaper board is made of very small wood fibers recycled from newspapers. Because it is very soft and not resistant to abrasion, this sheet material is usually covered with fabric when used as a finish wall material. It may also be a floor underlayment when sound reduction is important.

Strawboard—This board, not truly a wood product, is made from short pieces of straw, which are pressed and glued together to produce a structural product.

Cementitious backer board—Cementitious backer board is dense and very moisture resistant but not very strong. It has a cementitious core sandwiched between two layers of glass-fiber reinforcing mesh. It is usually $\frac{1}{2}$ in. thick and is commonly used on top of plywood substrate as a setting bed for thinbed tile installations.

APPENDIX C

FIRE & SAFETY CODES

Fire and safety issues are important at every stage of the design process, including the selection of finish materials. Recognition and familiarity with these concepts early on will help avoid a later redesign.

Fire Assemblies

Only certain construction types are allowed for various combinations of area and building height. A five-story 50,000-sq.-ft. building, for example, would probably be restricted by the Uniform Building Code to Type I or Type II fire-rated (F.R.) construction. Both Type I and Type II buildings must have a fireproofed primary structure, and all exterior bearing walls must be rated to resist fire for 4 hours. Other stringent measures designed to minimize combustibility and fire propagation are also enforced. Buildings with fewer stories or with less area may be built with other construction types requiring less extensive fireproofing measures.

For each construction type, fire-resistance ratings given in hours are used for each part of the building, including wall assemblies, floor/ceiling assemblies and openings. Hourly ratings can have an impact on the selection of materials for floors, ceilings and walls. Single-family residential construction generally falls within the least restrictive category and has few code requirements relating to the materials used for interior surfaces.

Fire Separation

Codes classify all buildings according to occupancy, which relates to the use of the building or rooms within a building. Larger spaces with the potential for bigger crowds generally have more restrictive requirements than smaller, less populated spaces.

It is common to find more than one type of occupancy in a given structure; such cases of mixed occupancy require special considerations with regard to fire safety. Codes generally take the approach that adjacent occupancies with different fire probabilities require wall or floor/ceiling assemblies to have a fire separation rated in hours. For example, a typical single-family

residence (UBC occupancy type R-3) with an attached garage (occupancy type M) will require a 1-hour fire separation between the garage and all living spaces. The drawing below illustrates one method of attaining such a separation in a wall:

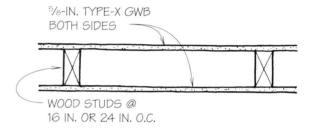

Once the ratings are ascertained, a designer in any region can choose from various construction assemblies approved by the ICBO (International Conference of Building Officials) to achieve the desired fire separation.

Flame Spread

Nearly all interior materials that may contribute to fire propagation and growth are rated by a uniform flame-spread test of the Underwriters Laboratories, Inc. (UL). The materials regulated by these criteria include large expansive covering materials, such as carpet and vinyl wallpaper. Trim and other small pieces are generally not rated, as they do not significantly contribute to fire growth or smoke generation.

Values are assigned to each material, comparing it to fixed values of 0 for asbestos and 100 or 200 for red oak (depending on the code used). Thus, each material can be judged according to its relative combustibility and evaluated against maximum flame-spread values assigned to each occupancy group. In general, rooms can have fairly high flame-spread values, while corridors and stairways have lower code allowances.

For a thorough treatment of this topic, review the comprehensive *Building Materials Directory* published by Underwriters Laboratories. ICBO's *Evaluation Reports* are also useful.

APPENDIX D

SOUND REDUCTION

Certain materials and assemblies can be used to attenuate or reduce sound transmission both within and between rooms. The primary classes of sound in building design are airborne sound and structure-borne sound. Airborne sound is generated by sources that rely on air to transmit the sound. Examples include the human voice, loudspeakers and musical instruments. Structure-borne sound is generated by sources that act directly on the building structure. Examples include footsteps, noisy plumbing and banging doors. Since most structure-borne sound results from impact with the structure, it is also referred to as impact sound.

Reducing Airborne Sound

Within rooms—The most effective method for reducing unwanted noise within a room is to place absorptive materials on the room surfaces. The performance of absorptive materials depends on their thickness, density, porosity and resistance to airflow. Sound is absorbed by friction produced by air moving in the small spaces within a fibrous or porous material. Since air must be able to move within an absorbing material, painting a surface meant for acoustic absorption is not recommended since it will seal the pores and render the material useless for absorbing sound.

Among the most common sound-absorptive materials are soundboard, acoustic tiles and carpet. Porous materials of this sort tend to be most effective at attentuating sounds in the high frequencies. Less frequently used are panel resonators, which are most effective at reducing low-frequency sounds. A typical panel resonator consists of a perforated membrane such as a wood or metal panel placed in front of an absorptive surface.

Between rooms—The transmission of noise between rooms depends upon both the nature of the barrier between the rooms, and the reverberation characteristics of the room in which the sound originates. Increasing the mass of a wall or ceiling

assembly is a simple way to reduce airborne sound because it reduces the assembly's ability to vibrate. Mass is most effective at blocking high-frequency sounds. Fibrous fill (such as batt insulation) within a wall or floor/ceiling assembly is effective at blocking sound within the mid- to high-frequency range. For attenuation of low-frequency sound between rooms, cavity resonators are useful. A cavity resonator consists of an airspace within a massive material such as a masonry party wall.

The sound transmission class (STC) provides a single-number rating by which to gauge how well an assembly can reduce the transmission of airborne sound between rooms. It is used primarily to rate walls but can also be applied to floor/ceiling assemblies.

Following are examples of sound-reducing assemblies for both walls and floor/ceiling assemblies:

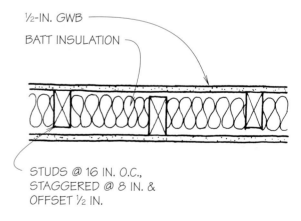

½-IN. GWB

BATT INSULATION

STUDS @ 16 IN. O.C., STAGGERED @ 8 IN. & OFFSET ½ IN.

SOUND-REDUCING WOOD-FRAME WALL

CARPET ON PAD

LIQUID-APPLIED GYPSUM

PLYWOOD SUBFLOOR ON
WOOD JOISTS

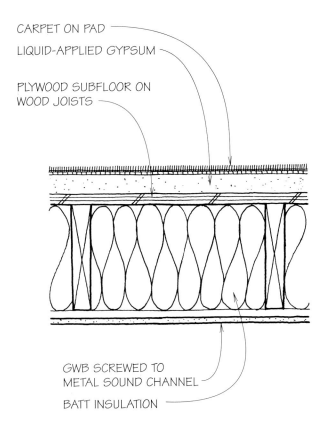

GWB SCREWED TO
METAL SOUND CHANNEL

BATT INSULATION

SOUND-REDUCING WOOD-FRAMED
FLOOR/CEILING ASSEMBLY

Reducing Structure-Borne Sound

The most effective method for reducing structure-borne sound is to isolate the noise-generating sources from the structure. If the amount of noise transmitted to the structure is reduced, the transmission of structure-borne sound is likewise reduced. In the case of mechanical equipment, this can be accomplished by careful selection, flexible mountings and antivibration pads. Flexible connections are also effective for reducing sound by reducing the energy transmitted through a material or assembly.

Impact insulation class (IIC) is similar to STC, and is used to rate the transmission reduction of sound caused by impact. It is used only for floor/ceiling assemblies. In both cases, the higher the number, the more effective the assembly at attenuating noise. STC and IIC ratings can be found in trade literature for various assemblies. For example, plumbing can be screwed to the structure with isolating clamps and bushings. Impact sound in floors can be reduced by resilient materials such as carpet, cushioned vinyl, rubber or cork. Floating floors can also significantly reduce the transmission of impact sound.

LIST OF ABBREVIATIONS

&	AND	‖	PARALLEL
@	AT	⊥	PERPENDICULAR
APPROX.	APPROXIMATE(LY)	PSF	POUNDS PER SQUARE FOOT
GA.	GAUGE	PSI	POUNDS PER SQUARE INCH
GWB	GYPSUM WALLBOARD	REBAR	REINFORCING STEEL
H	HEIGHT	REQ'D	REQUIRED
MAX.	MAXIMUM	T&G	TONGUE AND GROOVE
MIN.	MINIMUM	TYP.	TYPICAL
#	NUMBER	W	WIDTH
O.C.	ON CENTER	W/	WITH

RESOURCES

Trade and Professional Associations

American Concrete Institute
22400 W. Seven-Mile Road
Detroit, MI 48219
(313) 532-2600

American Hardboard Association
1210 W. Northwest Highway
Palatine, IL 60067
(708) 934-8800

American Institute of Architects
1735 New York Avenue, N.W.
Suite 700
Washington, DC 20006
(202) 626-7300

American Plywood Association
P.O. Box 11700
Tacoma, WA 98411
(206) 565-6600

American Society of Interior Designers
608 Massachusetts Avenue, N.E.
Washington, DC 20002
(202) 546-3480

Architectural Woodwork Institute
2310 S. Walter Reed Drive
Arlington, VA 22206
(703) 671-9100

Brick Institute of America
11490 Commerce Park Drive
Reston, VA 22091
(703) 620-0010

Door & Hardware Institute
7711 Old Springhouse Road
McLean, VA 22101
(703) 556-3990

Forest Products Laboratory
Forest Service, USDA
P.O. Box 5130
Madison, WI 53705
(608) 257-2211

Maple Flooring Manufacturers Association
60 Revere Drive, Suite 500
Northbrook, IL 60062
(708) 480-9138

Marble Institute of America
30 Eden Alley
Columbus, OH 43215
(614) 228-6194

National Association of Home Builders
15th and M Streets, N.W.
Washington, DC 20005
(800) 368-5242

National Concrete Masonry Association
2302 Horespen Road
Herndon, VA 22071-3406
(703) 435-4900

National Forest Products Association
1250 Connecticut Avenue, N.W.
Suite 200
Washington, DC 20036
(202) 463-2700

National Oak Flooring Manufacturers' Association
22 North Front Street
660 Falls Building
Memphis, TN 38103
(901) 526-5016

National Particleboard Association
18928 Premiere Court
Gaithersburg, MD 20879
(301) 670-0604

National Terrazzo and Mosaic Association, Inc.
3166 Des Plaines Avenue, Suite 132
Des Plaines, IL 60018
(800) 323-9736

National Wood Flooring Association
233 Old Meramec Station Road
Manchester, MO 63021
(800) 422-4556

Northeastern Lumber Manufacturers' Association
P.O. Box 87A
Cumberland Center, ME 04021
(207) 829-6901

Small Homes Council
University of Illinois at Urbana-Champaign
One East St. Mary's Road
Champaign, IL 61820
(217) 333-1801

Southern Forest Products Association
P. O. Box 52468
New Orleans, LA 70152
(504) 443-4464

Tile Council of America, Inc.
P.O. Box 326
Princeton, NJ 08542
(609) 921-7050

Western Wood Products Association
Yeon Building
522 S. W. 5th Avenue
Portland, OR 97204
(503) 224-3930

Wood Molding and Millwork Producers Association
P.O. Box 25278
Portland OR 97225
(503) 292-9288

READINGS & PRODUCT INFORMATION

Suggested Reading

American Institute of Architects. *Architectural Graphic Standards.* 8th ed. New York: John Wiley & Sons, 1988.

Bollinger, Don. *Hardwood Floors.* Newtown, Conn.: The Taunton Press, 1990.

Byrne, Michael. *Setting Tile.* Newtown, Conn.: The Taunton Press, 1995.

Dietz, Albert. *Dwelling House Construction.* 5th ed. Cambridge, Mass.: M.I.T. Press, 1991.

Environmental Building News. Brattleboro, Vt.: West River Communications (RR 1, Box 161, Brattleboro, Vt. 05301). Published bimonthly.

Fine Homebuilding. Newtown, Conn.: The Taunton Press (P.O. Box 5506, 63 South Main Street, Newtown, CT 06470-5506). Published bimonthly.

Leclair, Kim, and David Russo. *Environmental by Design.* Vancouver, B.C., Canada: Hartley & Marks, 1992.

Shuttner, Scott. *Basic Stairbuilding.* Newtown, Conn.: The Taunton Press, 1990.

Product Information

Architects' First Source for Products. Architects' First Source for Products (4126 Pleasantdale Road, Atlanta, GA 30340). Updated annually.

Sweet's Catalogue File. New York: McGraw-Hill. Updated annually.

Thomas Register of American Manufacturers and *Thomas Register Catalog File.* New York: Thomas Publishing Company. Updated annually.

INDEX

A

Adhesives:
  for gypsum wallboard, 6C
  for parquet flooring, 87A
  for plastic laminate, 133A
  for resilient sheet flooring, 69A,
    76A
  for tile, 29A
  for trim, 158A
  for wood floors, 80B, 81A
  See also Mastic.

B

Backsplashes:
  clip attachment for, for plastic-
    laminate countertop, 135D
  for concrete countertops, 145B,
    145C
  field-applied, for plastic-laminate
    countertop, 135B
  postformed, for plastic-laminate
    countertop, 133A, 135C
  shop-applied, for plastic-laminate
    countertop, 135A
  for solid-surface countertop, 143B
  for stainless-steel countertops, 146A
  for stone slab countertops, 140A,
    141B, 141C
  for tile countertops, 138D
  types of, 130B
  See also Countertops.
Banisters:
  building-code requirements for,
    181A
  closed, 181A, 182A, 183A
  with curb, 184A
  without curb, 185A
  glass, 183A
  open, 181A, 182A, 184A, 185A
  steel, 184A, 185A
  wood, 183A, 184A, 185A
  See also Stairs.

Baseboard:
  shoe and cap for, 154A
  wood, types of, 162A
Blind nailing, of tongue-and-groove
  floor boards, 80B
Brick:
  alternative, 17A
  bonding patterns for, 18B
  color of, 17A
  as flooring material, 93A
  types of, 17A
  veneer, on wood-framed wall, 19A

C

Cabinets:
  drawer and door pulls for, 120A
  drawer guides for, 121A
  face-frame, 109A, 112A, 113A
  frameless, 109A, 112A, 112B
  installing, 126A
  at juncture with wall, 127B
  modular vs. custom, 110A
  paint-grade, 111A
  plastic-laminate, 111A
  quality standards for, 108
  stain-grade, 111A
  standard dimensions for, 107
  toe kick for, 127A
  See also Hinges. Latches.
Carpet:
  acrylic, 62A
  backing for, 64A
  baseboard with, 67A
  blended-fiber, 62A
  characteristics of, 55
  dyeing methods for, 64B
  as flooring material, 60A
  fusion-bonded, 61A
  glue-down installation for, 66B,
    67B, 67C
  at juncture with wall, 67A
  natural-fiber, 62A
  nylon, 62A
  olefin, 62A

pads for, 65A
  peel-and-stick installation for, 66B
  polyester, 62A
  rolled-goods vs. modular-tile, 65B
  as stair finish material, 178A
  stretch-in installation for, 66A,
    67A, 67B
  tufted, 61A
  wool, 62A
  woven, 61A
  See also Pile.
Casings:
  bead joint for, 161A
  butt joint for, 161D
  corner block for, 161B
  for doors and windows, 160A, 160B
  mitered, 160C
  reveal joint for, 161C
Ceilings:
  acoustic-tile, 34A
  coffered, 2
  coved, 10B
  designing, 2
  gypsum-wallboard, 3A, 9C, 43D
  paneling for, 32A, 43C
  soffited, 2
  sound-reducing design for, 195
  suspended-grid, 42A, 43A, 43B
Cementitious backer board:
  discussed, 192
  as tile backing material, 28A
Chipboard. *See* Particleboard.
Composition board, discussed, 191
Concrete block:
  color of, 16A
  surface texture of, 16A
  types of, 16A
Concrete:
  characteristics of, 55
  pigmented, 101A
  as stair finish material, 180B
  as structural support for floors, 55
  as subflooring, 59
  surface texture of, 101A

Countertops:
    ceramic tile, 136A
        characteristics of, 128A
    concrete,
        cast-in place, 144A
        characteristics of, 128A
        finishing, 145D
        precast, 144A
        substrate for, 144A
    metal, 146A
    plastic laminate, 132C
        adhesives for, 133A
        characteristics of, 128A
        end cap for, 134D
        fabrication of, 133A
        postformed nosing for, 124B
        seams in, 133B
        self-edged nosing for, 134A
        substrates for, 132C
        wood nosing for, 134C
    solid-surface, 142A
        bevel-mount sink for, 143C
        characteristics of, 128A
        sinks for, 142A
        undermount sink for, 143D
        installation of, 142A
        seams in, 142A
    stainless steel, 146A
        characteristics of, 128A
    stone, 140A
        characteristics of, 128A
        substrates for, 140A
        undermount sink for, 141D
    substrates for, 129A
        attachment of, 129B
    tile,
        modular, 136A
        sealer for, 137A
        stone, 136A
        thick-bed installation of, 137A
        thinbed installation of, 137A
        types of, 136A
        See also Grout.
    wood,
        characteristics of, 128A
        finish for, 147A
        sinks for, 146A
    See also Backsplashes. Nosings.
        Sinks.

D

Doors:
    backset for, 52A
    base trim for, 163A
    bifold, 45A,
        hardware for, 53A
    bolts for, 53LA
    bypass, 45A
        hardware for, 53A
    cabinet,
        frame-and-panel, 110A, 114A
        inset, 111A, 115A
        lazy Susan, 125A
        lipped, 111A, 115A
        overlay, 111A, 115A
        single-piece, 110A, 114A
    casings for, 160A, 160B
    handles for, 52A
    hardware for, 50A
    hinged, 45A
    hollow metal, 48A
    hollow-core, 47B
    interior, 44A
    knock-down frames for, 49A
    locksets for, 52A
    metal frames for, 49A
    panel, 46A
    panic hardware for, 53A
    pocket, 45A
        hardware for, 53A, 124A
    self-closers for, 53A
    sliding, hardware for, 124A
    solid-core, 47A
    tambour, 124A
    trim for, 159A
    wood frames for, 48B
    See also Casings.

Drawers, cabinet:
    hardware for, 116A
    inset, 111A
    joinery for, 116A, 117A
    lipped, 111A
    materials for, 116A
    overlay, 111A
Drywall:
    seams in, finish for, 6A
    as three-coat process, 5A
    trim for, 8A
    vs. veneer plaster, 3A

F

Fiberboard (MDF), discussed, 191
Fillers, described, 189
Finishes:
    additives for, 189
    components of, 189-190
    dyes for, 189
    for end-grain block flooring, 89A
    pigments for, 189
    substrates for, 190
    toxicity of, 190
Fire codes, requirements of, 193-194
Flooring:
    and finish-floor level (FFL), 58
    brick, 93A
        joints in, 96A
    ceramic-tile, 92A
    concrete, 100A
        construction timing for, 101B
        expansion joints in, 101B
        control joints in, 102A
    cork, 72B
        characteristics of, 68A
    granite, 93A
        joints in, 96A
    hardwood plank, 85A
    hardwood strip, 85A
    Linoleum,
        characteristics of, 68A
        described, 75A

marble, 93A
    joints in, 96A, 95B
masonry, and transitions to other
    flooring, 96B
parquet,
    adhesive for, 87A
    characteristics of, 87A
    subfloor for, 87A
plank, grades of, 84A
resilient,
    adhesives for, 69A
    base trim for, 70B
    and moisture control, 69A
    and transitions to other
        flooring, 70C
    as stair finish material, 179A
    characteristics of, 55, 68A
    at juncture with wall, 70A
    sheet vs. tile, 69A
    types of, 68A
    underlayment for, 69A
resilient sheet, 74A
    adhesives for, 76A
    coved, 77A
    seams in, 76A
resilient tile, 71A
rubber, characteristics of, 68A
rubber tile, 73A
slate, 93A
slate, joints in, 96A
softwood plank, 85B
softwood strip, 85B
strip, grades of, 84A
terrazzo,
    base trim for, 105A-D
    characteristics of, 103A
    on concrete subfloor, 104B
    divider strips for, 103A
    installation sequence for, 104A
    on wood subfloor, 104C
tile,
    expansion joints in, 97A
    joints in, 96A
    at juncture with wall, 97A

at shower curb and at junction
    with wall, 99B
and transitions to other
    flooring, 96B
tub/shower drain detail for, 99A
tub/shower, 98A
vinyl, characteristics of, 68A
    vinyl sheet, 74A, 75A
    vinyl tile, 72A
wood,
    adhesive for, 80B, 81A
    borders in, 82A
    end-grain block, 89A
    fasteners for, 80B, 81A
    feature strips in, 82A
    grain orientation in, 84A
    hardwood vs. softwood, 79A
    at juncture with wall, 82C
    laminated, 88A
    moisture content of, 79B
    plank, 83A
    prefinished, 82D
    resilience of, 78A
    screws for, 81A
    site-finished, 82D
    square-edged, 80A
    strip, 83A
    subfloors for, 83A
    tongue-and-groove, 80A
    tongue-and-groove decking, 90A
    transitions in, 82B
    types of, 78A
wood-panel product, 91A
Floors:
    concrete, 56
    floating, 81A, 88B
    radiant-heet, 59
    sound-reducing design for, 195
    wood, 56
    wood/concrete hybrid, 56
    See also Subfloors.
Framing:
    and finish materials, 1
    of ceilings, 1
    of walls, 1

G

Glass block:
    anchors for, 23A
    edge detailing for, 24B
    expansion joint for, 24C
    mortar for, 23A
    mortar system for, 24A, 24B
    mortarless system for, 23A, 24D
    reinforcing for, 23A
    types of, 22A
    as wall material, 22A
Glazes, described, 189
Granite, as flooring material, 93A
Grout:
    joints in, 96B
        edge, 29B
        field, 29B
    for tile countertops, 137A
    as tile finishing material, 29B
    types of, 96A
Gypsum wallboard (GWB):
    adhesives for, 6C
    control joint in, 9C
    corner clips for, 7B
    coved, 10B
    curved, requirements for, 10C
    vs. lath and plaster, 11A
    nails for, 6C
    no-trim, 153A
    plywood-backed, for strength, 9D
    radius trim for, 10A
    resilient channel for, 7B
    screws for, 6C
    sizes of, 4A
    in suspended ceiling grids, 42A
    as tile backing material, 28A
    trim for,
        at inside corner, 8B
        at outside corner, 8B
    types of, 4A
    as wall and ceiling material, 3A

H

Handrails:
  building-code requirements for, 181A, 186A
  steel, 186A
  wood, 186A
  See also Stairs.
Hardboard (HDF), discussed, 191
Hardware:
  for adjustable shelves, 119B
  backsplash clip, for plastic-laminate countertop, 135D
  drawer and door pulls, 120A
  drawer guides, 121A
  for pocket doors, 124A
  for sliding doors, 124A
  See also Hinges. Latches.
Heat, radiant, 59
Hinges:
  for cabinet doors, 122A, 123A
  heavyweight bearing, 51A
  for interior doors, 50B
  plain non-bearing, 51A
  standard-weight bearing, 51A

J

Joint compound, taping vs. topping, 4A

L

Latches, for cabinet doors, 122A
Lath:
  metal, 11A, 12A
  and plaster, historic, 11A
  wood vs. metal, 11A, 11A, 12A

M

Marble, as flooring material, 93A
Masonry:
  types of, 15A
  as wall material, 15A
  as wall veneer, 19A
  See also Brick. Concrete. Concrete Block. Glass Block. Stone.
Mastic, as tile-setting adhesive, 95A
Molding:
  crown, 164B
  built-up, 150A
  corner-cap, 165D
  cove, 165D
  custom, 150A
  finger-jointed, 150A
  moisture content of, 150A
  profiles of, 151A
  quarter-round, 165D
  sanitary, 154A
  softwood vs. hardwood, 150A
  traditional, 164A, 164B, 165A-D
  See also Trim.
Mortar:
  for glass block, 23A
  joints in, 20B
  masonry-cement, 20A
  mudset, 95A
  portland cement-lime, 20A
  thick-bed, 95A
    installation for tile or masonry, 94A
  thinbed installation for tile or masonry, 94A
  thinset, 95A

N

Nailers, pneumatic, 158A
Nosings:
  for concrete countertops, 145A
  for face-frame cabinets/countertops, 129C
  for frameless cabinets/countertops, 129C
  postformed, for plastic-laminate countertop, 134B
  self-edged, for plastic-laminate countertop, 134A
  for solid-surface countertop, 143A
  for stainless steel countertops, 146A
  for stairs, 175A
  for stone slab countertops, 141A
  for tile countertops,
    thick-bed, 138A
    thinbed, 138B
  types of, 130A
  wood,
    for plastic-laminate countertop, 134C
    for tile countertops, 138C

O

Oriented-strand board (OSB), discussed, 192

P

Paints, described, 189
Paneling:
  ceiling, 42A
  edge details for, 35A
  fasteners for, 33A
  horizontal vs. vertical application for, 32A
  tongue-and-groove, 36A
    installation of, 37B
    at outside corner, 39C, 39D
    parallel to corner, 39A
    parallel to framing, 38A
    patterns for, 37A
    perpendicular to corner, 39B
    perpendicular to framing, 38B
  veneer, 34A, 38C
  as wall finish, 31A
Particleboard, discussed, 192

Picture rail, described, 164C
Pile (carpet):
    density of, 63A
    types of, 63A
Plaster:
    base coat, described, 13A
    curved, 14D
    edge trim for, 14C
    finish coat, described, 13A
    at radius corner, 14B
    at square corner, 14A
    three-coat system for, 13A
Plate rail, described, 165A
Plywood:
    discussed, 191
    as tile backing material, 28A
Primers, described, 189

R

Recycled newspaper board, discussed, 192

S

Sealers, described, 189
Shelves:
    adjustable, 119B
    fixed, 119A
    materials for, 118A
    quarter-turn, 125A
    roll-out, 125A
    thickness and span standards for, 118A
Showers, waterproof flooring for, 98A
Sinks:
    drop-in, 131A
    flush-mount, 131A, 139B
    integral, 131C
    self-rimming, 139A
    undermount, 131C, 139C, 141D
    See also Countertops.
Slate, as flooring material, 93A

Sound reduction, strategies for, 195-196
Soundboard, discussed, 192
Splines, with square-edged floor boards, 81A
Stains, described, 189
Stairs:
    base trim for, 163B
    building-code requirements for, 168B
    cantilevered, 169A
    carpeted, 178A
    ceiling-supported, 169A
    concrete, 172A
    curbed vs. curbless, 182A
    finish materials for, 174A
    free-spanning, 169A
    with housed treads and risers, 176A, 177B
    L-shaped, 167
    lighting for, 168A
    on grade, 169A
    open vs. closed risers for, 172C
    safety requirements for, 168A
    shop built, 177B
    side edges of, 175A
    site-built, 176B, 177A
        vs. shop-built, 170A
    space-saver, 167
    spiral, 167, 169A, 173A
        building-code restrictions with, 173A
        spatial requirements for, 173A
    steel, 171A
    straight, 167
    traction on, 175B
    with treads and risers applied to carriage, 176A, 176B, 177A
    U-shaped, 167
    wall-supported, 169A
    wood/steel, 172B
    See also Banisters. Handrails. Nosings.
Steel, as stair finish material, 180A

Stone:
    rubble vs. ashlar, 18A
    as stair finish material, 179B
    veneer, on concrete-block wall, 19A
Strawboard, discussed, 192
Subfloors:
    concrete, 57
        for radiant heat, 59
        for tile and masonry, 94A
        with strip and plank flooring, 83A
    for end-grain wood block, 89A
    for parquet, 87A
    plywood,
        on joists, 86A, 86B
        on slab, 86C
    sleepers on slab, 86D
    stability of, 58
    wood, 57
        with strip and plank flooring, 83A
        for tile and masonry, 94A

T

Terrazzo:
    characteristics of, 55
    as stair finish material, 180B
Tile:
    acoustic, 34A
    carpet, 66B
    ceramic, 26A
    characteristics of, 55
    as flooring material, 92A
    glazed, 26A
    grades of, and absorptivity, 25A
    grout for, 29B
    mortar setting bed for, 29A
    nonceramic, 26A
    organic adhesive setting bed for, 29A
    paver, 26A
    premounted, 26A
    quarry, 26A
    setting materials for, 28A

at shower-pan lip, 30C
as stair finish material, 179B
thick-bed installation for, 28A
thinbed installation for, 28A
trim, 27A
at tub edge, 30B
as wall material, 25
Trade and professional associations, addresses for, 199-200
Trim:
   adhesives for, 158A
   alignment of, 155A
   base, 162A
      at door casing, 163A
      at stair, 163B
      vinyl or rubber, 163C
   block joint for, 156A
   butted, 156A
   cope joint for, 156A, 157A
   discussed, 149
   for doors and windows, 159A
   filling holes in, 158A
   as gap concealer, 154A
   medium-density fiberboard (MDF), 152A
   at meeting surfaces, 154A
   mitered, 156A
   mitered and returned, 157A
   painted, 153B
   plaster, 152A
   plastic, 152A
   pneumatic nails for, 158A
   profiles of, 150A
   quarter-round, 154A
   rubber, 152A
   screws for, 158A
   scribed, 154A
   splicing, 155A
   square-cut, 157A
   stained, 153B
   vinyl, 152A

at wall and ceiling edges, 1-2
as wrap for structural members, 155A
See also Casings. Chair rail. Moldings. Picture rail. Plate rail. Wainscot cap.
Tubs, waterproof flooring under, 98A

Underlayment, for resilient flooring, 69A

Varnish, described, 189
Veneer plaster:
   described, 4A
   vs. drywall, 3A
   fiber-mesh tape for, 4A
   as one-coat process, 5B
   seams in, finish for, 6B
   trim for, 8A

Wainscot cap, described, 165C
Walls:
   brick-veneer, 19A, 21A-C
   corner details for, 14A-D
   corner trim for, 8B, 8C
   curved, 10C
   drywall system for, 5A, 6B
   edge trim for, 9A
   finishes for, maintaing consistent thickness of, 2
   frame-and-panel, 40A, 41A
   glass-block, 23A, 24A-D
   gypsum wallboard, 3A, 7A
   lath and plaster, 11A

masonry, 15A
paneled, 31A
reveal trim for, 9B
sound-reducing design for, 195
stone-veneer, 19A
tile, 25A
   at shower-pan lip, 30C
   at tub edge, 30B
   waterproofing systems for, 30A
veneer-plaster system for, 5B, 6B
Washes, described, 189
Waterproofing, for tile walls and ceilings, 30A
Waxes, described, 189
Windows:
   casings for, 160A, 160B
   trim for, 159A
   See also Casings. Moldings. Trim
Wood:
   characteristics of, 55
   as structural support for floors, 55

Yarn (for carpets), spinning proces for, 62A

Editor: Joanne Kellar Bouknight
Layout Artist: Christopher Casey
Copy/Production Editor: Saralyn F. Smith
Cover drawings: Vincent Babak

Typeface: Stone Serif/Tekton

Printer: Quebecor Printing/Kingsport, Tennessee